Palgrave Studies in European Union Politics

Edited by: **Michelle Egan**, American University USA, **Neill Nugent**, Manchester Metropolitan University, UK, **William Paterson**, University of Birmingham, UK

Editorial Board: **Christopher Hill**, Cambridge, UK, **Simon Hix**, London School of Economics, UK, **Mark Pollack**, Temple University, USA, **Kalypso Nicolaïdis**, Oxford UK, **Morten Egeberg**, University of Oslo, Norway, **Amy Verdun**, University of Victoria, Canada

Palgrave Macmillan is delighted to announce the launch of a new book series on the European Union. Following on the sustained success of the acclaimed *European Union Series*, which essentially publishes research-based textbooks, *Palgrave Studies in European Union Politics* will publish research-driven monographs.

The remit of the series is broadly defined, both in terms of subject and academic discipline. All topics of significance concerning the nature and operation of the European Union potentially fall within the scope of the series. The series is multidisciplinary to reflect the growing importance of the EU as a political and social phenomenon. We will welcome submissions from the areas of political studies, international relations, political economy, public and social policy and sociology

Titles include:

Derek Beach and Colette Mazzucelli (*editors*)
LEADERSHIP IN THE BIG BANGS OF EUROPEAN INTEGRATION

Morten Egeberg (*editor*)
MULTILEVEL UNION ADMINISTRATION
The Transformation of Executive Politics in Europe

Isabelle Garzon
REFORMING THE COMMON AGRICULTURAL POLICY
History of a Paradigm Change

Heather Grabbe
THE EU'S TRANSFORMATIVE POWER

Katie Verlin Laatikainen and Karen E. Smith (*editors*)
THE EUROPEAN UNION AND THE UNITED NATIONS

Hartmut Mayer and Henri Vogt (*editors*)
A RESPONSIBLE EUROPE?
Ethical Foundations of EU External Affairs

Lauren M. McLaren
IDENTITY, INTERESTS AND ATTITUDES TO EUROPEAN INTEGRATION

Justus Schönlau
DRAFTING THE EU CHARTER
Rights, Legitimacy and Process

Forthcoming titles in the series include:

Ian Bache and Andrew Jordan (*editors*)
THE EUROPEANIZATION OF BRITISH POLITICS

Also by Derek Beach

THE DYNAMICS OF EUROPEAN INTEGRATION: Why and When EU Institutions Matter

BETWEEN LAW AND POLITICS: The Relationship Between the Court of Justice and EU Member States

Also by Colette Mazzucelli

FRANCE AND GERMANY AT MAASTRICHT: Politics and Negotiations to Create the European Union

ETHICS AND GLOBAL POLITICS: The Active Learning Sourcebook (*co-editor with April Morgan and Lucinda Peach*)

THE EVOLUTION OF AN INTERNATIONAL ACTOR: Western Europe's New Assertiveness (*assistant editor to Reinhardt Rummel*)

Palgrave Studies in European Union Politics
Series Standing Order ISBN 1–4039–9511–7 (hardback) and
ISBN 1–4039–9512–5 (paperback)

You can receive future titles in this series as they are published by placing a standing order. Please contact your bookseller or, in case of difficulty, write to us at the address below with your name and address, the title of the series and one of the ISBNs quoted above.

Customer Services Department, Macmillan Distribution Ltd, Houndmills, Basingstoke, Hampshire RG21 6XS, England

Leadership in the Big Bangs of European Integration

Edited by

Derek Beach
Associate Professor, Department of Political Science
University of Aarhus, Denmark

and

Colette Mazzucelli
Assistant Professor, Department of History and Political Science
Molloy College, Rockville Centre, NY, USA
Adjunct Assistant Professor, Center for Global Affairs, New York University

First published 2007 by
PALGRAVE MACMILLAN
Houndmills, Basingstoke, Hampshire RG21 6XS and
175 Fifth Avenue, New York, N.Y. 10010
Companies and representatives throughout the world

PALGRAVE MACMILLAN is the global academic imprint of the Palgrave
Macmillan division of St. Martin's Press, LLC and of Palgrave Macmillan Ltd.
Macmillan® is a registered trademark in the United States, United Kingdom
and other countries. Palgrave is a registered trademark in the European
Union and other countries.

ISBN-13: 978–1–4039–9820–0 hardback
ISBN-10: 1–4039–9820–5 hardback

This book is printed on paper suitable for recycling and made from fully
managed and sustained forest sources.

A catalogue record for this book is available from the British Library.

Library of Congress Cataloging-in-Publication Data
Leadership in the big bangs of European integration / edited by Derek Beach
    and Colette Mazzucelli.
        p.   cm. — (Palgrave studies in European Union politics)
    Includes bibliographical references and index.
    ISBN 1–4039–9820–5 (cloth)
    1. European Union.   2. Political leadership—European Union countries.
    I. Beach, Derek.   II. Mazzucelli, Colette.   III. Series.
    JN30.L39 2007
    341.242′2—dc22   2006045748

10   9   8   7   6   5   4   3   2   1
16   15   14   13   12   11   10   09   08   07

Printed and bound in Great Britain by
Antony Rowe Ltd, Chippenham and Eastbourne

To our students throughout the world – who inspire us to learn, and to Europe's leaders – past, present and future

Contents

List of Tables

List of Figures

Foreword

Carlos Westendorp

My gratitude to the editors of this study analysing *leadership in European treaty reform* is twofold: first, because it will certainly help American readers to understand better the complex process of European integration; and, second, for having thought of me – I guess as a tribute to a lifelong dedication – to introduce such a serious, commendable effort.

My personal experience is that of someone who has taken part or closely followed the different intergovernmental conferences or their respective preparatory works since the 1980s – the Single European Act, Maastricht, Amsterdam, Nice, the Constitutional Treaty. My experience coincides with the main thesis of this study: leadership is crucial to attain the necessary compromises among the different actors who negotiate any revision of the Treaties. Leadership is even more important, as the authors point out, than the self-mechanisms for change built into the system (*functionalism*) or the political will to push the process forward – usually very weak or even nonexistent at the outset – of the main countries' governments (*intergovernmentalism*).

With this premise in mind, which in my opinion is the book's most original contribution, several experts analyze the role of different Presidencies – Dutch, French, Italian and Irish – in the final negotiations of the last four Intergovernmental Conferences (IGCs) to modify the EU Treaties – Maastricht, Amsterdam, Nice and the Constitutional Treaty. The role of the Commission, of the European Parliament, and that of the Council's Secretariat are also analyzed.

Attention is given, particularly in chapters analysing the Dutch Presidency and the Council Secretariat, to the *preparatory works* which usually precede each IGC. This is especially important given the volume's consistent focus throughout on leadership when an agreement is reached, thereby allowing a definitive text to be drafted and approved. This is, in fact, what makes history. Yet this volume also correctly underlines the importance of leadership in the phase prior to the launching of an IGC. It is precisely there when the scope, the agenda, and even the guidelines of a Conference are defined. The groups of persons in charge of such preparatory works have received different names: wise men, friends of the Presidency, working groups, personal representatives, reflection group or convention. Whatever their name, the most relevant ones have been those which received the mandate, normally exceeding the timeframe of a six-month Presidency, to produce a report to be submitted to, and discussed by, the IGC. Leadership is, of course, determinant in drafting and agreeing to such a text. Its real success, however, is measured by the degree of influence that text may have on the Conference's final outcome. In this respect, no one can deny that the Group of Wise Men chaired by Jacques Delors, the Reflection Group I had the honor to lead, and the Convention conducted by Giscard d'Estaing had a decisive influence on the IGCs leading, respectively, to Monetary Union in Maastricht, the Amsterdam Treaty, and the Constitutional Treaty or Rome II.

Allow me a few words on my own experience at the helm of the so-called Reflection Group, also known as The Westendorp Group, from June to December 1995. The mandate we received from the European Council in Corfu was both vague and a limited one: to prepare, for 1996, the Intergovernmental Conference foreseen in Maastricht to solve the problems which the Treaty signed in that city could not tackle, and to deal with decisions adopted by subsequent European Councils. My main task in the Chair was both to provide greater precision and to enlarge the agenda of the Conference, thereby enabling the European Union to cope with the huge challenges of a global world. This is a prerogative of any Presidency, of which I made full use. By so doing, my assumption was that I was better serving both Europe's and my own country's interests, which fortunately coincide. Needless to say, I had to confront the usual resistance of those who have a minimalist idea of European integration. The group dynamics ended, nonetheless, by overcoming all resistance except that of my British colleague. Given the alternative of either reaching a consensus to minimize the scope of the Conference at the level of the lowest common denominator or putting an asterisk near his name only, I chose the latter. It is my belief that by refusing any limitation in our work we were able to attain our initial goal. Our recommendations could be the basis of the Conference decisions in Amsterdam as well as in Nice and in the European Convention. Almost 90 per cent of the seeds we planted came to fruition in later years.

This experience, as well as other similar ones, shows how accurate the authors are when they put light on leadership as the main driving force in European construction.

Preface

Ezra Suleiman

The one thing that all specialists seem to agree upon when it comes to the European Union is that no matter how one defines the EU, it is always characterized as being one of a kind. No one is certain what this form of organization is, what it resembles, or into what it will evolve. Previous attempts to draw lessons or conclusions from the likes of regional alliances, federal-type structures, customs unions or other forms of cooperation and unions are generally rejected on the ground that the EU is *sui generis*. This necessarily has the advantage of allowing analysts considerable latitude since they can justifiably claim 'this is a different case.'

The excitement generated by the EU experiment and the difficulty of comprehending its complex structure has spawned a veritable industrial flow of books. For the most part, the works have largely been of a descriptive or institutional nature. Yet, more recently the EU has generated greater theoretical interest and applications, as well as valuable empirical work.

This is undoubtedly a healthy development allowing as it does for more careful and accurate assessments of the EU as a federal or a supranational structure, as a policy-making body, and as a player in international politics. No longer is it possible to make blanket statements or arguments about the Union's power, or lack thereof, or about its democratic form of governance or its lack of democracy. Given the numerous empirical studies based on theories of cooperation, of policy-making and of bargaining, we now have at our disposal more sophisticated answers to the questions we raise.

The work Derek Beach and Colette Mazzucelli have put together is one not content to rehash previous theories about the EU. The editors have set clear guidelines for the authors, which have, by and large, been followed. The first guideline was the imperative of escaping from the confines of the straightjacket into which a whole generation of students of the EU have been locked, namely, that of having to choose between the only two theories available on the EU studies menu: the neo-functional and inter-governmental theories.

The co-editors have taken their cue from the political process in democratic regimes. At the center of their model, they have placed the important phenomenon of leadership, which is a concept that has been rather vague in the political science literature. Beach and Mazzucelli have sought to provide leadership with rigor by placing the concept within the context of bargaining theory and rational choices made by the actors. Thus, they develop a model of leadership that helps explain how blockages of collective action and bargaining are unlocked. Indeed, they go further by arguing that treaty negotiations are so complex that it is really difficult for actors to be strictly 'rational.' At any rate, they can mostly hope on the basis of incomplete evidence that they are being rational. Hence, any actions based on rationality on the part of states are of necessity based on calculations that are rational only in a limited sense. Only a 'leader' can convince the parties that outcomes will be beneficial and acceptable to the collective.

With this theoretical framework, the authors in this volume examine in considerable detail the leadership exercised by the countries (France, the Netherlands, Ireland, Italy) holding the EU Presidency, and the leadership exercised by the key EU institutions (Parliament, Council Secretariat, Commission). The work carried out by contributing authors has permitted the editors to address comparatively the central institutional question confronting the analysis of the European Union: to whom does the leadership fall and what makes this possible?

I believe that Beach and Mazzucelli, aided by the contributors, have added an important volume to the vast literature on the EU because of the dynamic model that is developed by the editors. This is also a more realistic way of viewing the EU because the model is empirically grounded. Different times call for specific leadership needs. Hence different players can exercise leadership in different contexts for different reasons. Said in this way, the model may seem rather simple. Behind this model, however, lies a well-developed theory and substantial empirical evidence.

Acknowledgments

The origins of this volume date back to the International Studies Association (ISA) conference in New Orleans at the end of March 2002 where the
editors met during a panel analyzing multilateral negotiations. Derek Beach
was a post-doctoral research scholar at the University of Aarhus and Colette
Mazzucelli was a Program Officer in Education at the Carnegie Council on
Ethics and International Affairs. We both had written extensively with particular attention to the analysis of negotiations that led to successive European
treaty reforms. Our mutual interest sparked the idea for this volume, which
draws on the collective talents of colleagues and friends who are specialists
on this subject researching in Europe and the United States.

In an endeavor of this kind, there are many persons to thank. We express
our appreciation in particular to the University of Aarhus Foundation for its
generous support of the project. Professors Volker Berghahn, John Micgiel,
and Glenda Rosenthal, Institute for the Study of Europe, Columbia University, were instrumental as we contemplated a title for the volume and
assembled the group of contributors. The School of Advanced International
Studies (SAIS) at Johns Hopkins University in Washington, DC offered the
editors initial time to meet and discuss chapter revisions in September 2004
while Derek was a scholar in residence there. On the recommendation of
John Lotherington, Director, 21st Century Trust, Goodenough College and
its outstanding staff provided a wonderful venue in central London for our
authors' conference during January 2005. Each of the contributors offered
helpful criticisms and suggestions as we exchanged ideas analyzing the
content – thereby creating a wonderful learning community that continues
via email. In the editing process, we are grateful to Derek's research assistant,
Piet Juul Birch, who attended the Goodenough College meeting and took
extensive notes there, and also to Anne-Mette Lund who compiled the Index.
In the last stages of locating bibliographic references, Mr Cosimo Monda,
Lecturer and Head of Division Information, Documentation, Publications
Marketing Services, European Institute of Public Administration, Maastricht,
The Netherlands, provided timely assistance. We also wish to thank our
editor at Palgrave Macmillan, Alison Howson, for her wise counsel. All errors
are, of course, the contributors' responsibility.

The support of family and friends is also critical to the success of a tightly
edited volume, especially in the final stages. In particular Colette is grateful
to her parents, Silvio and Adeline Mazzucelli, whose encouragement is
unconditional. For his guidance through the years, Colette expresses her warm
appreciation to her mentor, Professor Emeritus Karl H. Cerny, Department
of Government, Georgetown University. The Robert Bosch Foundation

xviii *Acknowledgments*

in Stuttgart, Germany, has provided Colette with the opportunity to work in Europe, for which she is most grateful. A substantial amount of the research completing the volume occurred during Colette's initial year on full-time faculty at the John C. Whitehead School of Diplomacy and International Relations, Seton Hall University. For their assistance, Colette is appreciative to former Associate Dean Marilyn DiGiacobbe, Assistant Dean Ursula Sanjamino and Mrs Susan Malcolm. For her collegiality, good humor, and scholarship, Colette warmly thanks her fellow faculty member in European studies at Whitehead, Assistant Professor Cynthia M. Horne. The opportunity to learn and teach about European integration is invaluable to the research process. For this reason, Colette extends special appreciation to Associate Dean and Professor Carl Lebowitz, Office of Faculty and Academic Services, School of Continuing and Professional Studies (SCPS), New York University, and to Assistant Dean and Director, Center for Global Affairs, SCPS, Dr Vera Jelinek, for the opportunity to attend the Warsaw East European Conference, July 5–8, 2006, and present the research findings of this volume to an international audience. Derek would like to express thanks to the numerous academics for feedback on his arguments over time, including Thomas Christiansen, Finn Laursen, Jonas Tallberg and William I. Zartman. Editing this volume has been a wonderful intellectual journey – the first of many, we trust, in our quest to make sense of Europe.

DEREK BEACH   COLETTE MAZZUCELLI
Aarhus, Denmark   Brooklyn, New York

Notes on the Contributors

Derek Beach is Associate Professor in the Department of Political Science at the University of Aarhus in Denmark, and has been a visiting scholar at SAIS, Johns Hopkins in Washington DC. He has recently published articles on the Council Secretariat and an article explaining governmental compliance with EU law, and has published two books: one entitled *The Dynamics of European Integration: Why and when EU Institutions Matter* (2005), and *Between Law and Politics* (2001), along with several chapters in edited volumes.

Alasdair Blair is Jean Monnet Reader in International Relations at Coventry University. He has written on various aspects of European integration and Britain's European foreign policy. He is the author of *The European Union since 1945* (2005), *Saving the Pound? Britain's Road to Monetary Union* (2002) and co-author with Anthony Forster of *The Making of Britain's European Foreign Policy* (2002). Forthcoming publications include *The European Union Companion* (2006).

Krzysztof Bobiński is director of the Unia & Polska, a pro-European think tank in Warsaw and previously worked at the Polish Institute of International Affairs (PISM). He was the London *Financial Times* Warsaw Correspondent from 1976 to 2000, and published *Unia & Polska*, a bi-monthly devoted to European issues, from 1998 to 2003. He has contributed articles to *Poland into the new Millennium* (2001), *Ambivalent Neighbours* (2003) and *Obywatele Europy* (2005). He comments on Polish and EU issues in the Polish media and the BBC and has contributed to other major newspapers in the US and Western Europe.

Simone Bunse is a lecturer at the INCAE business school in Costa Rica. She completed her DPhil in Politics at Nuffield College, University of Oxford, and is a former visiting researcher at the Free University of Brussels. Her work focuses on small states in the EU and the Council Presidency. She has published on the 2003 Greek Presidency (*Mediterranean Politics*, Summer 2004) and co-published with Paul Magnette and Kalypso Nicolaïdis on small states and the Commission as well as on the Convention debates.

Ben Crum is Lecturer in Political Theory at the Vrije Universiteit Amsterdam. Earlier he worked at the Centre for European Policy Studies (CEPS) in Brussels, the University of Twente and a Dutch firm for policy-oriented research and consultancy. In recent years his research has concentrated on the proposed Constitutional Treaty for the European Union, the constitutional puzzles it has raised as well as the various stages in its conception and (non-)ratification. His writings on these issues have appeared in various edited volumes and in the *Journal of Common Market Studies*, *Politique Européenne*, *Politics* and *the European Law Journal*.

Renaud Dehousse is Jean Monnet Professor of European Law and Politics at the Institute of Political Studies (*Sciences Po*). He is Director of Sciences Po's Centre for European Studies and Scientific Advisor at *Notre Europe*, a Paris-based think tank established by former EU Commission President Jacques Delors. Dr Dehousse earned a PhD in Law from the European University Institute (Florence). He has held positions at the European University Institute and at the University of Pisa, Italy, and has been Visiting Professor at the University of Florence and the University of Michigan Law School. His main work has been on comparative federalism and on the institutional development of the European Union. He has been adviser to various units of the European Commission on institutional issues. His recent work has focused on the transformation of European governance, with reference to the growing importance of transnational bureaucratic structures (comitology) and on institutional reform.

Florence Deloche-Gaudez earned a PhD in political science, and is Secretary-General of the Center for European Studies, Institute of Political Studies (Sciences Po) Paris. She also lectures on EU decision-making at Sciences Po and is a member of the European Network of Excellence CONSENT. Dr. Deloche-Gaudez followed the European Convention's work very closely in Brussels and published a number of papers on the Convention method as well as a book on the Constitutional Treaty. She has worked with the French Ministry of Foreign Affairs, where she contributed, *inter alia*, to a French-German study on a 30-member European Union. Dr Deloche-Gaudez also collaborated on the 'Quermonne' report, analysing the future of the European institutions, for the French Government. She has published several articles on France's stance with regard to the enlargement of the Union and the reforms this requires, in particular within the framework of the Trans-European Policy Studies Association (TEPSA).

Dionyssis G. Dimitrakopoulos is Lecturer in Politics in the School of Politics and Sociology, Birkbeck College, University of London, which he joined in 2002 after holding an individual Marie Curie Post-Doctoral Fellowship at Oxford (Dept. of Politics & International Relations and Nuffield College). He has been educated in Athens (Panteion), Brussels (ULB), and Hull. His research interests are in institutionalist accounts of politics and the politics of European integration (especially the politics of preference formation, institutional change, executive politics and policy implementation). His work has appeared, *inter alia*, in *Political Studies*, the *Journal of Public Policy*, the *Journal of Common Market Studies*, the *European Journal of Political Research*, the *Journal of European Public Policy*, *Comparative European Politics* and the *European Law Journal*.

Ulrike Guérot has been a Senior Transatlantic Fellow – Europe in the Berlin Office at the German Marshall Fund (GMF) of the United States since 2004. From 2000 to 2003, she headed the European Union Unit at the German Council on Foreign Relations. Prior to her position at GMF, she was assistant professor in the European Studies Department, Paul H. Nitze School for Advanced International Studies (SAIS), Washington, DC.; senior research fellow at the Paris-based think-tank '*Notre Europe*,' working with Jacques Delors; and a staff member on the German *Bundestag's* Committee on Foreign Relations. Dr Guérot has published widely in European affairs and Transatlantic relations in European and American journals and newspapers. She is a commentator for European and American print-press, radio, and television stations. Dr Guérot has experience consulting with major European and American corporations and institutions, such as the, World Bank, and the French Ministry for Foreign Affairs, on their dealings with the European Union.

Hussein Kassim is Senior Lecturer in the School of Politics and Sociology at Birkbeck College, University of London. He was educated at New College, Oxford, and Nuffield College, Oxford. He has taught at Oxford University and Nottingham University, held visiting positions at Sciences Po Paris, Harvard University, New York University and Columbia University, and is currently political science mentor at the Centre for Competition Policy at UEA. His publications examine relations between the EU and the member states, preference formation and the future of Europe, and the development and operation of EU institutions, in particular the European Commission. He is currently working on projects analyzing the Europeanization of civil aviation, EU coordination, delegation and credibility, and EU competition policy.

Paul Magnette is professor of political science and Director of the Institute for European Studies at the Université Libre de Bruxelles. He also teaches at Sciences Po Paris and has been a visiting professor at Bordeaux, Pisa and Lausanne. Professor Magnette has published on European citizenship, democratic accountability and institutional change in the European Union, and is currently working on a book that analyzes Constitutionalism in the European Union. His last book was *What is the European Union?* (Palgrave 2005).

Andreas Maurer is Project Manager for CONVEU-30 – From the Convention to the IGC: Mapping Cross-National Views towards an EU-30 at the German Institute for International and Security Affairs (SWP) in Berlin. From 2002 to 2004 he was Adviser to the European Constitutional Convention. Dr Maurer is the recipient of the 2003 Science Award from the German Parliament. In the period 2000–02 he was Project Director at the Trans European Policy Studies Association in Brussels. From 1997 to 2002 Dr Maurer was Jean Monnet Chair for Political Science at the University of Cologne. In 1996–97 he was a member of the Task Force 'Intergovernmental Conference' of the European Parliament.

Colette Mazzucelli is Assistant Professor in the Department of History and Political Science at Molloy College on Long Island, NY. She conducts research in Paris at the Centre for European Studies, Sciences Po, and the German Historical Institute. Professor Mazzucelli has taught on graduate faculty at New York University's Center for Global Affairs. Her experience includes work in Program Development at Teachers College Columbia University and Education at the Carnegie Council on Ethics and International Affairs. She taught the first technology-mediated learning seminar for Sciences Po analyzing Balkans conflicts and was a visiting lecturer with a joint appointment at the Budapest University of Economic Sciences and the Budapest Institute for Graduate International and Diplomatic Studies. As a speaker for the United States Information Service, Dr Mazzucelli toured France, Germany and Poland. A Robert Bosch Foundation Fellow in the Foreign Office, she assisted with the ratification of the Treaty on European Union in Germany.

Almut Metz, M.A., is a political scientist and researcher and the Center for Applied Policy Research (CAP) at Ludwig-Maximilians-University in Munich, working on institutions and procedures of EU policymaking and Franco-German relations.

Kalypso Nicolaïdis is University Lecturer in International Relations at Oxford University and a fellow at the European Studies Center at St Antony's College. She held the Vincent Wright Chair at Sciences-Po Paris during 2004–2005. Previously Dr Nicolaïdis was Associate Professor at Harvard University and taught at the Ecole Nationale d'Administration in Paris. She was the chair of the international group of experts on the European Constitution for the Greek foreign ministry. Dr Nicolaïdis has published extensively on the European Union and issues of global governance. Her latest book is *The Federal Vision: Legitimacy and Levels of Governance in the US and the EU* (co-edited with Rob Howse).

Ezra Suleiman is the IBM Professor of International Studies, Professor of Politics, and Director of the Program in European Politics and Society at Princeton University. He is the author of numerous books on European politics, the most recent being *Dismantling Democratic States* (2003).

Jonas Tallberg is Associate Professor at Stockholm University. He has published numerous articles on European Union politics in international journals and is the author of *Leadership and Negotiation in the European Union: The Power of the Presidency* (2006) and *European Governance and Supranational Institutions: Making States Comply* (2003).

Carlos Westendorp is a Spanish politician and a career diplomat. Most of his professional life has been dedicated to European affairs. He was a member of the team that negotiated Spain's accession to the European Union, the first Ambassador to serve as Permanent Representative of his country in Brussels from 1986 to 1991, and Secretary of State for European Affairs from 1991 to 1995. He also chaired the Reflection Group, which prepared the Amsterdam Treaty. He was subsequently Minister of Foreign Affairs in the last Socialist Government headed by Felipe González, Ambassador to the United Nations, and High Representative of the International Community in Bosnia-Herzegovina. A member of the European Parliament and the Madrid Autonomous Assembly, he is currently Ambassador of Spain to the United States.

1
Introduction

Derek Beach and Colette Mazzucelli

1.1 Constitutional reform or the 'big bangs' of European integration

Since 1985 the European Union (EU) has been marked by an almost continual formal revision of its founding treaties. These rounds of constitutional reform, also known as intergovernmental conferences (IGCs), have over time become the key forum determining the scope and direction of the Union.[1] Major intergovernmental conferences transformed the EU from a stagnant common market in the early 1980s into a present-day nascent quasi-federal Union. Successive IGCs led to the introduction of a single currency, the Euro, in 12 member states, and the creation of a Common Foreign and Security Policy (CFSP), which, over time, resulted in the EU having military command over several peacekeeping and policing missions. In addition, these IGCs resulted in the expansion of supranational cooperation to deal with a range of new policies, including the environment, as well as immigration and asylum policies.

The basic question is whether these history-making decisions have been a series of French-German compromises, or whether the European Commission and other actors have played a significant role. These questions have been at the core of integration theory, but the answers provided reflect the different theoretical assumptions of the theories.

Neo-functionalists argue that after the initial founding compromise, the integration process develops a dynamic, which, under certain conditions, can lead to the creation of a self-sustaining process leading to more integration that is driven by three types of 'spillover' (Haas 1958, 1961; Lindberg 1963). Functional spillover refers to the process whereby pressures for further integration are created by past decisions. An oft-used example was the functional spillover of the single European market, with the argument being that in order for governments to reap the full benefits of the integrated market, a further step of creating a single currency was necessary. Political spillover related to the pro-EU shifts of national actor loyalties and activities, as the locus of policymaking increasingly moved from national capitals to Brussels.

Entrepreneurial supranational institutions in the EU are viewed as playing a strong integrative role in cultivating further demands for integration by playing upon functional and political spillover mechanisms. The European Commission in neo-functionalism is viewed as the motor of integration process. The Commission is able to provide leadership that 'upgrades the common interest' by advancing and building support for creative integrative proposals.

Intergovernmentalists and realists argue, in contrast, that the governments of the largest EU member states are firmly in control of major constitutional reform negotiations. According to them, integration is the result of deliberate choices made by these governments, with outcomes determined by patterns of relative state power and preferences. Therefore, the motors of the integration process are viewed as those actors with the most power. In realist theory, the most powerful actors in the EU are viewed as the states with a preponderance of material resources (Grieco 1985; Pedersen 1998). The other main intergovernmentalist position, liberal intergovernmentalism (LI), argues, based upon bargaining theory, that actor power reflects actor dependence upon an agreement (Moravcsik 1998). Germany, while being the strongest power in the EU, was, for example, dependent upon securing a burden-sharing agreement in asylum/immigration policies, and, therefore, was not the strongest actor in negotiations addressing this policy area. Both approaches expect, however, major treaty bargains to be driven by compromises among the preferences of France, Germany and the United Kingdom.

Our volume attempts to go beyond this tired either–or dichotomy that still plagues integration theory by proposing a theory that bridges the gap. The leadership model explains under which circumstances we expect certain types of actors to be able to exercise leadership in EU constitutional negotiations. Based upon mainstream negotiation theory and rational choice institutionalism, a three-stage model is developed to explain when and why different actors are able to provide guidance or leadership in European Union treaty reform negotiations. Leadership is seen as a crucial factor in overcoming the strong collective action problems and high bargaining costs that exist within these history-making negotiations (Mazzucelli 1997, 1999; Beach 2005). Leadership is defined here relatively broadly as *any action undertaken by an actor in order to attempt to solve collective action problems through the use of leadership resources.* Although the provision of leadership is often motivated by an interest in *collective* gains, it is also directed at influencing outcomes for *private* gain.

The first stage of the model hypothesizes which types of leadership resources are relevant for treaty reform negotiations. Second, the model describes how the negotiation context impacts upon the ability of different actors to provide leadership. The final step of the model looks at whether actors choose appropriate leadership strategies to match these contexts.

The leadership model does not attempt to develop a multi-stage model similar to Moravcsik's liberal intergovernmentalism, which includes three different mid-range theories that explain domestic preference formation, inter-state bargaining, and institutional choice by actors. The leadership model is a mid-range theory that attempts to explain why leadership can be necessary in EU constitutional bargaining, and when we should expect specific actors endowed with certain leadership resources and institutional positions to be able to provide leadership successfully.

This model serves as the theoretical baseline for the empirical contributions in this volume that are written by leading scholars in the field. The chapters assess what leadership resources are possessed by specific actors, how different negotiating contexts mattered, and then analyze what types of leadership they attempted to provide as well as the effects of their leadership attempts. In particular, the chapters analyze what factors determined the success of a given leadership attempt, and, most importantly, whether the supply of a leadership matched the demand created by the specific negotiating situation.

In the initial section of this introductory chapter, we briefly present the focus of our studies – intergovernmental conferences to address European constitutional reform. The second section presents the theoretical framework that guides the empirical chapters. The first question answered is why leadership is necessary in complex EU treaty reform negotiations. The chapter then develops the core assumptions of our leadership model, and details the three stages of the model, as well as the theoretical variables in each stage. This chapter concludes with a brief description of the content of this volume.

1.2 Intergovernmental conferences in the European Union[2]

There are currently three major EU treaties: the Treaty establishing the European Community; the Treaty establishing the European Atomic Energy Community (EURATOM); and the Treaty on European Union, otherwise known as the Maastricht Treaty. The fourth Treaty, the European Coal and Steel Community (ECSC), expired in 2002. There are also a series of minor treaties, including Accession Treaties.

No major intergovernmental conferences were held from 1957 until 1985, although minor IGCs had been convened for accessions and for other revisions, like changes to the budgetary procedure. In these minor IGCs, the substantial negotiations took place within the Council, followed by a ceremonial IGC that was convened to adopt the final Treaty. Since 1985, the EU has convened six major IGCs where the negotiations took place *within* the IGC itself. In effect, IGCs are 'constitutional conventions,' in which history-making decisions are taken by governmental representatives from the member states that alter the competences of the Union, its decision-making procedures, and the relative balance of power among EU institutions and between the EU and its member states (Peterson and Bomberg 1999).

IGCs are based upon Article 48 EU (ex Article N), which states that:

1. The government of any Member State or the Commission may submit to the Council proposals for the amendment of the Treaties on which the Union is founded.

If the Council, after consulting the Parliament and, where appropriate, the Commission, delivers an opinion in favour of calling a conference of representatives of the governments of the Member States, the conference shall be convened by the President of the Council for the purposes of determining by common accord the amendments to be made to those Treaties. The European Central Bank should also be consulted in the case of institutional changes in the monetary area.

The amendments shall enter into force after being ratified by all the Member States in accordance with their respective constitutional requirements.

Intergovernmental conferences are convened either by agreement in the Council under Article 48 EU, or by a binding legal commitment included in a treaty. A proposal to convene an IGC can come from either a member state or from the Commission. The decision to convene an IGC is taken by a simple majority vote in the Council. The use of the vote was seen in 1985, when the British, Danish and Greek governments voted against convening an IGC. In that case, the three governments were outvoted, which allowed the 1985 IGC to negotiate the Single European Act to be convened. There are no formal provisions as to how the agenda for an IGC should be prepared. In the past agendas were prepared by specific committees, reflection groups, and *ad hoc* COREPER discussions. In a major break with experience until that time, the 2003–04 IGC was preceded by a European Convention, which produced an actual draft Constitutional Treaty. This relegated the IGC itself to being a tidying-up exercise with the exception of a handful of contentious issues (Norman 2003; Beach 2005; Magnette and Nicolaïdis 2004; see also the chapters in this volume).

There are also no provisions in the Treaties regarding how IGC negotiations are to be conducted although a set of norms has developed – the *acquis conferencielle*. IGCs are formally outside the institutional framework of the Union, and in effect are both *international* and *intergovernmental* negotiations among national governmental representatives. Nonetheless, these conferences do draw upon and involve EU institutions to varying degrees, as analyzed in the following chapters. IGCs are chaired by the member state holding the six-month rotating Council Presidency. The Presidency prepares and chairs all the meetings, and controls the drafting process of the single negotiating text.

Since 1985, IGCs have been conducted at three or four different levels, with the exception of the 2003–04 IGC, where negotiations were formally only at the political levels of foreign ministers and heads of state and government. The four levels are: (1) heads of state and government, (2) foreign ministers, (3) ambassadorial-level meetings within the Preparatory Group, and (4) technical meetings among 'Friends of the Presidency.'

The highest level of the IGC is the heads of state or government meeting within the European Council. It is at this level that key deals are brokered and the final treaty concluded. The next level is that of the foreign ministers, who have the overall political responsibility for the IGC. But they are often sandwiched between two levels, and lack the informational skills to follow the lower-level discussions, while also lacking the political weight of the heads of state and government to strike key deals (McDonagh 1998: 20). In the EMU IGC during 1990–91, the ministerial-level negotiations were held among economic and finance ministers (ECOFIN).

The Preparatory Group level is compromised of representatives of foreign ministers at the ambassadorial level. The group meets frequently during IGCs. Most of the IGC negotiations are dealt with at this level, with discussions focusing on detailed and technical questions in what is often characterized as a problem-solving environment. At the lowest level are the Friends of the Presidency, a forum that is used to prepare technical questions for the personal representatives. In the 1990–91 Political Union IGC, the Friends of the Presidency assisted the personal representatives by clarifying points and asking questions on key issues (Mazzucelli 1997: 61–2, 136). In the 1996–97 IGC, this group was charged with discussing questions of simplifying the treaty.

The final outcome of an IGC negotiation is a treaty that revises or replaces the existing treaties. Following the logic of two-level games (Putnam 1988), the final treaty must then be ratified by member states according to their respective constitutional requirements.

1.3 Theoretical orientation – when and why leadership matters

This chapter develops a theoretical framework of inquiry for why leadership is necessary in EU constitutional negotiations, and which type of actors can successfully provide leadership in specific circumstances. The basic argument in this volume is that EU constitutional negotiations are very complex, unpredictable and messy affairs with high bargaining (transaction) costs. Therefore, leadership is often necessary in order for the parties to find and agree upon a mutually acceptable outcome. However, various types of leadership are demanded in different types of circumstances, and who provides leadership does affect the shape of the final outcome.

Two questions are answered in this initial chapter. First, why is leadership necessary in EU constitutional negotiations? The chapter then introduces a theoretical model of inquiry that puts forward hypotheses regarding circumstances in which we expect specific actors to be able to provide leadership in EU treaty reform negotiations.

How should we define leadership? There are a variety of different definitions in the international negotiation and integration theory literature. Lindberg and Scheingold view leadership as being a 'crucial activator of coalitions,' and a 'key determinant in translating demands for integration into outcomes within the EU political system' (Lindberg and Scheingold 1970: 128). Zartman defines leadership as the management of complexity (Zartman 2003). Underdal defines leadership as an, 'asymmetrical relationship of influence in which one actor guides or directs the behavior of others towards a certain goal over a certain period of time' (Underdal 1994:178).

Leadership involves the exercise of *influence* over other actors. Yet, as Underdal and many others define leadership, it is seen as a subset of 'influence' that is differentiated from influence per se by being aimed at overcoming *collective action problems* for the *common good* (ibid; Sjöstedt 1999: 228–9). Here we agree with Lindberg and Scheingold's less restrictive definition of leadership, where the *common good* element is replaced with a broader and slightly less altruistic sounding *collective* element. In this context, the supply of leadership ensures that demands for integration deriving from *some or all* of the EU governments are translated into an agreement. Leadership in this definition has two elements. First, leadership by an actor can ensure that all of the potential gains on the table are achieved (*efficiency or integrative dimension*); yet the leader can also have private interests in pushing a specific outcome. Further, in this definition, the 'collective good' is not necessarily the 'good' of the whole group, and can merely be the collective good of a smaller coalition of actors (ibid.).

Therefore, leadership is defined relatively broadly in this volume. It is defined as *any action by one actor to guide or direct the behavior of other actors (be they the whole group or only a smaller coalition) toward a certain collective goal*. For example, in this definition of leadership, when a laggard such as the UK merely vetoes or threatens to veto an outcome, that actor is *not* providing leadership, as there is no collective element. If the laggard on the other hand attempts to build a coalition in an effort to fight for the status quo, this would be categorized as a leadership attempt. An example of this type of 'negative' leadership is analyzed in the Polish chapter. As will be seen, Poland unsuccessfully attempted to build a coalition of governments around the position of preserving the Nice compromise on Council voting weights.

1.4 Why leadership is necessary

Why is leadership necessary in EU constitutional negotiations? Is the provision of leadership by any one actor redundant, as Moravcsik and other intergovernmentalists argue? Or are EU treaty negotiations more complex affairs with a higher demand for leadership?

Realists and intergovernmentalists argue that there is usually a low demand for leadership in international negotiations since it is relatively easy for governments to sit down at the negotiating table and agree upon a mutually acceptable outcome. Moravcsik argues further that there is usually an overabundance in the supply of leadership, making the provision of leadership by any one actor redundant (Moravcsik 1999a).

The realist/intergovernmentalist arguments are based upon two assumptions about negotiations. First, national governments are viewed as being 'comprehensively' or 'fully' rational. This means that governments have close to perfect information about their own preferences across the multitude of issues under discussion, and possess the necessary analytical and substantive knowledge first to find the Pareto frontier of efficient agreements, and then agree upon an outcome on the Pareto frontier (Moravcsik, 1998: 23; Milward and Sørensen 1993). Second, they argue that negotiations have low bargaining costs, or, as Moravcsik argues, that bargaining (transaction) costs are low relative to the potential gains from agreement (Moravcsik 1999a). Governments are therefore relatively easily able to agree upon a Pareto-efficient and mutually acceptable outcome. Questions regarding the distribution of gains that exist will be resolved in favor of the most powerful actors. Therefore, grand constitutional bargains in the European Union are explained by realists/intergovernmentalists as a series of French-German compromises, with the UK acting as the brake (Grieco 1995; Moravcsik 1998, 1999a; Pedersen 1998, 2002).

If we do not accept that the realist/intergovernmentalist assumptions of low bargaining costs and comprehensive rationality are substantiated by the empirical evidence, leadership can be necessary to overcome two major bargaining impediments in treaty reform. These impediments in can prevent the parties to a negotiation (governments) from achieving collective gains.

In complex, multi-party negotiations such as EU constitutional reform, it is by no means certain that parties will be able to first find a zone of possible agreements, and then subsequently agree upon an outcome within this zone (Melchoir 1998; Raiffa 1982; Sandholtz 1992: 20–8; Sebenius 1992: 338; Young 1991, 1999). Despite the large potential gains of agreement, there are also substantial bargaining costs and other bargaining impediments that can create collective action problems. This can lead either to less efficient agreements or even to bargaining failure (Hopmann 1996: 258; Stubb 2002; Tallberg 2003). Rational choice institutionalist theory also suggests that there are factors intrinsic to the negotiation process, such as the possession of a privileged institutional position, which also can open opportunities for actors to provide leadership (see Pollack 1997, 2003; Tallberg 2003).

We argue in this volume that EU constitutional reforms are complex multilateral negotiations with many cross-cutting cleavages across a range of highly complex and technical issues. Despite extensive preparation at both the national and EU level, treaty reform negotiations are often poorly defined negotiating situations, and actors are often unclear and/or disagree about what 'problems' need to be solved in a given EU constitutional negotiation, what possible solutions are available, and what their own positions are along with those of others (Underdal 1983, 1994: 191; Stubb 2002).

If actors could be treated as being comprehensively rational, then these bargaining costs arising from complexity would not matter. However, in EU constitutional negotiations, as in other complex international negotiations, actors can realistically be seen as only 'boundedly' rational (Simon 1997; Jones 2001; Rosati 2001). This means that there are natural limits to the cognitive abilities of actors, and they do not necessarily possess the necessary substantive and analytical skills to see through the fog of uncertainty to find a mutually acceptable and efficient outcome (Underdal 1983; Kassim 2004: 275). One well-informed EU insider who has taken part in several rounds of constitutional reform describes the typical IGC negotiating situation: 'Governments and their negotiators do not always know what they want and the situation changes unpredictably with the dynamics of the negotiations where written and oral proposals are floated around the table by all the participants at frequent intervals.' (Stubb 2002: 27). In such circumstances, leadership is often necessary to help the parties *find* the Pareto frontier of mutually acceptable agreements (see Figure 1.1).

Once the Pareto frontier is found, there is still the question of the *distribution* of gains along the frontier (see Figure 1.1). Although competing solutions

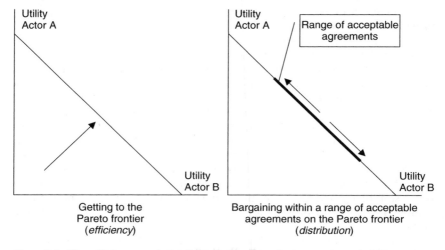

Figure 1.1 The efficiency and distributive elements of a two-party negotiation

to problems often exist along the frontier, agreement does not always emerge by itself (Krasner 1991). Leadership is often needed to create a 'focal point' around which agreement can converge (Garrett and Weingast 1993: 176; Tallberg 2002: 7). There are two principal problems in these types of situations: agenda instability and the negotiator's dilemma. First, as illustrated in the rational choice institutionalist literature, it is often necessary for one actor to have formal control of the agenda in complex multilateral negotiations to prevent agenda instability (Riker 1980; Scharpf 1997: 156–61). In EU constitutional negotiations, an unstable agenda would mean that actors would continue tabling their own proposals, and in the absence of a leader possessing agenda control, the agenda will listlessly continue to cycle among these different competing proposals. The solution to this problem is to formalize control of the agenda with an actor, such as the Presidency, enabling the actor to provide leadership by creating a focal point on the Pareto frontier around which agreement can (at least potentially) converge.

Another substantial collective action problem in EU constitutional negotiations is the negotiator's dilemma (Lax and Sebenius 1986: 29–45; Young 1991: 284). Cooperative moves in negotiations can increase the size of the pie, yet they can also be exploited by other parties through competitive moves to claim value for themselves (ibid.). Therefore, actors often have incentives not to reveal their true bottom-lines, and to distort information – for example, by exaggerating the value of their own concessions. In such circumstances, a trusted intervener can discuss with each party the nature and intensity of its preferences in an attempt to find the Pareto frontier of mutually acceptable agreements (Scharpf 1997: 145; Raiffa 1982; Metcalfe 1998: 424–5; Stenelo 1972: 54; Tallberg 2003). By gaining privileged information, this actor, be it a smaller EU government, the Presidency, or an EU institution, can provide leadership by crafting a mutually acceptable and efficient agreement. This inside information, however, can also be exploited to craft an agreement closer to the intervener's preferred outcome.

1.5   The provision of leadership in EU constitutional negotiations

The basic point of the theoretical model developed in this chapter is that actors possess leadership resources that can grant them opportunities to supply leadership in order to help the parties find and agree upon a mutually acceptable outcome. This will be successful if: they meet a demand for leadership that varies according to the negotiating context; and they are able skillfully to provide the appropriate type of leadership. By providing leadership that matches the demand, the actions of the successful leader can increase the overall collective gains from agreement. The leader can, however, also exploit his/her position to increase private gains.

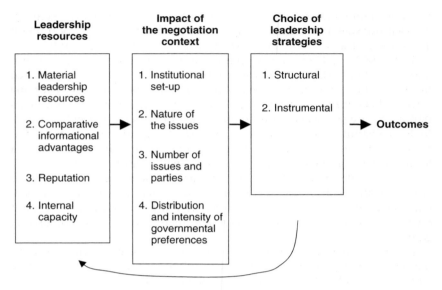

Figure 1.2   The provision of leadership in EU constitutional negotiations

The model is divided into three analytical categories (see Figure 1.2). *Leadership resources* are the relevant capacities a leader possesses, which can be used to supply leadership. The *context* of a specific treaty negotiation determines the opportunities that a given actor has to provide the different types of leadership and the size of the bargaining impediments creating a demand for leadership. In other words, the context of a given negotiation describes the level of demand for specific types of leadership. The third category focuses upon whether the specific actor actually supplied the type of leadership that was demanded in the negotiation. For example, a situation like the deadlock during the Nice European Council in December 2000 was arguably one in which structural leadership from a position of obvious strength was necessary to 'muscle' governments to concede in the sensitive discussions on revising Council voting weights (chapters 2 and 8). In this negotiating context, if an actor attempted to supply instrumental leadership, for example, by tabling creative compromise proposals, the supplied leadership would not match the demand, and, therefore, would be unsuccessful.

1.6   Leadership resources

There are four overall categories of leadership resources, which actors can potentially use to provide leadership in negotiations. Whether they are relevant in a specific negotiation is contingent upon the demand for leadership created by the negotiating context.

Material leadership resources

In order to provide what Young terms as *structural leadership*, the given actor must possess significant material resources that can be translated into bargaining leverage in order to push actors to agree to something to which they otherwise would not have agreed to (Young 1991). In the EU treaty reform context, relevant material leadership resources are resources deriving from actor capabilities such as material wealth or the ability to change other actors' dependence upon an agreement (Underdal 1994). Based upon material leadership resources, we expect that large member states, like Germany, have more leverage vis-à-vis other parties than smaller member states like Denmark or Portugal. EU institutions will only have material leadership resources when they are able credibly to link resources they control in daily EU policymaking, such as the EP's power of assent over enlargements, with outcomes in constitutional negotiations.

Informational leadership resources

When there are high bargaining costs in a given negotiation, the possession of comparative informational advantages, be they substantive expertise or bargaining skills, can be a strategic asset that allows the actor to provide *instrumental leadership* in order to forge an outcome.

This is because realistically not all actors are equal regarding their levels of substantive knowledge of the issues under discussion (content expertise), their analytical skills (process expertise), and their knowledge of the state of play of the negotiations (Wall and Lynn 1993; Sandholtz 1992: 27–8; Cox and Jacobson 1973: 20; Finnemore and Sikkink 1998: 899–900). Regarding *content expertise*, technical and legal knowledge are most relevant in EU constitutional negotiations. Technical expertise is based upon the possession of detailed substantive knowledge of how a certain treaty provision works at present, and/or the anticipated consequences of possible changes. Legal expertise is the possession of extensive knowledge of the way in which EU law works, which is vital when deciding how specific constitutional provisions should be formulated.

Not all delegations in EU constitutional negotiations possess the analytical skills and negotiating experience necessary to digest the hundreds of very complicated and technical proposals on the many different issues under discussion. Another type of process expertise deals with the possession of the necessary procedural skills to steer a negotiation effectively towards an efficient outcome. These skills are usually based upon the institutional memory of a given actor, and learning curves are often present.

Finally, we turn to the importance of *information on actor preferences and the state of play of negotiations*. There are two reasons why delegates in EU treaty negotiations often do not have detailed information about the nature and intensity of other actors' preferences regarding the myriad issues under discussion. First, it is often difficult for a single delegation to keep track of different actor preferences regarding the large number of very detailed issues under discussion. Second, governmental representatives, despite publishing opinions prior to a negotiation and presenting arguments and proposals during negotiations, are often reluctant to reveal their 'true' preferences in an EU treaty negotiation.[3] Delegates can have strategic reasons for holding their cards, waiting to see how an issue plays out before revealing their hand, or in order to distort other actors' perceptions of their true preferences (Underdal 2002: 115; Tallberg 2003). In this situation, a trusted intervener, like the Council Secretariat or a small state Presidency, can discuss with each party the nature and intensity of its preferences in an attempt to find a mutually acceptable, Pareto-efficient outcome (Scharpf 1997: 145; Raiffa 1982; Metcalfe 1998: 424–5; Stenelo 1972: 54; Tallberg 2003). By gaining private information about the zone of possible agreement, however, the intervening actor can also craft an agreement within this zone that is closest to its own preferred outcome (Lax and Sebenius 1986).

Reputation

In the third category, a further type of resource actors can possess in EU constitutional negotiations is the reputation for providing relatively acceptable leadership. Levels of acceptance can be based on recognition of the utility of the actor's contributions, the legitimacy, and/or reputation of the actor (Wehr and Lederach 1996; Bercovitch and Houston 1996: 25–7; Hampson 1995: 18; Tallberg 2003; Hopmann 1996: 225; Haas 1990: 87–8; Underdal 1994: 190). Note that 'neutrality' and 'acceptability' are not necessarily synonymous in this context, and a partial mediator/broker can be acceptable in certain circumstances.

The acceptability of an actor can be threatened if the actor is seen to be excessively partial either in the way in which he/she fulfills a specific institutional role (procedural bias), or with regard to excessively promoting a particularly unwelcome outcome (outcome bias) (Bercovitch 1996b: 5). If an actor is perceived by the parties to be excessively pursuing his/her own interests, this may undermine the actor's ability to provide leadership in a given situation. The distinction in perceptions between acceptability and excessive partiality is an invisible red line. The effects of crossing this are often very evident, as will be seen in the chapter on the Dutch Presidency (chapter 3). Actions that cross this line can have a negative impact on future attempts to provide leadership; this is modeled as a feedback loop in Figure 1.2.

Internal capacity

The fourth category of leadership resources is the ability of a given actor to mobilize all of his/her relevant resources behind leadership attempts. The ability to mobilize resources, or, in other words, whether the actor has the actual *capacity* to provide leadership, is dependent upon the internal organization of the actor (Dimitrakopoulos and Kassim 2004). Factors relevant here are the structure of the given political system, including the number of 'veto points,' and the relative power of different domestic actors (ibid. 251–2). For example, in Germany's federal system, a power struggle evolved in the 1990s between the federation and the *Länder*, as the *Länder* increasingly attempted to have a say over what they viewed as the transferal to Brussels of their prerogatives (Beuter 2001: 101). After the introduction of Article 23 in the Basic Law the *Länder* in the *Bundesrat* had a veto power of the transfer of sovereign powers, creating many problems for German European policy-making (Mazzucelli 2001). Another example occurred during the Constitutional Treaty negotiations, where Commission President Prodi was weak internally within the Commission, which prevented the Commission from fully mobilizing all of its otherwise considerable informational resources behind one position (chapter 6). These examples clearly illustrate that the possession of strong material or informational leadership resources is not enough – one must have the capacity to be able to mobilize them effectively during the negotiations.

1.7 The impact of the negotiating context

The context of a specific EU treaty negotiation matters in that it determines the extent of the collective action problems that create a demand for leadership, and whether an actor possesses a privileged institutional position – in effect what *opportunities* specific actors have to supply leadership successfully.

Institutional set-up

Looking first at the importance of the specific negotiation structure, a widely held conjecture in negotiation theory and rational choice institutionalism holds that how negotiations are structured affects how actor power resources are translated into influence over outcomes (Zartman 2002). This is particularly evident when we are dealing with highly institutionalized, multilateral negotiations like EU constitutional negotiations. Therefore, the institutional set-up of the given negotiation can matter. Actors can either start with or gain a privileged position during a negotiation. This position can grant the actor a range of powers, which can be exploited to influence outcomes (Watkins 1999: 257–8; Sebenius 1984, 1991). Examples of privileged institutional positions in EU constitutional negotiations include agenda control or controlling the actual drafting process. Different institutional positions affect the opportunities and constraints upon the ability of actors to supply leadership. Based upon general conjectures in negotiation theory and in rational choice institutionalism, we expect the ability of actors successfully to provide leadership increases with the level of their involvement in the negotiation and drafting process. The Presidency that chairs the IGC negotiations will therefore, other things being equal, have much greater opportunities to provide leadership than a normal delegation.

The nature of the issues

We take the empirically verified assumption that delegates in a constitutional negotiation often do *not* have perfect knowledge of the very complex institutional and legal implications of the many issues under discussion. This is due to high costs of gaining information and the cognitive limitations of actors. Therefore, we expect that in complex and/or technical issues there would be a stronger demand for instrumental leadership provided by actors possessing comparative informational advantages, with the aim of helping the parties sort out the issues and craft agreement (Meier 1989: 280; Pollack 1997: 126–7).

The number of issues and parties in the negotiations

Thirdly, the number of issues and parties to the negotiations both can increase the *level of complexity* of a negotiation if they increase the number of cleavages in a given negotiation situation (Midgaard and Underdal 1977; Hampson 1995: 28–9). In highly complex, multilateral negotiations, characterized by many cross cutting cleavages, it is difficult for the parties to identify possible agreements. Meaningful communication among parties also becomes increasingly difficult (Hampson 1995: 28–9; Raiffa 1982; Midgaard and Underdal 1977; Hopmann 1996). In these types of complex situations, there is often a demand for instrumental leadership in order to help the parties find and craft a mutually agreeable outcome.

In a traditional IGC setting, this type of mediation and brokerage can be provided by different actors, including the Presidency, European Commission or Council Secretariat, or a specific government, usually a smaller member state. What is critical to the provision of this type of leadership is the possession of process expertise and a reputation for being 'acceptable' as a mediator/broker. Note again that acceptability is not necessarily the same thing as neutrality. We therefore expect the ability of actors to provide instrumental leadership increases with the number of issues and parties to a given negotiation.

Distribution and intensity of governmental preferences

Governmental preferences determine at the end of the day what outcome is the result of an intergovernmental conference. However, due to high bargaining costs and boundedly rationality, there is a considerable range within which agreement can be reached, and there is also the distinct possibility of negotiation failure. The demand for leadership to help the parties find and agree upon an outcome within this range varies according to four factors.

First, when governments have strongly held and irreconcilable positions, no zone of possible agreement exists. When faced with such a deadlock, only strong structural leadership attempts can potentially push governments towards agreement by shifting actor positions to create a zone of possible agreements. In the consensual EU, this is usually not an option for even the most powerful governments.

Secondly, the strength of governmental preferences also matters for the ability of actors to provide leadership. We can expect that very salient issues will be kept firmly under the control of materially powerful national delegations. In these high stakes issues, governments would have incentives to mobilize the necessary resources to reduce bargaining costs, thereby weakening the informational bargaining advantages of expert actors (Moravcsik 1999a). Therefore, outcomes in these issues will often reflect patterns of material power, and tend to reflect the preferences of Britain, France and Germany, as argued by Moravcsik (ibid.).

Further, we expect in high stakes issues negotiations will be dominated by a 'hard bargaining' atmosphere (Hopmann 1995; Elgström and Jönsson 2000), in which material leadership resources are more important than other types of resources. In less salient issues we would expect, in contrast, that EU institutional actors, as well as other actors possessing strong informational leadership resources, would have more discretion in shaping the discussions and outcomes (Epstein and Segal 2000; Meier 1989: 279).

Thirdly, there is a strong demand for instrumental leadership when the parties are strongly interested in agreement and a zone of possible agreements exists, but where the parties have difficulties choosing a specific solution on the Pareto frontier (see Figure 1.1). In this type of situation, a window of opportunity is created by the demand for leadership, which can enable a trusted mediator/broker such as a EU institution or a small government to step in and broker an agreement (Young 1991; Kressel and Pruit 1989; Carnevale and Arad 1996). This type of situation is identified as 'ripeness' in the negotiation literature, as the parties are prepared to find and agree upon a solution. Yet, they are dependent upon the provision of leadership in order to conclude agreement (Zartman 2000; Hopmann 1996).

One example of such a window of opportunity for leadership was the 1985 IGC, which negotiated the Single European Act. In these negotiations, there was a strong majority of governments that wanted to create a working Internal Market. However, there were multiple potential ways to achieve this outcome. The European Commission exploited the window of opportunity and was able to use the institutional position delegated by the Luxembourg Presidency to supply instrumental leadership. The Commission successfully

Table 1.1   Conjectures on the impact of the negotiation context for the demand for leadership in EU constitutional negotiations

---

Institutional position
- The more privileged an institutional position an actor possesses, the greater are the opportunities for the actor to translate his/her leadership resources into influence over outcomes.

Nature of the issues
- As the level of issue technicality increases, this increases the demand for instrumental leadership.

Number of issues and parties
- As the number of parties and issues increases in a given negotiation, this increases the demand for instrumental leadership to forge order out of chaos.

Distribution and intensity of governmental preferences
- When there is no zone of possible agreements, only strong structural leadership can be used to force parties to change their preferences to create a zone of possible agreements.
- When issues are politically sensitive, governments have incentives to mobilize the necessary resources to overcome bargaining costs, thereby lowering the demand for instrumental leadership.
- When governments want an agreement, yet are hindered in achieving it by bargaining impediments, a strong demand for instrumental leadership exists.

---

created a focal point closer to its own preferences than the outcome upon which governments, left to themselves, would most likely have agreed (Beach 2005: 54).

In conclusion, the negotiating context matters in that it can both grant actors privileged institutional positions that can act as a platform for leadership attempts, and as variations in the context determine the level of demand for specific types of leadership (see Table 1.1). As argued above, when the negotiating context is very complex, with many technically complex issues on the agenda, we should expect there to be a strong demand for instrumental leadership. In contrast, intractable negotiating situations can often only be resolved using 'muscles,' forcing governments to change their positions in order to create a zone of possible agreements.

1.8   A typology of leadership strategies

The literature abounds with different typologies of leadership strategies. Of greatest relevance for EU constitutional negotiations are the following two overall categories of leadership strategies. Each analysis evaluates whether the type of leadership supplied by a given actor matched the demand created by the specific negotiating context. In specific negotiations, however, we will often see a mix of strategies used by different actors (Underdal 1994: 192–3).

Unilateral actions such as 'go-it-alone' leadership, where a hegemon or group of powerful states imposes its own institutional choices upon other actors (Gruber 2000), are not included in the following, as they are rarely, if ever, seen in the EU. One notable exception was arguably the creation by France and Germany of the EMS (ibid.).

Structural leadership

Structural leadership is based upon the use of material leadership resources to forge a zone of possible agreements where none existed (Young 1991).[4] Types of tactics in structural leadership include the threat or use of negative or positive sanctions (sticks and carrots) in order to affect the incentives of other actors in relation to the proposed terms of an agreement, or to induce actors to make concessions (Malnes 1995; Young 1991). For these types of leadership strategies to work, actors must possess strong material leadership resources, and there must be collective action problems that prevent the achievement of consensus in the absence of structural leadership.

The provision of structural leadership can impact upon both the efficiency and distributive dimensions of a given negotiation (see Figure 1.1). An example of structural leadership upon the efficiency of an agreement could be the use of threats or side payments by a materially strong leader to 'buy off' a laggard in order to push an agreement away from a lowest-common denominator towards the Pareto frontier. Structural leadership usually has strong distributive effects, as materially powerful actors such as Britain, France and Germany tend to attempt to push outcomes closer to their own preferred outcomes. This was clearly seen in the endgame of the 2000 IGC, during which the French Presidency used structural leadership to push the solution on the issue of the re-weighting of Council votes closer towards its own preferred outcome (chapter 2).

Instrumental leadership

The second form of leadership is *instrumental*, where the leader attempts to fulfill certain key functions such as managing agendas, crafting compromises, building coalitions, and brokering deals. Negotiating skill, substantive expertise and political vision are used first to develop possible substantive solutions and then engineer consensus, putting together a deal that eludes other actors. In order to be able to exercise instrumental leadership, the potential leader must possess strong informational leadership resources, and its leadership attempts must be broadly perceived to be acceptable by the parties to the negotiations.

The strong demand for instrumental leadership exists when there are high bargaining costs and strong bargaining impediments; for instance, when actors have incentives to hide their true preferences. Instrumental leadership is, of course, not relevant in situations where a zone of possible agreement does not exist, as was arguably the case in the 1996–97 IGC regarding sensitive institutional questions (Underdal 1994: 192; Beach 2005).

The demand for specific types of instrumental leadership varies during the course of negotiations. Zartman and Berman split the negotiation process into three phases: (1) the diagnosis phase; (2) the construction of a possible solution in the formula phase; and (3) agreement on details (Zartman and Berman 1982).

During the diagnosis or agenda-setting phase, the agenda is often quite open, and the parties are frequently unsure of their own preferences (Stenelo 1972: 129–30). We expect the most successful instrumental leadership strategies during this phase would be attempts to create the preconditions for a favorable solution (Young 1991).[5] An example was the role played by the European Commission in the agenda-setting phase of the EMU intergovernmental conference, where the Commission actively attempted to link progress with the popular Internal Market program with further economic and monetary integration. This was most evident in the publication of the 'One Market, One Money' paper in 1988 (Dyson and Featherstone 1999; Beach 2005).

In the formula phase, the most important tactics involve attempts to craft a possible feasible solution, and also efforts to build coalitions supporting deals. Regarding crafting possible solutions, this is where we most often see the Presidency providing leadership, assisted by the Council Secretariat and/or the Commission. Once a possible solution has been crafted, however, leadership is also often necessary in order to build consensus (Young 1991; Sjöstedt 1994: 242; Metcalfe 1998: 430; Tallberg 2003; Zartman 2003).[6] Coalitions do not build themselves – they need direction (leadership) in order to form around specific outcomes (Zartman 2003: 185).

The final agreement stage is where actors haggle over the details of the agreement (Zartman and Berman 1982: 95, 147). The demand for instrumental leadership in the form of brokerage usually increases during this phase, and brokerage is often necessary to help the parties find a mutually acceptable outcome and remove unrealistic options from the table (Stenelo 1972: 143).

The impact of instrumental leadership usually is mostly seen on the efficiency dimension. This ensures that all possible gains are made. Instrumental leadership can however also impact upon the distribution of gains, particularly in highly complex negotiations on relatively low salience issues. Here the leader is able to craft a deal closer to his/her own preferred outcome than would otherwise have been the case.

1.9 Summary

The basic argument of this volume is that agreement does not come about by itself in EU constitutional negotiations. Agreement is dependent upon the provision of leadership. Leadership is often necessary to help parties find and agree upon mutually acceptable outcomes. It can be provided by numerous different actors and depends upon their resources as well as the specific negotiation context. The success of leadership attempts is dependent on whether the type of leadership supplied matches the demand for leadership created by the negotiating context. Leadership is often not neutral; therefore, who supplies leadership matters both for the efficiency of a given agreement and the distribution of gains.

In each specific EU constitutional negotiation, we can distinguish between material resource-based leadership strategies (structural), and information resource-based strategies (instrumental). For heuristic purposes, these two categories of strategy can be delineated by the following image. The supply of material resource-based leadership can be thought of as forging a zone of possible agreements where none existed. This is accomplished by changing actor preferences, in effect creating the 'outer bounds' for possible agreements (Figure 1.3). Within these outer bounds, the provision of instrumental leadership is usually necessary to find and agree upon an actual treaty during what are often very complex situations, and where strong bargaining impediments exist.

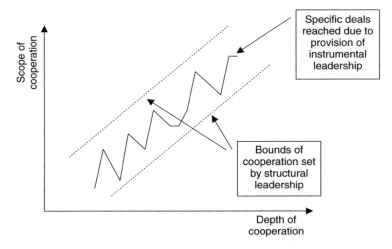

Figure 1.3 A hypothesis on the mix of leadership modes in EU constitutional negotiations

This is depicted in Figure 1.3, where instrumental leadership is crucial to find a specific deal within these outer bounds. While it is theoretically possible for one actor to provide both types of leadership, it is also hypothesized that there is often a distribution of labor, with materially strong actors, like France and Germany, usually setting the outer bounds for agreement. This is achieved through the provision of structural leadership. Then other actors, such as smaller member states, the EU Presidency, or the EU institutions, provide the instrumental leadership necessary to reach a specific agreement among many competing options.

1.10   Outline of the book

The chapters in this volume are grouped into two clusters: those focusing upon specific EU institutions, and those chapters analyzing individual member states. The initial chapters investigate the leadership role of the EU Presidency in recent rounds of EU treaty reform. Jonas Tallberg focuses on the French Presidency in the IGC 2000 and the extent to which the strong material resources of the Presidency were significant. Colette Mazzucelli analyses the learning curve experienced by the Dutch Presidency during the 1990–91 IGC and assesses the impact of that experience on the outcome of the 1996–97 IGC in terms of efficiency and distributive outcomes. Ben Crum compares the Italian and Irish Presidencies in the 2003–04 IGC, analyzing the results of the Italians in the Chair and the degree to which that outcome impacted upon the ability of the Irish to provide effective leadership at the helm.

In the three chapters analyzing the EU institutions, Derek Beach focuses attention on the overlooked Council Secretariat as the 'unseen hand' in treaty reform, whose possession of unrivaled bargaining skills and experience with EU constitutional negotiations meant that it played a key instrumental leader role, oiling the wheels of compromise. Hussein Kassim and Dionyssis Dimitrakopoulos analyze the changing influence of the European Commission in treaty reform by assessing the importance of its technocratic expertise and its reputation in this regard on the outcomes achieved. Andreas Maurer focuses on the European Parliament, the most vocal supporter of federal solutions, and assesses the extent to which its impact was dependent upon its acceptance by key member states as an IGC participant.

The chapters analyzing the EU governments ask which governments have driven the integration process. Simone Bunse, Paul Magnette, and Kalypso Nicolaïdis analyze whether small states matter in the context of the cleavage between the 'bigs' and the 'smalls,' which has increasingly dominated the debate on the institutional balance of power in the EU. Colette Mazzucelli, Ulrike Guérot and Almut Metz explain the changing influence of the French-German tandem, which has driven the integration process for decades and is now emerging as an 'improbable core' unable to lead an enlarged Union. Alasdair Blair analyses Great Britain's role in treaty negotiations, focusing upon the UK's 'outlier' position, and how the UK usually succeeded in acting as a 'laggard leader' by applying the brake on more ambitious proposals for reform. Christopher Bobínski focuses on Poland, which, as a larger and new member state, attempted to carve out a role early on the European Convention by allying with Spain to preserve the Nice formula on weighted voting in the Council. Renaud Dehousse and Florence Deloche-Gaudez offer a perspective on the future of leadership in the European Union in the aftermath of the rejection of the Constitutional Treaty in two founding member states, France and the Netherlands, and as the Union contemplates further enlargements to the southeast of the Continent.

The use of a common framework throughout the volume allows the concluding comparative analysis chapter to provide some tentative answers to the following empirical questions: which actors have driven the European integration process in the last two decades?; and, more importantly, what factors allowed specific actors to provide leadership in a given context? These conclusions provide a major step forward in the literature on the history-making bargains in the EU, enabling us to answer with more confidence the question of *which* actors have guided the 'big bangs' in the European integration process in the past two decades, and *why*.

Notes

1. While there is considerable debate about whether the European Treaties are true constitutions, only 'partial constitutions', or just international treaties, we use the terms treaty and constitutional reforms as synonyms in this work. For an extended discussion of this question, see Church and Phinnemore 2002.
2. This section draws extensively on Beach (2005).
3. See above. Moravcsik (1999a: 279) points out that actors with incentives to with-hold information from one another would also have incentives to withhold information from other actors such as an EU institutional actor. However, as the Council Secretariat sits at the center of a web of communications in an EU treaty negotiation, and given its reputation as a trusted insider, national governments often are more open with the Secretariat than they are with other national delegations (Beach 2004).
4. This is termed 'coercive' leadership by Underdal (1994: 186).
5. This aspect is defined intellectual leadership by Young.
6. Young terms this type of strategy entrepreneurial leadership.

2
The EU Presidency: France in the 2000 IGC

Jonas Tallberg

2.1 Introduction

Negotiations over treaty reform in the European Union are subject to one of the classic dilemmas of bargaining. For purposes of achieving maximum gain and securing themselves against exploitation, EU governments tend to be secretive about their true preferences and present tactical positions that go well beyond their actual bottom-lines. While common negotiation behavior, this practice risks producing breakdown by eliminating the perceived zone of agreement that is necessary for the parties to strike an accord and realize joint benefits. This chapter argues that the Presidency – the rotating chairmanship of the EU's intergovernmental negotiation bodies – provides the government in office with unique opportunities to help states overcome this ubiquitous bargaining problem and arrive at new constitutional treaties.

More specifically, this chapter advances two arguments. First, the institutional position of the Presidency endows the incumbent with informational advantages and a set of procedural powers that permit the government at the helm to shape both the efficiency and distributional implications of negotiated outcomes. Presidencies enjoy comparative informational advantages, as well as asymmetrical control of the negotiation process. Expressed in the terminology of this volume, EU Presidencies typically engage in instrumental leadership, sounding out state concerns, drafting compromise proposals, and constructing package-agreements. Second, as opposed to what is commonly assumed in the literature on negotiation and mediation (e.g., Young 1967; Carnevale and Arad 1996), the influence of the Presidency is not conditional on other parties' acceptance of Presidency leadership as legitimate and fair. Rather, Presidencies regularly exploit their privileged institutional position in ways that run counter to widespread norms of neutrality and impartiality. The French government's chairing of the IGC 2000 negotiations, examined in the empirical section of this chapter, demonstrates that EU Presidencies can be dominant, biased and disliked – and still achieve mutually acceptable outcomes. In sum, this chapter, just like the following one, underscores the leadership potential of the Presidency. Yet, contrary to Colette Mazzucelli's examination of the Dutch Presidencies in 1991 and 1997, this chapter speaks against neutrality/legitimacy as a necessary condition for instrumental leadership in EU treaty negotiations.

The argument in this chapter builds on a rational choice institutionalist theory of formal leadership in international cooperation presented in detail elsewhere (see, for example, Tallberg 2004b, 2005). The principal claim of this theory is that states in international cooperation create and empower the institution of the chairmanship in order to address collective-action problems that otherwise risk paralyzing multilateral negotiations. By executing functions of agenda management, brokerage, and representation, negotiation chairs help states reach efficient agreements. Yet these functions, and the informational advantages and procedural powers that come with them, may be exploited for private gain as well. Constrained and enabled by formal rules and procedures, opportunistic chairs typically steer negotiations toward their most preferred outcome, thus influencing both the efficiency and distributional implications of international cooperation.

This rationalist perspective on the power of the chair challenges the dominant interpretation of the Presidency in the literature on EU negotiations. With the exception of a limited number of recent studies (Wurzel 1996; Metcalfe 1998; Elgström 2003a; Tallberg 2003, 2004a), the existing body of literature specifically devoted to the EU Presidency tends to be a-theoretical and descriptive in orientation (e.g., O Nuallain 1985; Bassompierre 1988; Kirchner 1992). Partly because of its lack of communication with general theoretical traditions in political science, this literature has tended to underestimate the influence of the EU Presidency on political outcomes; in fact, it is commonly asserted that this office carries adverse consequences for its occupant's capacity to secure national interests.

In this vein, two observers assert that 'the real opportunity to promote initiatives or to deliver to domestic expectations is heavily constrained' (Hayes-Renshaw and Wallace 1997: 146), whereas another scholar and practitioner notes that 'Presidencies come and go [...] and the individual impact of each one on the European Union, provided they avoid disaster, is limited' (Corbett 1998: 1). One student of EU politics even submits that 'the presidency lacks most vital attributes and possesses most of the worst defects typically pertaining to executive power' (Coombes 1998: 7). This pessimistic perspective is summarized in a frequently quoted phrase by Jean-Louis Dewost, the former head of the Council's Legal Service, describing the Presidency as a *responsabilité sans pouvoir* – a responsibility without power (Dewost 1984: 31).

The remainder of this chapter is organized in three sections. In the next section, I apply the theoretical reasoning of this volume to the Presidency, and then identify the functions of and constraints upon the EU Presidency.

Section three presents the empirical analysis of the IGC 2000 and traces the influence of the French Presidency. I conclude with a discussion of the implications of this chapter for the study of leadership and negotiation in the EU.

2.2   Presidency leadership in EU negotiations[1]

The role and influence of the Presidency in EU negotiations are anchored in general processes of demand for, and supply of, brokerage in multilateral bargaining. This section first introduces the general theoretical logic of these processes, before identifying the strategic environment in which the EU Presidency operates.

The power of the chair: a rationalist theory

As discussed in chapter 1, general bargaining theory identifies negotiation failure as a standard problem in collective decisionmaking (e.g., Luce and Raiffa 1957; Walton and McKersie1965; Lax and Sebenius 1986; Young 1991). In order to reach an agreement that is satisfying to all participants, parties must signal what they can and cannot accept. Yet revealing information about one's true preferences is risky and non-tactical; risky, because it exposes a party to exploitation, and non-tactical because it deprives a party of concessions as a weapon for extracting favors from others. Negotiators therefore have incentives to be secretive or dishonest about their true preferences. The result is a distorted picture of preferences that either reduces the contract zone, with the effect that 'gains are left on the table,' or eliminates it, with the effect that negotiations break down. This bargaining problem is amplified in the multilateral setting, with its particular difficulties of communicating preferences among a large number of participants.

The functional solution to this problem is the involvement of a third party – a broker – who can act as a channel of reliable information about the nature of preferences. In multilateral negotiations, this is a role often assigned to the chair, who is delegated certain formal or informal process functions. The chair is then endowed with a set of advantages that permit it facilitate collective agreement. Analytically, these advantages split into two forms: asymmetrical control of information and procedural powers.

By virtue of its position, the chair gains access to information that is unavailable to the negotiating parties. Bilateral encounters allow the chair to obtain information about the parties' true preferences and resistance points. Through the management of the agenda and the search for viable compromises, the chair acquires an expertise in the dossiers under negotiation. In addition, the chair tends to develop an unusual command of the formal procedures of negotiation. The chair's asymmetrical control of the negotiation process encompasses both the general procedure and individual sessions. As process manager, the chair enjoys privileged control over decisions on the sequence of negotiations, the frequency of negotiation sessions, and the method of negotiation. As manager of individual negotiation sessions, the chair opens and concludes meetings, shapes the meeting agenda, allots the right to speak, directs voting procedures, and summarizes the results obtained. Expressed in more political terms, the chair enjoys asymmetrical control over who gets to say what, when, how, and to what effect.

By using these advantages, the chair can help negotiating parties overcome bargaining impediments that prevent the realization of collective gains. Privileged access to information about the parties' true preferences enables the chair to construct viable compromise proposals. Privileged control of procedure permits the chair to structure the negotiation process and individual sessions in ways that are favorable to agreement.

Yet the very same advantages can also be exploited to pursue national gains. An opportunistic chair will seek to exploit its exclusive preference information and procedural control to promote agreements with certain distributional outcomes rather than others. The influence of the chair over bargaining outcomes is therefore best conceived of in terms of both efficiency and distribution: at a first analytical stage, the chair helps negotiating parties reach an efficient agreement; at a second analytical stage, the chair affects the distribution of gains by promoting the one agreement – among a range of efficient outcomes – that is closest to its own preferred position. Expressed in the rational choice terminology used in this volume, the chair moves outcomes first to, and then along, the Pareto frontier.

In the execution of its functions, the chair may be constrained by both formal rules and informal norms. Formal constraints come in two shapes: institutional procedures for the office of the chair, and decision rules for the adoption of proposals. Institutional procedures provide the formal basis of the office of the chair, and include appointment procedures, administrative procedures, and oversight procedures. Decision rules shape the ease with which the chair can promote proposals that satisfy the requirements of an efficient bargain, yet meet the partisan interests of the chair. Informal constraints consist of established norms about the appropriate behavior of the chair. Norms factor into the chair's calculation of gains from alternative courses of action, but do not affect its basic preferences. The existence of multiple, competing norms typically reduces the costs of violation and expands the range of acceptable behavior.

In summary, this theory suggests that multilateral bargaining creates a demand for brokerage by the chair, whose informational advantages and procedural powers enable this actor to influence the efficiency and distributional consequences of negotiated agreements, under the constraints of formal rules and informal norms. Based on this general theoretical logic, the remainder of this section identifies the specific functions of and constraints upon the EU Presidency.

2.3   Leadership resources of the EU Presidency

Comparative informational advantages

The EU Presidency enjoys access to a set of actors and practices that enable it to gain privileged information about EU governments' preferences. The General Secretariat of the Council plays a central role in the Presidency's gathering of information, and works side by side with the Presidency throughout negotiations (Stubb 2002; Beach 2005). The Secretariat provides three main kinds of information to the Presidency, thus granting the chair a competitive edge. First, and most importantly, the Council Secretariat tracks the preferences and negotiating positions of all member governments. Through the long-term involvement in a dossier and informal communication with government representatives, the Secretariat gains an in-depth and horizontal picture of state preferences. Second, no actor is as familiar with the complex decisionmaking procedures of the EU and the formal instruments available to the Presidency as the Council Secretariat. Tactical advice on negotiation procedure is part and parcel of the Secretariat's support function, as is legal advice on possible courses of action. Third, the Council Secretariat constitutes a source of expertise on the content of dossiers under negotiation. Much like Commission's officials gain intimate knowledge of a subject when preparing a proposal, the civil servants of the Secretariat develop an issue-specific expertise when tracing a dossier through the Council machinery.

The Council Secretariat communicates its information on preferences, procedure, and contents to the chair through so-called *notes au Président*. These confidential documents are drawn up exclusively for the Presidency and generally contain information on the background of a proposal, its legal basis, the voting procedure, the state of play in the negotiations, governments' negotiating positions and room for concessions, tactical brokerage advice, and alternative compromises that the Presidency may want to investigate.

The second important source of privileged information on state preferences is bilateral talks initiated by the Presidency. The 'confessional' is a bilateral encounter between the Presidency and a member state, designed to break deadlocks in negotiations. Confessionals may be convened either during the course of negotiations, by simply adjourning plenary talks for bilateral discussions, or in preparation of negotiation sessions. As suggested by the term confessional, these encounters are strictly confidential: 'The President is under oath not to reveal a Member State's "confessed" position to any other Member State, but his secret and privileged knowledge of the positions and the degree of flexibility of all Member States can enable him to make winning compromise proposals' (Westlake 1999: 115). The sharing of private information is the most important function of the confessional, but it also provides an opportunity to put additional pressure on recalcitrant delegations, and to offer unofficial side-payments.

The Presidency practice of *tours des capitales* serves the same purpose of collecting information and putting pressure to bear. These shuttle diplomacy tours take place at a number of levels in the political machinery. In addition to the prime ministers' visits to all EU capitals prior to summits, less high-profile tours are undertaken by the ministers for foreign and European affairs, as well as senior civil servants. The format of the bilateral encounter enables prime ministers to share information on their bottom lines with the Presidency, without granting the same favor to other bargaining parties, thus improving the chances of agreement at the summit without exposing themselves to exploitation.

Reputation

In its activities as broker, the EU Presidency has to relate to two well-established informal constraints: the norms of neutrality and effectiveness. Both norms have gained semi-official status and are frequently referred to among EU policymakers and in official documents. The existence of multiple, and often competing, norms expands the Presidency's room for maneuver, by enabling the Presidency to justify its potential violations of one norm, with reference to another.

Existing research points to the existence of a strong honest broker norm (Metcalfe 1998; Elgström 2003b). This is further evidenced by the Council Secretariat's handbook for Presidencies, which prescribes that '[t]he Presidency must, by definition, be neutral and impartial' (1997: 5). Presidency action in conflict with the expectation of neutrality can carry negative reputational consequences. Yet Presidencies only face incentives to violate this norm if their own preferred outcome differs from the expected outcome under neutral brokerage. A Presidency with extreme preferences should be most tempted to violate the norm of neutrality, whereas a Presidency with central preferences faces few reasons not to comply.

Furthermore, the norm of effectiveness is sufficiently established in the EU policy environment to be expressed in official documents. The report of the 'Three Wise Men' stated: 'The Presidency's basic duty in this process is simply to get results. [···] It must urge the debate towards conclusions by using the most appropriate combination of the weapons at its disposal' (1979: 36; see also Westlake 1999: 308; Elgström 2003b). The emphasis on results constrains the Presidency's capacity to promote its own optimal outcome, to the extent that deals with other distributive implications are more readily available. At the same time, the expectation of effective brokerage may enable and legitimize biased behavior. As one Commission official recognizes: 'A chairman cannot be neutral, then you would never get any decisions' (interview, December 6 2000).

2.4 Negotiating context

Institutional position – procedural powers of the Presidency

The EU Presidency enjoys asymmetrical control of the negotiation process due to the possession of a broad repertoire of delegated procedural powers.

As one observer notes: '[A]ll Council sessions are essentially stage-managed by the Presidency' (Sherrington 2000: 45).

First, the Presidency is central in determining the pace of Council negotiations. It is the Presidency that fixes the meeting schedule, and even if tradition imposes certain limits, the chair can shape the number and frequency of formal and informal negotiating sessions. The effect is a well-documented variation across Presidencies in the number of meetings in different working groups, committees, and ministerial configurations (Sherrington 2000). Control over the meeting schedule grants the Presidency a capacity to improve the chances of agreement, by speeding up negotiations. The Presidency can call further meetings at short notice, alter meeting agendas to allow greater room for negotiations on certain dossiers, and impose time pressure on the parties.

The Presidency's formal prerogative to decide the format of negotiation sessions constitutes a second procedural instrument. The standard format of a negotiation session at the ministerial level is a formal meeting in the Council's Brussels headquarters, where each minister is accompanied by an impressive contingent of officials. To facilitate agreement, the Presidency frequently chooses to shift meetings into restricted session, where only a few, or even no, officials are allowed to stay, thus expanding the ministers' room for maneuver. An additional variation on the negotiation format is the informal meetings that the Presidency may convene in the home country. The purpose of these meetings is to provide a more relaxed and collegial atmosphere that can improve the chances of reaching an agreement.

A third procedural power is the so-called Presidency compromise. The existence of a specific term for compromises proposed by the chair reflects the Commission's original role as mediator and the Presidency's subsequent development into the preferred broker. Part of the explanation rests with the Presidency's unusual capacity to conclude package deals, owing to its position as linchpin between the different bargaining arenas in the Council. Such deals may consist of a conventional trade of concessions within the same issue area, but the true value-added of the Presidency as broker is the ability to stitch together unorthodox deals that stretch across a number of issue areas.

In Community negotiations, the Presidency's compromise text competes with the original proposal of the Commission, but supplants the latter as single negotiating text if attracting sufficient support, in which case the Commission is put under pressure to revise its proposal. In intergovernmental negotiations, the Presidency's compromise document faces less competition for the position as single negotiating text. Once the Presidency's text has been established as the basis of negotiation, the chair's ability to engineer agreement around its preferred outcome expands considerably. Since it is also the Presidency's responsibility to determine when an issue is ripe for decision, negotiations generally continue until the Presidency assesses that a sufficient number of governments are on board. Typically, the Presidency does not make use of its authority to call a vote, but instead proceeds by noting the existence of sufficient support, and if nobody objects the proposal is considered adopted. Explains one European Parliament official: 'He who proposes is in the driver's seat. Member states only say no if they totally cannot buy it, which grants the Presidency quite some room to shape deals to its own liking' (interview, July 2 2001).

Constraints upon the powers of the Presidency – rules and preferences

Since the Presidency's role as broker is not a formal position, but an informal function that has evolved over time, its brokerage activities are not regulated through procedures of *ex ante* or *ex post* control. Instead, the most central formal constraints are the decision rule for the adoption of proposals, and the distribution of state preferences. The applicable decision rule conditions the chair's capacity to construct an agreement and to promote its own ideal solution. In contrast to EU policymaking, where qualified majority voting (QMV) is the most common decision rule, revisions of the treaties must be adopted unanimously.

When unanimous consent is required, the Presidency as broker must take into consideration the interests of all member states. The distribution of state preferences consequently becomes of central importance. Since even outliers must be brought on board, the Presidency is forced to seek solutions that accommodate the position of the most conservative state, wishing the least change to existing rules. Unless the Presidency's own position is close to that of the most conservative state, the capacity of the chair to promote its own preferred solution is simultaneously reduced. The Presidency's best chance of delivering agreements that go beyond lowest-common-denominator solutions rests with its ability to construct package agreements. If the Presidency can compensate outliers through side payments, it can conclude agreements that upgrade the common interest.

The next section illustrates the explanatory power of this theory by examining France's chairing of the IGC 2000 negotiations. The case presentation draws on a combination of primary material, in the shape of interviews, documents, and secondary material, in the form of detailed empirical accounts, often by participants or close observers of these negotiations and news reports.

2.5   France and IGC 2000

The rationale of IGC 2000 was to prepare the EU's institutions for an enlarged Union. The conference addressed four key issues: the size and composition of the Commission; the weighing of votes in the Council; the extension of QMV in the Council; and the methods for enhanced cooperation. The issues were extremely controversial, and it was no coincidence that EU governments had failed to find acceptable solutions when first considering these issues at the 1996–97 IGC. In the spring of 2000 the Portuguese Presidency had managed to define the agenda of the IGC, but little movement had taken place in the substantive negotiations on the four dossiers when France took over the chair on 1 July 2000. The conclusion of the IGC during the fall was the foremost priority of the French government (2000).

The negotiations

When the French Presidency reinitiated the negotiations, it launched a new approach, composed of a partially new structure for the overall negotiation process, as well as a specific brokerage strategy. The French government announced a fuller schedule of IGC meetings and a new format for the negotiations (Dinan and Vanhoonacker 2000–01). Next to the existing nego-tiation levels of state representatives in the Preparatory Group, foreign minis-ters in the General Affairs Council, and heads of state and government in the European Council, the Presidency added a fourth tier of extraordinary ministerial conclaves. Whereas the effectiveness of this move is contested, it illustrated the Presidency's autonomy in shaping the format of the nego-tiation process. A further step taken by the Presidency was to make the IGC negotiations the focus of several informal ministerial meetings.

The French brokerage strategy consisted of a number of consecutive steps (Galloway 2001: 33–6; Gray and Stubb 2001; Schout and Vanhoonacker 2001). Rather than moving directly to the stage of article drafting, the French began by issuing oriented questionnaires, in order to sound out state concerns. Over time, these questionnaires turned into papers that gradually acquired the form of draft treaty language. In early November, these papers were merged into a summary document that constituted a first outline of a draft treaty, which then was shaped over the coming month into the draft submitted for final negotiation in Nice. In terms of substance, the French Presidency devoted most of the early work to the less sensitive issues of QMV extension and enhanced cooperation. By contrast, the size of the Commis-sion and the reweighing of votes were largely left for the European Council summits in Biarritz and Nice.

There was no denying that France had a distinct preference for certain outcomes over others. Already at the previous IGC France had insisted on a Commission with a limited number of members. France also wanted to secure a reweighing of votes that would compensate large member states for their likely loss of one Commissioner, as well as maintain French parity with Germany. France was in favor of an extension of QMV, yet concerned to keep the national veto for provisions pertaining to visas, asylum, and immigration, as well as the common commercial policy. France was one of the strongest proponents for easier access to enhanced cooperation.

The size of the Commission quickly became the most controversial issue in the negotiations (*European Voice*, 20–26 July 2000; 21–27 Sept. 2000). The French Presidency presented a proposal and structured the negotiations in favor of a limited Commission, where each member state would not be allowed to keep a Commissioner, as desired by the smaller states. While criticized by many as unproductive, this move exposed the underlying fault line and prepared the ground for the informal summit in Biarritz. At the summit, the Presidency managed to gain the support of the other four large states for equal rotation of the posts in a restricted Commission. By declaring their own willingness to lose their final Commissioner, and promising equal treatment, the large states placed the ball firmly in the court of the small states. This proved to be a major breakthrough in the negotiations, which then shifted to the format of such a capping in the number of Commissioners (*European Voice*, 19–25 Oct. 2000; Gray and Stubb 2001).

The negotiations on the reweighing of votes lay dormant for much of the autumn. This was the most important issue for the large member states, which sought compensation for the loss of (at least) one Commissioner. Real bargaining was postponed by the Presidency to the concluding session in Nice, since any solution to this highly sensitive issue would require concessions that only heads of state and government could make (Gray and Stubb 2001). The fall negotiations largely consisted of an inventory of alternative reweighing systems.

From early September onwards, the Presidency devoted considerable time to the issue of QMV (Galloway 2001: 101–102). In order to facilitate trade-offs at later stages, the Presidency kept as many articles as possible on the list. It became clear that some articles were sufficiently sensitive that only part of the subject matter could realistically be moved to QMV. The Presidency developed consecutive draft proposals, in an effort to find texts that would respect national sensitivities, yet achieve maximum extension of QMV (interview, French government representative, February 9 2001). This work was particularly delicate in those areas where France itself held the strongest reservations; for instance, the article on the common commercial policy saw the greatest number of options, redrafts and proposals during the entire IGC (Galloway 2001: 118).

Enhanced cooperation was put high on the agenda when France took over the chair. The first ministerial conclave was partly dedicated to the issue, as were five of the first eight meetings of the Preparatory Group. The attention devoted to the issue yielded quick results, and the Presidency's handling of the dossier is generally considered a strong contributing factor (Gray and Stubb 2001; Schout and Vanhoonacker 2001; Stubb 2002: 115–22). Once agreement had been reached that flexibility would not be applicable in the core areas of the internal market and economic and social cohesion, relaxing the conditions for enhanced cooperation proved less controversial. In fact, the European Council summit at Biarritz reached political agreement on all parts of this dossier, save enhanced cooperation in foreign and security policy.

The Nice Summit and the Nice Treaty

As the end stage of the negotiations approached, the French Presidency sought to prepare the ground for a comprehensive agreement in Nice. Formal negotiations were increasingly supplemented with informal bargaining and brokerage (Gray and Stubb 2001). The Presidency engaged in bilateral talks at three levels: confessionals were held with the state representatives in the Preparatory Group, European Affairs Minister Pierre Moscovici met with his counterparts in other EU governments on a *tour des capitals*, as did President Jacques Chirac shortly before the summit. The likelihood of a deal in Nice improved considerably, when Chirac and German Chancellor Gerhard Schröder, after a bilateral *tête-à-tête*, could announce that they had agreed to agree (Dinan and Vanhoonecker 2001). French insistence on voting parity despite Germany's greater population had until then been seen as a potential impediment to final agreement.

The concluding negotiations in Nice on 8–11 December proved extremely tough and have generally been described as a tug of war over national interests, devoid of the honored Community spirit. The talks began on the Friday night with bilateral confessionals between the French Presidency and the delegations, on the basis of which a draft treaty was distributed for negotiation on Saturday morning. This draft was discarded by the small member states, which considered it biased in favor of the positions of the large states, both as regards the size of the Commission and the reweighing of votes. A second draft was presented Saturday afternoon and a third draft Sunday morning, the main outstanding question being the reweighing of votes. Sunday afternoon and night, multilateral deliberations were interrupted eight times for bilateral consultations with delegations and, one by one, member governments came on board (Gray and Stubb 2001). To facilitate the last necessary compromises, the Presidency moved the negotiations to restricted session, excluding all but the heads of state and government. The negotiations could be concluded early Monday morning, once Belgium had given its consent following side payments from the Presidency.

Member governments reached the compromise that each state would maintain one Commissioner until the EU reaches 27 members, when the number of Commissioners will be capped at a lower level than the number of member states and an equal rotation system will be introduced. While temporarily satisfying the small member states' insistence on one Commissioner each, the compromise is best considered a victory for the French line of reasoning. After Amsterdam, it was generally expected that the large states would lose their second Commissioner, but all states would keep one. The French campaign for capping the number of Commissioners, and the rallying of other large states around the principle of equal rotation, explain the turn of events (interview, Council official, 8 Feb. 2001).

The final outcome on the reweighing of votes was a complicated triple-majority compromise. According to the new rules, the adoption of an act by QMV requires the support of a qualified majority of votes, a majority of member states, and at least 62 percent of the EU's population. The large states obtained the expected rebalancing of voting weight in their favor, and France managed to gain the hotly desired German acceptance of continued parity in votes. The price for formal parity was the new demographic criterion, whereby Germany in effect, but not as visibly, was compensated for its larger population. Yet, in order to gain small state support for the demographic criterion, the Presidency had to introduce the new majority-of-states requirement. To ensure unanimous support, the Presidency also engaged in *ad hoc* deal making at the end, where Spain gained additional votes, as did the Netherlands in comparison to Belgium, which in turn was bought off with the decision that European Council meetings would take place in Brussels in the future (interview, French government representative, February 9 2001).

Member governments eventually agreed to transfer about 30 articles from unanimity to QMV. This was generally regarded a success in numerical terms, but less impressive in substantive terms, since certain key legislative articles remained under unanimity. For instance, QMV in taxation and social security coordination was blocked by the UK, and QMV in structural funds decisions prevented by Spain. In addition, the French government refused to surrender its national veto on some matters pertaining to visas, asylum, and immigration, and the common commercial policy.

The question of enhanced cooperation had largely been solved before the summit. The only outstanding issue was whether flexible cooperation should be possible in foreign and security policy. Governments eventually limited the scope in this domain, only enabling enhanced cooperation for the implementation of certain foreign policy instruments, while excluding matters with military or defense implications.

2.6   The power of the chair: assessing process and outcome

In the process of steering the negotiations toward a conclusion in Nice, the French Presidency made active use of the procedural powers and informational advantages of the chair. When taking over the Presidency, the French government exploited its control over the negotiation process by intensifying the formal meeting schedule, introducing a fourth tier in the negotiations, and moving the IGC to the top of the agenda of both formal and informal Council meetings. Toward the end of the process, the Presidency invited the parties to specific, informal negotiation sessions, in order to prepare the ground for a final agreement. Throughout the process, the Presidency's documents functioned as single negotiating texts. The negotiation process was structured so as to solve the easiest questions first – extension of QMV and enhanced cooperation – and save the exceedingly thorny matters–the size of the Commission and the reweighing of votes – to the heads of state and government.

The chair's control over negotiation sessions was used to collect inform-ation about state preferences, put pressure on recalcitrant parties, and present revised compromise proposals. The Presidency obtained information about member state preferences through questionnaires, and sought private information about the parties' resistance points through confessionals and *tours de capitales*. New compromise texts were formulated in response to reac-tions and new information, and the chair's prerogative of summing up nego-tiation sessions was used to steer the deliberations in the direction desired by the Presidency. In order to cajole recalcitrant parties into agreement at the end stage, institutional side payments were invented and distributed, in the absence of the traditional money purse.

France also exploited its position as chair to advance its own national interests – a source of significant criticism. While resolute in its ambition to deliver a treaty, the French government was equally adamant on the content of such a deal. It is striking how the French government scrupulously used the position of the chair to advance proposals that essentially constituted national position papers framed as Presidency compromises. 'France took its own proposal as a basis for discussion and assumed that any point on which objections were not raised had been accepted. Contrary to other Presidencies that would consider the different delegations' stands on a particular point, France contented itself with stating its views and asking opponents to stand up' (Costa, Couvidat, and Daloz 2003: 124).

The open use of the Presidency's assets to this end resulted in much negative publicity, which some observers interpret as a sign of failure for the French government. Yet if we assess the substantive outcome of the negotiations, the French were remarkably successful in protecting their own interests. 'France succeeded in what really mattered to her: holding the bottom line on issues of vital national interest' (Meunier and Nicolaïdis 2001: 7; see also interview, Commission official, February 8 2001). The French managed to produce a treaty in Nice, achieved a future capping in the number of Commissioners, secured a rebalancing of voting weight in favor of large states and formal vote parity with Germany, prevented QMV in nationally sensitive areas, and reached the goal of facilitating enhanced cooperation.

The French Presidency's handling of the IGC 2000 highlights the potential tension between the dual leadership objectives of concluding an agreement (efficiency) and securing national objectives (distribution). While eventually achieving an accord that no party found sufficiently problematic to veto, the French government simultaneously delayed the process toward an agree-ment through its insistence of terms that satisfied French national interests. Clearly, the Presidency could have concluded the IGC sooner, had it chosen to sacrifice French concerns. Previous work on Presidency leadership testifies to such examples of self-sacrifice, for instance, during the Finnish Presidency of 1999 (Tiilikainen 2003). Yet what sets the French case apart from such examples of countries that have 'paid the price of the Presidency' is the presence of extreme and intense national interests in the issues under negotiation. Sacrificing marginal concerns on policy issues is one thing, sacrificing key national interests in the shape of the long-term rules of the game an entirely different thing.

To address the counterfactual question of whether this distributional outcome would have been likely with another government at the helm, we can safely conclude that this probability is exceedingly low. The empirical analysis reveals how the French government used the power resources of the Presidency at key points in the negotiations to favor certain outcomes rather than others. For instance, it is unlikely that one of the EU's small and medium-sized states, had they enjoyed access to the Presidency position, would have tabled proposals and steered the negotiations toward a deal that eventually would leave them without a Commissioner – a key concern for these countries. Similarly, it is highly improbable that any other member state would have structured the end game of the negotiations so as to achieve the French objective of formal vote parity with Germany, which required the creation of a complicated triple-majority system for qualified majority voting and the invention of institutional side-payments.

The Presidency's brokerage activities were shaped by formal decision rules, the distribution of state preferences, and informal norms. The requirement of unanimous agreement for all provisions of the treaty left predictable imprints on the outcome. On the size of the Commission and the reweighing of votes, the brokerage efforts of the Presidency were facilitated by the absence of a status quo alternative. No agreement meant no arrangement after enlargement, and all states were therefore anxious to come to some sort of deal. By contrast, concrete status quo alternatives existed as regards QMV and enhanced cooperation – continuation as previously – which meant that the requirement of unanimity favored the most conservative states: the UK on taxation and social security, Spain on the structural funds, and France on visas, asylum, and immigration, as well as the common commercial policy. Except where France itself benefited, this logic reduced the Presidency's capacity to steer the negotiations toward its most preferred outcome.

Cognizant of the norm of neutrality, the French government paid certain lip service to the principle of the honest broker, but let its behavior be guided by other considerations. Whenever France's core interests were at stake, the role of neutral arbiter was unquestionably relegated to a position of secondary importance (Costa, Couvidat, and Daloz 2003). When accused by other member states of partiality, arrogance, and misuse of the Presidency, the French government referred to the necessities for achieving results, thus exploiting the tension between the norms of neutrality and efficiency.

2.7   Conclusion

When member states' bargaining positions are incompatible and no area for agreement can be discerned, the Presidency's brokerage efforts can help governments avoid negotiation failure. The sources of Presidency leadership are its privileged access to information about state preferences and its instruments of procedural control. Yet these leadership resources and procedural powers are not only used for collective gain, but also for promoting the Presidency government's national interests. Typically, Presidencies steer negotiations away from their worst alternative and toward their preferred outcome. As one former permanent representative testified, it is 'almost impossible' for the Council to arrive at decisions that go against the desires of the Presidency (quoted in Troy Johnston 1994: 25). This is confirmed by the IGC 2000 negotiations; despite negotiation conditions that worked against the capacity of the Presidency to engineer agreement and shape distributional outcomes, the French government managed to strike an accord that simultaneously secured key national interests.

In the following chapter of this volume, Colette Mazzucelli analyzes the capacity of the Dutch government to provide leadership at the 1991 and 1996–97 IGCs. This chapter underlines many of the same points, especially the optimistic perspective on the Presidency's ability to offer leadership and help governments overcome deadlock in EU treaty reform negotiations. Yet it differs in once central respect – whereas the analysis of the Dutch cases points to acceptability and legitimacy as necessary leadership resources, the French case speaks against such an interpretation. During the 2000 IGC, the French government paid little regard to norms of neutrality and impartiality, specifically favored French national interests, and was severely criticized for its exploitation of the chair, yet succeeded in crafting a compromise that eventually was accepted by all parties.

It is sometimes argued that EU member states differ in the extent to which they successfully can exploit the Presidency for national purposes, large states typically being more prone and able to seek private gains. The alternative outcomes of the Dutch and the French cases would support such an interpretation. However, evidence from small-state Presidencies on other high-profile dossiers suggest otherwise. Sweden affected both the efficiency and distributional consequences of the EU agreement on new transparency rules during its Presidency in the first half of 2001 (Bjurulf and Elgström 2004), just as the Belgian government secured agreement on an expanded agenda for the European Convention on constitutional reform during the fall of 2001 (Kerremans and Drieskens 2003), and Denmark was pivotal in brokering a final deal in the enlargement negotiations during the fall of 2002 (Friis 2003). Recent comparative research suggests that EU governments – irrespective of relative power positions, administrative resources, and historically salient identities – use the Presidency office as a vehicle for national political interests (Elgström 2003a; Bengtsson, Elgström, and Tallberg 2004).

The provision of leadership in international negotiations is seldom altruistic. Yet, as Oran Young (1991, p. 296) points out, this is a fact that should comfort rather than disappoint. 'Individuals who act out of self-interest are far more reliable and predictable than those who respond episodically to some other motivating force, a fact that bodes well for the prospects of constructing a robust theory of entrepreneurial leadership in international society.'

Note

1. This section and the following section draw on my article 'The Power of the Presidency: Brokerage, Efficiency, and Distribution in EU Negotiations,' published in *Journal of Common Market Studies*, 42(4): 999–1022.

3
Drawing Lessons in the Chair: Assessing the Dutch Presidency's Impact during the Maastricht and Amsterdam Conferences

Colette Mazzucelli

3.1 Introduction

From the Single European Act (SEA) in 1986 to the 2003–04 IGC that agreed to a European Constitutional Treaty, member states and institutions of the European Union (EU) have engaged in a process of almost continuous treaty revisions. As a participant in European Community (EC) treaty reform in the early 1990s observed: 'negotiation about the future direction of the EC is, in fact, the norm rather than the exception' (Corbett 1992). As a founding member of the European Communities,[1] the Netherlands evidences a traditional concern about domination by the large member states. The fear is that Dutch interests will be subordinate to those of the 'Big Three' – Germany, France and Britain. This serves as a historical and sociological basis for Dutch attitudes vis-à-vis the Presidency of the Council. It also explains why the Dutch traditionally sought an independent European Commission as an ally (Jensen 1985).

The Netherlands, which is the largest member of the BENELUX coalition, demonstrated a pro-integrationist line in negotiations that led to successive treaty reforms at Maastricht and Amsterdam. A diachronic comparison reveals significant findings about the learning curve experienced by the Dutch Presidency as well as the changes in Dutch attitudes toward European integration. This analysis explains the puzzle of the 'Black Monday' episode in 1991 during which the Dutch Presidency broke all the rules of European treaty reform. The Dutch chose a contentious instrumental leadership strategy in which a unified treaty structure was at the center of the controversy. Some analysts argue that this choice is indicative of an underlying normative 'federalist' preference structure.[2]

This chapter posits that the Dutch Presidency is the single best case of a small or medium-sized member state's practical ability to learn in the Chair in the specific context of European treaty revisions. Unlike the French case analyzed in Tallberg's chapter, no other small or medium-sized member state Presidency attempted to implement a contentious instrumental strategy during intergovernmental conference reform. During the 1997 endgame, the Presidency aimed to shift outcomes in treaty reform negotiations to ensure that agreement was reached (efficiency dimension); yet, Dutch representatives also sought to shape the final treaty along the lines of their own national preferences (distributive dimension) in institutional issues, and in the flexibility and Schengen policy areas. The Dutch Presidency clearly evidenced an outlier preference vis-à-vis the other member states on Schengen. This chapter posits that the incorporation of the Schengen Agreement into the Treaty was not a make or break issue like that of the unified treaty structure in 1991. Schengen has since though acquired particular significance though as one of three projects to generate integration momentum alongside the single European currency and successive enlargements (Guérot 2005).

This chapter makes some preliminary observations about the success and/or failure of leadership attempts by the Dutch Presidency as an 'agenda-shaper' that advances integration through its ability to bring together 'the recognition of a problem, the development of policy proposals, and a receptive political climate' (Tallberg 2003). The ways in which the Presidency set the agenda to incorporate the Schengen Agreement into the Treaty were its ability to raise the awareness of the problem of leaving Schengen outside the scope of the treaty structure, and then being able to follow this up with concrete proposals at the negotiation table. The findings in this chapter demonstrate that Dutch behavior as President supports both a rationalist as well as a sociological approach. As this behavior pertains to the three issues analyzed in this chapter: institutional questions, flexibility and Schengen, the Dutch Presidency acted in a strategic manner as a rational agent constrained and enabled by existing rules, procedures and norms (Elgström 2003). Nonetheless, the shadow cast by its 1991 experience in the Chair is a long one. The Dutch Presidency by many accounts is an identity-driven actor, which tried, particularly after 'Black Monday', to determine the appropriate response to a given situation. The Dutch case illustrates the ways in which national, historically formed identities provide a foundation for decisions just as role conceptions based on previous experience in the Chair provide another. Learning and path dependence are essential in this explanation (ibid.). In other words, the Netherlands activities in the Chair were influenced as much by perceptions of how it should behave (sociological) as by cost – benefit calculations (rationalist).

This chapter's findings also shed light on whether any attempt at excessively partial leadership, identified here as a contentious instrumental strategy, is destined to fail during negotiations on treaty reform. In contrast to Jonas Tallberg's findings on the French Presidency in this volume, this analysis suggests that depending on the issue and the size of the member state in question, legitimacy is a key part of a potential leader's resources, and a such is a necessary condition for effective leadership in EU treaty negotiations.

3.2   Dutch preferences

The Dutch Presidency is a long-standing proponent of the 'Community method'; relying on the European Commission as the 'guardian of the Treaties' and protector of the interests of smaller member states. This preference, which motivated its actions during the 1990–91 and 1996–97 IGCs, explains the Presidency's goal of a unified treaty structure during the Maastricht negotiations on political union. Its preferences to institutionalize flexibility in the Treaty and to integrate the Schengen Agreement into the first pillar of the Treaty on European Union (TEU) during the Amsterdam process are examples that further reveal a clear and consistent approach to treaty reform that reflects 45 years of experience with European integration. These preferences also point to the type of leadership strategy the Dutch Presidency eventually chose to achieve its objectives. This choice, and the ways in which the Netherlands made use of the resources at its disposal to achieve bargaining outcomes during the Maastricht and Amsterdam IGCs, illustrate the influence a small or medium-sized state Presidency exercises in treaty reform negotiations.

3.3   The resources of the Dutch Presidency in the Maastricht and Amsterdam IGCs

The next sections discuss the leadership resources at the disposal of the Dutch Presidency; its comparative informational advantages, reputation and internal capacity.

The Dutch Presidency's leadership resources

In comparison to its larger neighbors, Germany and France, or its ally on specific key policy issues, the United Kingdom, or some of the newer member states like Poland, the Netherlands is a relatively small member state Presidency. It does not exercise what Young terms 'structural leadership,' which is usually available only to those states with strong material resources. In the context of treaty reform, relevant material leadership resources are derived from a country's material wealth, as well as its ability to change other actors' dependence on an agreement. These resources enable a large state to push other governments towards the large state's own preferred outcome, as demonstrated by Tallberg's research on the French Presidency in the IGC 2000, which epitomizes the use of structural power to influence outcomes.

The Dutch Presidency's comparative informational advantages

Given its lack of diplomatic resources, the Netherlands, assuming the functions and role of the Presidency, must rely on the 'institutional 'memory' and personal experience with IGC negotiations that civil servants within the Council Secretariat and the European Commission possess (Beach 2005: 114–44). This is true in terms of substantive expertise as well as knowledge of how to broker compromises in the IGC context.

The Dutch experience also gives the analyst of intergovernmental conferences the opportunity to assess the extent to which the Presidency possesses imperfect knowledge of multiple, complex agenda issues, its own preferences, and those of other actors. It is important, therefore, to analyze the cognitive limitations that impact on the negotiating abilities of IGC actors that are only boundedly rational. The queries of relevance in this context relate to the possession of comparative informational advantages, either substantive expertise or bargaining skills, and the extent to which one or the other can potentially be translated into influence over outcomes.

During the Amsterdam IGC, the Dutch Presidency, learning from its previous experience, emphasized a working method that refrained from introducing draft legal texts until the last moment prior to the European Council in order to accomplish a specific objective. The lack of time guaranteed that national experts did not examine a Presidency proposal too closely before the European Council met. This gave the Presidency and the Secretariat opportunities to utilize the asymmetry of technical knowledge to their advantage to close negotiations on treaty reform.

In the analysis of its analytical skills to steer negotiations to a successful outcome (process expertise), the Netherlands is the only member state to experience successive attempts in the Chair to close negotiations on treaty revisions. The Dutch Presidency experienced a steep learning curve immediately after the failure of its contentious instrumental strategy to introduce a unified treaty structure in the 1990–91 IGC. The Dutch understand that strong actors are capable of translating material resources into leverage at the bargaining table. As the sociological approach to explain Presidency performance suggests, the Netherlands learned to use their acquired knowledge to organize successful Presidencies during the Maastricht and Amsterdam treaty revisions. As explained in the pages to follow, the Black Monday episode in September 1991 provided the most valuable instruction in this context, particularly regarding the significance of French support to achieve constructive results during intergovernmental conference diplomacy (Soetendorp and Andweg 2001).

Further, after 'Black Monday', the Dutch Presidency relied on the Council Secretariat for guidance through the conclusion of the Maastricht European Council. Its expertise included assistance to the Presidency in drafting legal texts and other documents for the IGC, offerings ideas to the Presidency about how to reach agreements based on its knowledge of the state of play of the negotiations, and giving advice about the legal aspects of Treaty amendment, ensuring respect for Community law. As the sociological approach posits, the Dutch Presidency also learned to accept the reality of the pillar structure and subsequently to work creatively within the first pillar to preserve the balance between the Community method and the intergovernmental approach. Constructive use was made of what Tallberg identifies in this volume as the 'brokerage resources of the EU Presidency,' specifically the reliance on the General Secretariat's role gathering information at the centre of a web of resources, which no single member state can access on its own. Of additional importance to the Presidency were the Council Secretariat's in-depth knowledge of state preferences, its tactical advice on negotiation procedure, and its source of expertise on the content of negotiations.

This chapter's analysis of the Dutch Presidency assesses the importance of information on actor preferences and the state of play of negotiations by exploring a situation in which, as a trusted intervener, the Presidency can engage in discussions with each member state about their particular preferences. This is a scenario in which the Presidency attempts to find mutually acceptable, Pareto-efficient outcomes. The initiatives taken by the Dutch Presidency to institutionalize flexibility in the Treaty and to integrate the Schengen accord into the first pillar of the Treaty on European Union (TEU) are examples that illustrate the extent to which a proactive Presidency, regardless of size or structural advantages, can skew agreements towards the positions it advances in the Chair.

Reputation: The Dutch Presidency's 'courage' and its inherent risks

In the third category of leadership resources, the level of acceptability of the Dutch Presidency's contributions among the member states is evaluated with reference to their perception of Presidency on the basis of its introduction of the new draft treaty in September 1991. This analysis takes into account the extent to which the Presidency was seen to be excessively partial in the way it fulfilled a specific institutional role (procedural bias) and the way in which it promoted a particular outcome that was not desired on the basis of consensus (outcome bias). Of particular relevance is the extent to which other member states were subsequently more skeptical toward the Dutch Presidency in 1997 precisely because of its actions at the start of the 1991 Presidency.

Internal capacity

A diachronic comparison of successive turns in the Chair by the Netherlands during IGC negotiations clarifies the influence of internal capacity on the evolution of treaty reform. The Dutch government, during the initial months of its Presidency in the fall of 1991, was divided in approach, tactics and strategy. This fact suggests there were contested viewpoints within the Presidency at the time rooted in its historical experience of European integration, with the Dutch Foreign Minister Dankert wanting to fight for a single Treaty, whereas the more pragmatic Prime Minister, and the Permanent Representation in Brussels, were more interested in securing a mutually acceptable outcome than in pursuing Dutch pro-integrative interests (Pijpers 1983: 166–81). Coalition dynamics in The Hague are one explanation for the Black Monday scenario.[3] The central role of Hans van den Broek and the institutional set-up of the Dutch political system, which buttresses the position of the foreign minister, left Prime Minister Ruud Lubbers in a somewhat strained relationship with his colleague. Both men belonged to the same political party, the Christian Democrats (CDA), and both had international ambitions. Piet Dankert, the State Minister for European affairs in the foreign ministry, was a former President of the European Parliament (EP) and a staunch federalist. His ambition was to limit the role of the European Council and to push through a unified treaty structure (Mazzucelli 1999).

Dankert, a powerful player in the Dutch coalition government, belonged to a new continental breed of 'European affairs ministers' who wield enough power to coordinate policies across several government departments (Brock 1991: 11). With the foreign minister bogged down in Yugoslav diplomacy, the job of steering the treaty was given to Dankert, who was close to Lubbers and a Socialist member of the coalition. The Socialists were under pressure to bring down the coalition over disputes about Dutch disability benefits. In order to keep the government together, the Cabinet gave Dankert most of his own way, with disastrous results (ibid.).

The reliance on the national administration in the Hague by the Dutch Presidency during its first months, without the input of the Council Secretariat, led to a fundamental miscalculation within the Maastricht conference negotiating political union. Officials within the Netherlands Permanent Representation in Brussels even foresaw a fundamental error in judgment as events unfolded, but were kept out of the loop by the Dutch Foreign Ministry.

By some accounts, 'Black Monday' was the result of the complexities introduced by the 'human factor' in intergovernmental conference negotiations. This can be explained by the fact that Minister Dankert in The Hague and Ambassador Nieman at the Dutch Permanent Representation were not on speaking terms (Interview, Matthijs van Bonzel 1999). The Hague's refusal to listen to advice from the Council machinery in Brussels illustrates the clear limits to a Presidency's capabilities to act on its own during an IGC process.

The Federal Republic of Germany's late ratification of the Treaty on European Union in October 1993 did not allow much time in the run-up to the 1996 process. The Dutch government, which realized the likelihood of another turn in the Chair to close a treaty revision process, used a series of reports as a basis for government policy in a conscientious effort to 'avoid Black Monday' (ibid.). These reports covered such issues as the institutional reform of the European Union, European foreign, security and defense policy, European cooperation in the fields of justice and home affairs (JHA) and the enlargement of the European Union.

The Netherlands government was comprised of liberals, represented by Michiel Patijn, and socialists, represented by Wim Kok. These two ideologies clashed in the IGC and within the government. In the clash, the Dutch made constructive use of the government's different ideologies to play with concepts in dialogue and to develop internal compromises before they were tested with their European partners. As it circulated its own internal reports, the Dutch Presidency was careful to work with the Council Secretariat as well as the European Commission. It also developed good relations with the preceding Irish Presidency.

3.4   The negotiation context from Maastricht to Amsterdam – the role and impact of the Dutch Presidency

Institutional set-up

There are certain perks that the institutional position of the Presidency offers. In this volume, the institutional position is defined as the functions delegated to a given actor that can be used to provide leadership. Of particular significance is the fact that the Presidency controls the drafting of the single negotiating text and possesses the ability to gain privileged information on the state of play in negotiations through confessionals with the member states.

After 'Black Monday' the Dutch Presidency made a conscious decision to delegate responsibility to the Council Secretariat when the Presidency believed the Secretariat possessed comparative informational and procedural advantages. Its constructive choice to try to identify ways to put together deals that eluded other actors and to use the tactics of agenda-shaping and coalition-building were relevant on dossiers for which there were high bargaining costs. Implicitly, the learning curve that the Presidency experienced acknowledges the degree to which the Dutch have accepted that a more effective Council structure, emphasizing the development of instrumental leadership skills in the Presidency, is a constructive evolution in a multilateral institutional set-up (Jensen 1985: 234).

The nature of the issues

When the negotiations dealt with complex and/or technical issues, the Dutch Presidency used the comparative informational advantages it enjoyed to provide leadership, assisted by the Council Secretariat, or, particularly in the case of the Schengen integration, the Legal Services of the European Commission.

The number of issues and parties in the negotiation

A distinction must be made between the 1991 and 1997 treaty negotiations given the dynamics of the negotiating situation – only 12 member states in 1991 and 15 members, including Austria, Sweden and Finland, around the table in 1997. Moreover, although the number of issues to be negotiated was greater during the 1996–97 IGC, the Maastricht agenda was the more complex one; particularly the EMU dossier.

The Presidency's role has been defined in large measure by *practice*, although marked aspects of national character can leave an imprint on its tenure (Council of the European Union 2001: 4). The Presidency requires its entire national administrative apparatus to prepare, coordinate and implement a six-month agenda. Its working methods are 'conditioned by its traditions and culture' (ibid.).

The preceding definition of the Presidency's role as a European institution underscores that it is likely to learn from experience shaping the initial agenda and defining the parameters of the debate during successive intergovernmental conference processes (Lodge 1998: 351). This institution provides the structure through which an increasing number of competing interests in different issue areas can be reconciled and context to reshape, slowly, national interests in a wider European perspective. The Dutch Presidency's institutional record demonstrates that it is not human nature that was changed as a result of its successive turns in the Chair to decide treaty reforms. Over time the experience of the actors in the intergovernmental conferences was progressively transformed (McDonagh 1998: 151). It is only possible in the context of a treaty negotiation process for this transformation to occur. In this context, we learn, as Derek Beach concludes in his chapter, that governments, while 'Masters of the Treaties,' are not always the masters of the treaty negotiation process.

Distribution and intensity of governmental preferences

The analysis of the Dutch Presidency's preferences indicates the tensions between the efficiency and distributional implications of negotiations. Many of the issue areas the Dutch Presidency aimed to influence in terms of outcome varied in degree of political salience from high to low. Institutional reform is one of the most sensitive areas to negotiate in the treaty revision process. The political saliency of institutional issues kept those questions under the firm control of materially powerful national delegations. The Union's institutions 'offer the context for slowly reshaping national interests in a wider European perspective' (ibid.). Despite considerable motivation for institutional change, in part the result of gains left on the table at the close of the Maastricht negotiations, there were two trends working against reform in the run-up to the Amsterdam European Council. Institutional questions brought up sensitivities about national sovereignty. And, in light of prospective enlargements, attempts to rebalance the institutions in favor of the larger member states led the smaller Union members to insist that broad institutional balances be preserved, as outlined by the Founding Fathers of European integration (ibid.).

Flexibility and the incorporation of Schengen into the Treaty were issues with a different political salience. Unlike the treaty structure, or the 'Bermuda triangle' of institutional issues (i.e. number of Commissioners, votes per member state in the Council, and scope of qualified majority voting), these were not 'make or break issues' at the table.

3.5   The Dutch Presidency's impact on Maastricht Treaty reform: from contentious to pragmatic instrumental leadership

This chapter highlights the Maastricht issue areas that were significant in terms of the Dutch Presidency's preferences and its learning curve: treaty structure and opt-outs.

It is in the context of the internal splits within the Dutch Presidency that we must explain Black Monday, an unprecedented incident that occurred during the early months of its 1991 turn in the Chair. Its predecessor, the Luxembourg Presidency, handed over to the Dutch a draft treaty to establish the European Union that included a three-pillar structure (temple) – the European Community pillar, the Common Foreign and Security Policy (CFSP), otherwise known as the second pillar, and Justice and Home Affairs (JHA) or the third pillar. The motivation for the Presidency to introduce a new draft treaty in September 1991 was due to the concern, expressed by some members of the Dutch government, and echoed by the Commission, that the pillar structure was a triumph of the intergovernmental approach over the Community method in the Luxembourg draft treaty. To some Dutch officials, this pillar structure was too intergovernmental in nature since two of the three pillars relied on that method of decisionmaking. To counter this influence, the Presidency decided to introduce a unified treaty structure (the tree) that would do away with the pillar structure. Evidence has indicated that the Dutch held fast to the ideal of a supranational Community for at least 25 years to the detriment of proposals to enhance the effectiveness of the Presidency. This ideal, which has been elevated to the status of principle, is one of the most difficult for the Netherlands to abandon (Jensen 1985: 234).

The fact that in the structure of the draft treaty, two of the three pillars strengthened the intergovernmental nature of the proposed European Union gave an important Dutch minister, Piet Dankert, the opportunity to take advantage of the Dutch Presidency's situation to ignore the Council Secretariat and the French[4] as he pushed forward his own draft text. Thus, for largely domestic political reasons, the Dutch Presidency's decision to present a new draft treaty relatively late in the IGC negotiations resulted in a brutal rejection of its work and a return to the Luxembourg draft treaty, which included the pillar structure.

Moreover, the Dutch believed there was German support for their text that would tilt the balance among the member states in the Presidency's favor. There was German backing at the administrative level below Genscher. The week before the ministerial meeting, French foreign minister Dumas convinced his German counterpart that the Dutch Presidency was showing *trop de zèle fédéraliste*. Difficult relations between Genscher and van den Broek did not help the Dutch initiative. The outcome demonstrated the extent to which the Dutch foreign minister and Commission President Delors completely misjudged the situation, and the steepness of the learning curve for the future (Mazzucelli 1999).

This incident demonstrates how high the stakes were for the Dutch Presidency and the degree to which the Dutch had more substantive national concerns to argue than Luxembourg. As Crum explains in his analysis of the Italian and Irish Presidencies, each member state in the chair inherits an agenda. In this case, the Presidency agenda forced on the Dutch was a difficult one to handle given all the external issues, most notably the Yugoslav crisis and the Soviet Union's collapse (Wallace 1994: 48). Given that the Dutch managed to succeed at all in the Chair is evidence of the learning curve the Presidency adopted during the later stages of the 1991 conferences and its representatives' abilities to manipulate the IGC text in the endgame (ibid.). The counterfactual to consider is how the Italians might have fared in the same situation.

In an instrumental leadership strategy, negotiating skills are used to create an agreement that eludes other actors through the use of agenda shaping and coalition building. The Presidency must possess strong informational resources and must intervene in a way that is broadly perceived as acceptable by the member states.

Already during the Maastricht European Council, Economic and Monetary Union (EMU) and the Social Agreement illustrated the extent to which some member states either did not want to participate in specific policies or wanted to proceed at different speeds. What eventually became known several years later as flexibility aims to preserve the coherence and common endeavor of the Union. In other words, policy objectives should remain shared, although the speed at which member states participate to attain these objectives is allowed to differ (McDonagh 1998: 141–2). This was the onset of the discussion about the need for an inner ring, or core Europe, which the Dutch Presidency thought was a good idea. In its view, the outer ring was of a purely economic nature.

The Dutch Presidency learned first hand about the necessity about being flexible when sitting in the chair during tough negotiations about social policy at Maastricht. Commission President Jacques Delors's powers of persuasion helped bring Major around to the idea of an eleven-country opt-in (Grant 1994: 202). The Dutch Presidency's decision to rely on materials produced in advance by the European Commission's Legal Services led to the creation of a legally binding Social Protocol. The Commission's intervention avoided a breakdown in negotiations and the threat of a veto by France and Italy if the treaty did not include strong social policy provisions (Beach 2005: 63–113).

Rather than water down the social plan to suit Britain, the Eleven agreed to move ahead on their own, outside the Treaty on Political Union, leaving the British out. The social chapter was excised from the body of the Treaty and called an 'agreement' to be signed by 11 governments. A protocol in an appendix to the Treaty stated that the Eleven would make social policy according to the rules of the 'agreement' and authorized the member states to use Community institutions and procedures to do so (Grant 1994: 202). Lubbers acknowledged that 'we did the best we could,' but the reaction to Major's intransigence was one of surprise.

The lesson for the Presidency in the brokerage role was to learn, in this case from the Commission's intervention, how to convince a heterogeneous group of 11 member states to opt-in to the agreement. This issue offered the Dutch Presidency valuable experience in how to advance the European agenda in the face of the obstacle provided by the lowest common denominator of member state interest. That experience is augmented by the fact that the Presidency must progressively learn to broker agreements relying on its gains in comparative informational advantage in bilateral ('confessional') and trilateral meetings concerning those issues that are the most disputed politically and the most technically complex.

Although the Treaty on European Union introduced clear exceptions for the United Kingdom on EMU and social policy, the institutionalization of flexibility as a basic treaty principle did not take place until the Amsterdam negotiations (Stubb 2002: 41).

During the 1990–91 IGCs, the Dutch learned valuable lessons in the chair, which challenged a normative (federalist) preference that was consistent with the Netherlands European policy since the 1950s. The issues of treaty structure and opt-outs showed the Dutch the limits of influence that the Presidency was able to exercise on both the efficiency and distributive dimensions. This experience was invaluable given the issues the Dutch chose to emphasize in agenda-setting during the 1997 Presidency, as the next section explains.

The Presidency as engineer of Amsterdam's policy agenda: learning dynamics to strengthen a pillar in the Union's temple

The Dutch Presidency had ambitious goals at the start of its term in office, particularly regarding institutional questions, flexibility and the incorporation of Schengen into the treaty structure. By one account, throughout its 1997 tenure in the Chair the Dutch Presidency ran at 'high steam' (Interview,

Klaus-Peter Nanz 1998). It produced five reports even before the IGC began and numerous papers were tabled which kept the personal representatives busy reading although their margin to negotiate was limited.

In the words of one German IGC participant, the result achieved at Amsterdam is about 'the skills of the Dutch President' (ibid.). In the opinion of another long-time observer of European Union affairs, the Dutch Presidency was operating as the key driving force, particularly in the management of the agenda.

Timing was critical though. Luxembourg, the Netherlands successor in the Chair, did not want to close the intergovernmental conference under its watch (Interview, Günter Schaefer 1999). The endgame was clearly sought during the Dutch Presidency given the prospect of the May 1997 British elections (Interview, Svend Olling 1997). Even more important was the prospect of the French elections (Interview, Günter Schaefer 1999). As early as the first Dutch Presidency's draft treaty during February–March 1997, about 90 per cent of the overall result envisaged at Amsterdam was on the table. This outcome speaks to the importance of the preparatory work underlined by Ambassador Carols Westendorp in the Foreword to this volume.

As the time drew closer and pressure mounted to broker a successful outcome at the Amsterdam IGC, reality set in, particularly on the issues of highest political salience: the composition of the European Commission; the weighting of votes in the Council; and the extension of qualified majority voting. In these matters, the Presidency discerned that the member states were not willing to move ahead. During the Amsterdam conference itself, occasionally the existence of national proposals significantly influenced the nature of the papers introduced by the Chair. Only very rarely, however, did national proposals 'actually form the basis for discussion at a meeting.' When this did occur, proposals brought forward by individual delegations fell outside the scope of the main subjects for discussion and 'in relation to which it was not yet clear whether a level of support would develop which would justify the tabling of proposals by the Presidency' (McDonagh 1998: 206).

Already at the informal IGC Conclave in Noordwijk, a few weeks before the Amsterdam European Council, the Presidency knew that an agreement might not be forthcoming on institutional matters. It was up to the Presidency to prepare the agenda and build coalitions. This prompted the Dutch to distinguish between A and B points in order to understand the issues that needed to be left for the real negotiations in Amsterdam in the European Council. This meant that the Netherlands also had to renounce a Commissioner; an important sacrifice for a smaller member state. The Presidency and France wanted German support for a rotating Commission with less than 15 members. Here the Dutch Presidency supported the majority view, which was most realistic given the distribution of preferences, 'in the interests of the Union.' This objective was linked to QMV and the weighting of votes. At Noordwijk the Federal Republic of Germany was under the pressure of enlargement. Kohl was interested in limiting the coming enlargement of the Union to Poland, Hungary and the Czech Republic. Chirac supported Kohl, to the surprise of the French administration. The Presidency's tactic was broken and the line the administrators were preparing went down the drain.

After Noordwijk the Dutch Presidency expected things to get better in the negotiations. The Presidency's line was to increase the pressure on the smaller states to accept a reweighting of votes. These member states would not continue to have a Commissioner, but there would be a price to be paid for the larger states having only one Commissioner. It is important to consider the psychological environment created in discussions about these points. Was a decrease in votes acceptable because the larger states would lose a second Commissioner?

The French supported the Dutch Presidency regarding a smaller Commission. As a number of analysts have suggested, the French did not mind weakening the Commission, which many national politicians and civil servants have been skeptical toward since de Gaulle's time. Even though France could not have a permanent Commissioner, this did not have to be written in the treaty. France could claim it made the Commission more efficient. Every state could rotate its Commissioner. Kohl, on the other hand, believed that no state should give up a Commissioner, indicating his sensitivity to the smaller members.

Later during the second night of negotiations, these points were not resolved when Spain demanded more weighted votes in exchange for giving up its second Commissioner. The situation came to a head in that Spain was difficult to negotiate with as a special case. Aznar demanded recognition as an equal with France, Germany, Britain and Italy, which, like Spain, had two Commissioners. This led Kohl to advocate closing the debate until after enlargement.

In the view of a seasoned practitioner of European diplomacy, since the 'Spanish' problem combined the issue of weights and the problem of threshold for a blocking minority, the Amsterdam European Council was faced with 'an impossible task in the absence of adequate preparation' (Ersbøll 1997: 12). Here the tendency of the foreign ministers to engage in discussions rather than negotiations left a significant number of points for the European Council to resolve. By one account, the Heads of State and Government were simply 'worn out' after 14 hours of negotiations, and therefore did not engage in finding a compromise that could ensure that all possible gains were achieved in the final deal (Williamson 1997). An observer inside the Dutch Presidency explained that so many side conversations were taking place in the corridors that no one could keep track of the things that were being given away.

A number of analysts believed that significant gains were left on the table while others contended that a certain delay was useful. The size of the Commission would be easier to address when the potential burdens of enlargement on the Commission became clear to all concerned (Ersbøll 1997: 12).

The two points left in abeyance, the size of the Commission and the weighting of votes, illustrated that political union is about power and prestige. These were zero-sum issues that made it hard for the Presidency to broker a compromise using instrumental leadership. How can each state win and go home with gains to present to its public? Some scholars have even argued that the 'primary lesson of Amsterdam for bargaining theory is thus that no amount of institutional facilitation or political entrepreneurship, supranational or otherwise, can overcome underlying divergence or ambivalence of national interests' (Moravcsik and Nicolaïdis 1999: 83).

The findings in this chapter assert that the role of the Presidency is to operate effectively in the IGC negotiating context by choosing the leadership strategy that matches its resources. In the case of institutional issues, its instrumental leadership resulted in a stalemate that delayed an agreement on treaty reform until the implications of enlargement were clearer for member states. The push for an agreement on institutional reform by the parties at the table was therefore simply not present in Amsterdam.

Despite the stalemate on institutional matters, this analysis confirms that during the Amsterdam conference only the Presidency, aided by the Council Secretariat and the Commission, was able to provide leadership to reach specific agreements. In these cases, the Presidency's objective was not to overcome the underlying divergence of national interests. Its goal was to lead the negotiations so that member states' national interests were reconciled in a way that these interests may be progressively transformed in the European context.

Another politically sensitive issue, flexibility, was more legally complex than many of the issues that previous IGCs had experienced (Stubb 2002: 57). The Presidency was required to use all its experience in agenda shaping and coalition building, which demonstrated the strength of its informational resources, to bring these negotiations to a successful conclusion. The high bargaining costs associated with the extremely complex issue, and the potential collective action problems in the absence of agreement on flexibility explain the Dutch Presidency's choice of an instrumentalist leadership strategy. The Presidency's interest in using its comparative informational resources in the Chair to address the flexibility issue in a way that clarified the Union's future direction also explains this choice.

There were specific reasons why the debate on flexibility emerged in the EU context: uncertainty about member state participation in EMU; the interest of certain member states to develop the Union's defense capabilities; a willingness to improve the work in the third pillar, otherwise known as justice and home affairs; the necessity to accommodate enlargement; and a desire to progress in spite of reluctant member states. With these issues all on the

1996–97 IGC agenda, the legacy of Maastricht indicated that a consensus on the goals of integration no longer existed (ibid.: 58–9).

During the period defined by Stubb as the agenda-setting stage, June 1994–March 1996, some of the most important questions that were raised about flexibility made the member states' delegations to the IGC grapple with differentiation. The key contributions by Schäuble and Lamers, Major and Balladur set the tone for the debate to follow and the Reflection Group advocated that flexibility be included on the agenda (ibid.: 69).

In the decisiontaking stage, which coincides with the Dutch Presidency in Stubb's analysis, the mandate was to complete the intergovernmental conference at Amsterdam in June 1997. The Dutch wasted no time emphasizing flexibility. The Presidency organized twice as many meetings to address this issue than the preceding Irish Presidency. There was a genuine need for time to debate flexibility early in the Dutch Presidency. There were at least two reasons why a thorough discussion was necessary. Flexibility was linked to other issues on the IGC agenda, namely the common foreign and security policy (CFSP) and justice and home affairs. In the debate on flexibility, the Presidency was concerned not to undermine those issues.

Secondly, the member states did not necessarily agree about the purpose of flexibility. Some member states understood the concept as an instrument for enlargement. Others saw flexibility as a way to bypass member states reluctant to advance integration. Still other members wanted to use flexibility as a way to 'opt out' of specific policy areas. Stubb's analysis explains that member state delegations were 'involved in a long learning process without any qualified teachers leading the way' in terms of the flexibility debate during the IGCs initial nine months (ibid.: 84).

The flexibility debate that occurred in the initial months of the Dutch Presidency was motivated by the intention to learn from its previous turn in the Chair so as not to repeat the experience of Black Monday. Echoing Beach's findings (Beach 2005: 114–44), this chapter asserts that the Council Secretariat provided an important draft paper on flexibility in December 1996, which provided the basis for the discussions to come. As negotiations proceeded, the Dutch Presidency exercised instrumental leadership to reconcile the differences among the member states in this issue area (Stubb 2002: 85). McDonagh explains that the Presidency's draft treaty text for an enabling clause approach to flexibility, tabled on February 17/18, became the reference for negotiation on this issue (McDonagh 1998: 148). Although this Presidency document relied on the earlier work of the Council Secretariat, Stubb asserts that the Secretariat's role was dependent on 'the strength, imagination and initiative of the Presidency' (Stubb 2002: 69).

It was the Dutch Presidency that forced the flexibility debate on the IGC agenda in a way that required the member states to begin reflecting upon and revealing their positions in detail. The task of sorting through hundreds of oral and written flexibility positions to establish the final agreements on flexibility was the responsibility of the Presidency and the Council Secretariat. The necessity for decisive influence in agenda shaping explains the choice of an instrumental leadership strategy by the Dutch Presidency to negotiate flexibility. The role of the Council Secretariat, assisting the chair to the extent Presidency officials deemed necessary, was significant in terms of drafting and coalition building.

The Dutch Presidency's initiative on flexibility was inextricably linked to its central role in JHA – and, especially, Schengen – questions. This linkage demonstrates the ways in which its learning curve determined leadership outcomes. The learning experienced by the Presidency took place within the IGC negotiating context and impacted on its choice of an instrumental strategy to incorporate Schengen into the *acquis communautaire*.

The procedures introduced in free movement, asylum and immigration by the Dutch Presidency illustrated how the chair used a strategy of instrumental leadership to put forward a draft treaty text and build support among the member states to make substantial progress in this area. This choice left the Presidency with the responsibility of using the information resources gathered in the course of intense discussions to persuade 'coalitions of interest' among the member states to agree at Amsterdam to a full transfer of these issues to the first pillar. The substantial efforts made by the Presidency to integrate Schengen into the Union Treaties have been attributed to the persistence of Michiel Patijn, the Netherlands Minister of State for Foreign Affairs. In the words of one of his compatriots, Patijn was convinced that it was necessary to bring Schengen into the *acquis communautaire* to cope with migration (Interview, Matthijs van Bonzel 1999). According to one analyst, 'concerning Schengen the Presidency actually had to make something of a new start . . . because it was mentioned only in passing in the Irish draft treaty' (Svensson 2000).

Since Patijn was also the Schengen coordinator for the Netherlands, he was able to place Schengen on the IGC agenda. This Patijn accomplished working from The Hague. He was supported in his conviction by the other party in the Dutch government that also underlined the need for the European Court of Justice (ECJ) to have a role in this area.

The general view of the Dutch government was that intergovernmental cooperation was not working. Policymaking was obscure, with no influence by either the European Commission or European Parliament. Patijn succeeded in his objectives largely because of his personal commitment. In his view, there was an opportunity to further the integration process that should not be missed (ibid.). This was an area in which the Dutch Presidency wanted to take a leadership role because it feared French-German initiatives (Interview, Matthijs van Bonzel 1998).

In the Presidency's view, in order to avoid a French-German directorate, the Presidency should be flexible and introduce creative solutions. In fact, the Presidency's proposals were constructed on French-German ideas.

One of the main decisions left to be negotiated during the Amsterdam European Council was the decisionmaking on the transitional period in the new Title, as set out in Article G. The Dutch Presidency had introduced an ambitious draft (Council Secretariat SN/539/97 (C40) EN 15). This draft stated that, after a transitional period of three years following the entry into force of the Treaty, 'the Council shall adopt the measures referred to in this Title acting by a qualified majority on a proposal from the Commission and after consulting the European Parliament.'

During the afternoon of the second day at the Amsterdam European Council, Wim Kok, using his prerogative to engineer an agreement in the chair, created a crisis atmosphere to achieve a broader scope for decision-making using qualified majority voting (QMV). Kohl initially agreed with Kok's approach, but he later realized that he had gone too far in his agreement. Given *Länder* responsibilities in certain areas, including those related to internal security, Kohl explained that he could not give away competences that were not his to give. Although tensions ran high and explosive tempers flared, the other leaders agreed to cover Kohl in the sensitive area of extension of QMV in Council decisionmaking.

In this context, the Dutch Presidency's ability to reach an agreement that could achieve consensus was a critical factor. In an acknowledgement of Chancellor Kohl's delicate domestic situation, a consensus was reached that after a transitional period of five years, a decision should be taken by the Council, acting unanimously, with a view to apply co-decision in all or parts of the areas covered by the new Title on freedom, security and justice within the European Community pillar.

The other aspect of the Presidency's work as engineer on this dossier relates to the Protocols negotiated during most of the second day to recognize the United Kingdom and Ireland and their particular requirements relating to control of persons at their external borders. Denmark also negotiated a Protocol taking into account its unique domestic situation and the requirements of its national ratification process.

Unlike during the 1990–91 IGC, in which the Dutch Presidency tabled its draft treaty as a unified 'tree' structure, its more pragmatic vision prevailed in the 1996–97 conference to strengthen the Community pillar in the Union's 'temple.' In short, there was less rigid orthodoxy and more flexible creativity to achieve a constructive outcome for all parties at the table. In order to demonstrate instrumental leadership, the Dutch Presidency used its time in the Chair wisely from the start to talk with all the main players to the intergovernmental conference. Prime Minister Wim Kok had an excellent team. During the initial two months, the Presidency identified those issues left out by the Irish Presidency, including the incorporation of Schengen into the Treaties (McDonagh 1998: 173–9).

During spring 1997, the Dutch Presidency played a double tactical game. The Presidency knew what it could get through during the negotiations. In the Chair, the Dutch also tabled a text relatively late after making the most of the initial two months to listen to the other delegations' concerns in bilateral talks (Interview, Klaus-Peter Nanz 1998).

These tactics, which represented a 180-degree turnaround for the Dutch from the previous time in the Chair, also illustrate the increasingly critical brokerage role the Presidency has to exercise during intergovernmental conferences. The incorporation of Schengen into the first pillar illustrated that the Presidency used privileged information, acquired in negotiations with the member states, to press for an agreement that was faithful to the Chair's own vision of the preferred outcome as well as mutually acceptable.

The Dutch Presidency was threading a very fine line. Its previous experience had demonstrated the ways in which excessive partiality led to failure in the Chair. By arguing forcefully about the inefficiencies of intergovernmental cooperation in free movement, asylum and immigration, gaining high levels of acceptability through its work program, and acquiring legitimacy through its consistent dedication to its objectives, the Presidency relied less on orthodoxy and more on the necessity for improvements in the broader European interest. Its choice of instrumental leadership, which made the case for the 'big bang' incorporation of Schengen into the first pillar, was decisive in achieving a successful outcome. In the absence of such leadership, change was likely to have been limited to a reinforcement of the third pillar to address this issue area (McDonagh 1998: 181). This was unacceptable to the Dutch Presidency in light of its commitment to integration on successive occasions as Chair.

The success of instrumental leadership in this area confirms that, in contrast to the Maastricht experience, the Amsterdam conference defined the Dutch Presidency's role as an 'engineering' Presidency (Svensson 2000: 9–10). As Svensson identifies this role, the Presidency as engineer aims or has the chance to influence not only process, but also outcome in negotiation, but the primary focus is upon securing an agreement; in other words improving the efficiency of the negotiations. An engineering Presidency has the objective to be more than the administrator and the facilitator (ibid.).

3.6 Conclusions

The Dutch Presidency's leadership during the Maastricht and Amsterdam conferences reveals a learning curve that impacted on its actions and influence in the Chair. The passage of time and the accumulation of experience contributed to the Presidency's ability to engineer agreements, thereby providing leadership in the forms of managing the agenda and brokerage. Its leadership resources, relatively weak materially and comparatively strong comparative informational advantages, were influenced by the negotiation context that conditioned the Dutch Presidency's latitude in the Chair and its behavior during IGCs. This conditioning relates directly to the Presidency's choice of strategy in the Chair, which, in turn, contributes to an explanation of mixed leadership outcomes.

During the 1991 negotiations, the Dutch Presidency supported a position on treaty structure outside the zone of any realistic agreement, thereby following a contentious instrumental strategy. During the Maastricht IGC, the complexities of Dutch coalition politics and the Presidency's failure to consult with the Council Secretariat led to 'Black Monday.' It is reasonable to argue that the choice of a contentious instrumental strategy was rooted as much in traditional Dutch attitudes about the supranational nature of the European Communities, and a reliance on a proactive European Commission as an ally in treaty reform, as in the failure of domestic officials to understand the IGC negotiating context. After this defeat, there was a conscious decision to avoid repeating this situation.

The lesson September 30 reveals, however, is significant for an understanding of negotiation and influence. The Dutch Presidency's failure demonstrates that, with successive IGCs, bargaining is increasingly taking place in national capitals where the impact of European treaty reforms on domestic political structures, in terms of both institutions and administrative cultures, is still in question.

Success was evident in cases in which the Dutch Presidency, exploiting its institutional position, was entrepreneurial in its initiatives to change actors' perceptions of their own interests. Consistent efforts in agenda-shaping and coalition-building reflected the choice of an instrumental leadership strategy on flexibility and the integration of Schengen into the *acquis communautaire*.

In the Dutch case, the government's judicious use of the time period between the Maastricht and Amsterdam IGCs to develop its position papers and line of negotiation was critical. The failure of the third pillar's intergovernmental mechanisms in the daily business of Community affairs led to the Presidency's initiative, spearheaded by Patijn, to persuade the other member states to integrate Schengen, lock, stock and barrel, into the Treaties.

The Dutch Presidency's success, and the decisive contributions it made to the final outcome brokering agreement, relates to its ability to conclude the Protocols for Ireland, the United Kingdom and Denmark that allowed the Union to move ahead in this area. In other words, the Dutch Presidency learned to avoid pushing the negotiations to the break point by elevating an idea to the status of principle.

For this reason, the Dutch Presidency over time demonstrates that its role is not limited to that of manager. Leadership is required and brokerage skills are needed during intergovernmental conferences. Those lessons the Dutch Presidency drew from the Maastricht and Amsterdam intergovernmental conferences increased its scope for instrumental leadership. During its 2004 turn in the Chair, however, significant changes in the Netherlands' political situation were apparent to the Presidency. As the rejection of the European Constitutional Treaty on 2 June 2005 illustrated, the Dutch Presidency was not able to translate its learning curve in leadership to forge a new domestic consensus on European treaty reform.

In the light of Tallberg's France and the IGC 2000 analysis, the learning experience of the Dutch Presidency during successive treaty negotiation processes confirms that blatant partiality in the Chair can succeed even for a small or medium-sized state Presidency in matters of low political salience. Schengen is a particularly significant case in the present context given the importance this policy area has acquired in the context of sustaining the future momentum of integration, along with the single European currency and successive enlargements. By utilizing its knowledge of IGC diplomacy as an informational resource, the Dutch Presidency chose its strategy wisely to provide instrumental leadership at Amsterdam that no single member state was in a position to offer.

Notes

1. European Coal and Steel Community (ECSC), European Economic Community (EEC) and EURATOM.
2. Ben Crum in particular has made this point in our discussions of the Dutch case (Chapter 4).
3. This fact confirms Moravcsik's thesis that 'an understanding of domestic politics is a precondition for, not a supplement to, the analysis of strategic interaction among states.' Cited in Rosamond (2000: 137). As Rosamond asserts, the question to address is the appropriate account of domestic politics. The theoretical implications of internal factors like: 1. coalition dynamics; 2. the provincialism of The Hague's bureaucratic culture; and 3. changes in the Netherlands domestic situation for Wessels' 'fusion hypothesis,' in terms of how integration 'locks in,' are particularly relevant, but are overlooked by Moravcsik's theory.
4. The French permanent representative to the intergovernmental conference, Pierre de Boissieu, was believed to be the originator of the pillar structure in the Luxembourg draft.

4
The EU Presidency – Comparing the Italian and Irish Presidencies of the 2003–04 Intergovernmental Conference*

Ben Crum

4.1 Introduction

This chapter explores whether the governments holding the EU Presidency during the 2003–04 IGC were able to exercise leadership over the negotiations on the EU Constitutional Treaty. The case of the 2003–04 IGC is a tempting one, as it was put in the hand of two consecutive Presidencies, the Italian and the Irish governments, that both had the ambition of concluding the negotiations but adopted strikingly different leadership strategies. The comparison becomes all the more interesting in the light of the unprecedented crisis that emerged when, contrary to the initial intentions, the negotiations failed to be concluded under the Italian Presidency in December 2003 and hence had to be continued under the Irish Presidency.

This situation in which two Presidencies faced one and the same challenge presents us with a unique opportunity to examine by way of comparative analysis the difference the Presidency can make. Even if there are important differences to be noted between the two Presidencies (not least their sequencing), they offer probably as close a comparison as one can get in EU politics. The question then is whether we can identify leadership (or the lack thereof)

* A first version of this chapter was presented in the Workshop 'The Role of Political Agency in the Constitutional Politics of the EU' at the ECPR Joint Sessions in Granada, 14–19 April 2005 convened by Derek Beach and Thomas Christiansen. I thank the participants of this workshop, and in particular Mareike Kleine who acted as a discussant, for their comments. I also gratefully acknowledge the help of a senior official of the Irish Department of Foreign Affairs for elucidating the strategy of the Irish Presidency in an interview. All representations remain however the sole responsibility of the author.

by demonstrating that at critical junctures in the negotiation process specific interventions by the Presidency have led to distinctive achievements either to the collective good of the parties involved (efficiency) or to its own individual private gain (distributive dimension) which would not have been secured under a Presidency pursuing a different strategy.

In examining the strategic choices of the two Presidencies, I will focus on four procedural powers that the Presidency enjoys due to a possessing a privileged institutional position (cf. Metcalfe 1998: 422f.; Tallberg 2004b: 1004f.):

(a) the setting of the timeframe;
(b) the control over the agenda of the negotiations;
(c) the management of the 'zone of possible agreement'; and
(d) the frequency and nature of meetings.

The two Presidencies made strikingly different choices in employing these powers to provide leadership in the IGC. Thus, this chapter seeks to reconstruct how these strategic choices came about; how they were pursued in practice; and whether and how the strategic choices of the Presidencies affected the proceedings and the outcome of the negotiations.

After a short section outlining the point of the departure of the IGC, sections 4.2 and 4.3 reconstruct the strategic choices and achievements of, respectively, the Italian and the Irish Presidency. Naturally, this analysis eventually raises the questions whether the Irish strategy might have succeeded where the Italian strategy failed? And, in the interests of fairness, might the Italian strategy have succeeded just as well given six months more? Given their counterfactual nature, these questions do not allow for an unequivocal answer (cf. Fearon 1991). In the conclusion I will, however, try to sum up the findings that can be brought to bear upon them.

4.2 The context of the 2003–04 IGC

In two crucial respects the Presidency of the 2003–04 IGC faced a rather different challenge from its predecessors that had presided over previous IGCs. This IGC was the very first EU decision-making process involving 25 member states (even if 10 of them only formally acceded to the Union two months before the end of the Conference) and three more acting as observers, making it a test-case for the practical workability of an EU of 25 and more.

Possibly an even more notable difference was that the 2003–04 IGC proceeded to work on the basis of a complete legal text that had been prepared for it by a European Convention. Previous IGCs had often been preceded by preparation groups that would survey the issues involved, such as the Reflection Group that prepared the agenda for the 1996–97 IGC (see chapter 1). But never had these groups presented complete legal draft texts ready to be adopted by the member states, and even less so had they had the courage to present such a document under the ambitious name of a 'Treaty establishing a Constitution for Europe'. What is more, in contrast to earlier preparation groups, the Convention had been a public affair involving more than 200 European and national politicians that had been meeting and deliberating for over one and half years (Norman 2003; Crum 2004; Magnette and Nicolaïdis 2004b).

Regardless of the consensus achieved among the Convention participants, they had no reason to expect their work to be simply accepted by the EU governments. The mandate of the Convention set out in the Laeken Declaration provided no more than that its 'final document will provide a starting point for discussions in the Intergovernmental Conference, which will take the ultimate decisions' (European Council 2001). Still, with the active involvement of representatives of all Heads of Government of the member states, it had also become clear in the course of the Convention that none of them could simply brush aside the Convention's draft to engage with the negotiations as if from scratch.

Upon receiving the Convention's conclusions from its President Valéry Giscard d'Estaing, the June 2003 European Council cautiously echoed the Laeken declaration in affirming that 'the text of the Draft Constitutional Treaty is a good basis for starting in the Intergovernmental Conference' (European Council 2003). A more forthcoming attitude could, however, be read into the declared intention that the IGC 'should complete its work and agree the Constitutional Treaty as soon as possible and in time for it to become known to European citizens before the June 2004 elections for the European Parliament' (European Council 2003). While this ambitious timeframe did not necessarily reflect the desires of all governments, given the festive spirit surrounding the successful conclusion of the Convention and the obvious appeal of the EP elections, none of them resisted the formulation of the Greek Presidency and the aspirations of the in-coming Italian Presidency.

Still, it was anything but self-evident on which basis the IGC would work. All governments had several or more issues that they would want to change in the draft. At the same time, they were well aware that if each of them was allowed to put their own grudges on the table, Pandora's box would be opened and the IGC might well come to have an infinite agenda. Thus the Presidency had its work cut out for it.

4.3   The negotiation of the 2003–04 IGC

The Italian Presidency

The strategic choices of the Italian Presidency

As the Italian government started to prepare for the IGC in summer 2003, the first strategic choice it made was to commit itself to finishing the negotiations within the term of its Presidency, i.e. by December 2003 at the latest. No doubt the idea to have a second 'Treaty of Rome' crown their term at the helm of the Union appealed to some Italian officials and statesmen. However, the choice for an ambitious timeframe also logically followed from the intention expressed by the Thessaloniki European Council to finalize the negotiations on the Constitutional Treaty well in time before the European elections of June 2004. In order to achieve this, the negotiations would have to be concluded three or four months in advance to allow for the legal finalization of the Treaty in all EU languages (Frattini interview August 28 2003). Moreover, it was felt that the momentum of the Convention was best preserved by a short IGC and the longer the negotiations would be drawn out, the more the Convention spirit was bound to be diluted.

The commitment to an ambitious timeframe led to a second strategic choice: an insistence on a strictly limited IGC agenda. While the Thessaloniki European Council had welcomed the Draft Constitutional Treaty as 'a good basis for starting in the Intergovernmental Conference' (European Council 2003), it had left it open whether the IGC would indeed use the Convention's draft as the basis of its work or whether it would still review the desirability of each and every reform proposed. Importantly, the Convention had provided an integral text that put the existing treaties in a completely new and systematic format. However, even if there was then a consensus on the *format* from which the IGC would depart, some governments (most notably the Spanish and the Polish) would insist that in terms of *substance* the negotiations were to depart from the agreements reached in Nice (cf. Palacio in *Corriere della Sera*, 30 September 2003).

The Italians made it quite clear that they were intent to use the Convention's text as the basis of negotiations. Besides the Italian government's desire to conclude the IGC still within its own term of Presidency, this stance also reflected its basic satisfaction with the contents of the Convention's draft. Thus the Presidency indicated in a note circulated ahead of the informal General Affairs Council at Rive del Garda where the organization of the IGC was to be discussed:

> The Thessaloniki European Council welcomed the text of the draft Constitutional Treaty drawn up by the Convention and considered it to be a good basis for starting the IGC. The Presidency is therefore of the firm view that *the IGC should maintain the same level of ambition*, especially in institutional matters, and should aim to depart as little as possible from a balanced text which is the result of 18 months of intense negotiation. (Presidency of the European Union, 2003: 1, original emphasis)

More specifically, the Italian Presidency identified three kinds of issues that still needed to be resolved by the IGC. First there was the task of finalizing the Constitutional Treaty in legal and technical terms. This task was relegated to a group of legal experts with representatives of all states under the chairmanship of the IGC secretariat and with assistance of the Commission (for more on this, see chapter 5). Secondly, following a round of consultations, the Presidency had identified three issues 'which are not in principle called into question, but on which some further clarification is required in order to allow them to be applied in practice': (1) the rotating presidency of Council formations, (2) the Foreign Minister and (3) the modalities of the European Security and Defense Policy (ESDP). Finally, the Presidency recognized four issues 'which cause substantive difficulties for one or more delegation': (4) Christian values in the preamble, (5) the definition of qualified majority voting (QMV) in the Council, (6) the scope of QMV and (7) the minimum number of seats per state in the European Parliament.

Thus, essentially, the Italian Presidency sought to start the IGC with a substantial agenda of no more than seven issues, three of which mainly involved matters of clarification rather than political disagreements. Notably, the Italians chose to ignore several issues that had previously been raised by other member states. One of them was explicitly mentioned in the note, namely the issue of the division between European Commissioners and (normal) Commissioners that the Convention had proposed. Typically, however, the Presidency asserted that it was 'of the view that further clarification on this would not be necessary'. Still, the Presidency had to concede that further points were being raised and in a letter following up on the Rive del Garda meeting, Foreign Minister Frattini granted that whereas the Presidency would be responsible for preparing the negotiations 'Any delegation may ask for additional questions to be raised during the IGC'.

However, in defining the conditions that such additional issues would have to meet before being put on the IGC agenda, the Presidency clearly signaled its preference for the Convention's text by putting the onus squarely upon the claimants. Frattini characterized the Italian stance as follows:

We will adopt a 'constructive dissent' approach and not an amendatory one that, in fact, would just become a 'shopping list' of individual Member requests. In practice, an issue will be discussed only if a counterproposal is presented and its ameliorative effect explained. The Italian Presidency will oppose steps backward to reopen institutional pillars. (Frattini interview of August 28 03 on www.ueitalia.it; cf. Frattini letter of September 16 2003)

Thus, basically, the Italians required any amendments that would be raised to already command wide support among the member states and to constitute a genuine and substantial improvement over the Convention's text.

Finally, as for the format in which the negotiations would take place, the Thessaloniki European Council had already indicated that the IGC would be conducted by the Heads of State and Government with the assistance of their Ministers for Foreign Affairs. Experience with previous IGCs showed that in practice only the most contentious issues are left to be resolved at the level of Heads of State and Government, while as much as possible is already agreed by the Foreign Ministers who have in turn most of their decisions prepared by officials representing them (who may negotiate either in plenum or in subgroups). However, in line with its rather strict manage- ment of the agenda, the Italian Presidency from the start insisted that 'the work of the IGC should be conducted at political level' (Note 1/9/2003). Basically, the Presidency ensured that the IGC would be organized around a series of Ministerial meetings (CIG 5/03).[1] Over the months of October and November, the Foreign Ministers were to meet five times (interspersed with the October European Council), culminating in a two-day 'Ministerial Conclave' at the end of November where basically the overall package was to be put together. After the usual preparatory General Affairs Council, the IGC would then be concluded by the Heads of State and Government on 13 December.

To sum up, the strategy adopted by the Italian Presidency towards the IGC can be characterized in the following terms: an ambitious timeframe, a strictly controled agenda, a progressive stance on the substance of proposals to be debated, and a concentration on the highest political level. The Italians thereby attempted to exploit the procedural powers of the Presidency in order to get their preferred outcome, which was to minimize the number of changes to the Convention text, and to get the text adopted during their Presidency.

The achievements of the Italian Presidency

The Italian strategy did not fully work out as planned; the IGC was not concluded by December and had to be carried on under the Irish Presidency. Still, up until the end the Presidency remained committed to its initial choices, even if it did make concessions on various accounts. By the time the IGC officially began in early October, the original agenda of seven substantial issues had already been extended to include another three: the Composition of the Commission, the revision procedure and the European Council and its President (CIG 5/03). As the issue of the European Council was eventually never pursued for lack of an acceptable alternative proposal, there remained nine key issues on the IGC agenda.

Over the first weeks of the official negotiations, the Presidency secured its first results on the two institutional issues that were least contested: on the very first afternoon of the negotiations the Foreign Ministers got rid of the Convention's proposal to concentrate legislative affairs in a separate Legislative Council (CIG 39/03) and with regard to the Foreign Minister and his or her distinctive position within the Commission, the IGC quickly moved towards a clarified legal arrangement that was acceptable to all (CIG 45/03). Later on, two more key issues were successfully resolved: ESDP and the revision procedure (CIG 60/3; CIG 62/03). Step-by-step the Presidency also moved toward a solution of the (UK's) concerns about the scope of QMV in various domains. Most notably in the fields of social security and criminal policy it provided for a 'safety mechanism' that would allow a member state to suspend the legislative procedure in the Council and put the issue before the European Council (CIG 52/03: Annex 14; CIG 60/03: Annexes 18 & 25).

However, the Presidency faced continuous pressure to release its grip on the IGC agenda. For one there were several issues brewing in the financial-economic field. When these were not picked up within the IGC, the Ecofin Council tabled a list of amendments to the Convention's proposals on issues like the budget procedure and financial planning of the Union and multilateral surveillance in the context of the Stability and Growth Pact. Thus around ten issues were added to the IGC agenda, some of which were accepted without much further debate, but some of which would continue to be debated up until the very end of the negotiations. Furthermore, an inventory by the Presidency in the course of October yielded a list of 91 'non-institutional issues' (CIG 37/03) and about 15–20 areas in which one or more member states or the Commission suggested that a move from unanimity to QMV or vice versa might be desirable (CIG 38/03). Still, the Presidency sought to limit the IGC agenda as much as possible. It interpreted 28 of the 91 'non-institutional issues' as involving matters of 'legal and technical clarification' and relegated them for that purpose to the group of Legal Experts under the condition that 'In no case such a clarification may be subject to negotiations and does not prejudice any political solution' (CIG 43/03: 2).

As the agenda expanded, the Presidency also came to revise its progressive stance. Indeed few would recognize the very first deal on the abolishment of the Legislative Council as a progressive step compared to the Convention's text. Similarly on several competences, most notably involving the British red lines on taxation, social security and criminal justice, the Presidency was forced to retreat from its more progressive stance. Still it did so only in very small steps, marginally amending the competences and introducing safety mechanisms. Also on other issues the Presidency's stance regularly shone through. Thus on the two key issues concerning the composition of the Commission and the European Parliament, the Presidency refrained from submitting any concrete proposals in the absence of an acceptable 'ameliorative' alternative. Similarly it was reluctant to pick up on three deeply contested issues that had been raised by the Ecofin Council: budget procedure, financial framework and multilateral surveillance (cf. CIG 52/03 ADD 1: 6). On the other hand, the Presidency's distinct ambitions came out in the bold proposal to extend the use of QMV in the Union's foreign policy.[2] The other pet issue of the Italian Presidency was its wish to include an explicit reference to Europe's 'Christian heritage' in the Constitution's Preamble. However, the Italians only made sure that this issue remained on the IGCs agenda without seeking to use the Presidency to impose their own views on this issue.

As the IGC agenda expanded, the Presidency also had to make concessions on its intention to concentrate the negotiations at the highest political level. At the beginning of the IGC it had already set up a 'network of focal-points' that it used for distributing questionnaires on key issues. These focal-points basically involved high-level officials close to the Foreign Ministers, many of which were also closely involved with the group of Legal Experts. As the mandate of the group of Legal Experts was widened, these officials moved more center stage in the negotiations. Thus, step by step, the Presidency saw the IGC adopting a form reminiscent of the Amsterdam and Nice IGCs in which backroom preparations were crucial for the political decisions to be taken.

The fact that the political meetings convened performed far below expectation further contributed to this development. As it was, the IGC was the first formal occasion in which the Union operated as a Union of 25 member states. The challenges involved already emerged quite clearly when at the formal opening of the IGC the traditional *'tour de table'* ran far over time without yielding any new insights. In fact, if anything, the tour de tables merely had a perverse effect as they served to reaffirm the distinct positions of the Member States rather than allowing them to become negotiable.

On the eve of the December summit, the IGC agenda had come to include 43 issues plus 11 minor ('miscellaneous') ones on which the Presidency put forward concrete proposals (CIG 60/03 ADD 1). Furthermore, there remained four original key issues that the Presidency expected to be the focus of discussions: Preamble, QMV-definition, Commission and EP composition (CIG 60/03 ADD 2). Of these four, it was clear that the issue of QMV-definition was farthest from a resolution with Spain and Poland insisting that some form of weighted voting *à la* Nice be maintained and Germany and France insisting on the double-majority formula put forward by the Convention.[3]

In the end, the high-level politics of the summit did not suffice to find a solution to this standoff. There are various accounts of why the summit failed (cf. Ludlow 2004). Certainly the differences between Spain and Poland on the one hand and Germany and France on the other ran deep. At the same time, it was quite clear that, one way or another, the Spanish and the Poles would have to succumb to some kind of double majority-formula. But as the decision to break off the negotiations was already taken by midday on Saturday 13 December, it could not be merely because of the intransigence of Spain and Poland that by then had hardly been tested. In fact reports suggest that the decision to break off the negotiations was initiated neither by the Spanish or Poles nor by the Italians but rather by French President Jacques Chirac (*Der Standard*) December 14 2003.

However, even if it was indeed Chirac, then he merely was the first who had the courage to express a sentiment that was shared much more widely. Much goes to suggest that the failure of the December summit was a direct reaction to the time pressure that had been at the basis of the Italian strategy. Concluding the negotiations in December came for most delegations as 'too much too soon.' Many small and medium-sized states had resisted the Italian time pressure from the start. The Italians' reluctance to include new issues on the IGC agenda, in particular regarding the composition of the Commission, had fueled their resentment. Moreover, as the list of proposals had rapidly expanded in the final weeks, many of the compromises were still fresh and not fully thought through.

The Italian strategy to keep negotiations at as high a political level as possible also backfired. The logical implication of this strategy was that it was eventually left to Prime Minister Berlusconi to conclude the final issues. Berlusconi's reputation – colored by the Nazi accusations with which he had started off the EU Presidency in the EP and the jocular comments on soccer and women that were reported from the lunch at the December summit – may not have secured him the highest regard among his peers. His assertion in the run-up to the summit that he held a solution up his sleeve (ANSA December 10 2003) turned out to be a bluff. In fact it appears that the Italian Presidency started the summit not only without a clear idea about a possible solution but also without any clear perspective on how to proceed (cf. Ludlow 2004), which indeed suggests that they themselves had little confidence in realizing the ambition they had set themselves half a year before (see chapter 5 on the relationship between the Italian Presidency and their lack of use of the Council Secretariat).

Still the failure to conclude the IGC should not distract from the results that the Italians did achieve in the course of three months of negotiations (see Table 4.1). They firmly established the Convention's draft as the undisputable basis of negotiations. To a considerable extent they also managed to contain the IGCs agenda. As said, apart from the four issues that were left open, they addressed 54 issues. In fact, the Italians even claimed that their proposals on these issues as 'a "negotiating acquis" [supported by a large majority of the member states and] not open to further discussion' (European Council 2004: 31). Even if this line was not fully adhered to, 24 of the amendments drafted under the Italian Presidency were without any substantial changes adopted by the end of the negotiations and another 10 only underwent some minor modifications.

In quantitative terms one can say then that the Italian Presidency delineated 80 per cent of all issues that were to be addressed in the IGC and finalized half of the total agenda. Still, in qualitative terms it left four key issues unresolved, including above all the definition of QMV. In the end, however, it were not just the remaining issues that prevented the Italian Presidency from meeting its own deadline, but also the fact that by the December summit the very strategy that had brought it that far, had exhausted the credit and the willingness of the other states to seal the deal.

Table 4.1 Constitutional issues under the Italian Presidency

Status after the December Summit	Number	(Main) issues
Left open	4	QMV, Commission, EP, Preamble
Finalized	24	Foreign Minister, ESDP, Revision procedure
As good as finalized	10	Union's values, Equality of Member States, Tourism
Substantial progress in comparison with final version	12	Council of Ministers, Charter, Financial Framework, Safety valves for criminal policy and social security
Minor progress in comparison with final version	7	Budget procedure, Multilateral surveillance, Taxation, Energy, Common Commercial Policy
Not raised, but adopted under Irish Presidency	15	Objectives of the Union, Coordination of Economic Policy, Own Resources, Eurojust, ECJ jurisdiction in CFSP
Raised, but abandoned under Irish Presidency	1	QMV in CFSP
Total	73	

Note: Numbers based on a comparison between CIG 60/03 and CIG 81/04 and 85/04.

The Irish Presidency

The strategic choices of the Irish Presidency

As the December summit failed, there was little of a fallback scenario. All that the summit provided by way of a pointer was that it requested the Irish Presidency 'on the basis of consultations to make an assessment of the prospects for progress and to report to the European Council in March'. The Irish decided to suspend the (plenary) IGC negotiations and to use the two-and-a-half months before the European Council as a 'cooling-down period.' Thus they adopted a distinctively pragmatic step-by-step stance, focusing on the first task that they had been assigned – presenting a progress report to the spring European Council – and leaving the rest of the process to be determined in due course only. In contrast to the Italians, the Irish opted for an open, indeterminate timeframe and eschewed any suggestion that they were set to succeed in concluding the negotiations. Typically, the Irish Taoiseach (Prime Minister) Bertie Ahern (statement of December 16 2003) submitted: 'I am certainly not going to promise that the IGC will finish in our Presidency. But, equally, it would be premature to conclude that it will not.'

The Irish handling of the IGC agenda obviously built upon the agenda as it had formed under the Italian Presidency. It was, however, a question to what extent the agenda, as well as certain agreements achieved under the

Italian Presidency, would be closed. The Irish approached these issues under the general line that 'nothing is agreed until everything is agreed' (cf. letter of Ahern of April 9 2004). Thus, it was basically left open to any delegation to add issues as long as the negotiations were not yet concluded. At the same time though, the work done by the Italians had delineated the agenda and thus it was up to the delegations to demonstrate that there were good reasons to add an issue to the agenda or that the Italians had unduly kept their concerns off the agenda.

No doubt, the definition of the qualified majority in the Council remained the key issue on which any agreement hinged. However, other issues also remained far from resolved. Indeed, addressing the Irish Parliament in early February, Ahern indicated that there were in fact about twenty issues still outstanding, including issues concerning the scope of QMV and several matters in the field of Justice and Home Affairs. Notwithstanding the principle that 'nothing is agreed until everything is agreed,' Ahern also underlined the imperative to resolve as many issues as possible, submitting that 'whoever, whether me or someone else, has to have an IGC with over 20 issues on the agenda would never get an agreement' (*Irish Times*, February 5 2004; cf. letter Ahern, April 9 2004).

Whereas the Italian Presidency had remained committed to 'a general desire to move towards a more integrated and more ambitious Union' (European Council 2004: 31), the Irish adopted a more pragmatic stance, focusing on the conclusion of the negotiations. If anything, especially after the traumatic experience with the referenda on the Treaty of Nice, the general Irish stance on integration, while basically rather positive, was marked by a number of reservations in certain policy domains: ESDP, taxation, social security, Justice and Home Affairs (cf. Laffan 2003: 13/4). Notably, apart from the issue of ESDP, these reservations coincided to a great extent with the UK's 'red lines'.

Maybe the most fundamental difference between the Italian and the Irish Presidency concerned the forum in which they choose to concentrate negotiations. The Italians, considering that the key issues were deeply political in nature, decided to concentrate negotiations at the highest political level and invested little in preparatory meetings at the level of officials and in bilateral contacts. The suspension period introduced by the Irish ruled out any plenary sessions at the political level. Instead, until 17 May, the moment that the IGC was formerly reconvened at the political level, the Irish concentrated all their efforts in bilateral contacts with the national delegations, many of which concentrated at the level of officials (see chapter 5 for more on the Irish cooperation with the Council Secretariat).

Much of the Irish approach could already be gleaned from Ahern's diagnosis of the failure of the December summit:

> The assessment was that the European Council was trying to do too much, too fast and it required to think out the issues more fully, [...] If I, at any

time in the next number of months, believe the atmosphere will present itself to finalise it, I'd take it. (But) that atmosphere is not there (now). (as cited by *Eubusiness*, December 14 2003).

In hindsight, much of the Irish Presidency's moves can be seen as aiming at the creation of a favorable atmosphere. Thus, compared to the Italians preceding them, the Irish Presidency adopted a fundamentally different strategy that was rather marked by an open timeframe, an agenda that built on the Italian legacy, a pragmatic stance, and an informal, bilateral approach aiming at goodwill first.

The achievements of the Irish Presidency

Looking back, it appears that the Irish Presidency only formally reconvened the IGC once it was confident that it would be able to conclude the negotiations. In the progress report to the March European Council, the Presidency limited itself to observing 'that there is a strong case for bringing the Intergovernmental Conference to an early conclusion, and that there is reason to believe that an overall agreement acceptable to all delegations is achievable if the necessary political will exists' (CIG 70/04: 5). Only by the end of April did Foreign Minister Cowen present a timetable and this timetable only had the IGC formally reconvene one month before the envisaged conclusion at the European Council of June 17/18 with only two Ministerial meetings in between. Notably, however, a fortnight before the formal reconvening of the IGC on May 17, the basis for the final talks was already laid at a meeting of top-level officials (generally referred to as 'focal points') of all member states in Dublin.

As indicated, there was only a limited number of new issues that appeared on the IGC agenda under the Irish Presidency. Some of these were technical issues concerning transitional arrangements and provisions to allow for the special status of certain member states. Others concerned various member states' concerns that had not been addressed under the Italian Presidency. The most notable new items on the IGC agenda dealt with concerns that appear rather close to the Irish interests in the fields of Justice and Home Affairs (such as the amendments on Eurojust), economic policy (the insertion of price stability in the objective of the Union and the changes in the formulation of the Union's role in the coordination of economic policy) and foreign policy (dealing with the role of the ECJ in CFSP). Notably, from an integrationist stance (such as the Italian one), these amendments might well be regarded as regressive in character.

In the course of the negotiations in April and May, most of the dossiers concerning competences and the scope of QMV were closed, even though details of some of them would still be reopened until the final hours of the negotiations. Besides the well-known institutional issues, there were eventually also a number of financial issues that turned out to be most burdensome, not least because of the instigation of the Ministers of Finance. Amongst other things they involved the spilling over into the IGC of the disagreements that had been exposed by Ecofin's refusal in November 2003 to impose sanctions on France and Germany for excessive deficits under the Stability and Growth Pact (SGP). Eventually this led to amendments that sharpened the division of roles between the Council and the Commission in the excessive deficit procedure accompanied by a political declaration on the SGP (CIG 84/04). Ecofin also pushed the move, for which the Italian Presidency had already paved the ground, of restoring unanimity in the case of the Multi-annual Financial Framework. A final financial issue that still required substantial negotiations concerned the budget procedure, where the main concern involved the establishment of the proper balance of power between the Council and the EP within the tight timeframe available. The Irish Presidency eventually resolved this issue by removing Parliament's ability to reconfirm its amendments if conciliation between the two institutions fails (CIG 78/04).

Of the key issues that the Italians had left behind, the Irish laid the issue of the Preamble to rest, as they removed the most rhetorical passages proposed by the Convention's President, added a reference to Europe's 'bitter experience' and reinserted the Heads of State as official parties to the Constitutional Treaty, but did not persist on the inclusion of a reference to Europe's Christian heritage. Eventually then there remained only three key issues: the composition of the Commission, the minimum number of seats in the EP and the definition of QMV. The Irish chose to tackle these one by one, foregoing any attempt to combine them into some kind of package deal. Furthermore, they were determined to find a substantial solution to each of them; any suggestion to postpone issues to be resolved at a later moment (so-called 'rendezvous clauses') was rejected.

On the European Parliament, the Italian Presidency had already signaled the possibility of a 'limited increase' in the minimum threshold of seats for the smallest states, which the Convention had set at four (CIG 60/03 ADD 2: 4). Eventually, on the eve of the June European Council, the Irish formally proposed to raise the minimum threshold to six EP seats (CIG 82/04: 3). As a consequence also the maximum number of seats in the EP had to be raised from 736 to 750. To limit the upward pressure on the size of the EP, the provision was added that 'No Member State shall be allocated more than ninety-six seats' (cf. the present share of Germany of 99 in an EP of 732 seats).

On the European Commission the central challenge was to satisfy those (smaller) member states who resented the loss of a permanent Commissioner of their own nationality and still to allow for a reduction of the size of the College (as was also already envisaged by the Treaty of Nice). The solution to this challenge came in a number of components. A first concession, which had already been suggested by the Italians (CIG 60/03: 3), was to postpone the start of the reduced Commission by one term – from 2009 to 2014. Secondly, the Irish abandoned the addition of a special category of non-voting (junior) Commissioners that the Convention had introduced to placate those states without a voting European Commissioner, as they realized that this distinction caused more disturbance than it contributed to a solution. Then, thirdly, the key to the eventual solution was the Irish proposal to raise the size of the College slightly – from the 15 members as proposed by the Convention to 18 'which would in a Union of twenty-seven result in a situation where the nationals of any one Member State were present in two out of every three colleges' (CIG 75/04: 33). In fact, while the Irish tried to set the number of Commissioners at 18, in the final hours of the negotiations they had to change this into 'two thirds of the number of the Member States' but with the addition that this figure may be revised by the European Council acting unanimously (CIG 84/04; cf. CIG 82/04).

Clearly, the definition of QMV remained the most challenging issue on the table. Obviously it did not harm the negotiations that the two strongest opponents of the Convention's proposal on this point resigned from office in the spring: José-Maria Aznar's *Partido Popular* had to leave office to the PSOE after having lost the Spanish elections of March 14 and Polish Prime Minister Leszek Miller stepped down on May 2 as popular support for his government crumbled. Still, the impact of these political changes should not be exaggerated. Also Aznar and Miller had showed themselves open to certain conciliatory moves. Moreover, the change in power in principle did not affect each country's interest in securing as large a share as possible of votes in the Council. Still the change of faces did lower the pressure on the negotiations and increased the confidence that a deal could be secured.

The basis of the negotiations was always going to be some form of double majority formula (CIG 70/04: 4; cf. CIG 60/03 ADD 2: 3). Where the Convention had proposed to define the qualified majority as 50 per cent of the member states representing at least 60 per cent of the Union's population, it was clear that the population key would need to be increased to accommodate Spain and Poland. However, the room for maneuver was limited as various small and medium-sized member states insisted on a balance between the share of states and the share of population (cf. CIG 70/04: 4).[4] To increase the population key from 60 per cent to 65 per cent (which was of particular value to Spain and Poland as it would allow them to form a blocking minority by going together with Germany and a third big country), the Irish Presidency thus saw itself forced to also increase the member states' key from 50 per cent to 55 per cent (cf. CIG 77/04: 2). However, they added the requirement that to block a decision a minority of at least four member states would be needed, to balance out the effects for small states and to prevent blocking minorities from emerging too easily (CIG, 82/04: 2).

However, something more was needed than the mere recalibrating of the percentages of the double majority formula to bring Spain and Poland on board (see also chapter 5 of this volume for more on this point). This was eventually found in harking back to the 'Ioannina compromise' of 1994 in which the EU member states committed themselves that they would always aim to reach decisions by consensus and that they would first fully explore all reasonable alternatives before employing QMV to impose a decision upon an opposing minority that is only marginally short of the size required to block the decision (cf. CIG 82/04: 3). The Irish Presidency already started floating this option in the course of the spring negotiations and carefully tested it in the final weeks before the June summit in bilateral contacts with the key states involved: France, Germany, UK, Poland and Spain. The complete amendment package on the QMV definition was only revealed at the June summit (CIG 83/04). There it still underwent some final fine-tuning, but eventually it was accepted without much further ado. Thus, the Irish Presidency succeeded in bringing the IGC to an end on the evening of June 18.

4.4   Conclusion

This chapter has identified a range of differences in both the leadership strategy adopted and the results achieved by the two Presidencies of the 2003–04 IGC (see Table 4.2). While the Italian Presidency used an ambitious instrumental leadership strategy that put a lot of pressure on the timeframe and the agenda of the IGC, the Irish Presidency adopted a distinctively open and more pragmatic stance. Before turning to an assessment of the impact of the Presidencies, one should observe, however, that the analysis suggests that the different strategies adopted were not merely a matter of choice. To a large extent they reflect the different conditions under which each Presidency came to the job. The Italian Presidency started its work in the slipstream of the Convention momentum and was politically committed to conclude the negotiations well in time before the EP elections. The Irish found themselves faced with a moment of suspension that essentially did not leave them much alternative but a 'wait-and-see' strategy. Indeed, in key respects it appears that each of the two Presidencies was well disposed to yield to the demands for leadership created by the negotiating context that they faced. Thus the leadership choices were in many respects appropriate – and maybe even necessary – responses to the situations they faced (see Table 4.2).

The basic criticism of the Italians may be that they ended up hostage to the strategic choices that were suggested by the circumstances under which they came to their task. A Presidency other than that of the Italians might have interpreted the demand for leadership created by the context differently; it might, for example, have been more relaxed about the timeframe of the IGC and also less strict about its commitment to concentrating negotiations at the political level. Furthermore, agenda management by the Italian Presidency may have been overdone, for instance in the way in which they

Table 4.2 Overview of leadership strategies and the results of the two Presidencies of the 2003–04 IGC

	Italian Presidency	*Irish Presidency*
Leadership Strategy		
Timeframe	An ambitious timeframe	An open timeframe
Agenda control	A strictly controlled agenda	An agenda that built on the Italian legacy
Management of agreement	A progressive stance	A pragmatic stance
Meetings	A concentration on the highest political level	An informal and bilateral approach aiming at goodwill first
Results		
Timeframe	Failure to conclude the Successful finalization of negotiations; even if ±50% of negotiations eventual IGC agenda was finalized	
Agenda control	A gradually expanding agenda covering ±80% of the total IGC agenda	A limited number of new issues
Management of agreement	Mostly a progressive orientation, but with concessions	A wide range of concessions with some nicely fitting the Irish preferences
Meetings	Substantial setbacks in handling political negotiations	Carefully prepared and contained political negotiations

sought to exclude the issue of the composition of the Commission, with the consequence that it eventually backfired in that it cost them in terms of reputation. Looking back, the major achievements of the Italian Presidency are that it succeeded in establishing the Convention's text as the indisputable basis for negotiations and that it ensured that the IGC agenda remained of manageable proportions. Where the Italian Presidency fell short in realizing its initial ambitions, in particular the conclusion of the IGC within its own term, it may well have been the unavoidable price to pay.

In any case, while the disillusion might have been smaller, it would appear very unlikely that an alternative strategy would have secured a successful conclusion of the negotiations in December. Eventually, the mere passage of time appears to have been a crucial factor in explaining the difference between the failure of the December summit and the success of the June summit. For most, if not all, governments a deal in December came as 'too much too soon.' They simply needed time to digest the Constitution as a whole and to accept the inevitable concessions they had to make.

In these circumstances, the rotation of the EU Presidency provided a safety valve. The Irish Presidency could start from a clean slate and it handled the cooling-down period very smoothly. Another Presidency than the Irish might have accelerated the negotiations once it had regained confidence at the spring European Council and might have adopted a more formal approach from that moment onwards. Possibly such an approach would also have led to completion of the negotiations, but it is hard to see how the Irish success in finalizing the negotiations could have been bettered. Still, this success is premised on three important lessons that are of more general use to the handling of the EU Presidency:

- Creating atmosphere and goodwill is of great importance, and should certainly not be treated secondary to the proper organization of the formal aspects of the negotiations;
- Be cautious with setting deadlines for the conclusion of negotiations;
- In an EU-25 or more, political '*tour de tables*' can no longer be relied upon to make a substantial contribution to negotiations, and may well have adverse effects.

Even for a Presidency following these lessons, the December summit would probably have come too soon. Conversely, had the Italians been given the chance to adopt these lessons and to conduct the negotiations six months longer, who knows, they might well have succeeded.

On one point the appreciation of the various strategies has to go beyond mere effectiveness and that is when it comes to a qualitative assessment of the deals secured. In fact, the Irish strategy very much put the realization of deals before any substantive concerns – in other words, Irish leadership was aimed primarily at the efficiency dimension. The Italian strategy, on the other hand, was premised on a progressive stance that sought to maintain, if not to increase, the level of ambition of the Convention's draft, thereby aiming to shift outcomes closer to what the Italians wanted

This brings us to the question whether the Presidencies have in fact been able to exert leadership with regard to the substance of the outcome of the negotiations. Considering the evolution of the key issues it would seem that, given the almost irreconcilable positions of the member states, the Presidencies enjoyed very little discretion in shaping the solutions beyond the ones that were eventually established. Looking at the larger picture of the total of 73 amendments to the Convention's text, we find that on the great majority of them the two Presidencies basically stuck to the same approach regardless of the differences in strategy and interests between them. Obviously, each Presidency did have its pet issues. Notably, however, the Italians were distinctively unsuccessful in securing their preferences on theirs: the Preamble and the extension of QMV in CFSP. The Irish Presidency has a better claim to having left its marks on the eventual substantial result, although even these involve mostly points of secondary importance. The most glaring examples of where the Irish Presidency may have bend the outcome to its own preferences is in the ('regressive') changes it got adopted on the EU competences in economic policy, foreign policy and Justice and Home Affairs. Even if these changes were prompted by other states, another Presidency than the Irish might well have been more reluctant in adopting them.

All in all, given the Convention's draft Treaty and the pressure on the negotiations, the Presidencies of the 2003–04 IGC enjoyed only limited room for maneuver. To a large extent the two Presidencies seem to have yielded to the exigencies of the situations they faced. At the same time, it would appear that the Irish success only became possible due to the achievements of the contrary strategy of its Italian predecessor. The Italian Presidency may have made a mistake in claiming that the IGC would be concluded within its term of Presidency. However, in a deeper sense it may have been right in imposing this much pressure on (the first phase of) the negotiations. One may indeed wonder whether with a less stringent opening leadership strategy, any successive Presidency would have been able to conclude the IGC.

Notes

1. All official IGC documents are indicated by their official CIG-number. They are available online at http://ue.eu.int/igc/doc_register.
2. Eventually, this proposal did not survive. It only leaves its trace in Annex 30 of CIG 81/04 that basically reproduces the original Convention text.
3. For technical elaborations of the issues involved see Baldwin and Widgrén 2003; Felsenthal and Machover 2004.
4. This follows the basic logic that the blocking power of small states increases the higher the required proportion of states is set, while an increase of the proportion of the population works mainly in the advantage of the more populated states (cf. Baldwin and Widgrén 2003).

5
Oiling the Wheels of Compromise: The Council Secretariat in the 1996–97 and 2003–4 IGCs

Derek Beach

5.1 Introduction

While the roles and impact of the European Commission and the European Parliament in the 'history-making' decisions of the EU integration process have been subjected to considerable academic scrutiny, the Council Secretariat[1] has been all but discounted in the literature (Christiansen 2002; Christiansen and Jørgensen 1998; Dinan 2000; Gray 2002; Maurer 2002a; Moravcsik 1999a; Petite 2000; Corbett 1998). The Council Secretariat is on paper relatively weak in comparison to the Commission, playing a role of both administrative and technical secretary in IGCs, and assisting the Presidency in seeking solutions (Article 23(3) of the Council's Rules of Procedure, June 2000; Christiansen 2002). The Secretariat is therefore in many respects a 'least likely' case for the impact of EU institutions upon EU history-making decisions (Eckstein 1975). But a careful analysis that takes into account the causal impact of the actual negotiation process shows that the Council Secretariat is not merely the 'neutral' assistant to member state governments as assumed by Moravcsik and others (e.g. Moravcsik 1999a, p. 292). The Secretariat has played an influential behind-the-scenes role in recent inter-governmental conferences (IGCs), and has shifted outcomes closer to its own vision of the EU on many occasions.

The argument in this chapter proceeds in three steps. First, in section 5.2 I discuss the institutional preferences of the Council Secretariat, and the leadership resources that the Secretariat possesses. Section 5.3 applies the leadership model to the negotiation of two major treaty reform negotiations (the 1996–97 and 2003–4 IGCs). The section shows when and why the Council Secretariat played an influential but overlooked role in the negotiations, and, equally importantly, when and why the Secretariat was unsuccessful in its attempts to influence outcomes. The concluding section compares the cases and summarizes the findings for when and why the Council Secretariat mattered in the two IGC negotiations.

5.2 The preferences and resources of the Council Secretariat in the 1996–97 and 2003–4 IGCs

I will first briefly discuss the institutional preferences of the Council Secretariat, showing that the Secretariat has an independent institutional identity and that their preferences do not always overlap with the preferences of member state governments. Thereafter the leadership resources of the Secretariat are reviewed.

The preferences of the Council Secretariat

There are many indications that the Secretariat has its own pro-integration agenda that does not merely reflect member state preferences. One must naturally be cautious when discussing the 'interests' or 'preferences' of civil servants who proclaim that they are 'neutral,' but one can discern clues about the general orientation of their institutional and personal preferences from their speeches and actions prior to and during the negotiations. The following is based upon interviews with current and retired Secretariat officials and other officials that have worked closely with them, supplemented by written sources such as articles penned by Secretariat officials. A further caveat is that the Secretariat is a small and relatively permeable institution without as strong an institutional culture as the Commission. This means that individuals are often very important, making it difficult to speak of a single 'Secretariat interest'.

With these caveats in mind, one can detect an institutional interest of the Secretariat in increasing the strength and scope of policy areas dealt with at the European level, but only if the role of the Council of Ministers in EU policymaking is strengthened in the process.[2] Institutional issues are especially important to the Secretariat, as they have intimate knowledge of what works and what does not work in the EU through their daily work in the Council.[3] They are also quite pragmatic in their views in contrast to the Commission or European Parliament, believing that an incremental first step is often a better way of achieving a final goal than a single 'big bang' that often will not be accepted by the member states.[4]

Regarding the two IGCs, several key officials in the Secretariat published articles prior to the 1996–97 IGC (most under pseudonyms such as Justus Lipsius, authored by head of Council Legal Services Jean-Claude Piris), making it much easier to illustrate the preferences of the Secretariat in relation to the issues on the IGC agenda (Lipsius 1995; Charlemagne 1994; Ersbøll 1994).

Looking at several of the issues on the agenda of the IGC, while the Secretariat was in favor of flexibility, they were also interested in strong safeguards in order to protect the *acquis communautaire* (Lipsius 1995). The Secretariat was interested in more QMV, with Piris arguing for the 'quasi-elimination' of unanimity, with the exception of sensitive issues such as taxation and CFSP (ibid. 258–9). Prior to his replacement in 1994 Ersbøll had advocated for extending the use of QMV in CFSP, but also pragmatically stated that if CFSP is 'communitarized', it would 'result in a complete blocking of the much-needed effort to build the Common Foreign and Security Policy foreseen by the Treaty' (Ersbøll 1994: 416). Piris argued in favor of a much simplified two-tiered treaty, with a short treaty that would merge the EU and the EC into one legal entity, and would only include the most fundamental provisions, whereas all of the other provisions of the treaties would be contained in protocols.

In the 2003–4 IGC, the Secretariat did not have real 'preferences' on the handful of contentious institutional issues. On more technical legal points, however, the head of Legal Services, Jean-Claude Piris, was not satisfied with certain elements of the Convention's draft Constitutional Treaty. In his words, the Convention text was legally 'not very good' (Piris personal communication 2005). These concerns ranged from the use of Roman numerals for the four parts of the Constitutional Treaty prior to the article number, to concerns about the practicality of the Legislative Council.[5]

The leadership resources of the Council Secretariat

The informational leadership resources of the Council Secretariat are a product of the role that the Council Secretariat plays in daily EU policy-making and the role that it has played in previous IGCs. While the staff of the Secretariat cannot compete with the Commission in their substantive knowledge of the workings of the Treaties, the Secretariat has a breadth of knowledge on conducting both daily EU negotiations and treaty reform and strong legal expertise.

As its name suggests, the Council Secretariat officially provides administrative and technical assistance to the Council of Ministers, and the national Presidency chairing the Council. Despite it not being a Treaty-based institution of the Union in the manner of the Commission or European Parliament, it does play a very important role in the day-to-day policy-making process by: (a) providing authoritative technical and legal advice to the Council itself and national representatives therein; (b) playing the role of *confidante* and advisor to national delegations (Westlake 1999: 318); and (c) stepping in and brokering compromise solutions in difficult impasse situations in the Council. Given this role of being the 'vital cog' in Council decisionmaking, this provides the Council Secretariat with detailed knowledge of the workings of the EU Treaties, the preferences of member states, and extensive and unsurpassed experience with brokering compromises in the EU (Westlake 1999; Metcalfe 1998). It is especially in the latter that the Secretariat has a comparative advantage in comparison to all other actors in an IGC.[6]

If we look at the staff of the Secretariat that has dealt with IGCs, there has been a core team that has taken part in every IGC since 1985, giving them an institutional memory and experience unparalleled by any other actor (Christiansen 2002: 47; Galloway 2001: 38–9). Further, the Secretariat gains extensive knowledge of the state of play during an IGC negotiation by following it at every level, including the bilateral 'confessionals' between the Presidency and each member state held prior to the final summit of each Presidency during an IGC.

Turning to look at the reputation of the Secretariat in the two IGCs, despite the Secretariat's role changing from that of an unimportant *'notaire'* to the 'right-hand man' of the Presidency during the 1980s (Westlake 1999: 313), most national delegates saw (and still see) the Secretariat as a relatively neutral institution that can be trusted to produce issue briefs of the highest quality, formulate fair compromises, and in general help the Member States achieve their wishes.[7] This did vary, however, across the two IGCs as will be seen below, and when the Secretariat attempted to openly pursue its own interests, its acceptability as a useful and trusted assistant to the Presidency declined. This was seen in the Spanish Presidency in the fall of 1995, and the Dutch Presidency in the spring of 1997 (see below).

5.3   The role and impact of the Council Secretariat in the negotiation of the 1996–97 and 2003–4 IGCs

As was pointed out in chapter 1 of this book, contextual variables define the range of opportunities and constraints upon the attempts by an actor to provide leadership. The following section will compare the contextual conditions in the two IGCs, and their impact upon the ability of the Council Secretariat to translate their leadership resources into influence. The section then turns to evaluating the success of different leadership strategies employed by the Council Secretariat in the two negotiations.

The impact of the institutional structure of the negotiations

Based upon negotiation theory, we expected that a privileged institutional position would give the Council Secretariat more opportunities to shape the agenda and broker key deals, and vice versa.

The Secretariat had a very privileged position in the 1996–97 IGC, with two of the Presidencies very dependent upon the informational resources of the Secretariat (the Irish and Dutch), while the third Presidency during the IGC was unable to provide leadership due to a political crisis (Italy). The Council Secretariat's role in the 1996–97 IGC was based upon a mandate given to it prior to the opening of the IGC by the European Council. Its basic function was to support the IGC and the Presidencies in charge of the negotiations.

First, the Secretariat offered advice to the Presidencies on what issues to include on the agenda for particular meetings, and more generally on how to conduct the negotiations based upon its estimate of the state of play drawn from its prior experience in daily EU policymaking and IGCs. Secretariat advice often took the form of tactical advice such as "the Danes can be isolated", and "there is strong resistance to this in Spain and Portugal so caution is advised". . . ' (Nugent 1999: 153).

The Presidency–Secretariat relationship is quite fluid, with some Presidencies relying extensively upon the Secretariat, and others going it alone. Therefore Secretariat influence is always *contingent* upon the role that a given Presidency allows it to play – a point in my argumentation that cannot be underlined too strongly. And as will be seen below, when the Secretariat was perceived by a given Presidency to be pursuing its own interests too openly, this fed back into the reputation of the Secretariat, and could and did lead Presidencies to take over functions normally delegated to the Secretariat. But as pointed out by principal–agent theory, principals such as the Presidency do not always have the necessary informational resources to detect shirking by their agent (the Council Secretariat) (Pollack 1997, 2003).

Second, during the drafting process member states often put forward relatively vague ideas that then have to be translated into draft legal text. In the 1996–97 IGC almost all of the draft texts were written and developed by the Secretariat. The Secretariat often formulates its advice to the Presidency on drafting in the manner that, 'If you want co-operation in this issue-area, then it can be done in this way, while you should also be careful about this . . . '.[8] The Secretariat then develops an initial draft legal text for the Presidency, which can be modified by the Presidency if so desired. Yet as insiders point out, and as can be seen when papers prepared by the Secretariat are carefully scrutinized, the drafts often contain points that either were not on the agenda or that were even opposed by a majority of member states.[9] These inclusions are though often masked by the opaque, legal language that they are written in – giving the Secretariat considerable leeway to exploit its informational advantages.

Third, the Secretariat provided assistance to Presidencies in brokering agreements based upon its extensive experience in brokering compromises in daily Council policymaking. This role is further facilitated by the centrality of the position of the Secretariat in IGCs, and its privileged knowledge of the state of play. For example, all proposals in an IGC go through the Secretariat, and national delegations in an IGC use the Secretariat as a *confidante* and advisor in a manner similar to they way they do in daily Council work. This puts the Secretariat at the center of a web of communications. This is referred to in the negotiation literature as a 'hub-and-spoke' communications pattern, where 'one actor stands at the center of a relatively nonhierarchical communications pattern . . . ', strengthening the ability of the actor to play a strong leadership role (Hopmann 1996, p. 265).

Finally, the Secretariat provides expert legal counsel to the IGC, with the head of the Secretariat's Legal Services taking part in all IGC meetings. Importantly, while the Secretariat itself only works through the Presidency, the head of the Legal Services is an independent actor in the IGC, acting as the legal adviser to the IGC with the function of answering questions from national delegates, and also taking the floor on his/her own initiative when he/she deems it necessary.

By being the primary interpreter of EU law during an IGC, this creates opportunities for the Secretariat's Legal Service to convert its expertise into influence.[10] EU law is often ambiguous and open to many differing interpretations ranging from a literal interpretation that tends to downplay the scope and strength of EU-level competences, to a teleological method of interpreting Treaty provisions in the light of the goal of building an 'ever-closer union' (Beach 2001; Hartley 2003). There are indications that given the pro-integration (but also pro-Council) preferences of key lawyers in the Legal Services, their interpretations of EU law are often teleological.[11] By having the role of the authoritative interpreter of EU law in an IGC (see Table 5.1), this strengthens the authority of their interventions by allowing them to draw upon the moral weight of 'the law.' This enables the Secretariat to say to governments that there is no other *legal* course of action other than its own standpoint – in effect, creating a focal point that cannot be refused.

Concluding, the Secretariat enjoyed a very central position in the 1996–97 IGC, especially through its power of the pen, with the Secretariat drafting most of the Presidency draft texts and briefs put before member state delegations during the negotiations, and by acting as the legal adviser to the IGC (see Table 5.1). If used actively, we should expect that these factors alone would have granted the Secretariat numerous opportunities to influence the IGC outcome.

During the 2003–4 IGC, the head of the Council Secretariat's Legal Services Piris chaired the group of legal experts that attempted to legally tidy up

Table 5.1 The institutional role played by the Council Secretariat in the two IGCs

1996–97 IGC	• privileged institutional position, including: 　• exclusive drafter of treaty texts 　• offering advice to Presidency 　• being the center of communication 　• and providing sole legal advice to the IGC
2003–4 IGC	• less privileged institutional position, due to the role that it was allowed to play during the Italian Presidency, but the Secretariat did chair the Legal Experts Working Group. More privileged behind-the-scenes during Irish Presidency, including: • drafting all treaty texts for the Irish • offering key tactical advice to Presidency • and providing legal advice to the IGC

the final Constitutional Treaty. Yet by giving Piris the chair, the Italian Presidency attempted to signal that the process was to be a technical and not political exercise. The mandate of the group was also restrictive, being intended to merely be a legal and technical clarification exercise, and not a political negotiation (CIG 4/1/03, 42/03, 43/03).

On a more political level, the Italian Presidency in the fall of 2003 had good relations with the Secretariat until the run-up to the Brussels Summit, which was intended to conclude the IGC negotiations. But in the weeks prior to Brussels, Berlusconi and Rome-based civil servants assumed the reins of the Presidency, and ignored advice and attempts by the Secretariat to assist the Presidency. This was fateful, as a Presidency run from a national capital is often more concerned with national interests than common European interests, and often does not have the informational skills to help find a mutually acceptable outcome in complex IGC negotiations.

The impact of the nature of the issue being negotiated

Based upon the leadership model described in chapter 1, we should expect that the Council Secretariat would be able to translate its informational advantages into influence in complex, technical issues. In the 1996–97 IGC, most of the issues were relatively complex, opening many opportunities for the Secretariat to translate its informational advantages into influence. Despite the fact that delegations had begun preparing national positions during the discussions within the Reflection Group, which was charged with setting the agenda for the IGC, national delegations did not begin to seriously think through the consequences of reform in most issues until the IGC was well underway, and even then most governments often concentrated their analytical resources on only a handful of issues.[12] Therefore, in most issues in the IGC, actors such as the Commission and the Council Secretariat were 'the experts'. In contrast, the agenda of the 2003–4 IGC was limited to only a handful of relatively simple topics (see Table 5.2).

The impact of the level of complexity of the negotiating situation

Based upon the leadership model, we should expect that the demand for leadership to help the member states find a mutually acceptable outcome

Table 5.2   The nature of the issues being negotiated in the two IGCs

1996–97 IGC	• most of the issues in the IGC were quite complex, such as flexibility and the communitarization of Justice and Home Affairs (JHA), although the most salient issues dealing with the so-called 'institutional triangle' were relatively simple issues
2003–4 IGC	• most of the main issues were relatively simple, such as re-weighting of Council votes

Table 5.3 The level of complexity of the negotiating situation in the two IGCs

1996–97 IGC	• highly complex situation, with numerous different cleavages
2003–4 IGC	• simple negotiating context, with two primary cleavages, though meaningful communication difficult in an EU-25

would increase as the number of parties and issues increase. The 2003–4 IGC was a relatively simple situation, with two primary cleavages. One cleavage was between supranationalists/federalists and intergovernmentalists, while the other split small and larger member states (European Parliament IGC Monitoring Group 2003). However, meaningful communication was very difficult due to 25 parties sitting around the negotiating table. In contrast, the 1996–97 IGC was an extremely complex negotiating situation, with dozens of cross-cutting cleavages on over 200 issues. This created a strong demand for brokerage and agenda-shaping among governments in order to help them find and/or create zones of possible agreements (see Table 5.3).

The distribution and intensity of governmental preferences

Many of the issues in the 1996–97 IGC were relatively low salience, but there were also many politically sensitive issues on the agenda, such as the negotiation of changes in the second pillar (CFSP), and the institutional triangle that dealt with re-weighting of Council votes, number of Commissioners, and the extension of QMV. In these sensitive institutional issues, 'Compromises did not lie in skillful drafting or the gradual refining of texts. These were points of gut difference and fundamental importance such as cannot be resolved until the end of any negotiation' (McDonagh 1998: 155). Therefore we would expect that the Secretariat would be strongly constrained in providing strong leadership in these types of issues.

Additionally, many of these key issues were either zero-sum issues and/or dealt with sensitive matters of national prestige, including the sensitive institutional issues that have plagued IGCs since the mid-1990s. In such issues, the potential for EU institutions to have an impact on the distribution dimension through the use of clever leadership strategies was much lower. Pulling in the other direction was the strong demand for agreement on the sensitive institutional questions created by the upcoming Eastern enlargement, which created a strong demand for instrumental leadership to help governments reach a mutually acceptable outcome by brokering deals.

There were two cross-cutting cleavages in the 2003–04 IGC. The first was between pro-integrative and more intergovernmentalist governments on issues such as whether to extend Union competences and extend QMV and co-decision. The second cleavage was even more sensitive, and dealt with the distribution of power between larger and smaller governments in the EU (see chapter 8 for more on this). In both of these categories of issues, the situation

Table 5.4 The distribution and intensity of governmental preferences in the two IGCs

1996–97 IGC	• few cross-cutting cleavages, making governments very dependent upon leadership in order to find zones of possible agreement
	• most issues were low salience, with the exception of the Common Foreign and Security Policy (CFSP) and JHA, and the so-called 'institutional triangle' (number of Commissioners, extension of QMV, and re-weighting of Council votes), which were high politics issues
2003–4 IGC	• two cross-cutting cleavages: 1) pro-integrative/ intergovernmentalists; 2) reduced power to smaller states/maintain present balance
	• most of the issues were very sensitive, as they dealt with distributive issues

was relatively simple, meaning that governments did not need assistance in *finding* possible compromises. But the high political stakes involved created a strong demand for brokerage in order to help the parties *reach* an agreement (see Table 5.4).

The impact of the choice of leadership strategies by the Council Secretariat

While the context of the 1996–97 IGC opened many opportunities for the Secretariat to attempt to gain influence, the context of the 2003–4 IGC provided a much more limited range of options for the Secretariat. Was the Secretariat able to successfully exploit the context of the 1996–97 IGC? Was the Secretariat able to use the limited instruments that it possessed to gain influence in the 2003–4 IGC? Was the Secretariat able to meet the strong demand for leadership in the sensitive institutional questions, helping governments overcome collective action problems by crafting a mutually acceptable compromise?

The following will discuss the empirical findings for the instrumental leadership strategies employed by the Secretariat, showing that low-profile agenda-shaping and brokerage tactics were more effective in translating leadership resources and the possibilities opened by the negotiating context into influence over outcomes in both IGCs.

The 1996–97 IGC

The context of the IGC created a range of opportunities for the Secretariat to provide instrumental leadership. During the Spanish Presidency in the fall of 1995, a Reflection Group (RG) was charged with preparing the negotiation agenda. The Secretariat wrote the questionnaires that formed the basis of discussions in the RG,[13] inserting several of its priority issues into the document, including legal personality and a hierarchy of norms.[14] The Secretariat also downplayed the issue of flexibility in the report, as it was concerned about the potential implications of flexibility without safeguards. The Spanish Presidency, however, perceived that the Secretariat was excessively promoting its own agenda in the texts, leading the Spanish Presidency to draft much of the later material for the RG without assistance from the Secretariat (Svensson 2000: 56). This corroborates the impact that the feedback loop described in chapter 1 from the choice of leadership strategy back into the reputation of the EU institution, demonstrating the contingent nature of leadership by EU institutions. After the Spanish Presidency took firmer control, there is no available evidence indicating that the Secretariat was able to significantly shape the agenda in the RG.

The Council Secretariat filled in the leadership vacuum created by the fall of the Italian government during the Italian Presidency in the spring of 1996. The Italian Presidency effectively gave the Secretariat a *carte blanche* regarding the preparation and presentation of negotiation materials to the IGC. This allowed the Secretariat to insert certain proposals that reflected its pro-integration and pro-Council agenda (Svensson 2000: 83). The pro-Council slant was especially evident in the papers produced on the powers of the Commission or EP.[15] For instance, the Secretariat produced a proposal on the powers of the EP prior to the start of the IGC in March 1996 that was not asked for by any national delegation.[16] The Secretariat also wrote the draft conclusions that were then adopted by the Florence European Council Summit in June (Gray 2002: 393).

The Irish Presidency in the second half of 1996 drew extensively upon the Secretariat, with most of the draft texts coming from Brussels, through the Presidency guided and sometimes amended Secretariat texts (McDonagh 1998: 44, 104–5; Gray 2002). However, there are no indications that the Irish gave the Secretariat a *carte blanche*, thereby preventing the Secretariat from pushing its own agenda as strongly as it had during the Italian Presidency (Gray 2002). The only example during the Irish Presidency where it can be argued that the Secretariat was able to 'openly' promote its own interests by drafting texts for the negotiations was when the Secretariat presented a non-paper on flexibility after the Dublin II Summit in December 1996 (SN/639/96 (C 31)). The general rule when the Secretariat distributes a paper in an IGC is that either the Presidency or a member state has asked for the proposal to be prepared. However the Secretariat's non-paper on flexibility was submitted on its own initiative – something that has not happened before or since in an IGC, although the Presidency did accept it after the fact.[17]

The non-paper on flexibility clearly echoed the Secretariat's relatively skeptical attitude towards flexibility,[18] arguing for strict conditions in order to protect the institutional framework of the Community. The view in the Secretariat was that the debates in the IGC were too 'theoretical,' and it was therefore seen to be necessary both to alert member states to the risk of unbal-ancing the institutional equilibrium, and to move the debate forward by proposing a practical institutional framework for flexibility.[19] A participant pointed out that delegates were in the dark over the issue, not knowing how it could be used, or what the implications of flexibility were.[20] While certain parts of the non-paper were clearly based upon the state of play in the IGC negotiations, with the proposal attempting to translate the vague political discussions into concrete legal texts, the Secretariat was also able to insert many of its own ideas, substantially shaping the agenda and thereby successfully translating informational advantages into influence in the very complex issue.

Of the innovative ideas presented by the Council Secretariat, the following formed significant focal points for further negotiation, and made their way into the final Treaty of Amsterdam.[21] Most prominently were the eight conditions that were proposed for the use of flexibility, which were included almost word-for-word in the subsequent Dutch draft article in February 1997, and in the final Treaty of Amsterdam (Stubb 1998: 218–19). Additionally, contrary to the state of the debate in the IGC at the time,[22] the Secretariat argued that flexibility should *not* be applicable in CFSP, which also turned out to be the final outcome in the Treaty of Amsterdam. The proposals for the financial provisions contained in the Secretariat's non-paper were also, with few exceptions, accepted.[23] Further, the Secretariat also suggested splitting the EP, only allowing MEPs from participating member states to vote (See SN 639/96 (C 31), Article F quater TEU (Dispositions institutionnelles)) – an idea that was opposed by a majority of the member states, but kept reappearing in Presidency drafts due to Secretariat advocacy (Gray 1999: 218–19 footnote). It was not adopted in the Treaty of Amsterdam.

Like the Irish, the Dutch Presidency in the first half of 1997 was dependent upon the informational resources of the Secretariat. But the Dutch chose not draw on the Secretariat in certain issues such as the integration of Schengen into the EU, and chose to ask for assistance from the Commission instead. The Dutch felt that the briefs and draft texts in these issues that were produced by the Secretariat were excessively partial to Secretariat interests.

In complex issues where the Dutch Presidency did not have strong interests, such as flexibility and legal personality, the Secretariat enjoyed substantial leeway in drafting texts, enabling them to draft texts that echoed the Secretariat's own institutional preferences. As seen above, the Secret-ariat's non-paper from December 1996 shaped the final outcome on flexib-ility. Regarding legal personality, the Secretariat, and in particular Director-General of the Secretariat's Legal Service, Jean-Claude Piris, was a strong advocate of creating an independent legal personality for the Union.[24] The question of legal personality was a very complex legal question – one in which Piris, as a highly respected international law expert, had a home ground advantage. Coupled with his authoritative position of Legal

Adviser to the IGC, this gave Piris's interventions significant weight. While several member states supported creating a legal personality for the Union, there were several prominent opponents (France and the United Kingdom) (European Parliament 1996a: 27), and given this weight of opposition and lack of interest that the Dutch Presidency had in it, the issue could very likely have fallen by the wayside if it had not been for the constant advocacy of the Secretariat for the creation of some form of legal personality.

In contrast, in issues where the Dutch Presidency had strong interests that did not overlap with the preferences of the Council Secretariat, the Secretariat's level of involvement in the drafting of texts was low – again corroborating the *contingent* nature of Secretariat influence upon the role that the Presidency allows it to play. This was particularly evident on the question of the integration of Schengen into the Community. The Secretariat was opposed to integrating Schengen into the EU for two reasons. First, the Secretariat was concerned about the legal implications of incorporating the entire Schengen *acquis* into the EU's *acquis communautaire*, as the Schengen *acquis* was developed in a different institutional setting than the EU. However, perhaps the real reason for Secretariat opposition was an institutional interest in not having the Schengen secretariat incorporated into the Council Secretariat. This hesitancy by the Secretariat could be seen in the draft texts they wrote for the Dutch Presidency, eventually leading the Dutch to partially exclude the Secretariat from the drafting of these provisions, choosing instead to use their own officials, assisted by Commission experts.

Turning to look at attempts to broker agreements by the Secretariat, in issues where Presidencies had weak interests, there is evidence suggesting that the Secretariat was able to craft compromises that in the process shifted outcomes closer to their own preferences. For example the Secretariat was able to build a coalition around its own position on the need for some form of legal personality of the Union (see above).

In the endgame of the 1996–97 IGC, the Secretariat was able to broker compromises on several highly politicized issues. In the negotiations on the common trade policy (Article 133 EC),[25] the main issue was a possible extension of Commission competences in international trade negotiations such as GATT/WTO. Here the insights of the Secretariat for what was acceptable by a majority of member states, together with its technical and legal knowledge of the present scope of Commission competences, allowed it to craft a successful compromise in the final Amsterdam Summit that the Secretariat preferred over the no-agreement outcome that would have been the case had the Secretariat not put forward the compromise proposal.[26] In the IGC endgame a consensus was emerging around a German proposal that would grant the Commission across-the-board exclusive competence, coupled with a long list of exceptions (CONF 3912/97). On the last day of negotiations, the Commission pulled back its support from this proposal due to the ever-growing list of exceptions (Gray 2002). The Secretariat's Legal Service then proposed a solution to the impasse that became the final outcome, crafting an agreement that arguably no other actor would have been able to create given the absence of national experts in the actual Summit meeting.[27] The only actors with the necessary expertise to draft a compromise text were the Dutch Presidency and the Commission. The Commission's ability to broker a deal was compromised by its strong interests in extending its competences, whereas the Dutch Presidency was more interested in an amendment that reintroduced the wording of ex Article 116 EC, which had been repealed by the Treaty of Maastricht.

Additionally, the Secretariat suggested a compromise solution on the placement of the High Representative for CFSP, brokering a compromise between French ideas for a strong independent CFSP representative, and those delegations who wanted to utilize the Secretary General of the Council (Beach 2002). Tellingly, the final deal placed the High Representative within the Council Secretariat by significantly upgrading the post of Secretary General of the Council, thereby also strengthening the institutional prestige of the Council Secretariat in the process.

Concluding, in the 1996–97 IGC, the Secretariat was able to successfully exploit the possibilities for influence opened by the negotiating context through the use of low-profile agenda-shaping tactics. The Secretariat used its power of the pen to gain influence in several salient issues, illustrating the, 'influence of those who provide draft texts for debate – they run the show' (Stubb, 1998: 219). There is also evidence showing that the Secretariat was able to utilize its comparative informational advantage through brokering strategies to shift outcomes closer to its own preferences. The ability of the Secretariat to provide leadership was, however, contingent upon the acquiescence of the Presidency, and when the Secretariat attempted to more openly advocate its own positions, these tactics proved unsuccessful, as was seen in the Schengen issue during the Dutch Presidency.

It is also important to stress that most Secretariat interventions affected agreements along the efficiency dimension, and where they had a distributory effect, they only skewed outcomes *within* the broad zone of what member states would accept. The most significant exception to this was in the negotiation of flexibility, where the Secretariat shifted the zone of possible agreements itself. At the start of the IGC, based upon national preferences we would have predicted that the final outcome in flexibility would have been the creation of a form of 'hard core,' and that it dealt primarily with CFSP. The Secretariat shifted this zone to create a complex legal formula that included many institutional safeguards, and even excluded CFSP!

The 2003–4 IGC

The Council Secretariat played a key role in the IGC, oiling the wheels of compromise and assisting governments in the technical cleaning-up of the Convention's draft text. But as most of the real negotiations during the

IGC were held at the highest political levels, the Council Secretariat mostly provided leadership that ensured the efficiency of the negotiations at this level (i.e. ensured that agreement was reached), and had few opportunities to shift outcomes closer to its own position (i.e. on the distributory dimension) given that the Secretariat is more effective at the technical levels of negotiation.

The Council Secretariat signaled that it viewed the IGC as a technical exercise by appointing head of Legal Services Jean-Claude Piris to head its IGC team instead of Keller-Noëllet, who had led the Secretariat's IGC Team in previous IGCs, and was more of a political operator.[28] Piris also actively attempted to downplay the political nature of the legal experts working group that he chaired.[29]

Looking first at the Secretariat's impact in the legal experts working group, there are few indications that Piris provided more than technical (instrumental) leadership that improved the efficiency of the negotiations.[30] All of the discussions used the draft text produced by the Council Secretariat (CIG 04/03), but there is no evidence that the Secretariat inserted unwanted elements into the text. In an attempt to ensure legal continuity, and to iterate that the Union is not a tabula rasa but builds on 50 years of treaty-making, the Council Secretariat suggested in CIG 04/03 that a paragraph be inserted into the preamble about past EU treaties.[31] This made its way into the final text.

One area where there is some evidence that Piris succeeded in pushing the group in issues where he had strong views was in the issue of the numbering of the Convention's draft into four parts using Roman numerals, followed by an article number. Piris was concerned that when article numbers were read aloud, that Article I-45 would sound like 145, which could be confused with Article III-145.[32] But removing the Roman numbering of the four parts involved sensitive questions relating to the Charter for the UK, who fought strongly to keep the Charter legally apart from the rest of the treaty.[33] Piris's constant advocacy in the group ensured a compromise solution, with the Convention's numbering being revised. The compromise was to keep the four parts separated using Roman numbering, but with consecutive numbering for the entire text of the Constitution, thereby ensuring that confusions would not arise. But the use of consecutive numbering also strengthens the impression of a single text, which was something the more pro-integrative governments such as Belgium were interested in.[34]

In the actual IGC, the Council Secretariat did play a role in the Italian Presidency prior to the final Brussels Summit. The Italians drew upon the Secretariat, but relations were not close, and the Secretariat did not agree with the way in which the Italians handled the negotiations.[35] The Secretariat was particularly concerned about the lack of papers being advanced on the key institutional issues, which were not seriously discussed prior to the Brussels Summit.[36] The Secretariat did, however, draft papers and texts for the Italians on minor issues which were then approved by the Presidency for circulation.[37] For example, the Italian Presidency prior to Naples proposed going further than the weak Convention text on the issue of the Union acceding to the ECHR that stated that the Union 'shall seek accession,' and instead wrote that the Union 'shall accede.'[38] The Council Secretariat was aware that this raised problems for several delegations, and after discussions with several delegations, they drafted a protocol to explain the conditions for accession.[39]

When Berlusconi took over the handling of the Italian Presidency in the run-up to Brussels, he did not use the Council Secretariat – with predictable results.[40] According to participants, Piris had a range of possible compromise solutions prepared for the Summit, but Berlusconi did not listen.[41]

The Irish Presidency handled the negotiations differently, and worked very close with the Council Secretariat.[42] The Council Secretariat was fully associated with the Irish Presidency at all levels.[43] The Secretariat was kept informed of results of the bilateral meetings held by Irish Taoiseach Ahern with his colleagues. At the focal point level of civil servants that prepared the high-level political meetings, the Council Secretariat took part in all of the meetings, and discussed with the Presidency both the outcome and ways forward. There was a mutual dialogue, where the Secretariat offered ideas and advice to the Irish Presidency on how the negotiations should be managed, and the state of play and possible compromises.[44] The Secretariat drafted all of the texts for the Irish, under their guidance.[45]

The overall strategy agreed upon between the Irish and the Council Secretariat was to gradually narrow the parameters for agreement by testing compromises with different parties, and then tabling papers on the sensitive issues.[46] For example, after bilateral meetings between the Irish and Polish prime ministers, where Poland indicated that they would not accept a re-weighting of votes that did not incorporate an Ioannina-like agreement on blocking thresholds, the Council Secretariat produced a Draft Decision on implementing the new majority rules that stated that if a minority slightly smaller than a formal blocking minority was against a proposal, the Council would attempt to reach 'a satisfactory solution'.[47] This enabled Poland to accept the final outcome. Other actors also accepted the outcome after the Council Secretariat pointed out that the rules were not legally binding. In this instance, the Secretariat had copied the legally non-binding Ioannina agreements insertion of a reference to the Council rules of procedure that stated that a simple majority can stop the Council's attempts to find a 'satisfactory solution' by calling for a vote.

5.4 Conclusions

The central argument of this chapter is that the Council Secretariat plays an important but much overlooked role in treaty reform negotiations. By playing the role of trusted assistant in IGCs, the Secretariat gains many opportunities to provide instrumental leadership to the parties. The Council Secretariat was influential in the two IGCs analyzed here due to a combination of its high level of expertise, the Secretariat's reputation of being a trusted intervening actor, its privileged institutional position, and the skilful use of pragmatic and behind-the-scenes agenda-shaping and brokering forms of instrumental leadership.

Most of the Secretariat's leadership is on the efficiency dimension, ensuring that mutually acceptable agreements are reached, and that no potential gains are left on the table. The Secretariat fares much worse when it attempts to affect agreements on the distribution dimension, and has only in a handful of technically complicated issues like flexibility played an important role. And this influence has been contingent upon the acceptance or acquiescence of the Presidency. The role that a Presidency allows the Secretariat to play is based upon two factors. First, the resources available to a Presidency determine how dependent the Presidency is upon assistance from the Secretariat. Small state Presidencies for instance often lack the necessary informational resources to effectively chair both IGC negotiations and daily Council policymaking, and are forced to delegate many tasks to the Secretariat in order to ensure the effective functioning of their chairmanship. Second, the level of delegation in specific matters is also affected by the preferences of the government holding the Presidency. As was seen in the Dutch Presidency in the spring of 1997, when the preferences of a Presidency and the Secretariat clash, the Presidency will often choose to not rely upon Secretariat assistance.

Further, the key to the success of Secretariat leadership in the two IGCs was the use of low-key instrumental leadership strategies, such as behind-the-scenes drafting and informational tactics, and the provision of tactical advice to Presidencies. When the Secretariat departed from these behind-the-scenes tactics and attempted to more openly pursue its own interests by using more politicized leadership tactics, this damaged the perceived acceptability of the Secretariat's interventions, and affected both the Presidency's and other governments' use of the Secretariat as a source of information and advice. In the words of Piris, 'the Secretariat would simply not be listened to by all Member States if it were not perceived by them as truly helpful and impartial.'[48]

Concluding, this chapter provides evidence that IGCs are not always purely intergovernmental affairs. Contrary to the still popular either–or dichotomy between intergovernmentalists and neo-functionalists that persists in studies of the history-making decisions of European integration (See e.g. Moravcsik 1998, 1999a, 1999b; and Stone Sweet and Sandholtz 1998), EU institutions such as the Council Secretariat do matter *vis-à-vis* governments, but their influence varies according to: (a) the leadership resources that they possess; (b) the context of the specific negotiation; and (c) the appropriateness of the leadership strategies that they employ. The argument is not that EU institutions are always influential, nor even that they are always necessary for the member states to reach an efficient agreement. But the chapter did find significant evidence for the contention that they matter *vis-à-vis* governments even in the 'least likely' case. While governments may at the end of the day be the 'Masters of the Treaties,' they are not always the masters of the treaty negotiation process.

Notes

1. The official name of the Council Secretariat is the General Secretariat of the Council of the European Union.
2. See Lipsius (1995), Charlemagne (1994) for the Secretariat's preferences in the 1996–97 IGC. See Piris (1999) for the 2000 IGC. See also Beach (2002b), Christiansen (2002) and Westlake (1999) for more.
3. Interviews with present and former Council Secretariat officials, Brussels, May 2001, January 2002 and February 2003.
4. Ibid.
5. Interviews with senior Council Secretariat officials, Brussels, January 27 and January 28, 2004. Also personal correspondence with Piris, 2005.
6. One former Secretariat official in an interview appropriately called the Secretariat the Council 'Negotiating' Secretariat.
7. Interview with former Council Secretariat official, Copenhagen, January 2002; interviews with national civil servants, Brussels, May 2001 and April 2002, and London, February 2002.
8. Interview with former Council Secretariat official, January 2002.
9. Interview with former Council Secretariat official, January, 2002; national civil servants, Brussels, May 2001 and April 2002 and London, February 2002.
10. They shared this role with the Commission in the SEA IGC, but have enjoyed a monopoly since (Christiansen 2002).
11. Interviews with two Council Secretariat Legal Service officials, Brussels, May 2001 and February 2003.
12. Based upon research undertaken in national foreign ministerial archives.
13. Letter from the Chairman of the Reflection Group to its Members, Madrid, 23 May 1995, SN 2488/1/95 Rev 1.
14. See points 6 and 8 of the document.
15. Interview with Commission official, Brussels, April 2002.
16. CONF/3812/96. The Secretariat proposed a significant strengthening of the EP by giving it a right of initiative, and also extending co-decision – reforms which would have weakened the institutional power of the Commission while maintaining the same level of power in the decisionmaking process for the Council of Ministers.
17. Stubb (1998: 217–18). Also interview with Council Secretariat official, Brussels, May 2001.
18. See the writings of the head of the Secretariat's Legal Service, Jean-Claude Piris, under the pseudonym Lipsius (1995). Piris in personal correspondence with the author has pointed out that he was 'very open' to the 'novel idea'. While the Lipsius article clearly is 'open' to the idea, it also makes it very clear that in order to avoid the 'dilution of the Union', a number of relatively *strict* principles would have to be respected (pp. 244–5).

19. Based on interviews with officials in the Council Secretariat, Brussels, May 2001, and a national civil servant, Brussels, April 2002.
20. Interview with national civil servant, Brussels, May 2001.
21. Stubb goes so far to say that the Council was not only an 'advocate' of flexibility, but also became the 'judge' of the form of flexibility embodied in the final Treaty (1998: 218).
22. Stubb (1998: 199–200). See also joint Franco-German letter in December 1996 (Agence Europe, *Europe Daily Bulletins*, No. 6871, 11/12/96); and European Parliament (1996b: 27). According to Stubb, the Member States favouring CFSP flexibility in November 1996 were Belgium, Finland, France, Germany, Italy, Luxembourg, the Netherlands, and Spain.
23. Ibid.
24. See for instance the suggesting wording produced by the Secretariat in Note 27 of April 26 1996, which states that the 'most straightforward option' is full legal personality (CONF/3827/96). Interview with two national civil servants, London, February and April 2002.
25. Then numbered Article 113 of the EC Treaty.
26. Interview with national civil servant, London, February 2002; and Council Secretariat official, February 2003.
27. Interview with national civil servant, London, February 2002; and Council Secretariat official, February 2003.
28. Interview with senior Council Secretariat official, Brussels, January 27 2004.
29. Ibid.
30. See the report from Piris to the IGC, CIG 51/03.
31. Interview with senior Council Secretariat official, Brussels, January 28 2004.
32. Interview with senior Council Secretariat official, Brussels, January 28 2004; NAT-19.
33. Ibid.
34. Interview with Belgian national official, Brussels, January 27 2004.
35. Interviews with Belgian national official, Brussels, January 27 2004; British officials, London December 16 2003 and February 2 2004; senior Council Secretariat officials, Brussels, January 27 and January 28 2004.
36. Interview with senior Council Secretariat official, Brussels, January 28 2004.
37. Interview with senior Council Secretariat officials, Brussels, January 27 and January 28 2004, EC-26.
38. CG 52/1/03 Rev 1.
39. Interview with senior Council Secretariat official, Brussels, January 28 2004. See protocol on the ECHR in CG 73/04 p. 112.
40. Interview with senior Council Secretariat official, Brussels, January 27 2004, senior Council Secretariat official, Brussels, January 28 2004, EC-26.
41. Interview with senior Council Secretariat official, Brussels, January 28 2004, NAT-16.
42. Interviews with senior Council Secretariat officials, Brussels, January 27 and January 28 2004.
43. Ibid.
44. Interview with senior Council Secretariat official, Brussels, January 28 2004.
45. Ibid.
46. Ibid.
47. CIG 83/04: 8–9; ibid.
48. Personal correspondence with the author, April 29 2005.

6
Leader or Bystander? The European Commission and EU Treaty Reform

Hussein Kassim and Dionyssis G. Dimitrakopoulos

6.1 Introduction[1]

The ability of the Commission to influence EU treaty reform is strongly contested. Most accounts of treaty-amending decisions – in particular, the adoption of the Single European Act and the Treaty of European Union – argue that it was a significant player. Many claim a leading role for the Commission. Some go even further, contending that entrepreneurship – or 'leadership' in the terms of this volume – on the Commission's part is a necessary condition for advancing European integration (Ross 1995; Grant 1994; Sandholtz and Zysman 1989). From the same standpoint, but with the ambition of developing an explicitly theoretical perspective, advocates of what might be termed a 'supranational agency' approach have argued for a conceptualization of treaty reform that takes account of the role played by the Commission, as well as other supranational and transnational actors (Christiansen 2002; Christiansen and Jørgensen 1998; Beach 2005).[2] Proponents of this approach contend that the Commission has often been a significant actor in treaty reform and that it has, on occasion, had an important impact on the final outcome. Liberal intergovernmentalism, by contrast, the main rival and target of the supranational agency approach, takes a resolutely state-centric view. Though conceding that, exceptionally, the Commission had an influence in the case of the SEA, liberal intergovernmentalism proposes a perspective that 'privilege[s] the role of national governments and domestic politics' (Moravcsik 1999a: 269) and dismisses supranational intervention at intergovernmental conferences (IGCs) as 'generally late, redundant, futile and sometimes even counterproductive' (Moravcsik 1999a: 269–70).

This chapter aims to contribute to this debate, but, in line with the argument made in the introduction of this volume, it challenges the rather narrow theoretical approaches that have hitherto dominated discussion of EU treaty-making. The chapter seeks to go beyond the existing literature in three ways. First, it responds to specific claims concerning supranational entrepreneurship made by Andrew Moravcsik (1999a). Although the supranational agency approach offers a persuasive critique of the liberal intergovernmentalist account of treaty reform, it does not address these particular contentions. The second is to identify the conditions under which the Commission can exercise leadership in the sense defined by the editors of this volume – that is, advancing collective bargaining with or without the achievement of private gain (see chapter 1, above). The third is to examine the Commission's impact in the most recent round of treaty reform and to consider whether the decision to hold a Convention on the Future of Europe to prepare the 2004 IGC strengthened or weakened the Commission's influence.

The chapter makes three arguments. The first, following Christiansen *et al.*, is that liberal intergovernmentalism's construal of treaty reform as nothing more than 'hard bargaining' between states, beginning and ending with the opening and closing of formal proceedings, is too narrow. A broader conception which encompasses agenda-setting and implementation is considerably more convincing. The second is that the Commission can exercise *influence* over episodes of treaty reform – usually, in the terminology outlined in the introduction, through an information-based instrumental leadership strategy – and that it has done so, but its ability to do it is highly dependent on contextual factors, such as the member states' openness to 'building Europe', the structure of the decisionmaking arena – an IGC offers greater opportunity for the Commission to influence proceedings than a Convention – and, because it does not have a formal role at the center of proceedings, the preparedness of the presiding authority and the secretariat charged with supporting the latter to seek recourse to the Commission for advice or information.[3] It contests liberal intergovernmentalism's rejection of a role for the supranational institutions in treaty reform and its contention that only states matter. The third argument is that the extent to which the Commission can exercise *leadership* is still more contingent and depends to a large degree on the personal qualities, style and standing within the organization of the Commission President. In other words, the process of preference formation within the Commission is an important, but overlooked, variable in most of the literature. In this volume it is defined as a component of the internal capacity of the potential leader.

The chapter is divided into two parts. The first critically reviews the contentions made by liberal intergovernmentalism (LI) and the critique presented by the supranational agency approach. It then considers two objections to LI's arguments concerning the Commission's ability to act as an informal entrepreneur or leader in treaty reform. Distinguishing between influence and leadership, a distinction which the supranational agency approach does not press, the second part discusses the contextual and internal conditions that allow the Commission to act as an informal entrepreneur. Examples are drawn from IGCs between 1985 and 2004 and the Convention on the Future of Europe.

6.2   Theorizing Commission influence in EU treaty reform

Although the Commission's impact in various rounds of treaty reform has been the object of empirical investigation since the SEA, serious theoretical consideration of the relative influence of political actors did not take place until the early 1990s. Proponents of a state-centric perspective – namely, LI – were first to move into the field, with Moravcsik arguing, first, that national governments controled treaty reform (1991, 1993, 1998) and, later, that the Commission's influence has, with the single exception of the SEA (Moravcsik 1999a: 270), been negligible. The supranational agency approach, which emerged some years later,[4] offers an important and largely convincing critique of the liberal intergovernmentalist account, but its response is directly more towards LI's conceptualization of treaty reform ('LI I') than its arguments about the leadership capabilities of the Commission ('LI II').

Liberal intergovernmentalism I: a state-centric perspective on treaty reform

LI leaves little room for input by supranational institutions. Contending that the European Union 'has developed through a series of intergovernmental bargains' (Moravcsik 1993: 473), it argues that integration 'can best be explained as a series of rational choices made by national leaders' (Moravcsik 1998: 18). States act 'instrumentally in pursuit of relatively stable and well-ordered interests', implying 'a division of major EC negotiations into three stages: national preference formation, inter-state bargaining, and the choice of international institutions' (ibid.), each of which is best explained by a different theory (Moravcsik 1993: 482; 1998: 19). For the purposes of the current discussion, only the first two are relevant.[5]

According to the liberal theory of preference formation – the first stage – 'preferences reflect the objectives of those domestic groups which influence the state apparatus' (1998: 24) and are 'exogenous to a specific international policy environment' (1998: 24). In advancing these preferences in negotiations at the EU level, governments represent, and are constrained by, the interests of domestic constituencies. The second stage – inter-state bargaining – is explained in terms of a Nash bargaining solution. According to Moravcsik (1993: 498), outcomes are likely to be efficient; that is 'conflicts are generally resolved Pareto-optimally' (1993: 499), because bargaining takes place 'in a non-coercive unanimity voting system', and an environment that is 'relatively information-rich', where 'transaction costs . . . are low'. In shaping the outcome, 'relative power matters' and is linked to the intensity of national preferences: '[t]he more intensely governments desire agreement, the more concessions and the greater effort they will expend to achieve it' (ibid.).[6]

The contention that 'bargaining outcomes should be efficient, in the sense that conflicts are generally resolved Pareto-optimally' (Moravcsik 1993: 499), relies on three assumptions (Moravcsik 1993: 498): that bargaining takes place 'in a non-coercive unanimity voting system', that the environment is 'relatively information-rich', and that 'the transaction costs... are low'. '[R]elative power matters' and is linked to the intensity of national preferences: '[t]he more intensely governments desire agreement, the more concessions and the greater effort they will expend to achieve it' (ibid.). Supranational institutions enter only in the third stage and then only as agents, entrusted by the member states with responsibility for implementation and enforcement of the agreement to ensure the credibility of commitments undertaken by the contracting parties.

Liberal intergovernmentalism II: against supranational entrepreneurship

Despite LI's claims, and often against them, studies of treaty reform have argued that the European Commission (and other non-state actors) have indeed been influential in treaty reform, and have outlined how this influence has been exercised. They have argued that the Commission's intervention has been instrumental to decisions to convene an IGC, that it has contributed to the definition of the reform agenda (Christiansen *et al.* 2002; Christiansen 2002; Christiansen and Jørgensen 1998), set down important markers against which other participants situate themselves (Dimitrakopoulos and Kassim 2005), contributed technical expertise that has informed negotiations (Gray and Stubb 2001), supplied key actors, particularly the Council Presidency and the Council Secretariat, with information and advice (Endo 1999), and that it has otherwise contributed to the content of the final settlement (Noël 1985; Sandholtz and Zysman 1989; Green Cowles 1995; Grant 1994; Ross 1995; Endo 1999: 141; Christiansen 2002: 41; Gray 2002: 389), as well as to the process of post-ratification implementation (Hix 2002).

Responding to the first wave of this literature in the late 1980s and 1990s, Moravcsik contested claims asserting Commission leadership in EU treaty negotiations as part of a broader 'nearly unchallenged consensus across theories of international regimes, law, negotiation and regional integration [in which international officials] regularly intervene to initiative new policies, mediate among governments, and mobilize domestic groups in ways that fundamentally alter the outcomes of multilateral negotiations' (Moravcsik 1999a: 267), questioning the ability of international officials to act as informal entrepreneurs. The difficulty was how 'supranational leaders and the international officials working under them' can play a decisive role in 'a classical diplomatic setting of unanimity voting' (ibid.), where they have no formal power, but also lack the resources most often employed by states, domestic actors and formally empowered international officials, specifically 'discretionary control over domestic policy concessions, financial side-payments, voting rights, formal agendas, [and] credible threats to employ coercion' (ibid.,: 271). Moravcsik reasoned that effective leadership (or, to use the term that he employs, 'informal entrepreneurship') could derive only from

> 'an asymmetrical control over informational and ideational resources unavailable to the principals of a negotiations, but necessary for effective initiation, mediation and mobilization – a principle that follows from non-cooperative bargaining theory, which predicts that negotiations will be efficient if all actors are fully informed about relevant parameters, not least the nature and intensity of one another's preferences' (ibid., p. 272)

Consequently, any plausible explanation of supranational influence must identify such a 'bottleneck', and 'then describe how and why international officials are in a unique position to overcome it' (ibid.,: 272).

Observing that '[n]owhere are claims about effective informal entrepreneurship more boldly advanced than among those who study the European Union' (ibid.,: 267), Moravcsik concentrates his attention on the European Commission and its role in treaty-amending decisions.[7] He makes three arguments: first, that the claims made by existing studies about supranational leadership are not subjected to theoretically and methodologically rigorous evaluation, and fail to demonstrate that action on the part of a supranational body has influenced policy initiation, led to the proposal of new options or compromises in ongoing negotiations between states (mediation), or mobilized domestic social support for an agreement; second, that analysis of forty years of treaty-amending negotiations shows that supranational intervention is not 'a necessary condition for efficient interstate negotiation in the EC', but is in fact 'generally late, redundant, futile and sometimes even counterproductive' (ibid., pp. 269–70);[8] and third, that only a two-level bargaining theory attentive to the dynamics of state – society relations, rather than a theory that focuses on interstate coordination problems, explains the intermittent and rare variation in the effectiveness of supranational entrepreneurship in the EC' (ibid.,: 270).

The supranational agency approach

The supranational agency approach challenges the liberal intergovernmentalist account of treaty reform, but directs its argument more toward LI I than to LI II (see above). Its critique is largely convincing.[9] First, it contests LI's conventionalization of integration as a series of 'big bangs' (Christiansen and Jørgensen 1999), each an isolated event and separate from routine policymaking. Rather, it argues, treaty-making is embedded in processes of day-to-day EU policymaking (Falkner 2002a; Sverdrup 2002).[10] Though decisions about technical areas are taken at IGCs, the context in which they are arrived at, and the terms in which issues are framed, are influenced by everyday policymaking (see, e.g., Falkner 2002b). Second, charging that LI's 'focus on bargaining is, in itself, a limited perspective which implicitly privileges the role of national governments in a particular phase of treaty reform' (Christiansen 2002: 34), the supranational agency approach observes that an IGC is only one stage in any episode of treaty reform. The case for an IGC has in the first instance to be made, for example, and a reform agenda defined. Whilst these arguments go back and forth, expectations are created about what will be achieved and, if agreement that an IGC should be called is reached, the terms in which issues are discussed when formal proceedings begin are framed at this time. In addition, once a treaty has been ratified, there is an implementation phase, during which its content may be subtly reinterpreted. By drawing attention to the phases of treaty reform before the formal proceedings of the IGC begin and after they close, the supranational agency approach draws attention to stages of the process where supranational institutions and transnational actors play a part and may have an impact. The Commission, in particular, can influence the agenda through advocacy or its right to deliver an opinion in advance of an IGC and how decisions are implemented afterwards.

The supranational approach also contests LI's image of how an IGC works – a third challenge. As well as pointing out that negotiations take place at several levels, including the technical level where the Commission can be influential, proponents of this perspective posit that the IGC itself is not the 'open arena' for governments to debate and bargain over their respective positions and institutional choices that LI assumes (Christiansen 2002: 34). They also stress the character of an IGC as an institution (Falkner 2000a; Closa 2002), a 'structured environment' (Christiansen *et al.* 2002: 15), with rules and norms that impose restrictions on all participants, including states, and that the interaction between states has a social dimension. In other words, it is not only about 'economic interests and formal bargaining' (Falkner 2002a; Christiansen 2002). The image of 'hard bargaining' offered by LI, as well as the claim that an IGC is effectively a 'spot market' (Moravcsik and Nicolaïdis 1999: 62), fails to take account of the change of preferences, interests and identities that typically take place at an IGC (Falkner 2002a).[11]

6.3 The Commission as a leader

Although the supranational agency approach offers an effective critique of the original formulation of LI (LI I), it does not respond as directly to Moravcsik's later arguments (LI II). This reflects its proponents' concern to show that supranational institutions can *influence* treaty reform rather than identifying the factors that determine when and how the Commission can act as a *leader* – the concern of this chapter and book. For this reason, LI II needs to be addressed.

According to Moravcsik, the 'primary task of any explanation of supra-national entrepreneurship must be to investigate the conditions under which supranational entrepreneurs enjoy . . . a comparative advantage over powerful and directly interested governments' (1999a: 273). Interpreting this task as a challenge to demonstrate that supranational entrepren-eurs benefit from informational or ideational asymmetries, he argues that scholars are too ready to equate *action* on the Commission's part with *influ-ence*, do not test alternative hypotheses, and fail to demonstrate that the Commission does in fact possess attributes that bestow advantages upon it. He contends that investigation of successive rounds of treaty reform shows that, with the single exception of the SEA, where the Commis-sion and the Parliament played a secondary part, supranational institutions have not been informal entrepreneurs/leaders in treaty-amending decisions, and that national governments have been the lead actors in each reform episode.

Although space does not permit a full or detailed critique of LI II, it is possible to draw attention to at least three serious weaknesses. First, LI II's characterization of the resources at the disposal of supranational institution is misleading and problematic. Few, if any, of the scholars that make the case for entrepreneurship of the European Commission base their argument on claims that the Commission Presidents have shown greater 'political creativity' than national leaders or on the organization's reputed imparti-ality, as Moravcsik suggests (1999a). Most in fact point to the Commission's technical and policy expertise rather than the size of its staff, but their argument is not based on numbers, as LI II claims when the institution's small size is cited as a factor that limits the Commission's influence. It is not, though, the number of officials commanded by the Commission that give it influence, but the specialist knowledge and experience of its offi-cials, which arise from the functions that the organization discharges and its position at the centre of EU business. As well as policy expertise, with offi-cials who, unlike their national counterparts,[12] need to know about policy arrangements across the Union, the Commission has legal expertise that member countries cannot be expected to rival and a greater knowledge of, and familiarity with, EU procedures. In addition, the Secretariat General provides a permanent home within the Commission for a unit that monitors treaty reform and treaty implementation (Kassim 2006). In contrast to the turnover evident in national capitals, the officials called upon to prepare and coordinate the Commission's input into treaty reform are typically veterans of previous negotiations.[13] Allied to the expectation that the Commission will, in line with its treaty-given mission, attempt to set out an agenda that advances the general European interest, the unique expertise at its disposal serves as a powerful resource.

Second, the Commission's role as an agenda-setter and problem-solver in matters of treaty reform has been accepted since the 1985 IGC and institutionalized since the Treaty of European Union. Although the Commission had no formal role in the round of treaty reform that led to the SEA, its tabling of three texts shortly after the first meeting of the IGC was regarded as legitimate by national capitals.[14] Governments were accustomed to reacting to proposals from the Commission as a matter of routine and, in its formal role as 'guardian of the Treaty,' the Commission 'was uniquely able to suggest detailed legal changes to the existing treaties' (see Budden 2002: 90). The Commission has also been able to influence negotiations by proposing solutions that national governments would not have put forward themselves, but which, given limited information, the costs involved in formulating and testing alternatives, and their desire not to prolong discussions excessively, they have been prepared to accept.

Third, LI II seriously overestimates member state capacities. Moravcsik asks: 'Why should governments, with millions of diverse and highly trained professional employees, massive information-gathering capacity, and long-standing experience with international negotiations at their disposal, *ever* require the services of a handful of supranational entrepreneurs to generate and disseminate useful information and ideas?' (1999a: 273). Though national administrations are far larger than the Commission, the overwhelming majority of their staffs are sectoral experts working in line ministries. Though some are involved in work with an EU dimension, many do not have an expertise that would enable them to negotiate at IGCs. Relatively few officials in national capitals have a general overview of their country's EU policy, while expertise about the requirements of EU treaty negotiations is surprisingly thin and the number of officials drafted in to work on an IGC team surprisingly meager.[15]

It is unclear, moreover, that the size of state bureaucracies translates into influence in the way that the question cited above implies. What LI needs to demonstrate, but fails to do, is that governments gather and synthesize information effectively, that neither political differences between ministers, 'bureaucratic politics' (Allison 1969; 1971; Allison and Halperin 1972), nor conflict between different layers of government in federal or devolved states impede these processes, and that governments act coherently. Empirical evidence seems to suggest the opposite. Comparative studies show that such coordination is rarely sought and that, where it is an ambition, it is costly, demanding and difficult to achieve (Kassim *et al.* 2000, 2001).

Summary

The above discussion examines both weaknesses in LI and the limitations of the critique of LI offered by the supranational agency approach. While the latter reveals problems with LI's conceptualization of treaty reform and 'reinstates' supranational institutions as actors in that process, its main concern is to demonstrate that players other than national governments are involved and that governments do not have the open-ended freedom that LI suggests. It does not, however, directly address LI's claims regarding the Commission's leadership capabilities, nor does it distinguish between influence and leadership, or discuss the factors that determine its impact.

The first part of this chapter has been concerned to directly challenge LI's argument about Commission leadership, while endorsing the supranational agency approach's image of treaty reform. In the second part, it argues that the Commission is able to influence this process, and even to play a leadership role. It considers the conditions under which it can do so, and identifies instances where the Commission has been a leader in constitutional negotiations.

6.4   The Commission and Treaty reform in an historical perspective[16]

Contrary to the claims of LI, the Commission is able to influence treaty reform, and even to act as a leader, as the consideration of past treaty-amending decisions presented below demonstrates. Its ability to do so, however, depends on three sets of factors identified in the introduction: (1) the reputation of the Commission and its President; (2) the Commission's internal capacity; and (3) the institutional position granted to the Commission.

The first key factor is the standing and reputation of the Commission and its President. Whereas Jacques Delors was admired for his technical abilities and his political skill, this has not been true of his successors. The second is related to effective advocacy on the part of the Commission President, and the ability of the Commission to define a clear message and present a united front in the negotiations. This is an internal factor that is a necessary and crucial precondition for Commission influence and leadership. In the absence of these conditions, the Commission lacks credibility and, therefore, influence.

The final factor is the institutional structure of the decisionmaking arena and the preparedness of the presiding authority and its secretariat to seek recourse to the Commission for advice. With respect to the former, this chapter argues that the Commission is more likely to be effective at an IGC, where the central authorities – the Council President and the Council Secretariat – are more likely to request its input and where its involvement is institutionalized, than at a Convention, which is characterized by a form of political discourse and interaction that does not suit a supranational actor, which does not directly represent an identifiable constituency. With respect to the latter, whether in the case of an IGC or a Convention, the extent of the Commission's influence during the negotiations will depend upon the preparedness of the country holding the Presidency or the President of the

Convention, or the Council Secretariat or the Convention's Secretariat, to call upon the Commission.

The discussion below looks at the Commission's ability to influence and to lead reform first in the case of IGCs and then at the Convention on the Future of Europe. It reflects on the different structure for opportunity presented by the two institutional contexts.

The Commission and IGCs

The way in which IGCs are organized and operate have remained remarkably unchanged,[17] even if the grounds on which they are called, the length of the agenda-setting phase, and the subjects brought before them have varied considerably (see also chapter 1). In several instances, action on the part of the Commission has been an important factor leading to the convening of an IGC. Though the formal power to call an IGC rests with member governments, the Commission has typically been a protagonist in calling for a new round of reform (Christiansen 2002: 41). The 1985 IGC and the 1990–91 IGC on EMU are particularly striking examples. That the Commission should mobilize in this way is unsurprising, since it actively monitors EU activities and the institutional development, and, as guardian of the treaties, is concerned that remedial action is taken where problems arise.

In addition, in arguing for an IGC, the Commission has been able to put particular topics on to the reform agenda.[18] In the case of the 1985 IGC, it was the Commission, and Delors in particular, that argued for the inseparability of institutional and policy reform (Noël 1985: 449; Ross 1995: 32) – a proposal that ran counter to national views as expressed in the Dooge Committee (Budden 2002: 83). Delors linked an expansion of qualified majority voting in the Council with a set of policy objectives,[19] notably liberalization, which persuaded national political leaders, including Margaret Thatcher, later to take a decision that they would not independently have chosen. Delors also championed a strengthening of the European Parliament's powers, not only giving itself an ally, but also launching a process that has turned the EP into the EU's co-legislator.

A further example of agenda-setting – which also illustrates why treating episodes of treaty reform as isolated events is misleading – is provided by the 1990–91 IGC on EMU, where Delors's incrementalist strategy begun in 1985 paid off.[20] Margaret Thatcher may have dismissed the Single European Act's short chapter on 'Cooperation in Economic and Monetary Policy (Economic and Monetary Union)' as meaningless words (Grant 1994: 74), but Delors used them once the process had been set in motion for the establishment of the single market. By skillfully exploiting both his own political capital and intra-national divisions he secured – during the 1988 German Presidency – the creation of the committee that paved the way for the establishment of EMU under the Maastricht Treaty. He was instrumental in persuading Chancellor Kohl – who was skeptical about monetary union and distrusted his

Vice Chancellor, Hans Dietrich Genscher (Grant 1994: 119) – not only to add this item to the agenda of the European Council in 1988 in Hanover, but also to support his proposal that the committee be composed of the governors of the central banks and that he (Delors) should chair it.[21] Unsurprisingly, even after Mrs Thatcher's intervention, the text referred to the EMU-related part of the SEA as a confirmation of 'the objective of the progressive realization of economic and monetary union' and ascribed to the Delors committee the responsibility for 'studying and proposing concrete steps leading towards this union' (cited in Grant 1994: 120). The committee came up with the three-step blueprint upon which the creation of EMU was subsequently based (see Endo 1999: 153–66). Furthermore, Delors's skilful use of 1992 as the 'deadline' for the creation of the single market was equally important in the post-IGC phase of the 1985 IGC.

The Commission has been able to influence formal proceedings and, thereby, the final outcome of negotiations, on several occasions. In these instances, the Commission has acted as an instrumental leader. Sometimes its proposals have merely created a 'focal point'. At other times, the Commission has shaped the final agreement. Examples include the adoption of the Commission's maximalist definition of the single market as 'an area without frontiers' at the 1985 IGC, despite opposition from all three largest member states (Budden 2002: 81–2). More dramatically, in response to a request from the Luxembourg Presidency, the Commission tabled around thirty proposals for the 1985 IGC (Endo 1999: 141). As a result, Delors and his staff are credited for drafting between 60 and 70 per cent of the final text of the SEA (Grant 1994: 75; see also Ross 1995: 32). Similarly, the Delors Report provided the basis for the provisions in the Treaty of European Union relating to EMU (Grant 1994; Ross 1995; Christiansen 2002: 41; Gray 2002: 389).

The negotiations that led to the Maastricht Treaty provide another example of Commission influence. When Delors realized that the weak Major government was willing to veto the draft treaty on the European Union in part because of the proposal regarding the enhancement of the social dimension, he proposed the creation of the 'social protocol' which meant that 11 states could proceed without being hampered by the Conservative British government (Ross 1995: 191; Falkner 2002b: 110). The Commission also mobilized peak associations representing labor and industry, who formulated their own proposals on the role of the 'social partners'. It was as a direct result of the Commission's intervention that the text that they elaborated became part of the Treaty (Falkner 2002b: 111).[22] Crucially, aware of the fact that some of its proposals were objected to, not because of their content, but because of their origin, the Commission channeled its proposal through a national government (Falkner 2002b: 111).

The Commission has even had an impact in more recent rounds of reform, despite member governments' determination to keep control of proceedings. During discussions at Amsterdam, for example, the Commission was influential both in the decision to extend co-decision (Christiansen and Gray

2003: 15) and in the major innovation introduced by that Treaty – the inclusion of a flexibility clause. The Commission lent credibility to the idea of such a provision, accompanied by appropriate safeguards, which subsequently found its way into the treaty (Stubb 2000: 166). As with QMV, it is difficult to see how such a change could be made without Commission support. The Commission has even influenced the third pillar, where it was instrumental in the decision to shift sections of Justice and Home Affairs across to the first pillar (Christiansen and Gray 2003: 15).

This brief discussion is not intended to suggest that the Commission has been able systematically or uniformly to influence treaty reform, but to highlight, contrary to LI, occasions where the Commission has intervened with effect. Indeed, there have been reform rounds, such as the 2000 IGC, where the Commission has been a peripheral actor, unable even to defend 'the general interest' (Gray and Stubb 2001: 13). The Commission's influence, still more its ability to act as informal entrepreneur, has varied over time. Ken Endo (1999: 153, 166) has suggested that Delors was able to 'succeed' in 1991 due to external contextual factors, such as the opportunity afforded by the ambitions of two of the larger member states (namely, France and Italy), and internal factors, such as Delors's ability to mobilize the support of Commission officials; and personal factors, such as Delors's technical expertise, his ability to contribute to discussion in the European Council, and high-level contacts with François Mitterrand and Helmut Kohl.

The argument made here is slightly different: Commission influence does depend on contextual and internal factors, but the key contextual factors, so far as leadership is concerned, are the extent to which the Council Presidency is prepared to seek recourse to the Commission for advice and initiatives, and the defensiveness of member governments. Where the Council President has shown such willingness, as, for example, in the case of the 1985 IGC and the 1990–91 IGC on EMU, the Commission has been able to provide instrumental leadership. Where it has been excluded, as in the case of the 2000 IGC, its opportunities to provide leadership have been much fewer.[23] Moreover, since 1991, member states have generally been defensive and less open to Commission proposals, fearing the domestic backlash should their action be interpreted as 'selling out' in Brussels (Kassim and Menon 2004). The main internal factor is whether the Commission President is able to mobilize the resources of the Commission effectively. While Delors was able to present and mobilize support for his proposals in 1985 and at the 1990–91 IGC on EMU, Jacques Santer took a minimalist approach to the 1996–97 IGC and Prodi did not offer a compelling vision at the 2000 IGC.

The Commission and the future of Europe

Although Romano Prodi was an enthusiastic advocate of the 'new method' of treaty reform, the Commission was not an influential actor, and certainly not a leader, at either the Convention on the Future of Europe or the IGC that followed. Indeed, the Commission performed poorly, even if it did not ultimately suffer a serious erosion of its powers or responsibilities (Dimitrako-poulos and Kassim 2006). Its inability to influence proceedings can be attrib-uted to a negotiating context that provided them with few opportunities to provide leadership, and the Commission's leadership resources, or lack thereof. With respect to the negotiating context, the nature and working methods of the Convention did not suit the Commission. As an organiza-tion whose legitimacy derives from its technical expertise, whose influence in treaty reform has usually been exerted behind the scenes, and which, because it does not directly represent an identifiable constituency, is without a 'sovereign no', the Commission found it difficult to engage in an exer-cise that was meant to be much more overtly political than any of the previous rounds of treaty reform.[24] In addition, the Commission was not regarded as an important interlocutor or source of advice or policy recom-mendations by the chair of the Praesidium, Valéry Giscard d'Estaing, or the Praesidium Secretariat. In regard to the Commission's leadership resources, the Commission was marred by strategic and tactical errors. Prodi therefore chose to advance a programme that reflected the Commission's institution-alized myth – 'the Community method', which places the institution at the heart of Europe and entrusts it with a key leadership role in daily EU policymaking – that, under the circumstances, was unlikely to command widespread support due to the distribution of governmental preferences in the negotiations. Moreover, the Commission was known to be intern-ally split and Prodi's actions only compounded its divisions. In addition, although Prodi's college included a significant number of 'political heavy-weights', this did not enable the Commission to overcome problems that stemmed from the nature of the negotiating context or, indeed, the legacy of the crisis that led to the resignation of the Santer college.[25]

The negotiating context – the Convention on the future of Europe

Despite Prodi's support for the new method of treaty reform,[26] the appoint-ment of two *conventionnels* from the Commission that also sat on the Prae-sidium, the Convention's executive and drafting body, the Commission's status as one of the *composantes* of the Convention, and a sympathetic majority in the Praesidium,[27] the Commission faced two serious problems. First, it confronted a very different structure of opportunity to that of an IGC. With no role for the Council President or the Council Secretariat, the Commission was deprived of its usual channels of influence. Whereas at an IGC the Commission could be assured that its opinion or any proposal it submitted would be discussed and taken notice of, the possibility that it could exercise similar agenda-setting power at the Convention was by no means assured. In addition, Giscard, who was clearly an influential figure in the Convention, was quick to announce his lack of sympathy for the

Commission as an institution and his scorn for the Commission President's view that it should become the government of Europe.[28] Not only did Giscard favor a more intergovernmentalist conception, but he calculated that the success of the Convention depended on his ability to retain the support of key national governments. He did not regard listening to the Commission or keeping Prodi on-board as priorities.

Second, the Convention was not an arena in which the Commission could operate effectively. It was not at all clear that the Commission, which was created as an *administration de mission* – a technocratic body designed to propose solutions to policy problems, broker deals and upgrade the common European interest in sectoral politics, was suited to the task of debating the EU's constitutional future. In contrast to previous treaty reforms, the discussion launched by Joschka Fischer's call to define the *finalité politique* of integration called for grand schemes and value judgments, not technocratic fixes. Moreover, unlike the Convention on the EU's Charter of Fundamental Rights, which had been tightly focused and low profile, the Convention on the Future of Europe was designed to be open and wide ranging. Thus, the content expertise that it possessed due to its institutional position as guardian of the treaties and Antonio Vitorino's not-inconsiderable process expertise (since he had successfully participated in the Convention that drafted the EU Charter of Fundamental Rights) had to be deployed in a new and much more demanding negotiating context than previous rounds of treaty reform.

Commission leadership: the interplay of internal capacity and negotiating context

The approach of the Prodi Commission to the Convention reflected three factors: the novelty of the exercise, the Commission's inexperience, and the dual *presidential* and *ministerial* logics that characterized the Commission between 1999 and 2004.[29] Although presidentialism and ministerialism can coexist at the level of normal policymaking, they are likely to lead to incoherence when 'high politics' are at stake. Faced with the choice between the defense of its institutionalized myth and the articulation of an alternative vision, more suited to the twenty-first century, the Commission opted for the former.

The Commission President took overall responsibility for the Commission's input into the Convention. Prodi set down a number of the main orientations to be defended by the Commission, such as the need to restore a clear division of labor between EU institutions and a refusal to take on new competencies, often carrying over ideas, including the defense of the Community method, familiar from the exercise that had produced the White Paper on European Governance and the Commission's contribution to Nice. He explicitly sought to avoid becoming involved in parts of the broader debate, such as the weighting of votes in the Council, which he believed that the Commission could not influence.[30] He gave speeches setting out the Commission's position to various audiences, including the European Parliament, spoke at the Convention, held meetings with Giscard, and discussed the Convention at meetings of the European Council. Within the Commission, Prodi sought to affirm his presidential authority, particularly through the tactical use of the *'principe existentiel'* of the Commission.[31] He also made extensive use of bilaterals within the College, a mechanism which, as well as allowing him to get a sense of the points that individual Commissioners were likely to raise in the College, provided a context that was more amenable to the exercise of his authority as Commission President.

Antonio Vitorino and Michel Barnier, the two Commissioners responsible for representing the Commission in the Convention, were allowed a measure of discretion but they were also constrained by the need to ensure that the positions that they adopted in the Convention would command the support of the College and President. They were active participants in Convention proceedings, members of the Praesidium, keen contributors to plenary debates, and attended the Hilton dinners that brought together 'movers and shakers' of the Convention (Norman 2003: 52).[32] Vitorino, in particular, was an impressive figure, and 'one of Convention's key problem solvers' (Norman 2003: 31). This demonstrates that despite the impact of the Santer débâcle on the Commission's reputation, individual members of the College retained a significant degree of legitimacy, process and content expertise.

Although in his opening speech to the Convention, Prodi had promised that the Commission would 'make a full and enthusiastic contribution, drawing on all its own experience and its expertise',[33] the Commission's first major intervention took until the spring of 2002 to arrive (CEC 2002a) and only then after it had met strong opposition in the College.[34] Commissioners were divided along ideological lines on the economic and social development chapter,[35] while a significant minority, including the holder of the office concerned, opposed the proposal to merge the functions of High Representative and Commissioner for External Relations.[36] The result was a text, which, in the words of a Task Force member, 'was not very good'.[37] It made little impact on discussions in the Convention.

The decision to make a second contribution – on institutions – later in the year was Prodi's, but it was shaped by the context in which the Commission had to operate. Although the paper might have had more of an impact on the debate on institutions initiated by Aznar, Blair and Chirac on the eve of the Convention if it had been produced in October, and could have filled the vacuum created by Giscard's decision to leave discussion of the Union's institutional architecture until the Convention had dealt with policies, the Commission President decided that it should appear after the summer so as not to interfere with the Irish referendum on the Nice Treaty.[38] In addition, Prodi had been reluctant to go to the College with a second document, because he (rightly) expected further opposition.

In the debate that took place, individual Commissioners chose to 'defend their national positions', thereby turning the College into 'something of an IGC'.[39] The proposal that the Commission President should be elected by the European Parliament – an idea supported by Prodi, but originating from Commissioners Lamy and Barnier, was opposed.[40] This was the main expression of ministerialism in the College, but it is important to note that this pattern was mainly focused on objections to Prodi's proposals and tactical choices that reflected, to a large extent, his federalist tendencies – or at least his support for the classic Community method.[41]

The President's willingness to put his mark on the Commission's contribution to the debate and his desire to influence the outcome of the Convention was best exemplified, however, by his creation of the so-called 'Penelope group'. Though the objective of the Convention was 'to consider the key issues arising for the Union's future development and try to identify the various possible responses' (European Council 2001: section III), it quickly became apparent that because of its composition and the openness of the process, it would not be easy for the member states to diverge from the outcome of the Convention. Thus by shaping the outcome of the Convention – which had become essentially a *drafting* exercise – the content of the new Treaty could be determined. During the 'listening phase', in July 2002, Prodi decided to create a small group of senior officials to prepare a draft Constitution in secret (CEC 2002c), to submit to the Convention at the beginning of the 'drafting phase'. The group met in secret over a five-week period to avoid any pressure from the outside, though both Barnier and Vitorino were aware of its existence.

The very existence of the 'Penelope' draft infuriated Giscard, who saw it as an attempt to do his job for him, and several Commissioners, who, in the words of one *cabinet* member, suffered 'betrayed husband syndrome' (interview, Brussels, 3 June 2003).[42] Some Commissioners were apparently informed about it the day before its presentation whereas others were presented with a *fait accompli* on the day of the official presentation of the document (interview, September 19 2003). The 'Penelope' draft was leaked to *Le Monde* and newspapers in Germany, Italy and Spain only hours before the official December document (CEC 2002b) was approved by the College (Norman 2003: 165). The virtually simultaneous appearance of these two texts, the official Commission submission and the 'Penelope' draft, seriously undermined the Commission's credibility, despite some significant overlap in substance ideas.

Although the Constitutional Treaty that ultimately emerged was not as threatening as it had feared, the Commission was not an influential player at the Convention. The Prodi Commission undoubtedly confronted a more difficult environment than, for example, the first or second Delors Commissions. As well as the damage to its reputation that followed the resignation of the Santer Commission, member states since 1991 have sought to limit the

Commission's power, and, while not totally abandoning the Community method, have shown increasing enthusiasm for new methods of decision-making (Kassim and Menon 2004). Crucially, the Convention, both in terms of its structures and organization, and its subject matter, presented challenges that the Commission found difficult to meet.

Internal factors also affected the Commission's capacity to play a leadership role and to influence the negotiations. A large part of the problem stemmed from the Prodi method with dealing with the Convention. Appeal to the Commission's founding idea may have strengthened the Commission President's hand in the internal process of preference formation and allowed consistency across Commission preferences to be achieved, but, as a response to the demands of a Convention on the Future of Europe, it condemned the Commission to a position in the sidelines. There were also tactical errors – the Commission's credibility was seriously weakened by the 'Penelope' saga – and organizational failings. The emergence, for example, of two chains of command – one from the Commission President, the other from the two Commission *conventionnels* – seriously complicated coordination and prevented the Commission from speaking with one voice with the result that it 'went missing' (Norman 2003: 265–8) in the final stages of the Convention.[43]

The 2003–4 IGC: the importance of institutional misfit, negotiating context and the exogeneity of domestic ratification processes

A number of important problems undermined the ability of the Commission to shape the outcome of the IGC that followed the Convention on the Future of Europe. First, the aforementioned inability of the Commission to define and present a blueprint for the future of Europe in the context of a new debate that called for explicit value judgments had become obvious. It was difficult for a body whose credibility depended on its technocratic expertise to formulate a view on whether a reference to Europe's 'religious' or 'Christian' heritage ought to be included in the preamble of the constitutional treaty.[44] Second, the search for a successor to the Prodi College was about to start; and when it did start, the acrimony surrounding the discussion of rejection of the candidacies of Guy Verhofstadt and Chris Patten further undermined the capacity of the Commission to influence the IGC. More importantly, the Commission had not recovered from its often unhappy experience in the Convention and did not have enough time to restore some of its old alliances (assuming it wanted to do so). Finally, it was unable to influence key decisions, including those regarding the national ratification processes (i.e. the use of referenda) which had added strength to the negotiating hand of those – like the British government – who called them.

6.5 Conclusion

The above discussion has shown that, contrary to the assertions of liberal intergovernmentalism, the Commission has not only influenced treaty reform, but has at times been a leader in constitutional negotiations. In the spirit of this volume's concern to extend discussion beyond claims on the part of specific actors, the chapter also considers different types of leadership, and identifies conditions that make it more or less likely that a particular actor will be able to assume a leadership role, thereby illustrating the problem of treating the relative influence of an institution as a conceptual rather than an empirical problem, since even a brief survey of rounds of treaty reform since 1985 reveals that the Commission's impact has varied considerably over time. That variation can partly be attributed to internal capacity of the institution to articulate and then defend a view. Indeed, unless the Commission appears united and is able to present clear and practical proposals, it is unlikely to be influential. The informational leadership resources and reputation of the Commission are also crucial factors that can grant the Commission resources that can be used to supply leadership.

Contextual factors – especially the institutional position enjoyed by the Commission – are also important, however. The suggestibility and defensiveness of national governments, the structure and organization of the decisionmaking setting, and the preparedness of the key executive body and the secretariat that supports it to solicit advice and policy suggestions from the Commission emerge as the most significant. Worryingly for the Commission, if the Convention method becomes dominant, it can expect to continue to be the *object* rather than the *subject* of treaty reform.

Notes

1. We thank the ten senior European Commission officials who kindly granted unattributable interviews to answer our questions on the issues examined in this chapter. We are grateful to the participants of workshops in London and Oxford for their comments on earlier drafts, and to the ESRC for a grant under its 'Future Governance' programme and the British Academy (award BCG-35160), which enabled us to hold a workshop at Birkbeck, University of London. Dionyssis G. Dimitrakopoulos thanks Birkbeck's Faculty of Arts for a College research grant.
2. They also argue that supranational bodies other than the Commission, notably, the Council Secretariat and the European Parliament, can be influential. See Granger (2005) for a discussion of how the European Court of Justice has influenced the content of treaty reform.
3. The significance of the negotiating setting is emphasized in the introduction.
4. See especially Gerda Falkner (ed.) (2002a) 'EU Treaty Reform as a Three-Level Process: Historical Institutionalist Perspectives', special issue of *Journal of European Public Policy*, 9:1.
5. For discussion of the third – credible commitments – see Moravcsik 1998: 67–77.

6. A government's bargaining power depends on its ability to make a credible threat to reject cooperation in favour of a better alternative, to be part of an effective alternative coalition, and to create side payments and issue linkages.

7. Moreover, Moravcsik contends that 'effective informal supranational entrepreneurs [are deemed by many theorists to be] one of two factors feeding self-sustaining and path dependent processes of unintended consequences that powers regional integration' (1999a: 297).

8. The roles of Monnet and Delors, for example, have, he argues, been much exaggerated.

9. Though this does not imply endorsement of its more radical claims, such as the view that constitutional politics is continuous. Space constraints do not allow further discussion here.

10. Falkner (2002a: 1–2) cites the observation made by Scharpf (2000b) that constitutional and day-to-day politics are ideal types rather than, as she puts it, 'separate processes in isolation'.

11. For this reason, Beach (2003: 410) argues that LI effectively 'black boxes' what actually happens at an IGC.

12. Moravcsik's assertion that, among Commission staff, 'almost none are technical experts,' is a strange way to describe a career civil service with wide-ranging responsibilities and competitive entry requirements.

13. Michel Petite, Francois Lamoureux and Paolo Ponzano, to name but three, are Commission officials who have all been involved in several rounds of reform.

14. The Commission was entrusted with the task of drawing up proposals by the Luxembourg Presidency (see Beach 2005: 48–9).

15. Witness the use of consultants by governments holding the Council Presidency or in advance of IGCs.

16. This section draws extensively on Dimitrakopoulos and Kassim (2005).

17. The way in which they are prepared has undergone a slight chance. However, the centrality of a committee or group of representatives of heads of state or government has remained constant.

18. A recent example is the Commission's call for the trade agreements negotiated with third countries to cover intellectual property.

19. In fact he did so in his 'inaugural' speech to the EP in January 1985 (Drake 2000: 98).

20. Delors described it thus: 'It's like the story of Tom Thumb lost in the forest, who left white stones so that he could be found. I put in white stones so we would find monetary union again' (cited in Grant 1994: 74).

21. Delors was also responsible for drafting the relevant part of the conclusion of that meeting.

22. At least one of these organisations (UNICE) agreed to the proposals at least in part because its standard internal organisational processes had been bypassed, a small price to pay for securing the access that the Commission's provided to the IGC proper (Falkner 2002b: 112).

23. The involvement of the Commission in the process that led to the Nice Treaty indicates the importance of the need for careful and balanced contextualization. Although it included a significant number of 'political heavyweights', the Commission led by Romano Prodi was easily sidelined for a number of reasons. The effects of the 1999 crisis that led to the resignation of the entire Santer College were still unfolding. The deep divisions between the member states on issues (such as the re-weighting of votes in the Council) over which the Commission could not hope to have an important role and the atmosphere of hostility, conflict and

acrimony created by the French Presidency's unskilful (see, for example, Gray and Stubb, 2001: 16) and undiplomatic handling of the negotiations prior to and during the acrimonious Nice summit contributed to the sidelining of an institution that was still ruing the recent blow to its credibility.

24. As Christiansen and Gray note (2003, p. 12), the Commission is more likely to get its way when it is 'prepared to concentrate on the 'low politics' of detailed legal provisions rather than on the grand political battles'.

25. Although a serious effort to reform the Commission was already under way when the second Convention begun its proceedings, the image of the Commission as a beleaguered institution remained dominant.

26. This was in part due to the fact that the Commission had successfully participated in the Convention on the EU's Charter of Fundamental Rights, and partly to the failure of the Nice European Council, which had strengthened Prodi's conviction that Europe's future needed to be debated by a wider circle of participants if the Union were to meet the challenge posed by the pending enlargement and public disillusionment with the European project.

27. Norman (2003, p. 161) estimates that eight of the 12 members of the Praesidium could be counted on to support the Commission.

28. Indeed, Giscard had voiced the opinion that, with the creation of the single market, the Commission had served its purpose (Norman 2003: 29).

29. The Commission under Prodi betrayed both traits. It was presidential in that Prodi was 'the political figurehead at the top of the Commission' (Peterson 2004: 17), and free to concentrate on major issues', and ministerial in that the College that Prodi was leading was an outstanding team of political 'heavyweights' who were relatively free in their areas of responsibility.

30. Interview with the authors, 19 September 2003, Brussels.

31. This was facilitated by proposals submitted by some national governments, even before the Convention opened, which advocated a reduced role for the Commission.

32. In that sense, it was not deprived of informational leadership resources.

33. 02/88, February 28 2002, CONV 4/02.

34. Interview with the authors, March 18 2003, Brussels.

35. Interviews with the authors, September 18 and 19 2003, Brussels.

36. Though the Commissioner for External Relations, Chris Patten, wrote to Prodi to express his view that coordination could be improved short of constitutional reform and that the Commission was not ready to assume responsibility for external affairs, several of his colleagues believed that the idea had gained broad support in the Convention, not least due to the impact of the report of the working group on external relations, chaired by Dehaene. It was also believed that neither Aznar nor Blair would oppose the proposal in the endgame (interview with the authors, March 18 2003, Brussels).

37. Interview with the authors, March 18 2003, Brussels.

38. Interviews with the authors, March 17 and 18 2003; 3 June 2003, Brussels.

39. Interview with the authors, September 19 2003, Brussels.

40. Interview with the authors, September 19 2003, Brussels.

41. Or 'penchant fédéraliste ou au moins communautaire classique,' as one interviewee put it (interview with the authors, September 19 2003, Brussels).

42. One of Prodi's collaborators justified the exercise on the grounds that the aim was to help the Convention, that 'it was never meant to be put to the College' since it was a merely technical exercise, a feasibility study, and that Delors 'never put

a draft Treaty to the College except EMU and that was a very painful experience. Interview with the authors, March 17 2003, Brussels.

43. One commentator notes that 'the number of Commission staff working on the Convention was greater than the Convention secretariat [but] they were split into different groups [which] seemed unable to work together' (Norman 2003: 267). He refers to the two Commissioners in the Convention, and their cabinets, the Commission President and his staff, and the group of policy advisors headed by Ricardo Levi.

44. This was one of the contentious issues identified by the Irish Presidency (Dinan 2005: 40).

7
A Formal Outsider Becomes an Effective Player: The European Parliament in the Negotiation of the Treaty of Amsterdam and the Constitutional Treaty*

Andreas Maurer

7.1 Supranational parliamentarism in a multi-level polity

Analysts who stress that national sovereignty is not significantly affected by European integration, and that decision-making in the EU rests primarily upon the member states within the Council of Ministers and, since Maastricht, the European Council, ascribe only a minor role to the European Parliament. However, since the entry into force of the Single European Act (SEA) and the introduction of the cooperation and assent procedures, the real distribution of powers between the institutions goes far beyond this conceptualization of the Union. Within the sphere of the European Communities, the Treaty revisions from 1985 on reveal a clear tendency towards a multi-level polity where competencies are not only shared between the Members of the Council but also between the Council and the European Parliament (Maurer 2002b).

This chapter analyses the European Parliament's leadership role with regard to its constitutional development function in the 1996–97 Amsterdam Intergovernmental Conference (IGC) and the recent 2002–04 Convention/IGC process. The European Parliament's constitutional development function refers to the participation of the European Parliament (EP) in

---

* The author would like to thank Roderick Parkes, PhD Fellow and Junior Researcher at the German Institute for International and Security Affairs, for his comments and assistance on finishing the manuscript.

the development of the EU's para-constitutional system (such as institutional reforms and the division of competencies). This constitutional
development function is here understood as a type of leadership provided
by the Parliament, and focuses upon the Parliament's ability to present,
promote and defend proposals for institutional reform, especially during
IGCs (Bourgignon-Wittke *et al.* 1985; Grabitz *et al.* 1988; Steppat 1988), but
also via other channels lying outside the *formal* IGC process (Maurer, Kietz
and Völkel 2005).

7.2   The European Parliament's own preferences in constitutional reform

The EP's agenda in the constitutional reform of the EU has been insti-
tutionally expansive – it has sought to maximize its role in future day-
to-day decisionmaking configurations. Although the Maastricht Treaty
upgraded the EP's role in decisionmaking, commentators and involved
actors – including the Parliament – criticized the Treaty as not moving far
enough in the right direction. Criticism occurred because the co-decision
procedure was conceived for just 15 out of the then 162 EC and 11 EU
articles containing procedural arrangements.[1] 140 of these articles dealt with
binding secondary legislation, whereas the remaining provisions concerned
quasi-constitutional questions such as enlargement or Treaty reform. In
other words, only 9.25 per cent of the EC Treaty arrangements were
conceived for co-decision and another 9.87 per cent for cooperation (Nickel
1993; Duff 1995; Maurer 2002b).

Besides those innovations introduced in the framework of the TEC, the
new fields of intergovernmental cooperation and coordination – Common
Foreign and Security Policy (CFSP) and cooperation in the fields of Justice and
Home Affairs (JHA) – constituted what was probably the EU's most obvious
parliamentary democratic deficit. The inadequacy of the Parliament's powers
of control was all the more serious since many governments escaped any
kind of parliamentary scrutiny at the national level. When acting under the
CFSP, the European Parliament obtained the right to ask questions, to put
forward recommendations to the Council, and to be informed by the Council
Presidency. In addition, the Commission had to inform Parliament about
progress made in CFSP. The scrutiny rights of Parliament were, however,
severely limited since its general participation in CFSP activities was specified
neither in the Treaty provisions on common positions nor in those relating
to the adoption of joint actions.

Where Justice and Home Affairs were concerned, the Maastricht Treaty
provisions on the European Parliament's role in JHA corresponded very
largely to the CFSP. A positive factor for Parliament in this context was
the fact that the Commission was at least given a right of initiative in the

areas listed under the then Article K.1 (1) to (6) TEU (now, after amendment, Articles 29 to 39 EU), although the Commission had to share this right with the member states. The latter, on the other hand, obtained the sole right of initiative in judicial cooperation on criminal matters, customs cooperation and police cooperation. There was thus a specific and effective opportunity for monitoring and censuring the Commission, but not the Council of Ministers.

The EP's own preferences on constitutional reform should not, however, be considered in isolation from other actors' priorities. Viewed from an intergovernmentalist perspective, the democratization of the EU will only occur when democratization does not strengthen the supranational character of the EU. Yet as the intergovernmentalist perspective questions whether the EP is capable of providing leadership by attempting to strengthen its own institutional prerogatives, it struggles to explain the current form of democratization at the European level, where the EP has been the major institutional 'winner' of the past twenty years of constitutional reform. This suggests that either the Parliament's preferences for constitutional change do significantly overlap with those of the other actors involved in treaty change, or that the EP is capable of exhibiting a greater degree of leadership than it is given credit for by intergovernmentalists, or indeed both together.

The main focus of this chapter is the question of whether a leadership strategy pursued by the EP during constitutional negotiations has allowed it to affect the scope of its powers in daily policymaking. However, it is important to iterate that this focus is not necessarily representative of the full range of areas where the Parliament can provide leadership: the Parliament also has preferences in other areas under negotiation – whether they concern constitutional reform or otherwise – that do not entail a significant extension of its powers. In such cases, the negotiating context (*nature of the issues*) and the Parliament's leadership resources (*reputation*) may permit it to play a rather different kind of leadership role compared with those times when it has an obvious vested interest in the outcome.

7.3 Rethinking the scope of the European Parliament's leadership role at IGCs

From an intergovernmentalist point of view, the evolution of the EU system takes place during the short phases of IGCs as 'big bargain decisions' (Moravcsik 1993: 473–524; Hurrell and Menon 1996: 386–402; Moravcsik and Nicolaïdis 1999: 59–85). From this perspective, the member states' governments are the dominant actors at the EU level – in daily politics as well as in treaty reform. In IGCs governments make all the decisions on the reform of the institutional system on the basis of their fixed national interests. Supranational institutions are only seen as having been established and endowed with powers in order to help maximize governmental interests, e.g. to resolve collective action problems and reduce transaction costs. However, the institutions remain at all times under the control of the member states, and therefore merely implement member states' decisions *without* having an autonomous reform agenda.

According to this analysis, the EP's material resources and the institutional set-up of the 'grand bargains' are not conducive to the EP playing a strong leadership role, let alone mobilizing coalitions around its own, autonomous preferences. The EP would perhaps be identified as an actor able to steer political debates, to create tension in some parts of the agenda, to make issues public, but it is not seen as a decisionmaker. According to this point of view, the influence of the EP is limited, and thus EP actions cannot explain the increase in the power of the EP.

Yet constitutional change in the Union does not take place exclusively at IGCs. Relations between Treaty reform and Treaty implementation are not one-directional, but characterized by 'mutual interdependencies between and within the many levels of governance within the EU' (Sverdrup 2000: 249). Both the EP's leadership resources and the negotiation context must therefore be understood within a broader context. Neo-institutionalists and structurationists argue that IGCs are just one step in the constitutional dynamic. In their broader vision of the institutional set-up of constitutional negotiations, the Parliament enjoys an autonomous and formative influence upon the agenda of IGCs that is overlooked by the intergovernmentalist focus upon the 'history-making' decisions (see also chapter 6 for similar arguments).

Neo-institutionalist explanations of institutional change of the EU systems challenge the view that member states' governments are the only key actors that determine the constitutional development of the EU. Neo-institutionalists assert that a plurality of actors participate in the decisionmaking process. They acknowledge the role of autonomously acting supranational institutions that pursue their own reform agendas, as well as a dense cluster of governmental and non-governmental actors at all levels of the EU. At the core of their arguments is the claim that the scope for action of all these actors is defined by the institutions (informal and formal rules, procedures, or norms) in which the policy-making process is embedded (Pierson 1998). Moreover, they view institutional change as a process unfolding over time. Restricting the analysis of institutional change of the EU to IGCs will therefore only yield a snapshot of constitutional development.

Their model of the 'path dependency' of policy preferences, institutions and procedures, policy outcomes and policy instruments (Pierson 1998) suggests that, in an institutionalized arrangement such as the EC/EU, 'past lines of policy [will] condition subsequent policy by encouraging societal forces to organize along some lines rather than others, to adapt particular identities or to develop interests in policies that are costly to shift' (Hall and Taylor 1996: 941). Hence, every introduction of new rules constrains the decisionmaking options for all actors, with further institutional changes developing incrementally along certain paths.

Importantly, therefore, this approach allows us to see the EP as an autonomous supranational actor with an independent reform agenda. Since its creation, the EP has been able to use the constraints and opportunities arising from the mass of decisionmaking procedures and the multitude of actors in the EU's policymaking process to subject more and more policy fields to parliamentary control and legislation. This vision of the institutional set-up of constitutional dynamics indicates that the EP has been able to exploit the need for leadership in complex bargaining situations in order to pursue its own preferences by linking decisions in EU daily politics with IGC outcomes – termed 'material leadership resources' in this volume (Maurer, Kietz and Völkel 2005).

Structurationist approaches to the evolution of the EU system (for example, Christiansen and Jørgensen 1999; Christiansen 1998) come to similar conclusions. Like historical institutionalists, they view the EU's constitutional development since the very inception of the EC as an *unceasing process of incremental change* with an (as yet) open end. They claim that instead of focusing on IGCs we must look at the process whereby member state interests are constructed. Following the notion of path dependency, the reform process in an IGC is structured by predefined demands, the convergence of beliefs about the outcome, and the constraints and opportunities established by past choices.

Treaty reforms do not come out of the blue as a 'deus ex machina' from some distant masters, but are reactions to prior trends. They 'ratify' or 'rubberstamp' institutional evolutions which have taken place within or outside the existing treaty provisions. They try to address institutional and procedural weaknesses identified during the implementation of previous provisions or aim at adapting the Union to new – external and/or internal – contexts (Christiansen and Jørgensen 1999).

Constitutional reform therefore takes place incrementally during the 'valley' of day-to-day EU politics. The resulting, incremental change suggests that treaty reform is subject to a wide range of actors (not only states) and to an unceasing process of discovering political preferences and 'problem solving' in an unstable setting (Risse-Kappen 1996). Member states identify their preferences not simply as a fixed set of demands, but also during the process of Treaty implementation and Treaty reform. The EP in this perspective is an important actor able to influence the rolling agenda of the very process of constitutional change.

7.4   Expectations concerning the European Parliament's leadership role

The potential leadership resources enjoyed by the European Parliament in the IGC context – and its autonomy in using them – appear, therefore, to be greater than intergovernmentalists acknowledge. Moreover, given the dynamic nature of European integration, these resources have not remained static. Above all, the EP's potential *material leadership resources* have grown. For example, by linking the use of its powers in daily decisionmaking or in quasi-constitutional proceedings, such as the conclusion of international agreements, with the outcomes of IGCs, the Parliament is able to translate potential material resources into bargaining leverage in constitutional negotiations. In line with the idea of 'path dependency', the relationship between the 'summits' and 'valleys' of European integration allows the Parliament to forge a mutually reinforcing dynamic of institutional expansion: an extension of its powers in daily decisionmaking can be translated into an expansion of its clout in constitutional negotiations, which in turn can impact favorably upon its future position in daily decisionmaking.

These resources should not, however, be overstated. Not only does the principal–agent relationship between parliament and electorate constrain the EP's margin for maneuver, so too the member states may be in a position to sanction the Parliament for making excessive attempts to use these resources in the IGC setting. The Parliament is also constrained by the practicalities of daily decisionmaking, which cannot always be made subservient to its priorities in IGCs. Underlying all these constraints is the concern that the EP's reputational leadership resources may be damaged by excessive resort to this kind of material resource.

Conversely, the Parliament enjoys considerable *content* and *process expertise*, particularly in comparison to some of the small and/or newer member states (although during the period under consideration the latter group had not yet acceded to the EU). Thanks to the relationship between the political parties making up the EU's national governments and those in the EP's own political groupings, the Parliament can potentially draw on significant informational resources. Such resources are precious in the complex bargaining context of IGCs, given that national governments' rationality is bounded. Further, as will be seen below, the MEPs' familiarity with working in a parliamentary-like setting debating EU issues was a key informational resource that assisted the EP in becoming an influential leader in the Convention on the Future of Europe.

Another set of resources enjoyed by the EP relates to its legitimizing function in the European polity, interpreted here as part of its reputation resources. Not only can it play a legitimizing function at IGCs, it can also tie its legitimizing function in daily policymaking to IGC outcomes concerning its future role. Yet this function has not been without its critics, particularly since Maastricht. Several deficits concerning the state reached in the execution of parliamentary democracy remained after Maastricht and led to a controversial dispute about the pros and cons of the Treaty with regard to the European Parliament but also to the national parliaments in the EU member states (Kohler-Koch 1997; Nickel 1993; Pliakos 1995; Reich 1992;

Smith 1996) and the democratic nature of the EU (Weiler 1995, 1997; Craig 1997). The most critical view argues that the European Parliament remains an artifact of elitist integration and cannot be considered as a '*Vollparlament*' (Lübbe 1994: 147; Schröder 1994: 318) (a fully fledged or 'real' parliament). Accordingly, strengthening the European Parliament by means of institutional and procedural reforms would not result in any strengthening of democracy at the EU level.

Yet, once again, the dependencies between different categories of leadership resource become clear. There is, for example, a dependency between the EP's material and its reputational resources: as the EP's material resources – and thus its leadership capacity – grow, member state governments may become wary of treating MEPs as privileged interlocutors. A second dependency is constituted by the relationship between the Parliament's informational resources and its *internal capacity*. It is by no means a given that privileged actors within the Parliament will make information, which they have received from national governments and parties, more generally available. Perhaps of less significance, but nonetheless important, is the fact that the exchange of information between national governments and MEPs is by no means one-directional: MEPs can also share information on the Parliament's preferences and strategy with national actors. The strength of the EP's internal capacity thus relates to the question of whether the EP can be considered a unitary actor – an issue addressed in more detail below.

The Parliament's leadership resources must also be understood in conjunction with the negotiation context in which they are exercised. It was argued above, for example, that the *institutional set-up* of constitutional negotiations should be examined over the *longue durée* – a perspective which takes account of the EP's broader material resources (Maurer, Kietz and Völkel 2005). It was noted that the links between the 'summits' and 'valleys' of European integration permit the European Parliament to exercise a degree of agenda control – both direct and indirect – over IGCs. Moreover, a significant innovation that gives the EP a more formal agenda-setting role was the Convention that preceded the latest round of constitutional negotiations. The Convention did not just afford the EP a stronger institutional position, but also allowed MEPs to draw on their experience with EU-level parliamentary negotiations, as the institutional structure and processes of the Convention bore similarities to those of the Parliament, thus boosting its potential process expertise.

In recognizing more fully the scope of the constitutional negotiating context, it is important not to lose sight of the IGCs themselves. Although intergovernmentalists would argue that the EP's capacity for leadership in IGCs is minimal, they base their assumptions upon quite heroic assumptions regarding the rationality of member states' governments. However, as European integration has progressed, IGCs have become even more complex affairs, with more actors becoming both formally and informally involved in negotiations. A growth in the number of actors involved, coupled with the technical complexity of the issues on the table, can translate into opportunities for the EP to supply leadership.

This overview of the EP's potential leadership resources and their interaction with the negotiating context gives rise to a number of expectations about the leadership strategies the EP is likely to employ in IGCs. Given the dynamism of the European system, the EP's strategy is likely to have evolved during the period considered. *Structural leadership* is, for example, a strategy open principally to those actors with a large degree of material resources. But with the consistent growth in those material resources deriving from the EP's increasing ability to link its role in everyday policymaking with events in IGCs, the EP finds itself better placed to pursue such a strategy. Equally though, the increasing complexity of constitutional negotiations and the wealth of its informational resources have also given the EP the kind of informational advantages required for the successful pursuit of an *instrumental leadership strategy*.

7.5   The participation of the European Parliament in the 1996–97 IGC[2]

In the prelude to the IGC, Dinan (1999: 8) asserts that the EP had been able to exploit a crisis over qualified majority voting in 1994. It was able to translate its material resources into bargaining leverage, and thus changed the institutional set-up of the bargaining context as a whole: unhappy with the Ioannina Compromise, the Parliament had used its power of assent over the 1995 enlargement as a tool to barter for a greater role at the next IGC – in the teeth of opposition from France and the UK.

Partly as a result of this activism, the institutional structure of the 1996–97 IGC was rather different from those that had preceded it. Two members of the European Parliament participated in the Reflection Group that prepared the IGC, alongside personal representatives of the Foreign Ministers of the EU-15, and one member from the Commission. Within this institutional set-up, both individually and as a pair, the two Parliament representatives (Elmar Brok, German Christian Democrat, and Elisabeth Guigou, French Socialist) were deemed to have acquitted themselves impressively (Interview with a Commission official, AM-Int. 1999-23a). Moreover, they learnt from the EP's past mistakes: the Parliament had effectively sidelined itself at Maastricht because of the extravagance of its demands. Now the two MEPs were careful to ensure that their contributions and requests were realistic. This gave a considerable boost to their 'reputational capital', and ensured that the EP was never isolated within the Group.

Within this amenable atmosphere, the EP felt able to raise the question of its role at the IGC itself. Its arguments were twofold: firstly it demanded a place at the Conference Table, reasoning that the IGC was supposed to prepare the Union for enlargement – a process which required the EP's assent; this assent could always be withheld (Lodge 1998: 486). Secondly, MEPs pointed to the legitimacy that the EP could lend to the IGC process, thanks to its position as the EC's only directly elected institution.

These arguments were somewhat shaky from a legal point of view, since the 1996–97 IGC was conducted under the terms of ex-Article N TEU which did not mention the European Parliament. Moreover forceful resistance emanated from French and British quarters: these two countries blocked suggestions from Benelux, Germany and Italy that the EP should gain permanent observer status (Petite 1997: 23). In March 1996, the Foreign Ministers agreed that (European Parliament 1995: 7):

- the Presidency would keep the European Parliament informed, orally or in writing.
- there would be an exchange of views between the EP President at the beginning of each ministerial session of the IGC, attended by EP representatives.
- when the representatives of the Ministers considered it desirable, and at least once a month, the Presidency of the Council would hold a working meeting on the occasion of the meetings of the IGC Representatives Group (Maurer 2001).

This compromise received a tepid welcome in the EP, with President Klaus Hänsch calling it 'reasonable' (*Agence Europe* 1996). Its implementation met with even less satisfaction, characterized as it was by 'a minimalist interpretation' (CONF/3847/97, confirmed by speech of the Portuguese State Secretary for European Affairs, 11 November 1999).

In the run-up to the 1996–97 IGC, the Parliament pursued – at different stages – a structural as well as an instrumental leadership strategy in seeking to shape both the institutional set-up of and the leadership resources it could draw upon during the IGC itself. Its threat to sanction member states by vetoing future enlargement showed that it was capable of translating material resources into bargaining leverage. By this means, the Parliament won for itself an agenda-setting role. Its actions gave rise to suggestions that the Parliament would follow a structural leadership strategy in the negotiations themselves. However, once the constitutional process entered the reflection stage the EP shifted toward an instrumental strategy. Here, negotiating skill, substantive expertise and reputation resources were key. Yet, although this may have pushed discussion of substantive issues somewhat closer to the EP's preferences at this preliminary stage, it did not suffice for the Parliament to gain a substantial role once negotiations in the IGC began. Moreover, a second attempt by the Parliament to link its capacity to block enlargement with bargaining leverage in the IGC was unsuccessful.

7.6   Influencing the outcome of the 1996–97 IGC

First amongst the EP's priorities at the IGC was the extension of its powers and rights (Nickel 1997). It called for changes to the decision-making process and, specifically, to the decisionmaking powers of the EP (CONF/3810/97; CONF/3891/97); it aspired to become an equal to the Council in decisionmaking. It thus proposed a simplification of decision-making procedures, establishing co-decision as the standard procedure (the remaining two procedures being consultation and assent). Qualified majority should become the rule in Council. Alongside these demands, the EP made reference to the statute of MEPs (CONF/3881/97), employment policy (CONF/3891/96), and to CFSP reform (CONF/3885/97).

In order to gain support for its demands, the EP could rely on four strategies. Each strategy called for a different approach toward the institutional set-up and a different use of the material resources at the EP's disposal:

- First, the EP could benefit from a partnership with national parliaments which had evolved since 1989 under different formats (COSAC, Joint Committee Meetings, and Joint Parliamentary Hearings etc.).
- A second way in which the Parliament could gain support was to use its contacts with intermediary groups and, through its parliamentary groups and European parties, with national political parties.
- Third, it could profit from alliances with certain national governments: due to pressure from their national parliaments the Belgian and Italian governments connected their signature of the Maastricht and the Amsterdam Treaty amendments to the vote of the EP. Both governments proclaimed that they would not accept the results of the IGC until the European Parliament had approved it. This proclamation put considerable pressure on the other European governments to take the view of the EP into account.
- Finally, a fourth strategy of the EP resulted from linking important decisions and enacting a kind of package deal. In the 1996–97 IGC, this last option had some influence. The European Parliament stated that if the results of the ongoing IGC were unsatisfactory, it would reject the future enlargement of the Union, which is a decisive right of the EP (Art. 49 TEU). As any future enlargement is subject to the assent procedure, Parliament's right embodies a tremendous potential.

The outcome of the 1996/1997 IGC for the EP was somewhat ambiguous (Nickel 1997, 1999; Maurer 2001). If, from an institutionalist perspective, the centrality of the European Parliament as the main actor securing indirect democracy in the European Union is accepted, then the Treaty of Amsterdam means a greatly improved setting. It widened the scope of application of the co-decision procedure extensively both with respect to those policy areas which it newly introduced into the EC sphere and with respect to policy areas which were already covered by the cooperation procedure. Following the Amsterdam reforms, the bulk of the EC's original secondary legislation was subject to the co-decision procedure.

Apart from those areas where co-decision applied immediately after the entry into force of Amsterdam, it was automatically extended to measures on the procedures and conditions for issuing visas by member states as well as to rules on uniform visa formats after five years. The assent procedure was extended to the new TEU provision on sanctions in the event of a serious and persistent breach of fundamental rights by a member state. Finally, the scope of application of the consultation procedure was expanded by nine treaty provisions.

However, the European Parliament remained excluded from dynamic and 'costly' policy areas such as agriculture (Article 37 TEC), tax harmonization (Article 93 TEC) and trade policy (Article 133 TEC). Apart from the extension of co-decision, the procedure itself was considerably simplified.

Improvements in Amsterdam were also made with regard to the European Parliament's elective function (Article 214 TEC). Not only had the Commission as a collegiate body, but also the President of the European Commission alone become subject to a vote of approval by the European Parliament (Notre Europe – European Steering Committee 1998; Notre Europe – European Steering Committee and Padoa-Schioppa 1998; Padoa-Schioppa 1998; Hix 1995; Nickel 1997).

As far as the institutional-procedural democratization of CJHA is concerned, the Amsterdam Treaty introduced the European Parliament for the first time as a consultative body within the new Title covering the 'Area of Freedom, Security and Justice' (AFSJ). Moreover, the Treaty stipulated a phasing-in of the Parliament's involvement with regard to AFSJ in general. Whilst for five years after ratification of the new Treaty the European Parliament was only to be consulted, Article 67(2) TEC allowed the Council to introduce the co-decision procedure after the end of this transitional period. For those two areas which remained in the third pillar (police cooperation and judicial cooperation in criminal matters) the European Parliament should be consulted when framework decisions, decisions and conventions were to be adopted.

As for CFSP, the European Parliament's role remained restricted to information: the revised CFSP Title emphasized the predominant position of the European Council as a quasi-legislative body. As the common strategies of the European Council form the basis of joint actions and other measures to be decided by the Council of Ministers, the European Council achieved a *de facto* right of initiative which was not open to censure. Thus, Parliament's active participation in shaping the substance of the CFSP rested at the entire discretion of the member states' governments.

7.7 The European Parliament's strategies for the 2002–04 Convention and IGC

Just as it had done in the run-up to the 1996–97 IGC, the European Parliament made a proactive effort to shape the negotiating context for the constitutional negotiations in 2002–04. This time, though, it employed an instrumental strategy instead of trying to link daily EU policymaking decisions with constitutional reform. In its first Resolution on the Nice Treaty, the Parliament underlined that the traditional IGC method appeared unable to create a more democratic EU that had a greater capacity to act. The Parliament called for a change in the decisiontaking process on Treaty reform along the lines of, and with a similar mandate to, the Convention that drew up the Charter of Fundamental Rights (European Parliament 2001b).

The EP thrashed out its conception of the convocation and tasks of the Convention with representatives of national parliaments, particularly within the framework of the Conference of Community and European Affairs Committees of Parliaments of the European Union (COSAC) (Maurer 2004). The EP's call for a new Convention met receptive ears in the Belgian Presidency in the fall of 2001, and helped build momentum behind the decision to hold Convention (Ludlow 2002; Norman 2003).

The subsequent Convention, which had no formally binding effect upon the IGC, presented a very favorable negotiating context for the Parliament. New actors were also involved in the Convention's decisionmaking process. Representatives of the Commission, national parliaments and the European Parliament, as well as representatives of the Heads of State and Governments, were to take part in the Convention, bringing new aspects to the consultation process due to their different institutional backgrounds. The greater heterogeneity of the whole group made the use of traditional methods of IGC negotiation, which revolve around national positions, far more complicated. In this novel but complex decisionmaking situation, the potential for the EP to provide leadership was great.

The beginnings of the Convention, its working groups and the first phase of drawing up the Constitutional Treaty (CT) were marked by strong, paraparliamentary characteristics that lasted until April 2003. Members of the national parliaments and the EP came together in meetings of the Parliament and European parties in order to elaborate responses to the questions inherent in the Convention's mandate which had been drawn up at Laeken.

7.8 The 2002–04 Convention–IGC process

In the run-up to the 2002–04 Convention/IGC-process, the Parliament laid particular stress upon the following elements of constitutional reform (Scelo 2002; Schunz 2005):

- the creation of a normative hierarchy for a universal classification of individual policy areas, the decisionmaking processes derived from them and the organs empowered to take those decisions,
- the introduction of a power of parliamentary consent for every amendment to the founding Treaties,
- the extension of co-decision to every legislative area,
- the application of co-decision to the adoption of the EU's annual budget and the discharge of the financial regulation applicable to the general budget,
- the fusion of the European Union and the European Community to create a single legal personality, and
- the further development of the provisions contained in the Treaties relating to the EP.

At this stage of the constitutional process, the Parliament flexed its ideational muscles in pursuit of an instrumental leadership strategy. To lend weight to its demands for upgrading the EP to the position of co-legislator with the Council, the Parliament grappled first of all with the legislative functioning of the Council. According to a clear majority of parliamentarians, the Council should be structured as a semi-parliamentary chamber of states (a Legislative Council). It is in this context that the Parliament's Report and Resolution on the Council advocated a stronger role for the 'General Affairs Council'. This latter body should gain stronger coordinatory functions *vis-à-vis* the other Council formations, and in the future be comprised of government figures that were closely involved in the coordination of national EU policies, rather than, as a matter of principle, the foreign ministers (European Parliament 1999).

Following this Resolution, the EP reinforced its conception that, in order to be able to coordinate and give political guidance to COREPER, the General Affairs Council must meet more regularly, preferably every week (European Parliament 2001a). The frequency of the meetings demanded by this kind of system of coordination could be introduced within the framework of the Council's implied powers. Yet the limits of this 'soft' change quickly were apparent, since most member states do not have a minister who could deal exclusively with European policy at such frequent intervals. The Parliament thus consistently argued for the General Affairs Council to be made up of ministers with a coordinating role and who wielded the necessary political authority (European Parliament 2001a).

These two Own Initiative Reports and Resolutions constitute milestones in the EP's work on constitutional reform. Up until that point, the parliamentarians had not publicly expressed an opinion about the internal organization of the Council, nor had it submitted proposals for Council reform. The fact that the Parliament now – after Maastricht, Amsterdam and Nice – presented plans for a reorganization of the Council as well as for the reform of governments' powers of self-organization reflects a trend which has grown in recent years: a large group of parliamentarians have shown that they are no longer satisfied with making proposals for reform which essentially consist of 'navel-gazing' exercises that are limited to their own institution and its position in the EU system. Since the development of relations between Parliament and Commission can be driven through without Treaty change, and depend more upon the goodwill of the parties than on rules anchored in the Treaties, the parliamentarians started turning the focus of their attention to the web of relations between EP and Council.

The context of the Convention

The Convention worked in three phases: a 'listening phase/*phase d'écoute*' in the plenary, a 'study phase/*phase d'étude*' characterized by work groups and an editorial phase, and the 'reflection phase/*phase de réflexion*' that drafted the Constitutional Treaty.

During the *phase d'écoute*, the numbers and heterogeneity of the involved actors and the prompt publication of all contributions, speeches and protocols on the Convention's website, coupled with the novelty of the negotiating situation (Zimbardo and Leippe 1991: 31), created an atmosphere without clear cleavages and coalitions, but from which the strands of the future debate could be drawn. In this kind of complex but collegial situation, the actors best placed to play an instrumental leadership role were those – like the EP – with experience in working in parliamentary-style environments. One indication of the importance of familiarity with this type of negotiating context was that parliamentary contributions – be they from the EP or from national Parliaments – outnumbered the contributions from representatives of governments or other institutions.

Whilst these deliberations were still going on within the plenary, a new working method took over during the beginning of the study phase. The key factor in this second phase was the creation of the 11 working groups dealing with different themes.

The most important difference between the plenary and the working groups was how they were set up. Working in smaller groups that were relatively shielded from outside attention made the participants more willing to examine and consider the arguments of other participants. Alongside the size of the groups and the segmentation of the plenary into thematic groups, an important function of the working groups was to encourage a focus on thematic roles amongst the actors. Unlike in the plenary, not only were new actors attached to the working groups but certain actors were also 'excluded'. This was because Convention members could not take part in different working groups simultaneously (CONV 52/02). For this reason only a portion of the national governments or the parliaments were represented in a working group at any one time. Thanks to this exclusionary mechanism it became clear during the work phase of the Convention that decision-taking would not follow the normal rules of intergovernmental bargaining. This context was, then, potentially favorable to the EP.

The results of this phase certainly mirrored to a large extent the EP's preferences on constitutional reform. The working groups called for: the clarification of the differences between obligatory and non-obligatory spending; a clear separation of the EP's and Council's responsibilities, with the Council retaining its hegemony on matters of income and the Parliament having the final say over expenditure; and the creation of a new legal basis for mid-term financial planning instead of using inter-institutional agreements.

The introduction of a clear hierarchy of norms was due in part to the set-up of the working groups (European Parliament 2002b; Arnauld 2003; Maurer 2003). Since the Convention had no stand-alone group dealing with the reform of the institutions and processes, the only point from which to illuminate the tangle of processes and types of act was in the group on the 'simplification of procedures and instruments' (Häberle 2003). This group dealt first with the qualification of the individual EC/EU instruments. Expectations about the sensitivity of the issue proved misplaced, as the discussion in the working group was far less controversial than had been expected. The context of this second phase therefore proved favorable to the EP as well.

The release of the first draft articles by the Praesidium in February 2003 marked the start of the third phase – the editorial phase or *phase de réflexion*. During this phase, the consensual results of the previous phase were to be translated into concrete articles and the question of institutional reform, which had not yet been properly dealt with, was to be tackled. National divisions, which had previously been all but absent, now began to play a greater role in this more concrete consultation phase. Thus, the interaction between the nature of the issues and the institutional set-up of this third phase created a context that was rather less congenial to the EP and its potential leadership role. Moreover, the governmental representatives began to buttress their central role. The change of communication and consultation style was evidenced by coalition-building on the part of national governments outside the Convention. The resulting bi- and multilateral initiatives began to flow into the Convention.[3] The previously open and discursive style which had characterized the opening phases of the Convention was now implicitly put in question. These bi- and multilateral initiatives simultaneously meant that the Heads of State and Government – or rather their representatives – gained a key role within the Convention. The formerly consensus-oriented working style of the Convention now increasingly resembled that of an IGC (see Magnette and Nicolaïdis 2004 and chapter 8 in this volume).

The representatives of the European Parliament

The delegation of the European Parliament perceived itself as the representative of the institution that sent it; much more so than did the national parliamentarians. This meant that the European Parliament assumed a large proportion of the work of the Convention and introduced various proposals via its delegation. In this regard, it displayed impressive informational resources as well as the internal capacity to mobilize them.

In relation to the Convention plenary, the majority of the representatives of the European Parliament performed a collective instrumental leadership role. The positions adopted in plenary sessions by the Parliament on issues such as the legal personality of the EU (European Parliament 2002a), the role of the national parliaments in the EU (European Parliament 2002b), the division of competences (European Parliament 2002c), and the hierarchy of norms (European Parliament 2002d), were used as the definitive points of reference in the Convention working groups and plenary sessions. Even the publication of proposals by the Heads of State and Government were sometimes 'cited' less than the decisions of the European Parliament.

The circle of European parliamentarians centered on the Parliament's Constitutional Affairs Committee grew, and the contributions emanating from the Parliament also enjoyed a greater authority than those produced by the Convention Presidium and its secretariat. This gain in authority was also grounded in the structural advantages of European parliamentarians' membership of the Convention: They could fall back on personal and financial support from an institution 'on the spot.' Further, the European parliamentarians were used to the modus operandi of the negotiating committees, in which solutions were sought on a party-political basis, but also across partisan lines or specifically within committees. The European parliamentarians were thus the only Convention cohort to enjoy institutionalized and functioning work-structures that could help with the preparation for Convention meetings. Further, the vast majority of its members are accustomed to the mechanisms of what Weber termed a 'working parliament', in which most decisionmaking is based on the search for common solutions between committees, fractions and party political groups. They were thus able to exploit their considerable informational resources quite effectively in the Convention setting.

Within the Parliament, the group motions from the European Socialist, and also the European People's Party groupings, were a focus for activity. Members of national parliaments behaved in many different ways. National parliamentarians – particularly those from the Benelux states, Sweden, Lithuania, Latvia, Slovakia and Malta – often threw their weight behind amendments from the representatives of their national governments. Parliamentarians from Portugal and Estonia made joint amendments. Many national parliamentarians also signed the motions made by groupings from the European Parliament.

The influence of the Parliament nevertheless depended largely on the definition of the Convention's role in relation to the intergovernmental conference. If a large group of its members had decided from the start that the Convention should simply present a range of reform options and to leave it to the intergovernmental conference to draft the new Treaty, which was envisioned in the Laeken Declaration, the Parliament's influence would have remained marginal. The Parliament's relative gain in influence in the Convention process could then have been reversed by the IGC if the heads of state and government had treated the Convention's result as an important point of reference, but only one of several in their agenda for the IGC. Yet, in the complex bargaining situation of the IGC, the Convention decision to draft a 'Constitution' that replaced the existing Treaties created a strong focal point that proved impossible to move away from except in certain sensitive institutional questions.

7.9 The participation of the EP at the IGC 2003–04

Drawing on the EP's participation modes agreed for the Amsterdam and Nice IGCs, the EP also participated as an observer in the work of the IGC 2003–04. When the IGC met at the level of Heads of State and Governments, the EP was represented by its President, Pat Cox. By decision of the EP's Conference of Presidents, the parliamentary representatives in the IGCs minister for foreign affairs meetings were MEPs Iñigo Méndez de Vigo (replaced by Elmar Brok in November 2003) and Klaus Hänsch, who were former EP representatives in the Praesidium of the Convention. The Conference of Presidents also decided to back up the two MEPs by creating an IGC monitoring committee, and further stipulated that the two representatives must regularly inform the Conference of Presidents, the Committee on Constitutional Affairs, and the IGC monitoring committee about the proceedings of the IGC. In substance, the main focus of the EP's work within the IGC was to prevent it from unraveling the consensus achieved by the Convention. Neither the EP's President nor the two EP representatives therefore tried to reopen any parts of the Convention's draft CT. In the end, the EP endorsed the final Constitutional Treaty on 12 January 2005 by an overwhelmingly majority. 500 MEPs voted in favor of the text signed by the 25 governments on 29 October 2004 in Rome, while 137 voted against and 40 abstained.

7.10 Conclusions

Constitutional reform appears to be the most pressing concern for the EP, considering that the Parliament has to improve both its situation within the institutional framework and advance the community's policies. Constitutional reform functions *à longue durée*. The EP still has to make use of a leadership strategy entailing supporting small steps, together with compromises with powerful partners. These compromises only rest, however, on a thin layer of ice. A position of the EP which is too inflexible and rigid could obstruct further improvements. An attitude too weak, however, could prevent far-reaching solutions. To date, the European Parliament has showed a relatively constructive attitude in EU constitutional negotiations (Wessels 1996: 893).

This chapter has indicated that the Parliament is capable of displaying a greater degree of leadership than it is given credit for by intergovernmentalists. Although the EP remains *formally* marginalized in the actual IGC process, the process of constitutional reform must be viewed through a broader lens that takes into account both the 'summits' and 'valleys' of European integration. Exploiting its growing powers in day-to-day policymaking, the Parliament has employed its resources in order to gain more privileged institutional positions, and in general to create a context more amenable to its attempts to provide leadership. This has, in turn, permitted the EP to play a greater leadership role in the negotiations themselves than would otherwise have been the case.

Given the dynamic nature of the EU's institutional structure, it is unsurprising that the EP's leadership strategy has developed over time. The relationship between the Parliament's resources in daily policymaking and those it enjoys in constitutional negotiations has permitted the EP to play a greater role in constitutional negotiations. This has allowed it to turn its previously rather passive observer role in constitutional negotiations into a more active instrumental leadership role. Similarly, its growing capacity to sanction and reward member states through its behavior *outside* constitutional negotiations has allowed it to play a more active structural leadership role.

Conversely, the growth in its material resources and its capacity to play a leadership role appear in some respects to have actually reduced the Parliament's scope to pursue its own preferences in EU constitutional negotiations. The general European public perceives that the MEPs are no longer democratic opponents of 'EU bureaucracy', but are increasingly seen to be a part of the European political 'establishment'. Has this gradual strategy of participation turned the EP from a potential troublemaker into a tame partner?

One thing is clear: without personalizing itself or defining its profile *vis-à-vis* national actors, i.e. without establishing itself as an independent, political and politicized actor, it is hard to make the EP's role clear to citizens. By following a strategy of 'containment' towards the Commission and Council, the EP's capacity to act increasingly resembles that of national parliamentary majorities that have lost their profile *vis-à-vis* the governments that they have appointed, except in crisis situations.

Nevertheless – and although the extension of the EP's powers through the Constitutional Treaty was not one of the prime points of controversy during the ratification process – the more general question arises of whether or not the growth in the Parliament's leadership role in the elaboration of the Constitutional Treaty contributed to the subsequent ratification crisis. In pushing for the Convention, and in arguing that the Convention should adopt a Constitution, the Parliament arguably exaggerated its resources, especially its legitimizing function. Whether the Parliament will turn out to have been a victim of its own success in mobilizing coalitions around its own preferences in the negotiation of the Constitutional Treaty remains though to be seen.

Notes

1. For a general discussion on the legal aspects of the different decisionmaking procedures, see Kapteyn and VerLoren van Themaat (1998: 408–46); Schoo (1997).
2. This section essentially builds on an earlier article by the author on the European Parliament and the Amsterdam IGC. See: Maurer (2002a: 419–22).
3. See the Common Franco-German Initiative on Institutional Reform (CONV 489/03), the relevant Hispano-British Proposal (CONV 591/03), the Memorandum of the Benelux states (CONV 457/02) as well as the initiatives of many smaller states, which should be understood as a response to the first two initiatives (CONV 646/03).

8
Big versus Small: Shared Leadership in the EU and Power Politics in the Convention

Simone Bunse, Paul Magnette and Kalypso Nicolaïdis

8.1 Introduction

The European Union (EU) is a strange mix. A political construct conceived as a guard against the temptation of hegemony by any member state against any other(s), it relies most fundamentally on the ideal of shared leadership. In the EU, therefore, the principle of equality between states is not mainly grounded in the sovereignty norm as in classic intergovernmental organizations, but rather in the attempt to constrain power. At the same time, however, the EU obeys a stringent reality principle, whereby institutions and decisionmaking procedures must reflect power realities in order to be effective and credible. It would thus be hard to argue that the EU has transcended power politics: the taming of power is the best it can do. Thus, behind the 'big versus small problem', the conflicting views over institutional design between more and less populated member states, lies an age-old dilemma faced by all political communities, especially federal constructs (Magnette and Nicolaïdis 2004a).

The EU's founding bargain was meant to address this dilemma. It relies on a delicate institutional balance guarding on the one hand equality between its member states and the ideal of shared leadership, and on the other hand the principle of proportionality and the underlying reality of relative power among member states. In part, this balance is achieved through a purposeful diffusion of political authority between supranational and inter-governmental institutions. In part it is obtained through the special characteristics of each one of these institutions.

Nonetheless, with successive enlargements with predominantly small states and the extension of qualified majority voting (QMV), the original founding bargain became increasingly contentious. The big countries fell prey to the 'Gulliver syndrome', picturing themselves as giants held back by a crowd of mini-countries (Magnette and Nicolaïdis 2004a). As they started to push for a fundamental revision of the EU's delicate founding equilibrium, the division between the big and the small, which had been latent until the Nice negotiations, became ever more explicit. Thus, the rational of the Convention on the Future of Europe was not only to ensure that preparations for the forthcoming IGC would be more 'broadly based and transparent,' but to resolve this increasingly stark divide.

This chapter examines the 'big vs small' cleavage in the Convention which – rather than rectifying it, as its mission suggested – almost caused its breakdown. The key questions the chapter seeks to address are who won and who lost in the Convention debates on the institutional balance of power in the Union, and, most importantly, why. It begins with an examination of the EU's historical institutional balance. This is followed by an analysis of the Convention endgame which was dominated by the passionate debate over the future shape of the Council Presidency. While the bigs favored the creation of a permanent European Council president, the smalls fiercely defended the rotation principle. The analysis pays particular attention to the negotiating context, the resources which both coalitions had at their disposal, and the strategies that they applied.

We argue that power politics as it was practiced in the Convention greatly undermined the principle of shared leadership that had been part of the EU construct since the beginning. While France and Germany responded to a strong demand for leadership to bridge the impasse over the issue of institutional balance, their response was not to forge a consensus but rather to impose their own bilateral bargain on the Convention (see also chapter 9 for more on the Franco-German tandem). Relying mainly on their material resources, reputation, and the support they enjoyed in the Convention Praesidium, they tried to set the agenda, construct a coalition around their compromise proposal, and induce the other states to make concessions. The Benelux-led opposition, in turn, concentrated on convincing the bigs of the importance of the equality ideal for the EU. However, given the intensity of the preferences of the bigs, the Praesidium's support of the Franco-German compromise, and the lack of coherence of the small state coalition, despite being in the majority in the Convention, the bigs were able effectively to exploit their strong material resources, providing successful structural leadership in the Convention that resulted in a pro-big state institutional outcome.

8.2 The EU's institutional balance

The EU's institutional balance rests on three complementary mechanisms to guarantee a fair balance between big and small: weighted votes in the Council of Ministers; independent supranational institutions; and a rotating Council Presidency.

8.2.1   Weighted votes in the Council of Ministers

Weighted votes offer a degree of security for small state interests while giving the largest members a greater say in the decision. The EC's initial system of QMV is a perfect illustration of this logic of 'regressive proportionality' – a midway house between the principles of 'one country, one vote' and 'one citizen, one vote.' The three large states were given four votes each, Belgium and the Netherlands two votes each, and Luxembourg one vote. This implied that the largest states were 25 times 'under-represented' compared to the smallest one. A decision could be blocked by six votes, i.e. two large states or one large and at least one small state, but not by a small state alliance or one state alone. The qualified majority (QM) represented about 70 per cent of the population.

The 1973 enlargement called for a first revision of this bargain: while the UK received the same votes as the three large founders, Denmark and Ireland were given a smaller weight than Belgium and the Netherlands. The four big states now had 10 votes, Belgium and the Netherlands 5, Denmark and Ireland 3, and Luxembourg 2. The original idea of a 'blocking minority' (BM) was preserved. Successive enlargements with Greece, Portugal, Spain, Finland, Sweden and Austria followed the same logic (see Table 8.1). In May 2004, Poland, the Czech Republic, Hungary, Slovakia, Lithuania, Latvia, Slovenia, Estonia, Cyprus, and Malta were accommodated into this system. While the BM became more complex with each enlargement, the relative scale of representation – with a factor of one to five between the smallest and biggest state – remained unchanged.

However, with the growing number of 'smalls', favoring them became more contentious. Thus, the Nice Treaty, whose institutional provisions have been in force since November 2004, redesigned three parameters of the EU's traditional voting system: the number of votes of the big states increased from five to almost ten times that of the smallest member; the majority threshold was raised from 71 to 74 per cent; and it adopted additional voting criteria. Acting upon a Commission proposal, the votes must be cast by a majority of the member states; otherwise the Council requires votes by at least two-thirds of the members. In addition, the QM must represent at least 62 per cent of the EU population. Above all, this was the first revision of the relative weight of member states in favor of the big states bringing the system closer to the principle of one person, one vote than in the original 1958 bargain (see e.g. Raunio and Wiberg 1998).

8.2.2   The independence of the EU's supranational institutions

Similarly, supranational law and institutions – supposed, disproportionately, to serve weaker actors – have been essential to obtain a degree of equality between the EU members. The independent supranational Commission was granted the monopoly right to initiate legislation and make proposals to

Table 8.1 The evolution of member states' weight in the Council of Ministers

Bigs	Weighted Votes								Double Majority 2009[4]	Pop. (million)
	1958	1973	1981	1986	1995	May 2004	Nov. 2004[1]	2007[2]		
D	4 (23.5%)	10 (17.2%)	10 (15.9%)	10 (13.2%)	10 (11.5%)	10 (8.1%)	29 (9%)	29 (8.4%)	17.0% (+8.6)	82.398
F	4 (23.5%)	10 (17.2%)	10 (15.9%)	10 (13.2%)	10 (11.5%)	10 (8.1%)	29 (9%)	29 (8.4%)	12.4% (+4)	60.181
I	4 (23.5%)	10 (17.2%)	10 (15.9%)	10 (13.2%)	10 (11.5%)	10 (8.1%)	29 (9%)	29 (8.4%)	12.0% (+3.6)	57.998
GB	—	10 (17.2%)	10 (15.9%)	10 (13.2%)	10 (11.5%)	10 (8.1%)	29 (9%)	29 (8.4%)	12.4% (+4)	60.065
E	—	—	—	8 (10.5%)	8 (9.2%)	8 (6.5%)	27 (8.4%)	27 (7.8%)	8.3% (+0.5)	40.217
Pl	—	—	—	—	—	—	27 (8.4%)	27 (7.8%)	8.0% (+0.2)	38.623
Total	12 (70.6%)	40 (69%)	40 (63.5%)	48 (63.2%)	48 (55.2%)	56 (45.2%)	170 (53%)	170 (49.3%)	70.1% (+20.8)	339.482
Smalls										
R	—	—	—	—	—	—	—	14 (4.1)	4.6% (+0.5)	22.272
NL	2 (11.8%)	5 (8.6%)	5 (7.9%)	5 (6.6%)	5 (5.7%)	5 (4%)	13 (4%)	13 (3.8%)	3.3% (−0.5)	16.151
B	2 (11.8%)	5 (8.6%)	5 (7.9%)	5 (6.6%)	5 (5.7%)	5 (4%)	12 (3.7%)	12 (3.5%)	2.1% (−1.4)	10.289
Gr	—	—	5 (7.9%)	5 (6.6%)	5 (5.7%)	5 (4%)	12 (3.7%)	12 (3.5%)	2.2% (−1.3)	10.666
P	—	—	—	5 (6.6%)	5 (5.7%)	5 (4%)	12 (3.7%)	12 (3.5%)	2.1% (−1.4)	10.249
CR	—	—	—	—	—	—	12 (3.7%)	12 (3.5%)	2.1% (−1.4)	10.249
H	—	—	—	—	—	—	12 (3.7%)	12 (3.5%)	2.1% (−1.4)	10.045
S	—	—	—	—	4 (4.6%)	4 (3.2%)	10 (3.1%)	10 (2.9)	1.8% (−1.1)	8.878
A	—	—	—	—	4 (4.6%)	4 (3.2%)	10 (3.1%)	10 (2.9)	1.7% (−1.2)	8.188
Bu	—	—	—	—	—	—	—	10 (2.9)	1.6% (−1.3)	7.538

Table 8.1 (Continued)

	(1)	(2)	(3)	(4)	(5)	(6)	(7)	(8)	%	
DK	—	3 (5.2%)	3 (4.8%)	3 (3.9%)	3 (3.4%)				1.1% (−0.9)	5.384
Ire	—	—	—						0.8% (−1.2)	3.924
Fin	—	—	—	—		7 (2.2%)	7 (2%)		1.0% (−1)	5.191
SR	—	—	—	—	—				1.1% (−0.9)	8.878
Li	—	—	—	—	3 (2.4%)				0.7% (−1.3)	3.593
La	—	—	—	—			4 (1.2%)		0.5% (−0.7)	2.349
Slo	—	—	—	—			4 (1.2%)		0.4% (−0.8)	1.936
Es	—	—	—	—			4 (1.2%)	4 (1.2%)	0.3% (−0.9)	1.409
Cy	—	—	—	—					0.2% (−1)	0.772
L	1 (5.9%)	2 (3.4%)	2 (3.2%)	2 (2.6%)	2 (2.3%)	2 (1.6%)	3 (0.9%)	3 (0.9%)	0.1% (−1.1)	0.454
M	—	—					3 (0.9%)	3 (0.9%)	0.1% (−0.8)	0.400
Total	5 (29.4%)	18 (31%)	23 (36.5%)	28 (36.8%)	39 (44.8%)	68 (54.8%)	151 (47%)	175 (50.7%)	29.9%	145.220
QM	12 (70.6%)	41 (70.7%)	45 (71.4%)	54 (71.1%)	62 (71.3%)	88[3] (71%)	232[3] (72.3%)	258[3] (74.8%)	65% of pop./55% of MS[5]	—
BM	6 (35.3%)	18 (31%)	19 (30.2%)	23 (30.3%)	26 (29.9%)	37 (29.9%)	90 (28%)	88 (25.5%)	4 MS	—
Total	17	58	63	76	87	124	321	345	100	484.702

Notes: [1] Nice rules enter into force; [2] expected accession of Bulgaria and Romania; [3] cast by a majority of Council Members on a proposal from the Commission (in other cases, cast by at least two-thirds of MS). 62% of the EU's total population; [4] Constitutional Treaty; [5] Where the Council is not acting on a proposal of the Commission or initiative of the proposed Union Minister for Foreign Affairs, the QM is obtained with 72% of the MS representing 65% of the EU population. Council members representing at least three-quarters of a BM (either at the level of MS or population) can demand that the Council should further discuss the issue. The Council may decide to withdraw the latter measure in 2014. Population estimates July 2003, CIA World Factbook 2003. QM=Qualified Majority, BM=Blocking Minority, MS=member state, Pop.=Population.
Source: Bunse (forthcoming DPhil thesis, University of Oxford).

the Council of Ministers. The intergovernmental Council of Ministers has to accept them before becoming law and can in most cases only amend them unanimously. The European Parliament (EP) gradually developed into an independent co-legislator alongside the Council. The relative power of these three institutions depends on the underlying legislative procedure and voting arrangements (e.g. Tsebelis 1994). Finally, the European Court of Justice (ECJ) was set up to interpret the treaties and bind all member states equally to EU law. This combination of functions and the independence of the Commission, EP, and ECJ were to ensure that size would not be mathematically related to influence.

Although the small states initially feared Franco-German dominance of the Commission, the collegiality rule has prevented the Commissioners from systematically defending their member state's interest. Developing the reputation of a guarantor of the 'general interest' against the weight of the large states, the small states have generally come to see it as their strongest ally, while big states tend to assert their power in the Council. In addition, the composition of the Commission explains, in part, its support by the smalls. Each small state was guaranteed one Commissioner, while the large states have – until November 2004 – had two. Despite this strongly degressive rule of proportionality in the Commission, this asymmetry did not tip the balance of support. The fact that the Commission has always included one member for each state is not merely understood in terms of representation, but as a guarantee that the peculiar situation of the small states can be understood in the college.

Once the EU consists of 27 states, the number of Commissioners is to be less than the number of member states.[1] While bigger states can compensate for the lack of a Commissioner through their weight in the other EU institutions, smaller countries will find themselves at a greater disadvantage. In short, here, too, representation is moving away from the equality principle.

De facto inequality is also visible in the EP whose attribution of seats is degressively proportional, half way between equal representation and population proportionality. As a result, most small states are either three or four times less represented in the EP than the big ones (see Table 8.2). Nonetheless, the EP's more fluid nature offers small states the possibility of forming *ad hoc* coalitions within transnational political groups. Thus, smaller state representatives tend to promote their interest better in the EP than in a rigid intergovernmental Council – explaining their defense of the Commission–EP pair.

8.2.3 Avoidance of a permanent presidency

The principles of equality and shared leadership are exemplified most 'purely' by the rotating Council Presidency (Bunse forthcoming). Upon its creation, small countries feared that if they gave the EC a single figurehead, this person would be in the sway of the big and powerful. Thankfully, such

Table 8.2 The evolution of member states' representation in the European Parliament

Bigs	Number of MEPs: 1958	1973	1976	1981	1986	1991	1995	2004	2007	2009	Representing % of EU27
D	36 (25.4%)	36 (18.2%)	81 (19.8%)	81 (18.7%)	81(15.6%)	99 (18.5%)	99 (15.8%)	99 (13.5%)	99 (13.5%)	Max. 96 (12.8%)	17.0
F	36 (25.4%)	36 (18.2%)	81 (18.7%)	81 (18.7%)	81 (15.6%)	81 (15.1%)	87 (13.9%)	78 (10.7%)	72 (9.8%)	To be defined	12.4
I	36 (25.4%)	36 (18.2%)	81 (19.8%)	81 (18.7%)	81 (15.6%)	81 (15.1%)	87 (13.9%)	78 (10.7%)	72 (9.8%)		12.4
GB	-	36 (18.2%)	81 (19.8%)	81 (18.7%)	81 (15.6%)	81 (15.1%)	87 (13.9%)	78 (10.7%)	72 (9.8%)		12.0
E	-	-	-	-	60 (11.6%)	60 (11.2%)	64 (10.2%)	54 (7.4%)	54 (7.4%)		8.3
P	-	-	-	-	-	-	-	54 (7.4%)	50 (6.8%)		8.0
Seats	108 (76.1%)	144 (72.7%)	324 (79%)	324 (74.7%)	384 (74%)	402 (75%)	424 (67.7%)	441 (60.2%)	415 (56.7%)		70.1
Smalls											
R	-	-	-	-	-	-	-	-	33 (4.5%)		4.6
NL	14 (9.9%)	14 (7.1%)	25 (6.1%)	25 (5.8%)	25 (4.8%)	25 (4.7%)	31 (5%)	27 (3.7%)	25 (3.4%)	Min.6 (0.8%)	3.3
B	14 (9.9%)	14 (7.1%)	24 (5.9%)	24 (5.5%)	24 (4.6%)	24 (4.5%)	25 (4%)	24 (3.3%)	25 (3.4%)		2.2
Gr	-	-	-	24 (5.5%)	24 (4.6%)	24 (4.5%)	25 (4%)	24 (3.3%)	22 (3%)		2.1
P	-	-	-	-	24 (4.6%)	24 (4.5%)	25 (4%)	24 (3.3%)	22 (3%)	To be defined	2.1
CR	-	-	-	-	-	-	-	24 (3.3%)	20 (2.7%)		2.1
H	-	-	-	-	-	-	-	24 (3.3%)	20 (2.7%)		2.1
S	-	-	-	-	-	-	22 (3.5%)	19 (2.6%)	18 (2.5%)		1.8
A	-	-	-	-	-	-	21 (3.4%)	18 (2.5%)	17		1.7
Bu	-	-	-	-	-	-	-	-	(2.3%)		1.6
DK	-	10 (5.1%)	16 (3.9%)	16 (3.7%)	16 (3.1%)	16 (3%)	16 (2.6%)	14 (1.9%)	13 (1.8%)		1.1
Fin	-	-	-	-	-	-	16 (2.6%)	14 (1.9%)	13 (1.8%)		1.1
SR	-	-	-	-	-	-	-	14 (1.9%)	13 (1.8%)		1.0
Ire	-	10 (5.1%)	15 (3.7%)	15 (3.5%)	15 (2.9%)	15 (2.8%)	15 (2.4%)	13 (1.8%)	12		0.8
Li	-	-	-	-	-	-	-	13 (1.8%)	12 (1.6%)		0.7
La	-	-	-	-	-	-	-	9 (1.2%)	8 (1.1%)		0.5
Slo	-	-	-	-	-	-	-	7 (1%)	7 (1%)		0.4
L	6 (4.2%)	6 (3%)	6 (1.5%)	6 (1.4%)	6 (1.2%)	6 (1.1%)	6 (1%)	6 (0.8%)	6 (0.8%)		0.3
Es	-	-	-	-	-	-	-	6 (0.8%)	6 (0.8%)		0.2
Cy	-	-	-	-	-	-	-	-	-		0.1
M	-	-	-	-	-	-	-	5 (0.7%)	5 (0.7%)		0.1
Seats	34 (23.9%)	54 (27.3%)	86 (21%)	110 (25.3%)	134 (26%)	134 (25%)	202 (32.3%)	291 (39.8%)	317 (43.3%)		29.9
Total	142	198	410	434	518	536	626	732	732	Max. 750	100

Source: Bunse (forthcoming DPhil thesis, University of Oxford).

a fear chimed with that of big countries who wanted to avoid the emergence of an autonomous leader that could have undermined their own prestige. There was also widely shared agreement that a permanent presidency would risk generating rivalry with the young Commission. Thus, the original model established a system of equal rotation among the member governments to chair the different Council formations regardless of size, economic power, or merit (Wallace 1985: 2; Westlake 1995: 37).

The rotation principle allowed the member states equal access to an institution which – rather unexpectedly – evolved from a 'fairly passive [manager]' (Wallace and Edwards 1976: 576) and mere administrative function into a crucial agenda setter, a promoter of political initiatives, and a compromise shaper (Kirchner 1992; Westlake 1995; Hayes-Renshaw and Wallace 1995; Sherrington 2002). Enabling states to make diplomatic contributions independent of their political and economic weight (*Financial Times* April 12 2000), the office has been particularly important for the smalls:

> 'The most positive aspect of the rotating presidency is that it gives us a chance to hold an influential role and that you manage to get totally different people to look at the same issue which you move into the spotlight.' (Interview European Parliament (April 26 2004) in Bunse forthcoming).

Unsurprisingly, proposals that could potentially upset the EU's historical institutional balance, particularly replacing the rotating presidency with a more permanent arrangement, were to cause an outcry by the smalls.

8.3 Power politics in the Convention: the small versus big divide

The idea for a permanent European Council president was initially put forward by a three big state coalition: former Spanish Prime Minister José Maria Aznar, British Prime Minister Tony Blair, and French President Jacques Chirac (hence the ABC proposal). Contrary to the Community's original bargain it advocated the election of a full-time European Council Presidency from among former government heads for a period of up to five years. Its proclaimed rationale was to enhance the effectiveness of the Council by having a full-time person in charge of managing it; to ensure greater continuity in terms of priority and long-term planning; and to give a more permanent face to the EU in the rest of the world. Particularly the first rationale remained paramount in the debate.

The Benelux, supported by a coalition of smalls opposed to a permanent presidency (the self-styled 'friends of the Community method'), countered the ABC proposal in December 2002.[2] In addition to prioritizing the reinforcement of the Community method, electing the Commission president by the EP, enhancing the Commission's executive powers and strengthening the Commission by eventually reducing its size, its key focus was the defense of the rotation principle. To enhance the Council's effectiveness the Benelux suggested another approach: a clearer distinction between the executive and legislative functions of the Council. Executive functions (the coordination of national policies) should be chaired by the Commission while rotation would be maintained at European Council level and the specialized ministerial Councils performing legislative functions.

Not inconsequential, politicians and the media framed the issue of the Council Presidency as that of 'Presidency of the Union.' This ambiguous semantics conveyed both the intent of the bigs and the fears of the smalls. For the bigs, this new European Council president should indeed be seen as the president of the Union as a whole reflecting the role of the revamped European Council as the superior authority in the EU, directing and overseeing the work of other institutions. For the opposing small states, this was exactly the outcome to be avoided: the concentration of power in a single individual leading the EU in the name of the most powerful heads of state in the EU.

To solve the conflict that almost led to the breakdown of the Convention a compromise was needed that could develop into the focal point around which an agreement could converge. Such a compromise (see below) was presented by France and Germany in January 2003 (Schröder and Chirac 2003). Although their proposal was not formally put on the Convention agenda and generated widespread opposition within it, it immediately turned into the reference point of reform. It became clear that the bargaining space, i.e., the set of settlements potentially acceptable to the Convention, were bounded by the positions and bottom lines of the most powerful member states and that the very salient issues, such as the EU's institutions, were firmly kept under their control. To understand why, their resources, the negotiating context, and strategies the opposing coalitions used are examined next.

8.3.1   Leadership resources of the Franco-German axis and the Benelux-led small state coalition

Like previous treaty changes, the Convention centered on 'power issues' and was dominated by intra-state bargains. In this type of negotiation, a member state's size is the major resource (Moravcsik and Nicolaïdis 1999). Second, reputational resources played a role: in the presence of lots of new participants, the Franco-German tandem on the one hand, and the Benelux on the other hand were expected to take the lead. Informational resources, in turn, were much less important since: (a) this was the fourth big bargain in ten years and the member states' preferences were well known; and (b) the member states made their views public much before the Convention.

Material leadership resources: the importance of size

Germany with a population of over 80 million is the EU's largest economy and most populous nation. Together with France with 60 million people, the two countries' material leadership resources could not be matched by any other two Convention members (for example, the UK and Spain who also presented a joint proposal on the Union institutions) (Palacio and Hain 2003). The size of their population was a crucial resource in the Convention's institutional debate as Giscard – contrary to the EU's historic compromise – defined consensus in terms of the majority of the EU population.[3] Representing over 30 per cent of the EU's population, France and Germany only needed the support of two other big states to generate a majority and hence translate their material resources into bargaining power. Indeed, as Mazzucelli, Guérot and Metz argue in this volume, on many occasions French-German compromises have been a precondition for further EU integration.

The material resources of the small state coalition, in contrast, were much weaker. The 16 smalls who opposed the permanent presidency particularly fiercely (see below) only represented around 25 per cent of the EU population. Without big state support their bargaining power was weak.

Reputation

A second resource on which the French-German axis could rely was its past reputation. The French-German couple has long provided leadership in the EU and IGC negotiations although its strength has varied throughout history and its nature seems to be changing (see chapter 9). Since its early beginnings, European integration rested on a bargain between France and Germany and their relations 'appeared so fundamental in the negotiations for the first European Treaties that from this fact they derived a kind of original legitimacy.' (de Schoutheete 1990: 110). In addition, the EU as a whole has usually reaped beneficial results from French-German initiatives – a prominent example being Economic and Monetary Union (EMU) (Cameron 2004: 12). Finally, the other EU member states have traditionally seen the French-German relationship as a way of containing 'the danger emanating from Gaullist ideas on European Affairs and Atlantic solidarity' (de Schoutheete 1990: 19). Although not enjoying the reputation of providing impartial leadership, Germany has in the past frequently sided with small states and their fight for strengthening the supranational over the intergovernmental elements in the EU.[4] Thus, the country has often been seen as a defender of the smalls and 'the revival of the French-German partnership in the final two months of 2002 (after both countries' general elections) was welcomed by many conventionnels' (Norman 2003: 174; Allen 2004).

While the Benelux countries were also founding members and thus had a greater claim to leadership than all the other small newcomers, their alliance has mostly served to co-ordinate and defend their common positions rather than taking initiatives shaping the EU's integration path. Since the creation of the EC, they have been the defender of small countries' interests and developed a reputation of the 'guardian of the Community method' which had worked well in the past even after successive enlargements.

Informational resources

For both coalitions informational resources were less relevant in the Convention's institutional debate than at previous IGCs. Theoretically, France and Germany's informational resources are greater than those of the smaller states. The size of their administrations and material resources allow them to invest more heavily in developing content and process expertise and networks of contacts within the EU institutions than small states. However, after the Maastricht, Nice and Amsterdam negotiations, the member states' preferences were well known, they made their views public much before the Convention, and given the issue of the EU's future institutional set-up was of key interest to conventionnels and politically highly sensitive, all actors, including the small member states, invested heavily: 'Those who are most affected by a proposal get most active. If something is against our interest we act as vehemently as big states' (Interview, Belgian Permanent Representation, February 17 2005).

In addition, the set-up and workings of the Convention allowed each member state the same number of seats regardless of size (one government representative and two national parliamentarians), and all parties could present proposals, suggest amendments, and rally support for them in the Convention.

8.3.2   The negotiation context

France and Germany had greater opportunities to exercise leadership in the Convention not only because of their greater resources, but also because of the negotiation context they were facing. Here the institutional set-up, the number of the parties in the Convention and the distribution and intensity of preference were of particular relevance.

The institutional set-up

Key to the Convention's functioning was its Praesidium consisting of a Chair (former French President Valéry Giscard d'Estaing), two Vice Chairs (the former Italian and Belgian prime ministers Giuliano Amato and Jean-Luc Dehaene), and nine other Conventionnels, including representatives of the governments holding the Council Presidency during the Convention (Spain, Denmark, and Greece) and two representatives each from national parliaments, the EP, and the Commission. In addition, the Convention's representative of the Slovene Parliament was invited on behalf of the candidate countries. The Praesidium's role was defined as lending impetus to the Convention and providing it with a basis on which to work. To do so it was granted considerable procedural powers including preparing agendas for each plenary and working group session and a Convention Secretariat (under the former head of the British civil service, John Kerr) was set up to assist it. As Laeken had left the process and procedures of the Convention undefined, Giscard had ample room for maneuver to outline its operating style and flesh out a powerful role for himself.

Crucially, while the Convention was supposed to remain sovereign in the process of developing the Constitutional Treaty, the Praesidium acted as the interpreter of the dominant view and was the sole drafter of the actual text presented to the floor. As Allen finds, Giscard 'monopolised reporting of the work of the Convention to both member states and the public,' 'it was usually Giscard's or Kerr's summary of proceedings that formed the ongoing basis for further negotiation', and he cleverly 'created controversies [. . .] or negotiating positions that were designed to be conceded in return for consensus on more important items' (Allen 2004: 24).[5] In addition, it was Giscard who – perhaps daunted by its highly divisive nature or as a strategic means to exert pressure to compromise – decided not to put the EU's future institutional design on the Convention agenda until the very end, determined that no voting would take place in the Convention, that a single text would be agreed rather than options proposed, how consensus and the majority was to be defined, and when a consensus existed. While operating within the constraints of the other Praesidium members, this gave him considerable leverage to steer the result towards his most preferred option. Given that Giscard was pro-large member states, their proposals were guaranteed a dominant position in the debates.

The number of parties in the Convention

One of the rationales behind the creation of the Convention had been to create a more representative body than IGCs that would openly debate all the issues and interests at stake. Thus, its members (105 altogether) included not only government representatives (and their alternates), but also members of national parliaments, the European Parliament (MEPs), and Commission representatives. Similarly, the candidate states were granted government and parliamentary representatives.[6] The Economic and Social Committee (Ecosoc), the European social partners, the Committee of the Regions and the European Ombudsman were invited as observers.

This produced a negotiating context in which the number of actors was much higher than in previous EU constitutional negotiations, making it potentially more difficult to broker compromises and find zones of agreement. At the same time the incentive was high to present a single – and therefore more influential – constitutional draft treaty to the IGC rather than options.

For a number of reasons leadership in the institutional issues could most effectively be provided by the member states rather than the MEPs or the

Commission. Most importantly, the Convention did not replace the IGC and took place in its shadow, i.e. the outcome faced the potential veto by the member states. Once concrete issues were put on the table, the representatives of the governments loyally defended their interests – as did most of the national parliamentarians nominated by the governments. By the autumn of 2002 they started to build coalitions and invoke their veto in the pending IGC.[7] The other Convention members, anticipating the IGC, adapted their behavior to this constraint. Hence, the MEPs were largely ineffective when it comes to the hard-core institutional issues.

In addition, the Commission lost credibility in the Convention due to Commission President Prodi's secret drafting of his own ambitious draft EU constitution, the so-called Penelope document (see chapter 6). By intending to put his vision of the Commission as a European government at the center of the Convention's endgame, he offended his colleagues who did not accept political responsibility for its content and alienated potential supporters in the Praesidium. Kassim and Menon (2004: 101) argue: 'In tactical terms, by declaring such ambitious objectives, the Commission President may have committed a serious error, by effectively playing the Commission out of the game.' The Commission's capacity to shape the final outcomes of the Convention also declined sharply after it backed the small country coalition (Norman 2003: 266).

With the MEPs and the Commission mostly marginalized, the Convention was on institutional issues not radically different from IGCs and much of its endgame was dominated by the kind of hegemonic compromises that have characterized EU politics since its inception (see Magnette and Nicolaïdis 2004b). What then was this compromise about and what was the basic cleavage in the negotiation?

The distribution and intensity of preferences

The French-German contribution included the controversial creation of what became referred to as a 'dual EU Presidency.' A permanent European Council president elected from amongst its members for a period of up to five years would provide the EU's overall guidance and a directly elected Commission president by the EP would put together the reduced Commission college considering the geographical and demographic diversity of the EU.[8] Foreign affairs would be chaired by a permanent European foreign minister and two-year chairs would be created for Ecofin, the Eurogroup, and Justice and Home Affairs (JHA). Rotation would only be kept for the remaining Council of Minister formations.

Italy, Spain and the UK strongly supported the creation of the permanent European Council Presidency. Aznar had already used the 2002 Spanish Council Presidency to advocate this idea:

'Allow me, [. . .] after four months of experience of the Spanish Presidency of the European Union, to tell you that it is necessary to modify the current system of presidencies. [...] I agree with those who think that a good solution to this problem would consist of the President of the European Council having a longer mandate. A choice could be made between a mandate of five years or a shorter one of two and a half. In order for that to be possible, the President of the European Council should not have other political responsibilities in his own country. An option could be the requirement that candidates should have previously held the position of Head of State or Government. [...] My prime motivation in defending this new system of presidencies is the effective future working of the Union. [...] Presided over in this way, the European Council should continue to be the political apex of the Union. (Aznar (2002), Speech made at St Antony's College, University of Oxford, 20 May 2003)

Similarly, a British government official argued:

The rotating presidency has had its day. The current crisis over the EU's common foreign and security policy shows the limitations of pillar two. We are seeking a more permanent system that provides greater continuity and leadership. (Interview, UK Permanent Representation, February 10 2003)

However, although the UK welcomed the French-German contribution, it was skeptical about other aspects of the French-German plan. For example, it had consistently been opposed to replacing a Commission President chosen by the member states with an elected one.

Denmark and Sweden – who have taken a more intergovernmental approach to European integration – were the only two small countries that warmed to the creation of a permanent European Council Presidency:

'I can see a number of arguments in favour of an elected president. It will create continuity. And it may – if the model is correctly attuned – ensure clarity and balance in relation to the EU Commission.' (Rasmussen, Speech held at the Institute for International Studies, Copenhagen January 15 2003)

The other small states (particularly Belgium, Luxembourg, Ireland, Finland, Austria, the Netherlands, and Portugal) reacted in a very hostile manner to the French-German compromise. This skepticism was shared by politicians from the ten Central and Eastern European countries, as well as national parliaments, the European Commission, and the EP. At the January plenary on institutional issues most Conventioneers regretted a state of affairs where positions were adopted in advance and the Convention was transformed into an IGC. Dutch Christian Democrat MEP Hanja Maij-Wegen announced for the record that 64 speakers had spoken against the dual-presidency plans, 11 in favor, and 15 had remained neutral (Maij-Wegen, cited in *EU Observer* 21 January 2003). Others counted 55 speakers against, 18 in favor, and 15 somewhat against. Thus, the proportion against the appointment of a president of the European Council at that point was roughly 3 to 1.

The fears by the opposition centered on some of the same concerns raised in the original bargain: the importance of avoiding the creation of two competing power centers (the Commission and Council) and the potential damage a dual presidency could have for the EU's institutional balance by undermining the Commission. A Benelux position issued on January 21 summarizes these concerns:

> As far as the European Council is concerned, the Benelux favour maintaining rotation at European Council as well as Council of Minister level. We reiterate our opposition to the principle of an elected full time European Council Presidency that risks changing the institutional balance to the detriment of the Commission and provokes a confusion of competences as well as rivalry between the institutions. The Benelux think that a further European actor on the international stage will give rise to confusion who represents the EU in the different international arenas. (Benelux January 21 2003).[9]

However, not all aspects of the Benelux counterproposal enjoyed the coalition's support. For example, contrary to the Benelux compromise, other small countries continued to support the maintenance of rotation for the General Affairs Council rather than its chairing by the Commission President. Some also opposed the chairing of the Foreign Affairs Council by the Foreign Affairs minister, arguing that the latter could not chair a body that was supposed to hold him accountable. In addition, particularly the accession states fiercely rejected a future Commission that would not consist of one Commissioner per member state.

In sum, there was a strong demand for mediation both between the coalitions and within them.

8.4   Strategies and outcomes

8.4.1   The strategic approach of the French-German axis

To turn its proposal into a viable focal point France and Germany pursued a threefold strategy. First, the timing of their French-German compromise was chosen carefully to fully exploit the 'reputation' factor. It was put forward on the occasion of the 40th anniversary of their bilateral friendship (Élysée) treaty in January 2003. Shortly before, in October 2002, France and Germany had replaced their government representatives with their foreign ministers, thereby increasing their political weight in the Convention. Shortly afterwards the EU's future institutional set-up was also put officially on the Convention agenda for the first time.

Second, while first and foremost being a compromise between the two founding states, their proposal also reconciled the ABC suggestions with the aspects from the Benelux proposal that were supported by Germany. The election of the Commission President by the EP, for example, reflected Benelux suggestions and had broad support in the Convention. Moreover, a consensus had emerged on the double-hatted foreign affairs minister as included in the French-German proposal and supported in the autumn by a narrow majority in plenary. Enjoying Italian, British and Spanish support on the permanent presidency (and thus the support by the largest part of the European population – as Giscard pointed out in various interviews), the key strategy here was to induce the smalls to make concessions on the permanent presidency in return for an elected Commission president and European foreign minister. To convince the smalls that the French-German compromise was sensitive to small state concerns, respected the Community method and its intention was not the weakening of the Commission, France issued, together with the Netherlands, a joint statement on the importance of the reinforcement of the Commission.[10]

Crucially, the British position evolved with regard to the Commission. Apparently, its traditional opposition to electing the Commission President could be traded off against the 'strategic prize' of a stronger leader representing EU governments on the world stage. As Peter Hain, the Convention's British government representative, put it to his Parliament:

> in the end there will have to be an agreement and a necessary process of adjustment by all parties. We have, for example, been willing to look at, with certain very big safeguards, electing the Commission President through some method, provided that does not involve being hostage to a particular political faction and provided that the outcome is one that the Council can accept. So it is not something we sought and we remain deeply sceptical about it, but if, as part of the end game, getting an elected President of the Council, which is very much a priority for us, involves doing something with the Commission President with those very important safeguards that I mentioned, then that is something that we might have to adjust to. (Hain, 'Interview in the European Affairs Committee of the House of Commons' March 25 2003).[11]

The coordination between the big five, which had started with informal meetings at the 2000 IGC and continued since then, was now bearing fruit.

Third, France and Germany sought to exploit their privileged access to the Convention Praesidium, in particular Giscard d'Estaing. Indeed, at the January 20 and 21 plenary Giscard reacted favorably, calling their compromise 'a positive proposal [that is] going in the right direction [. . .] guaranteeing the stability of EU institutions' (Convention Plenary, January 20–1 2003).[12] He was personally much closer to the French-German compromise than to the Benelux proposals and sensitive to British concerns about the election of the Commission President. His detractors recalled the fact that he had become the Convention's chair on the insistence of Chirac, Blair, and German Chancellor Gerhard Schroeder. In addition, he himself 'created' the European Council in 1974 and would therefore naturally want to make it the apex of the European system. They pointed out, further-more, that this dual presidency set-up resembled the peculiar French political system in which the president is the 'leader of the nation' and the 'ulti-mate arbitrator of the national interest', while the prime minister heads the government (Wright 1989). Finally, they argued that his two foremost goals have been to support the claims of big countries and to weaken the Commission. His defenders, in turn, retorted that this only appeared to be the case because he tried to ensure that 'his' Constitution would not be radically altered by the IGC, and therefore the most powerful member states. Whatever the motivation, at some point before the official tabling of the draft articles on institutions, he chose to take sides and to support the idea of a permanent Council Presidency. Amato and the Spanish and Danish Praesidium representatives agreed with him.

It proved difficult for the smalls to split the big country coalition promoting the permanent presidency or gain similar influence in the Prae-sidium. Thus, the big country camp remained strong – the only wedge appeared on the definition of QMV and the proposed replacement of weighted votes by a double majority system as well as the Commission composition when Spain and Poland, joined quietly by some new members, started waging a 'give Nice a chance' campaign towards the end. This position later explained the difficulties of the IGC and the failure of the December 2003 Brussels Summit.

8.4.2   The strategic approach of the small state coalition

The Friends of the Community method had met since April 2002 to flesh out common positions across issues. By sometimes leading the coalition of smalls (when presenting their counter proposal) and sometimes following a more autonomous line the Benelux countries tried to position themselves as a mediating force. To generate support for their counterproposal their key strategy was threefold: first, to convince the other conventionnels of the shortcomings of the dual presidency and the value of the rotation principle; second, to generate a coherent coalition that comprised up to 19 states; and third to build strong alliances with the supranational institutions to defend the Community method.

As to the shortcomings of the dual presidency system, they criticized the lack of a clear division of labor between the two presidents and mechan-isms to mediate between them, its potential to unbalance the position of the High Representative/Minister for Foreign Affairs, and its failure to bring the EU closer to its citizens. It would move closer to the French system where leadership is torn between the head of state and the prime minister with obvious adverse effects in terms of efficiency (Nicolaïdis 2004). Further, the proposal was attacked as inconsistent. On what grounds it was asked, did its promoters believe that EU heads of states and governments would recognize the authority of one among them, a former peer most likely from a big member state. This was all the more true with regard to foreign policy in the context of the Iraq War. Would a former Prime Minister – the likely pedigree of a European Council president – have the political clout to represent the EU on the world stage? Would the French accept being represented by a British citizen in Washington or vice versa?

Their most radical argument against the dual presidency proposal was, however, that the rotating presidency had for almost fifty years been the symbol of equality between the EU's member states. Not only would the Council President most likely be selected from among the bigger countries but he or she, whoever they might be, would be the big countries' voice, and would therefore marginalize the smalls. This would endanger the future functioning of the EU which rests on shared leadership and harmonious relations between the bigs and the smalls. On similar grounds, Giscard's logic of consensus was fiercely rejected. It introduced in the procedure of the Convention a majoritarian logic (as in majority of population rather than member states), which was alien to the EU's traditional modus operandi, had not been foreseen by the Laeken mandate, and had not governed their work so far. If this became the Convention's rule, all the minorities could feel that the process does not respect their rights, and this could ruin the legitimacy of the whole enterprise.

In the run-up to the formal debates on institutions, they issued a paper at the end of March to reiterate their common stance in favor of the community method.[13] Most importantly, they spelled out where the distinction between big and small states ought to be relevant and where not: yes, demographic factors are relevant for representation in the European Parliament and to voting weights in the Council of Ministers; no, they should not lead to 'any hierarchy of member states' or 'differentiate between them in terms of their entitlement to involvement in the operations of the institutions.' On the Council, while they acknowledged less than full consensus, this meant that a rotating presidency ought to be the predominant aspect of a new system.

However, their arguments were weakened significantly by the fact that Denmark and Sweden were not sharing their fears of a more permanent presidency arrangement. In addition, given the strong preferences by the coalition of bigs and by Giscard, they failed to convince them, despite the weight of their arguments. Neither the big states reconsidered their position nor Giscard changed his strategy and small state concerns about the permanent presidency were pushed more and more into the background.

This can partly be explained by the fact that – as in the past – the Benelux-led camp was a defensive coalition. While able to issue joint statements and united in its opposition to the permanent presidency, it proved unable to draw up a comprehensive set of articles together (Norman 2003: 244). At a meeting in Luxembourg in early April, the smalls merely confirmed their rejection of the permanent Council Presidency. Similarly, at the Athens meeting of the European Council on 16 April 2003, each country laid out its argument once again with little or no visible attempt to bridge the existing divide between big and small countries.

This leads us to the second strategy by the Benelux countries. As seen above, the apparent unity of the small state coalition was far from perfect. Constructing a coherent coalition was difficult due to the number of smalls involved and the lack of experience of the candidate states. Thus, despite mediating attempts it became increasingly fragile. When the Benelux countries produced an updated proposal on the institutions in May 2003, the other 16 small countries did not officially go along with it. In addition, another option for consideration in the plenary (the election of the president of the European Council by universal suffrage or an electoral college) was put forward by Greek Foreign Minister George Papandreou. The proposal had little chance to fly in the short run but was meant, in part, to reintroduce the central consideration of democratic legitimacy in the Convention debate. If the Convention was to get rid of democratically elected prime ministers and heads of states to head the European Council, the least it should do was to give the new figurehead a democratic pedigree. Moreover, such an election would give the president a source of legitimacy separate from the Commission and therefore reduce the potential rivalry between the two bodies by making the Council president a more supranational figure. Papandreou's proposal drew some support from Bruton, the Irish representative and a couple of other conventioneers. Most importantly, it served to signal in the plenary that there was no full agreement in the Praesidium. However, rather questioning Giscard's 'consensus' on the permanent presidency and the broad features of the French-German compromise, the increased heterogeneity of viewpoints towards the end curbed the small state coalition's leadership potential.

Finally, given the weakness of the Commission and the EP on institutional issues the small camps' alliance with them did not increase their leadership capacity in the debate on the institutions.

8.4.3   The final compromise: trumping the smalls

Consequently, the Praesidium's draft articles on the EU's institutional framework resembled the French-German compromise and ignored the key criticisms of the smalls (see Table 8.3). While the Praesidium constrained Giscard somewhat (it was split along the same lines as the Convention) and revised the initial highly intergovernmental institutional design that Giscard had

Table 8.3 Synopsis of small versus big divide and the Convention/IGC outcomes

Institution	Position of majority of bigs	Position of majority of smalls	Convention outcome	IGC outcome	Favors
European Council Presidency	Permanent	Rotating	Permanent	Permanent	Bigs
Council of Ministers Presidency	Some form of rotation except for general and foreign affairs, JHA, Ecofin, and the Eurogroup	Rotating	Except foreign affairs, 1-yearly rotation	Except foreign affairs, rotation in accordance with decision by European Council	Status quo
QMV	Double majority (except Spain and Poland)	Prefer weighted votes as per Nice Treaty or sufficient guarantees for smalls	Double majority: 60% of population and a majority or 2/3 of the MS	Double majority: 65% of population and 55% or 72% of MS	Bigs
Commission composition	Less than one Commissioner per MS	One Commissioner per MS (except Benelux)	No blocking minority President, Union Minister for Foreign Affairs (Vice-president) and 13 Commissioners selected on basis of equal rotation reflecting demographic and geographical range of MS	Blocking minority: 4 MS Two-thirds of the number of MS (unless Council decides otherwise) selected on the basis of equal rotation reflecting demographic and geographical range of MS	Bigs
Voting	Not opposed to non-voting Commissioners	Opposed to non-voting Commissioners	Non-voting Commissioners chosen by President according to same criteria that apply for composition	Commission acts as a collegiate body	Status quo
Presidency	Council proposes, EP elects	EP elects, Council confirms	Council proposes, EP elects	Council proposes, EP elects	Status quo
Parliament composition	Greater proportionality	At least 1 MEP per EP faction (i.e. 7 MEPs per MS)	Degressive proportionality minimum of 4 MEPs per MS Max. of MEPs 736 Council to decide precise allocation of MEPs	Degressive proportionality minimum 6, maximum 96 MEPs Max of MEPs 750 Council to decide precise allocation of MEPs	Status quo

devised primarily with Kerr, the main reforms opposed by small and medium states were left in: a smaller Commission, a Commission president – although elected by the Parliament – presented to it by the Council, and the abolition of the rotating presidency. The smalls were to lose on all sides.

The final compromise was reached in June 2003. By applying the 'single negotiating text' approach and bypassing veto threats, the Praesidium played an important role in the final outcome (Magnette and Nicolaïdis 2004b). It leveraged its hybrid nature as a secretariat/mediator and a college to the fullest. On the one hand, like presidencies in IGCs, it acted as an organizer and mediator. Supported by the Convention Secretariat, it sought to forge a compromise on a step-by-step basis. But it chose to do so not by leaving options open until a last-minute package deal but by submitting a single negotiating text. This text became the reference or status quo, with the burden of proof being put on the dissenters. More often than not, after the submission of the initial draft articles, the Secretariat in its explanatory comments was able to pit one set of amendments against another, and represent its initial version with only cosmetic alterations. Since, on the other hand, the Praesidium was a collective organ rather than a single presiding member state, it had enough authority to impose its viewpoints as 'consensual' or at least 'the best possible compromise.' This made it harder for the other conventionnels to question its proposals. In this context, potential vetoes were forestalled and actual ones ignored.

These informal tactics worked in reaching a 'consensus,' but they also left a definite 'bad taste' among many delegates, which in the end might have deprived the Praesidium proposal of the kind of legitimacy that a more negotiated text would have achieved. By debating in absolute secrecy, without displaying the textual basis for its own sessions, the Praesidium conveyed the idea that the grounds for its decisions were not purely objective. Moreover, within the Praesidium itself, the Chair acted with an iron fist, controling relations with the Secretariat and often submitting proposals to his colleagues only a few hours before discussion. By requiring that once a topic had been tabled in the Praesidium, members were not allowed to present amendments for debate in the plenary, he sought to signal consensus even where it did not exist. It is little wonder, then, that these provisions never commanded the support of a majority of member states in the Convention, with obvious implications for the IGC.

The failure of the December 2003 Brussels Summit revealed the limits of this strategy. France and Germany strongly supported the Convention text which strengthened their own power. Spain and Poland continued to oppose the new system of weighting votes. A majority of the small states refused to abandon their 'representation' in the Commission and the presidency issue remained thorny. Although a dozen compromises were put forward, the Convention solution adopted by consensus proved fragile and its attempt to surpass the intricate logic of intergovernmental bargains short-lived.

8.5 Conclusion

European integration has been based on a sophisticated concept of shared leadership to manage the inherent tensions between large and small countries. This is particularly reflected in its system of weighed votes in the Council, the role and composition of the EU's supranational institutions, and the rotating presidency which preserved the basic principle of equality among member states, while giving the larger ones a preponderant role. Successive enlargements have made these three mechanisms ever less adapted to the functioning of the Union. As the number of small states has grown much more rapidly than the number of large states, the institutions which guaranteed equality among states have seemed less defendable to the larger ones. By the time the Convention was convened and the EU was about to enlarge to 10 new – mostly small – member states, a new bargain was needed to reconcile the principles of equality among states and proportional democratic representation in the EU.

However, the Convention did not manage to narrow the divide between large and small. Once the EU's institutions were tackled, the Convention soon divided along this line, reproducing a classic feature of former IGCs. Agreeing on a new bargain proved highly difficult. At the center of the conflict was the reform of the rotating Council Presidency which had been the only institutional mechanism in the EU that guarded equality in its pure form and – due to its increasing importance and influence – was much appreciated by the smalls. While most of the large states tried to strengthen the role of the European Council (and thus the role of governments) by providing it with a permanent chair, most of the small states defended the status quo and the rotation principle.

To bridge the fierce differences over the institutional set-up France and Germany put forward a compromise which immediately became the focal point. The reasons for this include their strong material leadership resources and reputation, and the relative coherence of their alliance with the other big states. But, most crucially, their proposal enjoyed support by the Praesidium and its chair responsible for drafting the Constitutional Treaty. This seems to confirm that the ability of actors to successfully provide leadership increases with the level of their involvement in, or access to, the drafting process.

Despite a large opposing small state coalition led by the Benelux countries, their 'numerosity' did not translate into bargaining power. Given that Giscard had defined the majority in terms of population size rather than in absolute terms, the smalls had to resort to leadership strategies involving convincing the big state coalition of the value of rotation and attempting to change big state preferences. However, the logic of the negotiations in the Convention and its outcome were primarily governed by the initial distribution of preferences and their intensity (Magnette and Nicolaïdis 2003). Thus, this strategy was doomed to failure. Strong structural leadership had to be applied in this hard bargaining atmosphere on 'high politics' issues such as the EU's future institutional design to push governments toward an agreement and to ensure that the Convention would not break down. Thus, material leadership resources and influence in the Praesidium, which the smalls lacked, proved most important and the final compromise trumped the interests of the smalls. The large states won the permanent presidency of the European Council, compromising the principle of equality for the EU's most powerful guiding institution, while the smalls won the election of the Commission President by the EP that was also requested by Germany, and managed to preserve some form of rotation in the Council and in the composition of the Commission. Which parts of this compromise may survive after the rejection of the Constitutional Treaty by referenda in France and the Netherlands and whether the new deal will preserve the balances of the Union remains to be seen.

Notes

1. The Commissioners are then to be chosen according to a rotation system based on the principle of equality and reflecting the demographic and geographical range of all states. Treaty of Nice, Protocol on enlargement, Art. 4, Provisions concerning the Commission.
2. In its fullest configuration, the group included all member states and candidate countries except the six big states, Romania and Greece – the latter became an observer when it took on the Council Presidency.
3. Theoretically a majority could have represented a very small minority of the EU's population. In addition, the fact that each component of the Convention was to form part of a final consensus, gave the small states a potential collective veto. Unsurprisingly, small states had supported the idea of a Convention from the outset – they had good reasons to think that the Convention process would strengthen their position compared to the previous IGCs at which their capacity to shape the final outcomes had been marginal with only a theoretical recourse to the veto.
4. It has also accepted more readily than France to be outvoted.
5. Interestingly, Ludlow finds that the Convention which drafted the Charter of Fundamental Rights only succeeded because its chair Roman Herzog was able to dominate the process (see Ludlow 2001a).
6. Their only restriction was not to obstruct any emerging compromise.
7. In most states, one of the 2 national parliamentarians was drawn from the opposition. This did not mean that they did not defend national interests. The British Conservative MPs, for example, were more critical than the representative of the government, helping them to play on the 'domestic constraint.'
8. The precise composition of the Commission was left unclear, but – by mentioning the demographic and geographical diversity of the member states – the French-German contribution implicitly assumed the future size of the Commission would be less than the number of member states.
9. Authors' own translation. See also Finnish Ministerial Committee for EU Affairs, January 17 2003.

10. Contribution franco-néerlandaise à la Convention: renforcement du role de la Commission, 25.3.2003. Available at: http://europa.eu.int/constitution/futurum/ documents/contrib/cont250303_fr.pdf.
11. Available at: http://www.publications.parliament.uk/pa/cm200203/cmselect/ cmeuleg/63-xxvi/3032502.htm.
12. Available at: http://www.europarl.eu.int/europe2004/index_en.htm.
13. 'Reforming the Institutions: Principles and Premises' (CONV 646/03 (March 28 2003)).

9

Cooperative Hegemon, Missing Engine or Improbable Core? Explaining French–German Influence in European Treaty Reform

Colette Mazzucelli, Ulrike Guérot and Almut Metz

9.1 Introduction

While the influence of smaller or newer member states on European Union treaty reform has not always received sufficient attention, the impact of France and Germany, acting either separately or in concert, is the subject of substantial analysis in the literature. The largest and arguably most influential original members of the European Communities are therefore an obvious case to assess the influence of the member states during EU negotiations to revise the founding treaties.

A purposeful analysis that accounts for the causal impact of the actual negotiation process demonstrates that the significant material resources which France and Germany possess individually and when acting in tandem have not consistently translated into a leadership asset or bargaining power at the table. This observation suggests that the occasions on which France and Germany acting together have been able to shift outcomes in treaty reform negotiations to conclude an agreement (efficiency) or to secure their national objectives (distribution) must be analysed more closely.

This chapter questions the extent to which unparalleled material leadership resources allow France and Germany jointly to provide leadership in European treaty reform. In addition, we analyze the impact of the comparative informational advantages which the French–German tandem have at its disposal. We next assess the reputation of French–German institutionalized cooperation, otherwise described as a 'sub-system.' How is this sub-system changing and what impact does this evolution have on French–German leadership and influence in European treaty reform?

Traditionally, when French and German interests in European integration and treaty reform diverged, their leadership translated into bargaining power when compromises were created as 'focal points' around which other member states converged, i.e., Single European Market and Economic and Monetary Union. Schild distinguishes among three possible conditions for French–German leadership: (1) a grand common project (such as EMU), (2) coordinated operational proposals and (3) bilateral compromises that were accepted by the other member states (Schild 2001). In successive intergovernmental conferences (IGCs), French–German leadership was most effective when the two member states were able to bridge the key cleavages in a given issue and create a compromise that neatly bridged the gap. This created opportunities to increase the efficiency of constitutional bargains, as it enabled the parties to find and agree upon agreements closer to the Pareto frontier. In other issue areas, the main result of French–German leadership was on the distributive dimension, where national objectives were achieved, i.e., the pillar structure in the Treaty on European Union (France) and the third pillar, otherwise known as justice and home affairs (Germany). In other words, France and Germany needed to dispute each other's positions in order to avoid fixed positions with which the other member states did not identify. Simply put, French–German disputes were healthy for the tandem, allowing its leadership dynamic to thrive without dominating the rest of the European partners in a dysfunctional way (Guérot 2004).

In recent years, France and Germany have tried to define their cooperation in the context of participation in the 'big three' – along with the United Kingdom – and in so doing are not bringing the other member states along to follow their lead. In this context, traditional French–German leadership has been absent. It has been evident for some considerable time that the engine that allowed European integration to advance is missing. In fact the change from divergence to convergence makes French–German leadership less that of a cooperative hegemon and more of an improbable core in European treaty reform. It is a significant evolution in that France and Germany are less likely in an enlarged Union to challenge the Presidency to provide the alternative leadership that can broker deals to determine the momentum of integration (Schild 2004). Their emphasis of late is on policies that accentuate a tendency to play by their own rules and to privilege national objectives at the expense of Union policies.

It is a paradox of French–German leadership that the two countries, in spite of their divergent preferences, cooperate. Neo-realist analyses predict that France would balance against Germany (Grieco 1995). Why does this not happen? Our analysis demonstrates unequivocally that a balancing dynamic for France is not possible. When acting independently, France is not strong enough to balance simultaneously Germany and to be constructive in its European policy. History explains when and why France acted on its own during the empty chair policy in 1965–66, which led to the Luxembourg

Compromise. This form of Community blackmail was hardly constructive and led to twenty years of paralysis in Community decisionmaking until the European 'relaunch' during the 1980s and the Single European Act, which redressed the institutional dynamics along functionalist lines. In historical perspective until the present day, Germany has not wanted a *Sonderweg*, a policy of going its own way. The Federal Republic does not want to give in to a policy of a 'German Europe,' which explains why successive governments, regardless of political orientation, have relied on France as a partner to act on the European scene.

Clearly it is also essential to understand the changing dynamics of this relationship. In the 15 years following unification, Germany has not been willing to pay the bill for Europe. France cooperates with Germany out of necessity. It is less fortunate as a hegemon. As a country, France is losing influence and does not have the power to achieve its preferred outcomes in Europe without cooperating closely with Germany. This is all the more true in light of its failed referendum on the European Constitutional Treaty, which leaves open the question of Germany's role in the coming years, i.e., is the Federal Republic likely to be more content with the role of the Union's hegemon?

In this chapter, we proceed as follows. First, we discuss what France and Germany have wanted in treaty reforms, then we turn to look at their leadership resources, including the material and comparative informational advantages, reputation and internal capacity France and Germany possessed in consecutive treaty revisions. The impact of the negotiation context follows. The subsequent section applies the leadership model to the negotiation of a number of significant issues on the table during the Nice IGC and the Constitutional Treaty process. This analysis highlights when and why France and Germany, while they were cooperating, were unable to dictate outcomes to other governments, thereby limiting their role as the hegemonic engine of Europe. The closing section relies on our chapter findings to explain when and why France and Germany are likely to make a difference in treaty reform in the changed European context after the rejection of the Constitutional Treaty.

9.2   French and German preferences in EU constitutional negotiations

French preferences

France has traditionally demonstrated a strong preference for an intergovernmental approach to European integration, which allows those countries with strong material resources to preserve their power of veto on matters of vital national interest and to dominate in sensitive areas touching upon sovereignty such as European institutional issues, security/defense and economic/monetary policy (Jabko 2004). Institutional questions are particularly important in that France consistently defends its preference for a strong Council structure and limited influence for the more integrationist institutions, the European Commission and the European Parliament. As one French negotiator explained in the early 1990s, 'qualified majority voting in the Council is preferable to the presence of the Commission everywhere' (Interview 1991).

This French preference is in line with a traditional Gaullist definition of Europe for which the 'empty chair' crisis serves as a reference point in the intergovernmental/supranational debate that has divided member states into camps regarding the question of the future of integration. As French–German cooperation intensified, the tension between France's preference for a more Gaullist approach and Germany's federal vision strained their relationship.

There is also a pragmatic quality in France's preferences. The degree of integration achieved in certain issue areas that are at the heart of national sovereignty, such as the single European currency, was accomplished with strong French support. France has also demonstrated a willingness to support a higher degree of integration over time in specific aspects related to justice and home affairs, particularly in those policy areas like visa policy that were transferred from the third to the European Community pillar during the 1996–97 IGC.

Pragmatism notwithstanding, the famous debate on the treaty structure during the 1990–91 treaty reform process asserted the French preference for pillars that retained an intergovernmental approach to decisionmaking in CFSP and JHA. France retains its preference for a strong Council in which the interests of the larger member states in the Union can dominate policymaking in matters of security and defense. It is also one of the countries that introduced the concept of flexibility on the European treaty reform agenda to allow those member states that want to advance key policies to move ahead. This indicates that France perceives itself as a core member state whose preferences are integral to the decisions taken in treaty reform.

German preferences

German preferences in European treaty reform have undergone an evolution since the 1950s. Successive federal governments have tried to maintain a pro-Europeanist stance that has its origins in the European politics of Chancellor Konrad Adenauer. The generational change introduced by Chancellor Gerhard Schroeder demonstrated a shift in basic principles of German European policy, particularly regarding German sensitivity to relations with the Union's smaller member states. The Schroeder government likewise attempted to retain some of Germany's traditional preferences, like that of strengthening the European Parliament, in the Nice treaty reform process and the more recent negotiations on the European Constitutional Treaty (Thielemann 2004: 359). However, Schroeder, unlike Kohl, lacked the close ties with German representatives in the European Parliament, which are essential to take care of Germany's relationship with that institution.

German preferences have consistently supported a federal vision of Europe's future. The fall of the Berlin Wall and the advent of German unification in 1989–90 led to German support, in tandem with France, for a stronger European political union. The fundamental decision on European economic and monetary union was taken beforehand, however, with Chancellor Kohl articulating the German preference for a single European currency that, in his perception, anchored a united Germany to a 'union' closer to the peoples of Europe, thereby making the integration process 'irreversible.' It was within the treaty reform process on political union throughout 1991 that the Chancellor articulated a number of German preferences, especially on institutional questions, to which the Schroeder government has remained faithful, particularly regarding its commitment to the 2004 enlargement.

What Pedersen defines as Germany's search for 'institutionalized hegemony' (Pedersen 1998) has been thwarted, given the unwillingness of key member states, most notably France, to accept the German institutional preference in support of a federal system that defines Europe's political union. Without France, Germany does not possess sufficient negotiating power to enable it to shape the European institutions to its advantage. The debate on the European Constitutional Treaty as well as the subsequent referendums in France and the Netherlands demonstrated that the 'constituent treaty' preference articulated by Joschka Fischer in his famous speech at Humboldt University, Berlin, in May 2000, proved to be 'a bridge too far' in the history of European integration.

Our analysis reveals another influence that changed German preferences for the type of federal model for Europe's future. Since the mid-1990s, the *Länder* have sought to prevent a gradual loss of power and influence in domestic policymaking *vis-à-vis* the federal government in those issue areas that are specified in the German Basic Law as either shared national-regional or entirely regional competences (Goetz 1996). This power struggle has led the *Länder* to shift their preferences from a 'let us in' approach regarding policymaking in the European Union to a 'keep Europe out' of domestic affairs mentality, particularly regarding the interference of the European Commission in those issue areas, like competition policy and state aid, that are legally defined within their jurisdiction (Thielemann 2004: 364).

9.3   The resources of France and Germany

French material leadership resources

As a large founding member state of the original Communities, France possesses unparalleled material resources, particularly of a political and administrative nature. France's relative economic weight, its demographic growth, and its geopolitical power provide additional resources. France has specific resource advantages in those policy areas where its large military and permanent seat on the United Nations Security Council give the country a strong voice in international affairs.

German material leadership resources

In contrast, Germany possesses relatively less resources in that its administration is smaller and more decentralized among those representing the large member states. Politically, the Federal Republic acquired sovereignty after unification; yet as the country with the largest number of neighbors on the Continent, Germany does not aspire to the roles played by France or Great Britain within the European Union.

Traditionally, as the strongest economy in Europe, Germany was able and willing to use material advantages, particularly its financial resources, to provide side payments to other member states as 'carrots' in support of German preferences in European treaty reform. The strength of German financial leverage was evident in 1988 when Kohl agreed to use German material resources to double the size of structural funds as a means of enhancing poorer Member States' participation in the single European market. In exchange for the Spanish agreement during the 1990–91 treaty reform negotiations, Kohl also provided German financial backing for cohesion funds to the 'Club Med' states – Spain, Portugal, Greece and Ireland.

In the aftermath of unification, Germany has reconsidered its financial contributions to Europe. The willingness of its leaders to use side payments as a material resource to convince other member states to follow the German negotiating line is no longer evident. This change is directly related to the different priorities of Chancellors Helmut Kohl and his successor, Gerhard Schroeder, as well as the different economic situation in Germany owing to the heavy financial burden of unification. Kohl knew there was a price to pay for the compromises he sought to make with France to push for more integration. Under Kohl, Germany's contributions to the European Union's budget made the country the largest net contributor (Dempsey 2005).

French and German material leadership resources

The preponderance of structural resources that France and Germany possess offers the tandem unparalleled opportunities to 'go-it-alone' with two caveats that are in line with the *asymmetric interdependence approach* (Beach 2002): in the initiatives taken to lead Europe, France and Germany are dependent on European agreements in order to achieve their preferred outcomes. In the case of the internal market, the Euro, and the CFSP, the duo were dependent on the integration dynamic to introduce new policy initiatives that would not have been conceivable in a purely national context, i.e., completion of the single market, nor achievable without the rationale of the European project, i.e., the loss of the Deutsche Mark, which embodied for the national population the stability and success of the postwar Federal Republic. France and Germany, moreover, need the willingness, and subsequent quick support, of other member states to follow their line.

In the case of Schengen, for example, which created a European space free of internal physical borders, France and Germany promoted a key European agreement not by depending on all of the other member states; only reliance on Benelux was necessary. The success of the motor, however, was in its intrinsic ability to drive the train, including most of the other cars, on the European track.

Asymmetric interdependence posits that 'the strongest actor on paper is not necessarily the strongest in practice'; what is crucial for actor power is how dependent an actor is upon an agreement (Beach 2002). This position to explain actor power is illuminating in the German case. Kohl's decision to give up the national currency, the Deutsche Mark, in favor of the Euro was only grudgingly accepted by most Germans during the course of the 1990s. They believed it weakened a country already reeling from the impact of national unification. Kohl's commitment to the Euro, and German dependency on agreement, intended to make the European integration process irreversible, linking Germany's destiny with that of France and the other European member states. Yet, fundamental differences existed between a France committed to equality with Germany in monetary affairs and a German partner determined not to sacrifice price stability or risk inflation for the sake of imposed deadlines to achieve monetary union. The creation of the Euro was notable for the sharp tensions in the relationship between France and Germany starting during the period 1996–97. The minimalist reform that Amsterdam made possible was quickly overshadowed by the tandem's struggles on EMU and the employment chapter. Observers of the European scene observe Germany's lack of 'engagement and input', the progressive emphasis on the intergovernmental approach in its EU policy, and an excessive reliance on France 'without getting that much in return that could benefit Europe' (Dempsey 2005).

French and German comparative informational advantages

France and Germany have very different organizational approaches and institutional structures to handle European treaty negotiations. The French are much more centralized in the internal workings of their administration in contrast to the Germans, whose administrative apparatus must cope with the difficulties of Federal–State, *Bund–Länder*, relations. In Paris, European treaty reform is in the hands of very few national civil servants in the *Quai d'Orsay*, the French foreign ministry. This administrative coterie of persons, who are usually trained at the *Ecole Nationale d'Administration* (ENA), one of France's elite schools, makes up part of the core of its administrative resources. A small number of highly qualified officials influential in treaty reform subsequently move from Paris to positions in Brussels. These officials provide an extension of French structural resources and establish the close linkages, national capital–Brussels, which distinguish the Union's hybrid system of policy governance.

French negotiators take pride in the introduction of a few key goals, which are consistently defended over time with the aim of persuading the others to agree, i.e., the importance of the European Council at the apex of the Union's system, or the need for a greater voice for national parliaments in European integration. Further, their energy, intellect and time are devoted exclusively to maintaining a strong French presence during IGC negotiations. As successive IGCs took place, French negotiators relied more on the material advantages that France possesses vis-à-vis the other member states; e.g. by forcing its own negotiating line while in the Chair during the Nice reform (see chapter 2).

As the largest member state, Germany has significant administrative resources although its civil servants in the Foreign Office are not as numerous as those of either France or the United Kingdom. The federal government also has to contend with the civil servant representations of each of the *Länder*, which are increasingly active in the treaty reform process.

Reputation: the French–German 'sub-system' and its discontents

France and Germany share a history of enmity as well as a specific institutionalized partnership (Krotz 2002), which led one respected observer to identify the unique nature of their relationship as a Community 'subsystem,' based on its 'intensity, duration, formalization, effectiveness and acceptability' (de Schoutheete 1990). This 'sub-system' has changed fundamentally over the years. In terms of leadership, which is defined as the translation of political energy into constructive outcomes in integration, there are distinct periods of which we are cognizant. After 2001, a dysfunctional French–German relationship emerged. In the earlier period of creative dynamism, other member states were able to locate their own interests within the space that France and Germany, the engine of integration, created in order to move the IGC negotiation process forward. In recent years, other member states perceive France and Germany as an inward-looking couple, 'a locomotive without cars' (Guérot 2004) that is more concerned with its own bilateral dynamics than with the larger integration process.

The recent reality was one in which Chancellor Schroeder's Germany assumed a co-leadership role with France, much to the consternation of the smaller member states. This is particularly sensitive to the extent that IGC negotiations post-Maastricht were concerned primarily with the adaptation of the original institutional system to accommodate an enlargement process that disrupts European order. The co-leadership role identified in this chapter is one that increasingly called an outdated, status quo oriented institutional set-up into question. In this role, France and Germany were perceived by the smaller member states as exercising 'cooperative hegemony' as their 'sub-system' deviated increasingly from the rules to establish parity among the member states within the larger European system. In this context, the degree to which 'Germany has consistently pursued a grand strategy of cooperative hegemony in which France and European integration have played an essential role' must be analyzed (Pedersen 1998).

This point is especially relevant in terms of a Community sub-system because successive IGC processes illustrate an inverse relationship between German willingness to assume a co-leadership role with France which ignores the interests of the smaller member states, and the level of acceptability of that role by those countries. Rightly or wrongly, France and Germany have been perceived as anti-American and anti-liberal, as they claimed moral leadership of the Union without complying with its rules. The mistrust this perpetuated *vis-à-vis* the tandem among the other countries is particularly significant in a larger Union of 25 that includes 19 smaller member states.

Internal capacity

The ability to mobilize resources, or in other words the capacity to actually provide leadership, is dependent upon the internal organization of the actor (Dimitrakopoulos and Kassim 2004). Factors included here that are relevant include the structure of the given political system, including the number of 'veto points,' and the relative power of different domestic actors.

The President of the Fifth Republic is meant under the design of the Constitution of 1958 to have unfettered power in the negotiation of European treaty reform. It is his responsibility to define French preferences and control all the levers of the state apparatus that are implicated in the treaty revision process. During times of cohabitation, when the French President hailed from one political party and his Prime Minister represented the opposition, there were tensions in domestic politics that made it difficult for the government to mobilize its resources in order to provide leadership. This impacted on France's leadership during the Single European Act (SEA), Amsterdam and Nice intergovernmental conferences.

In the federal system exemplified by Germany, a power struggle evolved in the 1990s between the federation and the *Länder*. The *Länder* continue to demand a stronger voice in the EU treaty negotiation process. In their view, many of the competences transferred to Brussels by the federal government are their prerogatives (Beuter 2001: 101). These pressures resulted in the introduction of Article 23 in the Basic Law, which gives the *Länder* in the *Bundesrat* a veto power over the transfer of sovereign powers. The introduction of a strong domestic veto point has, however, created many problems for German European policymaking (Mazzucelli 2001).

The *Länder*, which retain significant powers in key policy areas under the Federal Constitution, the Basic Law, demand increasingly greater influence in the European constitutional treaty process over time and wield the power of the veto to block treaty revisions. Since the agreement on Article 23 in the Basic Law as a result of the Treaty on European Union, Germany has struggled with a domestic European policymaking problem (Mazzucelli

1999). In each successive IGC, the *Länder* have become more prominent veto players, and have increasingly constrained German representatives.

This situation has consistently led to conflicting positions, most notably, during the 1996–97 conference when former Chancellor Helmut Kohl pushed for more qualified majority voting (QMV) and was blocked by a complicated internal context (Mazzucelli 2001; Guérot 2004). Germany has consistently tried to find a solution at the European level for its difficulties with the *Länder* within the constitutional treaty process, thereby introducing a systemic problem. This evolution is particularly relevant to the volume's analysis of the extent to which materially strong actors like France and Germany set the outer bounds for agreement through the provision of structural leadership.

The French Nice negotiating style is therefore inconceivable for the Germans because of their internal constraints (chapter 2). In Bonn, and later Berlin, the decentralized nature of the federal system means that numerous ministries have to be involved in the internal discussions on treaty reform negotiations, depending on the issue in question. A complicated interministerial coordination is required. In the German system, almost 90 per cent of the energy and work in European treaty reform negotiations is devoted to thorough internal preparation of the German negotiating line, which is supported by a larger view of the goals of specific domestic actors, the *Gesamtkonzept* (Smyser 2004). Germany, the largest Union member state and the one surrounded by the most neighbors, also holds informal, and at times secret, meetings at the ambassador or second-in-charge level with other member states during the IGCs, as documented in the foreign office's archives.

9.4   French–German leadership in European constitutional negotiations

The Nice IGC Negotiations

In stark contrast to the earlier IGCs, the situation before and during the Nice European Council signaled a major crisis in French–German relations. The engine failed to play its role in paving the way for an enlarged Union with regard to financing or the future institutional structure. During the Berlin European Council in spring 1999, the German Presidency did not manage to overcome French resistance to Common Agricultural Policy (CAP) reform. The Nice IGC, which aimed to prepare the Union's institutions and procedures for the upcoming accessions, turned out, on some issues, to be a French–German battlefield.

The IGC agenda was limited, but extremely controversial: the future size and composition of the Commission; the system of weighed votes for qualified majority voting (QMV) in the Council, the extension of QMV and, at a later stage of negotiations, the modification of enhanced cooperation.

To start with the future size of the Commission, France and Germany, for different reasons, supported the model of a reduced College that did not mirror the number of member states. The French position on the Commission stands in line with its intergovernmental approach to reduce that institution's influence and status in the eyes of the member states. Germany, in contrast, sees in a limited College with a strong President an opportunity to strengthen the Commission, which is part of the German supranational approach. Although inspired by different approaches, France and Germany agreed on their objective to reduce the number of European Commissioners. As a first step, both countries were willing to give up their second Commissioner for that purpose. However, France and Germany were among the few members that wanted to go even further and accepted losing a permanent French or German Commissioner (Giering 2001). The French strategy might have been that as one of the largest member states, even without its 'own' Commissioner, it would still be relatively superior to the smaller members. For this same reason, smaller countries insisted on one Commissioner for each member state in order to maintain their voice in Brussels' supranational College.

Since the issue was extremely controversial during the work at the Preparatory Group level, the French Presidency decided in September 2000 to deal with the size of the Commission only during informal meetings (Metz and Möller 2001). The big versus small cleavage widened when the larger members presented a joint initiative for a limited Commission and a principle of rotation in mid-October. Even among the larger members, there was no consensus on the details of the provisions, above all the question of a permanent representation of the large members and the details for rotation, alphabetical or geographical order. The French Presidency responded by taking the issue off the agenda. When it presented its first synthesis paper in the beginning of November, the most controversial issues, among them the size and internal organization of the Commission, where almost completely excluded. The French Presidency considered waiting for the Nice European Council, where conditions for a solution would be better.

The compromise on the Commission that was forged in Nice did not take French and German preferences fully into account. Following the smaller members' position, the heads of state and government agreed to maintain one Commissioner for each member state until the Union expanded to 27 members. Only then would the number of Commissioners be limited and a system of equal rotation established with a veto for each member on the details of the provisions. The larger members also had to give up their second Commissioner. A success from a German perspective, qualified majority was introduced in the election of the Commission President, a position also strengthened in its organizational competences.

It is pointless to ask if and how France and Germany could have modeled an outcome closer to their preferences in Nice. Yet one can observe that

Germany and France's positions were probably too similar regarding the Commission. In the French–German case, consensus is often not the clue for success. To convince other member states to join a French–German initiative usually requires overcoming differences and presenting a compromise. On the Commission issue, there was no suitable dynamic available for the engine to succeed.

With regard to the distribution of votes in the Council, the picture was different. France and Germany strongly disagreed on this issue. France did not want to give up parity with Germany. Germany, in contrast, wanted a higher number of votes to reflect its larger population. Whereas France saw this issue as a question of power, Germany insisted on the aspect of democratic legitimacy (Schild 2001). France publicly stated on numerous occasions during its Presidency that it would not accept a decoupling from Germany. As a result, the *marge de manoeuvre* for France in the Presidency was limited. Here France played a double game. As Chair it argued to the smaller and medium-sized members that a new distribution of votes according to demographic criteria was necessary. At the same time, to Germany, France argued that demography was not accepted as a relevant criterion. This example supports Tallberg's findings in this volume: the French Presidency exploited its informational and procedural advantages quite successfully to support its preferences. Germany pointed out that it would accept either a re-weighting of votes according to 'demographic facts' or the introduction of a new system of voting – a double majority of member states and population – which would also benefit Germany as the largest member state. Germany might have expected to be able to convince France of the double majority as the lesser evil since it excluded the contentious distribution of votes (Janning 2001). If this was the German consideration, it failed, as an overly complicated triple majority of votes, member states and population was introduced into the Nice Treaty.

On the surface the solution on the Council voting system was a success for France since voting parity with Germany was maintained. The two countries, along with Italy and the United Kingdom, were allocated 29 votes each. At the same time, France had to accept a demographic criterion that reflected Germany's preference: QMV had to cover not only a majority of votes and member states, but also had to overcome the hurdle of 62 per cent of the Union's population. One might argue from a French perspective that the new QMV provisions were a greater success for France than for Germany: the number of votes was a more visible provision than the demographic hurdle. The introduction of the demographic criterion though was a first step toward the double majority that was finally introduced during the Constitutional Treaty negotiations. The French *victoire* in Nice was, therefore, only a short-term success.

The third issue, the extension of qualified majority voting, was a shared French–German objective. On the eve of enlargement this was seen as a means to guarantee the effectiveness of the decisionmaking procedures. Even though this was agreed in a broader perspective by all member states, when it came to details, i.e. the specific cases to transfer voting to qualified majority in the Council, the picture was different. The French Presidency played an ambivalent role. Since it refused to accept QMV voting in the field of trade agreements on services and intellectual property to protect the French film and culture industry (Deloche-Gaudez and Lequesne 2001), France was not able to put pressure on other member states that also had their respective preferences. The specific fields of application of QMV voting therefore remained extremely controversial in the second half of 2000 (Metz and Möller 2001). Britain insisted on unanimity in social and tax policy, whereas Germany and France jointly claimed QMV in taxation. Spain was able to postpone the decision on the structural funds until 2013, another defeat for Germany. Germany successfully claimed unanimity in asylum and immigration policy, at least for agreement on a basic concept, which might then be followed by QMV. The Treaty of Nice reflects these preferences in its patchwork style on QMV. The nature of the issue had resisted a systematic approach to QMV and made leadership almost impossible.

In summary, several obstacles prevented the engine from gathering steam on the Nice institutional triangle: extremely controversial institutional issues, consensus on the reform of the Commission which prevented the tandem from bridging the cleavage on the issue, dissent on the distribution of weighed votes, a French Presidency exploiting its institutional perogatives for its own private gain, and disagreements about extending QMV.

On the fourth major IGC issue, enhanced cooperation, the picture is slightly different. The introduction of enhanced cooperation in the Treaty in Amsterdam was a main interest of France and Germany. It is not surprising that these two countries supported modifications on enhanced cooperation, which was difficult to use given the restrictive nature of the Amsterdam provisions (Janning 2001). The French proposal on enhanced cooperation, presented in early September 2000 (CONFER 4766/00), had changed the minds of critical members by underlining that the instrument was meant to be an 'integrating factor' rather than a means to establish a 'hard core' within the Union.

The technical modifications of enhanced cooperation – the reduction of the number of member states required from half of the members to eight regardless of the total number, the extension of enhanced cooperation to the field of CFSP (except for military aspects) and the elimination of the veto in the first and third pillars – can be interpreted as a success for the French Presidency that was clearly supported by the German delegation. Was it an example, however, of French–German leadership? As the new provisions on enhanced cooperation were not extremely revolutionary, the support of the other members was not difficult to organize. There was no real need for leadership on the issue. Enhanced cooperation in Nice is therefore much more a success of French–German agenda-setting in a long-term perspective than an example of leadership during this specific IGC. In the 2000 speeches on the Union's finality, Foreign Minister Fischer and President Chirac had both discussed the future role of flexibility (Janning 2001; Schild 2000). Their goal was to shape the future by suggesting possible alternative institutional options for the Union's evolution. Even though France wanted the finality debate to stay outside the IGC agenda, this parallel discourse demonstrated leadership by France and Germany.

Did the French role as President during July–December 2000 impact on the leadership abilities of the tandem during the Nice IGC? A Presidency possesses leadership resources and institutional powers that the other parties do not have (see chapter 2). These resources are meant to facilitate a brokerage role in negotiations. Yet, in the French–German case, the French Presidency blocked the tandem since it was suddenly transformed into a tandem of unequal partners. France vis-à-vis its most important ally possessed comparative informational advantages and institutional powers during the end-phase of negotiations. Since equality is an important source of mutual trust, the tandem was challenged by this fact. When, in addition, France exploited its advantage to further its national interests, confidence as the basis for a successful joint leadership was gone. An incoherent strategy not only affected France's reputation as an 'honest broker'; it also affected French–German relations in Nice.

Is the tandem able to provide leadership if one of the partners holds the Presidency? We argue that the French–German relationship could hardly stand this degree of asymmetry. Since the Presidency is supposed to be neutral, listening to other member states during the months preparing a draft agreement, a public French–German position, beyond 'we have agreed to agree' would have damaged the French reputation as an objective Presidency. By playing its own game behind closed doors, the French choice to 'go-it-alone' during the decisive days in Nice was definitely the more successful one at first glance. Yet, over time the French strategy in Nice proved questionable in terms of general acceptability and the stability of the agreement reached there as well as the rather negative perception by the other member states of France's use of its influence in the Chair to broker a treaty close to its own preferences.

The Constitutional Treaty process

The Declaration on the Future of the European Union was introduced through a German–Italian initiative to the Treaty of Nice, claiming a Union-wide debate on four aspects: the separation of competences, the future of the non-binding EU Charter of Fundamental Rights, the simplification of the Treaties, and the role of the national parliaments in the Union. At that time, it was thought to be quite improbable that four years later the Union would have a single-text constitutional treaty.

Since Maastricht, and most obviously in Nice, relations between Berlin and Paris underwent a period of exhaustion (Schild 2003; Zervakis van Gossler 2003). General elections occurred during 2002 in both countries, which also ended the paralyzing period of French cohabitation. On the eve of the 40th anniversary of the *Élysée* Treaty, and at the time of the common position of the two countries regarding the Iraq conflict, French–German cooperation was revived through a Schröder–Chirac initiative. French–German relations depend to a large extent on the personal commitment of the political leaders (Janning 2003: 329). Although the French–German relationship is institutionalized on different levels, it cannot be taken for granted that the tandem will actually work.

The French and German governments played a comparatively passive role in the early work of the European Convention. Only in late 2002 did the tandem mechanism start to work when the two governments replaced their representatives in the Convention with their foreign ministers, Joschka Fischer and Dominique de Villepin. France and Germany formed a coalition on a number of issues above all institutional questions. De Villepin, in a speech in Marseille in December 2002, supported, for the first time during the Convention, strengthening the European Parliament and the Commission in the Constitutional Treaty, a position that Germany had claimed several times before (Guérot 2004). During November 2002 and January 2003, Fischer and de Villepin presented four joint contributions to the Convention: a paper on ESDP (CONV 422/02), a JHA proposal (CONV 435/02), a joint statement on economic governance (CONV 470/02), and a concept on the Union's institutional architecture (CONV 489/03). The contribution on institutions, including proposals on a permanent presidency and the Commission, gained much attention because negotiations were blocked on these questions. A coalition of larger member states supporting the so-called 'ABC proposal,' an initiative by José Maria Aznar and Tony Blair for an elected presidency of the European Council that was quickly joined by Chirac in May 2002, came into dispute with the small and medium sized members, which were united in defending the Benelux proposal (analysed in Chapter 6).

From a German perspective, a coalition with the Benelux countries on institutions would have been a promising strategy. These countries are traditionally much closer to the German position than France (Schild 2003). Germany decided, however, to ally with France. This strategy was in part a reaction to French activities rather than a proactive 'choice for the tandem'. Since France had quickly supported the 'ABC proposal,' reviving the tandem implied, from a German perspective, hindering the French from forging an intergovernmental set-up of institutions in a coalition of large members that Germany – supporting strong supranational institutions and still known as an advocate of the smaller member states – could have only joined with high opportunity costs. Furthermore, joining the Benelux-led coalition would have meant for Germany to support one Commissioner per member state.

This position was supported by the smaller members, but definitely not by Germany. Finally, Germany needed French support in order to come out of its isolation during the Iraq crisis: a joint contribution, including ideas on ESDP, would demonstrate French–German partnership.

From a French perspective, the choice for Germany was a strategic one. As there seemed to be no way to overcome the cleavage between the ABC and Benelux proposals, coalescing with Germany provided a way out. An intergovernmentalist French approach, inherent in the ABC proposal, could be reconciled – at least on the surface – with a supranational German one. France and Germany would be able to take the lead in a deadlocked situation that France alone would have not been able to overcome, with both countries demonstrating their leadership abilities even in the EU-25. In that sense, the choice for the tandem can be interpreted in the context of the enlargement process. As the constitutional treaty process was the first grand project of the enlarged Union, France and Germany felt the need to demonstrate their alliance in a Union that would soon become more heterogeneous.

Public and media attention for the *Élysée* celebrations on 22 January 2003 provided a good opportunity for French–German reconciliation. The French–German proposal on institutions presented to the Convention on 16 January 2003 probably gained more attention and credibility in the context of those celebrations than it would have otherwise.

In their contribution to the Convention, France and Germany followed the ABC proposal in the way that they also suggested a permanent presidency for the European Council, elected by qualified majority for five years or 2.5 years with a possible second term, to guarantee stability and continuity within that institution. As a counterpart to the President of the European Council, France and Germany claimed to strengthen the President of the European Commission by reorganizing that position's election and strengthening its internal competences. The President of the Commission, following the French-German proposal, had to be elected in light of the elections to the European Parliament by QMV in Parliament and then confirmed by the European Council, again by QMV. This proposal reversed the procedure of the Treaty of Nice and aimed at providing greater legitimacy to the Commission President.

Some analysts underline that the French–German initiative was a typical compromise, as it mixed a French sovereignty-intergovernmental stereotype and a German federal-Community oriented approach (Dehousse *et al.* 2003). In its hybrid structure though, it was a masterpiece of French–German diplomacy (Guérot 2004). France accepted *nolens volens* a stronger Commission and Parliament. On the Commission, there might have been a shift in the traditional French position since France understood that for issues like economic governance, which France frequently asks the EU to create, might better be realized with a strong Commission. Germany supported the elected Presidency even though it was still extremely controversial amongst the coalition of the small and medium-sized members.

The French–German institutional compromise overcame the deadlock on the permanent Presidency, but it was not able to close the gap between larger and smaller members: the preceding chapter argues that the French–German proposal was a 'hegemonic compromise,' which successfully laid the ground for the final provisions on the Presidency for three reasons: privileged access for France and Germany as materially strong member states to the Praesidium; President Giscard d'Estaing in his position as President and his support for the proposal; the additional backing of other large members, namely Spain and the UK, and their reputation as credible architects of EU integration. In addition, we underline that the strength of the tandem's proposal derived from the fact that it was a compromise, which made it at least on the surface more acceptable for the negotiating parties.

In contrast to the preceding chapter, we argue that by the beginning of 2003 the French–German tandem had already started to lose its reputation. During the *Élysée* celebrations France and Germany publicly rejected their support for a military intervention in Iraq. Even though this French–German position was less a result of shared preferences than specific circumstances (Vogel 2004), the joint stance provoked the so-called 'Letter of the Eight' that split the Union. Germany and France as traditionally strong CFSP supporters were criticized for having damaged the 'European voice'. The reputation of the tandem as acting for the benefit of EU integration was challenged even more in the following months as the two countries, both facing economic decline, raised questions about the Stability and Growth Pact. In so doing, France and Germany lost more authority. The tandem nevertheless proved to be quite strong during the IGC, which suggests that reputation is not an extremely relevant criterion for successful structural leadership, echoing other findings in this volume (see chapter 2).

In this sense, the issue of defining QMV is an interesting case for analysis. Since the conclusion of the Convention in July 2003, France and Germany had been united in the mantra of consolidating the draft Treaty, including the provisions on the new system of qualified majority voting. From a German perspective, double majority, which included a demographic criterion, responded to German preferences. Germany, by far the largest member state, was, for the first time, offered representation in the Council proportional to its size. The same was true for France as the third largest member state. Yet the French were nevertheless challenged by the new system of voting. The double majority, which dropped the distribution of votes, implied giving up parity with Germany in the Council. Parity with Germany was from the very beginning of European integration a strong pillar of French European Policy. It was indeed surprising that the French government remained silent on this issue. Why did France accept a decoupling from Germany? We argue that the French farewell to the system of weighed votes had already begun in Nice, when France had to accept the demographic criterion to QMV for the benefit of its larger neighbor, Germany.

During the IGC, only Poland and Spain, who benefited disproportionately from the Nice provisions in that both countries were given a rather high number of votes compared to their demographic size, defended going back to the Nice system. Support for the Nice formula would have been a predictable failure for France, and 'double majority' was a system that France, as well as Germany, could live with as one of the largest member states. Clearly though, accepting double majority meant that France had to give up one of its strong preferences, which was hardly discussed in the French press and public during the constitutional treaty process.

1Can we identify leadership by France and Germany on the new QMV formula, even when taking the collapse of negotiations in December 2003 into account? If we define leadership following the volume's theoretical framework, we can also expect leadership in a situation that from an integrationist perspective was disastrous since leadership does *not* necessarily imply Pareto-improvement. In our understanding, leadership is rather defined as any action one actor takes to guide or direct the behavior of other actors toward a certain goal. A complete failure of the IGC was certainly not a French–German interest. The two countries wanted the double majority for an effective Council though. On the eve of enlargement and the negotiations on the Financial Perspective 2007–2013, they also wanted to use this issue as a warning to Poland and other new members to respect 'the rules of the game.' Lastly, France and Germany apparently felt they had to show their muscles toward Poland and Spain because these countries had supported the 'Letter of the Eight.' In this context, to run the risk of collapse during the negotiations was also an act of French–German self-assertion in the expanding Union. It is often argued that Poland and Spain, as well as a bleak Italian Presidency, were responsible for breaking off the negotiations because they did not accept the 'double majority' and wanted to go back to Nice. However, France and Germany, as demonstrated previously, also successfully played their game. In June 2004, the IGC was finally concluded under the Irish Presidency with a modification of the provisions on QMV as presented by the Convention. Hurdles were raised, yet given that the double structure itself was not touched, there was no return to the triple formula of Nice (see chapter 4).

The years 2002–03 witnessed a successful revival of the tandem after the disastrous performance in Nice, and were also a turning point for the tandem's role. France and Germany had caused the split during the Iraq war, lost credibility on the Stability and Growth Pact, snubbed the smaller members on the permanent Presidency issue, thereby widening the big versus small cleavage, and had failed to use the Weimar Triangle to integrate Poland on the double majority.

9.5   Closing remarks

What can we expect from the French–German tandem? In 2005, both countries have seen fundamental domestic changes. France was the first member state where a referendum on the Constitutional Treaty failed. This was followed by a crisis of government and a replacement of the French prime minister. President Chirac emerged from this political earthquake as a weak monarch. On the other side of the Rhine, Chancellor Schroeder decided to call for early general elections in autumn 2005 because of a series of regional elections lost by the Social Democrats, which culminated in a historic defeat of his party in North-Rhine Westphalia just days before the French referendum.

After an autumn of political turbulence following the German elections in September 2005, a new coalition government of Christian and Social Democrats ('Grand Coalition') was created under the leadership of Christian Democratic Chancellor Angela Merkel in November 2005.

What are the implications for the leadership abilities of the tandem? Will the French–German locomotive without cars be further weakened, leaving a leadership vacuum in the enlarged Union? Or will the new political leaders bring a different leadership introducing dynamism to European integration again, including an improvement in Transatlantic relations?

The new German government will be one of continuity rather than change with regard to French–German relations and European construction. The German commitment to the US is likely to be normalized under Chancellor Merkel. After the French *'non'* to the European Constitutional Treaty, Germany must take the lead to guide France out of the political chaos the referendum created. The essential point is to get back the triggering effect French–German relations always had for the whole Union instead of the present state of affairs in which other member states reject joint leadership by the 'privileged partnership.'

It is, however, questionable whether the Merkel coalition government will be able to create a new and positive dynamic for the French–German engine. In a way, France and Germany remain mentally committed to the European debate of the 1990s, the *'Europe de Charlemagne,'* the small Europe, and its debate about a core EU. Their fundamental choice is to embrace a modernized discourse with a strong emphasis on geo-strategy or to remain the Union's missing engine. The debate to resurrect the European Constitutional Treaty, which emerged under the Austrian Presidency in 2006, is likely to continue under the German Presidency in 2007. This emphasis, however, is contingent on potential changes in government resulting from elections in France and the Netherlands during spring 2007. This evolution may well provide one indication of the possible success of French–German initiatives in the short-to-medium term. To date, there have been fundamental differences in views as to how the Constitutional Treaty may be salvaged. The Federal Republic advocates an approach that keeps the Treaty structure intact. This is in contrast to France, which prefers to approve only specific Treaty articles that the country believes necessary for the Union to function effectively.

This chapter's analysis concludes that joint leadership by the Union's two largest member states is not likely to challenge that of the Presidency, given the divergences in their fundamental preferences. Their effectiveness as an engine in the integration process is dependent on the extent to which France and Germany address the dysfunctional nature of their relationship. In other words, can they provide the negotiating space to allow other member states to locate their own interests in the compromise solutions the duo identify, thereby creating a focal point around which the others converge? This leadership question is a serious one. Despite incremental progress, a long 'muddling-through period' before French–German relations regain their traditional *élan*, and the EU gets back on track, is possible. During this period, their leadership is likely to remain that of an improbable core in Europe's larger Union.

This is as much a significant development for the future as a break with the past. Given the challenges the EU has to face, consolidation of its political system after the 2004 'big bang' enlargement as well as the future expansion to Romania, Bulgaria, Croatia, and Turkey, and identifying a solution to move beyond the rejection of the Constitutional Treaty, leadership which exercises a triggering effect toward convergence is urgently needed by European institutions and member states.

10
Britain and the European Union: A Laggard Leader?

Alasdair Blair

10.1 Introduction

Numerous studies have portrayed Britain as an 'awkward,' 'reluctant' and 'semi-detached' European Union (EU) member state that has been 'at odds with Europe' (see, inter alia, George 1998; Gowland and Turner 2000; Wallace 1997). It has even been suggested that Britain is an 'allergic European' (Aspinwall 2004). Such views have been shaped by Britain's unwillingness to participate in the initial steps toward European integration in the 1950s and its inability to offer wholehearted commitment to the European project since its accession in 1973. A review of British 'awkwardness' since 1973 includes the 1974 renegotiation of terms of membership, the 1975 referendum on the renegotiated terms, the debate over the budget contributions that was eventually settled at the 1984 Fontainebleau European Council, hostility toward the development of a European social policy and Economic and Monetary Union, the 1996 policy of noncooperation over the ban on British beef, and the inability of the Labour government led by Tony Blair to endorse fully the single currency. A direct implication of these developments is that Britain has often been perceived to be on the sidelines of key policy developments at the European level.

This chapter explores a particular dimension of Britain's European policy by focusing on government behavior in the intergovernmental conference (IGC) negotiations that have resulted in the Single European Act (SEA), Treaty on European Union, Treaty of Amsterdam, Treaty of Nice, and finally the Constitutional Treaty. The chapter argues that despite the hesitancy of British governments to offer a wholehearted commitment to European integration, Britain has achieved considerable success in obtaining satisfactory outcomes in IGC negotiations. In taking this approach, the chapter emphasizes Britain's unique position within the EU and focuses on the extent to which it can be considered 'a laggard leader.'

The chapter proceeds as follows. First, it examines the policy preferences that British governments have tended to advocate in IGC negotiations. In particular, it pays attention to the impact that the domestic context has had in shaping government behavior. Second, it discusses the general leadership resources that British governments have brought to the IGC arena. These resources are wide-ranging and include such factors as the influence afforded by the size of the British economy, its status as a major security power, its position as a bridge between Europe and the United States, the diplomatic resources attained from the presence that it maintains in most countries of the world, and the strategic role that it plays in a number of international organizations, including the Commonwealth, the UN and NATO. In addition, Britain's ability to bring pressure to bear upon IGC negotiations is shaped by its own material and informational resources that are influenced by the work of relevant government departments and Cabinet committees. Third, the chapter investigates the strategies that British governments have used in IGC negotiations. Apart from a tendency to adopt an awkward negotiating style, British governments have regularly challenged the transfer of sovereignty to the European level. That is not to say that successive British governments have been unwilling to compromise. The chapter then goes on, finally, to assess the relative influence of British governments in IGC negotiations and to explore why governments have been willing to compromise on some issues rather than others.

10.2 Understanding British preferences in treaty reform

Let us first look briefly at the factors that serve to underpin the formation of British foreign policy preferences in EU negotiations. In line with other member states, British negotiating preferences in IGC negotiations have for the most part been shaped by the domestic political context. This has primarily taken the form of the views advanced within the Palace of Westminster and the views held by the electorate. That British negotiating preferences have often been in contrast to other member states has been influenced by two key factors.

First, the lack of overwhelming support for European integration among an electorate which 'neither seem to see themselves as, nor to feel, particularly European' (Geddes 2004: 210). In the most recent European Commission 'Eurobarometer' survey gauging pan-EU public opinion, Britain had the lowest level of support for EU membership among the 25 member states, with only 38 per cent of the population considering the EU to be a 'good thing' (see Figure 10.1). And when asked the question of whether they felt that Britain had benefited from EU membership, less than 50 per cent of the population believed that membership had been beneficial (see Figure 10.2).

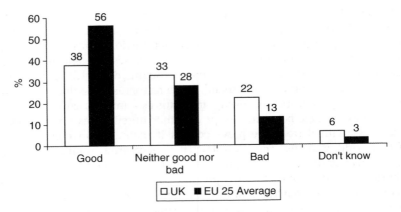

Figure 10.1   Support for European Union membership (%)
Source: Data from *Eurobarometer Standard Report 62*, December 2004, p. 8.

Although it can be seen from Figures 10.1 and 10.2 that there is a lack
of support for European integration in British politics, the reality of over 30
years of membership is that Britain has become even more integrated into
the EU. Whereas at the outset European policy was concerned with a limited
number of subjects, such as external trade, competition policy, agriculture
and financial and budgetary affairs, many more policies have arisen, especially in the last two decades. A direct effect of these developments is that
there are few issues of a national interest that are not also of a European
interest, and vice versa. Within government, this is reflected in the reality

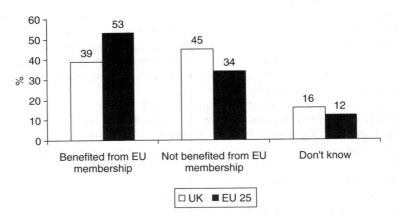

Figure 10.2   Benefit from European Union membership (%)
Source: Data from *Eurobarometer Standard Report 62*, December 2004, p. 10.

that every department is somehow affected by policy developments at the European level and that domestic parliamentarians are regularly involved in debating and shaping policy that has a European dimension. Yet, despite the fact that Britain has become more intertwined with the EU, there has been a conspicuous absence of a consistent policy towards European integration by the two main political parties.

The second key factor that has therefore shaped the negotiating preferences advanced by governments has been the impact of party politics, whereby there has been a lack of a common viewpoint on European integration across all political parties. The main components here have been:

- *The absence of a consistent European policy in each of the two main political parties.* The broadly pro-European policy of Tony Blair's government contrasts with Labour's opposition to European integration in the 1970s and early 1980s. This was marked by it contesting the 1972 entry negotiations, pursuing renegotiation of the terms of entry in 1974 and culminated in the 1983 general election manifesto that called for Britain's withdrawal from the Community. Such stances were in themselves paradoxical given that in 1967 it was the Labour government of Harold Wilson which made the second application to join the Community. The record of the Conservative Party is no better. Once the natural party of Europe, Edward Heath's pro-European leadership of the Conservative Party which secured Britain's accession to the Community in 1973 has been followed by a succession of Conservative leaders that have for the most part been lukewarm to further European integration. This has been particularly true since the Conservative's defeat in the 1997 general election, with William Hague, Iain Duncan Smith and Michael Howard having tended to oppose the Labour government's position on European affairs. The reality of this state of affairs has meant that although it is broadly true that the UK has had a difficult relationship with the EU, there have nevertheless been variances in the UK's European policy (Kassim 2004: 263).
- *The presence of significant intra-party conflict over the issue of European integration.* Within the Labour and Conservative parties there has consistently been a number of MPs that have held strong views on European integration and who have been willing to voice their own views during parliamentary ratifications. As has been noted elsewhere, 'Europe is one of the few issues on which it has become acceptable to put an MP's personal view before party loyalty' (Forster and Blair 2002: 112) and as such 'British policy on European integration is constrained by the need for party leaders to manage unwieldy and often warring wings of their parties' (Aspinwall 2004: 3). Party leaders are regularly faced with the difficult task of achieving a balance between pro-integrationist and anti-integrationist MPs. John Major commented that 'From the moment I crossed the threshold of Number 10 as prime minister I had dreaded the

potential impact of Europe on the Conservative Party' (Major 1999: 583). And while the European issue is particularly critical when a government has a low parliamentary majority, it is a circumstance that has nonetheless dominated Britain's membership of the Community. The fact that Treaty changes brought about by IGC negotiations require the government to secure parliamentary ratification only heightens the tension surrounding party management. Britain's negotiating strategy in the Maastricht Treaty was heavily influenced by the need to secure an agreement that would be palatable to a Euroskeptic Conservative Party (and at the same time the need to show a degree of goodwill towards other member states). John Major would later reflect as the negotiations came to and end, 'politically the position I faced was dire' (Major 1999: 275). As a result the 'the crucial question asked was whether any proposal would hold the Conservative Party together in the House of Commons, not whether it responded to international developments' (Forster and Wallace 2001: 142).

- *The willingness of opposition political parties to use European debates as important opportunities to challenge the government of the day irrespective of the worthiness of the policy being discussed.* In opposition the Labour party opposed the single market program that Margaret Thatcher negotiated in the SEA, and even though the Labour Party was broadly in favor of European integration by the time of the 1990–1991 Maastricht Treaty on European Union negotiations, it nevertheless exploited the Conservative government's difficulty in ratifying the Treaty. This opportunity to attack the government of the day is particularly acute when governments have a low parliamentary majority. This helps to explain why, despite Labour's opposition, the large parliamentary majority of 140 enjoyed by Margaret Thatcher in 1986 ensured that she was able to push the SEA through the House of Commons over a weekend. In contrast, John Major was returned to government with a Conservative majority of 21 after the 1992 general election and as a result his task of ratifying the Maastricht Treaty was far more complicated.

In arriving at these conclusions there is a considerable body of literature that has emphasized the political effects of the British 'first-past-the-post' electoral system which, in contrast to proportional representation systems (that are more common in continental Europe), has a greater tendency to produce a non-centrist government where there are more acute divisions between parties on European integration (Powell 2000). It is with this in mind that Mark Aspinwall has argued 'that the electoral system in the UK empowers Euroskeptic backbench MPs, a feature which is rarely if ever present in other member states' (Aspinwall 2000: 416). The situation has additionally not been assisted by large sections of the media being opposed to European integration.

These issues have been translated into a number of objectives that have dominated Britain's negotiating preferences. The first of these has been the advocacy of intergovernmental forms of cooperation that have defended the role of national governments. Grounded in a concern about the erosion of national sovereignty, there has been a tendency on the part of all British governments in the postwar period to attach prominence to the theme of the nation being detached and independent from other European countries. For instance, in October 2000 Tony Blair described Britain as 'a proud and independent-minded island race (though with much European blood flowing in our veins)' (Blair, T. 2000).

Second, successive British governments have been unwilling to support the continental preference for grand European projects. In part, this position has been shaped by the domestic political climate in Britain, whereby grand projects such as Economic and Monetary Union by their very nature create awkward debates about the nature, scope, speed and direction of European integration. In other words, whereas the continental vision of European integration has often been underpinned by ideological considerations, Britain's views have tended to be determined by the practical realities of these objectives.

Third, in contrast to such grand projects, British governments have tended to prefer quieter, more informal and pragmatic developments that do not attract the same degree of domestic scrutiny about the implications of the transfer of power away from member states. Prior to the Single European Act negotiations, Prime Minister Thatcher had argued that the realization of the objectives of a single market and closer political cooperation did not require the negotiation of a new treaty, not least because she was only too aware that any such treaty had the potential to raise other issues that impacted on the authority of nation states. 'What I did not want to do, however, was to have a new treaty grafted on to the Treaty of Rome. I believed that we could achieve both closer political co-operation – as well as make progress toward a Single Market – without such a treaty; and all my instincts warned me of what federalist fantasies might appear if we opened this Pandora's box' (Thatcher 1993: 548–9).

Fourth, Britain's commitment to European integration has been set within a broader set of foreign policy priorities that have included the prominence attached to the relationship with the United States. For John Major, this meant that Britain 'straddled the divide between the United States and Europe' (Major 1999: 578). It is a theme that has continued under the Labour government, with the former Europe Minister, Peter Hain, commenting in 2001 that 'Britain can be a leading member of the EU and be proud to be a European power, while still valuing and benefiting immensely from our special relationship with America' (Hain 2001). Thus, while the process of European integration has had a notable impact on British sovereignty, one of the most significant factors that has shaped British foreign policy in the postwar period has been the influence of the United States.

Finally, Britain's role as a world trader has resulted in it campaigning against excessive EU regulations that impact on economic competitiveness in a globalized marketplace. To a large extent this is a view that is based in an Anglo-American model of capitalism that has differed from the Rhine-Alpine model that has tended to dominate debates in continental Europe (Albert 1993), and which has most recently been reflected in British unwillingness to participate in the single currency.

Yet while these foreign policy priorities lend support to the awkward partner thesis and suggest that Britain has been somehow hampered in its ability to take a leadership role within the EU, it is nevertheless the case that successive British governments have in fact been able to effectively promote their policy preferences at the EU table. This has particularly applied to the economic arena, whereby Britain has campaigned against protectionism and has been a key advocate of deregulation, labor market flexibility, and trade liberalization. Thus, whereas France, Germany and Italy imposed restrictions on the free movement of workers from the ten new member states that joined the EU in 2004, Britain was one of only three countries that allowed unrestricted access to its labor markets. At the same time, Britain has a better record than France, Germany and Italy in terms of the transposition of European legislation into national law. Moreover, whereas British governments have championed the cause of EU enlargement, it is a position that has not always been shared with other member states. This has most recently been evident in the case of Turkey, whereby British support for Turkey's membership of the EU has contrasted with Germany's reticence.

10.3 Leadership resources

As the second largest economy in the EU and the fourth largest economy in the world, Britain is able to bring considerable material leadership resources to the European negotiating table (Clarke 1992: 42–71). Apart from the fact that the size of the British economy means that its 'voice matters,' the British economy is a truly international one. The country has significant trading relations outside of the EU. In certain specific areas, such as finance, Britain occupies a key world position. The influence of British negotiators is also maximized by Britain's broader world role, as signified by its position as a permanent member of the UN Security Council, membership of NATO, leadership of the Commonwealth, and the 'special relationship' that it enjoys with the United States. The latter has played into British concerns that any moves toward an integrated European security identity should not jeopardize the Atlantic link which has provided the bedrock of stability within Europe in the postwar era (Blair, A. 1998b). Britain's ability to influence events is backed up by its continued role (albeit depleted) as a significant security power, not least through its role as a nuclear power, and the considerable diplomatic expertise that Britain is able to draw on from the presence that it occupies in most countries of the world.

Within the EU, this state of affairs has ensured that Britain is able to exercise its influence across a broad range of policy issues and contrasts with smaller member states who are generally only able to influence one or two issues in EU negotiations. British influence is specifically felt on those policies where it has particular abilities and resources that are of value to the EU. This is evident in the case of discussions on foreign and security policy where Britain's position as one of the two main EU security powers (the other being France) has ensured that any developments relating to foreign and security policy at the EU level have to take into consideration British interests. While the combination of these issues has been a strength to Britain's influence within the EU, they have at the same time also been a weakness because this wider global role has led to a view that it has been a semi-detached member that has offered a halfhearted commitment towards European integration. For the most part this has been the product of the difficultly that British governments have encountered in setting out clear political priorities rather than its record of responding to and enacting European legislation. Indeed, Britain's perceived 'awkwardness' does not fit with its record as one of the best implementers of European legislation. Nevertheless, the underlying current of political apprehension towards the EU has meant that British negotiators have often been more concerned with responding to debates at the negotiating table. The UK's position as a 'laggard leader' is therefore reflective of a tendency to be reactive within the negotiating context.

Where successful outcomes have been achieved, they have been greatly assisted by the informational resources that have underpinned the construction of Britain's European policy. In tandem with other member states, the structure and operation of British government has been impacted on by the process of European integration as the spread of the EU's competencies has meant that greater numbers of ministers and civil servants have experience and knowledge of European affairs (Blair, A. 1998a; Bulmer and Burch 1998; Kassim 2000; Forster and Blair 2002). Initially, the impact on government from EU membership was concentrated on a small group of ministries, including the Foreign and Commonwealth Office (FCO), the Ministry of Agriculture, Fisheries and Food (MAFF – now DEFRA), the Treasury and the Department of Trade and Industry (DTI). In recent years this grouping has expanded to include all aspects of government, including ministries such as the Home Office which had no dealings with the EU prior to the Treaty on European Union.

In order to ensure that matters relating to European policy could – where possible – be coordinated across Whitehall, the Cabinet Office European Secretariat (COES) was established with the sole responsibility of providing a neutral steer to the government's European policy. And while some individuals may have concluded that the task of coordinating European issues should have been entrusted to the FCO, it was decided that this would be impossible because a significant amount of European business was concerned with domestic issues that were not directly relevant to the FCO. As a former head of the European Secretariat has emphasized, the 'FCO has – and wishes to argue – a particular departmental point of view on EC issues. It could not do this and at the same time hold the ring in Whitehall' (Bender 1991: 18). The work of projecting Britain's European policy on a day-to-day basis has been entrusted to the Brussels-based UK Permanent Representation to the EU (UKRep). It essentially acts as a 'mini-Whitehall', with its staff coming from a range of domestic government departments that have an input into the shaping of EU policy (Blair, A. 2001). Finally, an expansion in the number of policy advisers in No. 10 Downing Street has meant that there is increasing Prime Ministerial involvement on matters relating to foreign policy.

Of these bodies, the 'golden triangle' centering on the FCO, COES, and UKRep are crucial to the organization, construction and projection of Britain's European policy. The FCO plays a key negotiating role on policies that are particular to its own interests such as foreign and security policy, and by taking a leading role in negotiations with other member states and the EU institutions. The Foreign Secretary also represents Britain in the crucial General Affairs Council and is responsible at the domestic level for chairing the leading Cabinet Committee that deals with European policy (the Overseas and Defence Policy Committee, or OPD(E)). The FCO's involvement also stretches to UKRep where it contributes a considerable number of staff, including the Permanent Representative. UKRep is particularly important because it is entrusted with representing Britain in debates with other member states and the EU institutions and as a result considerable importance is attached to the appointment of a Permanent Representative who has always been one of the most senior members of the diplomatic service.

The ability of Britain to exercise influence in European negotiations has been greatly assisted by a practice of sending negotiators to work in Brussels for a considerable period of time where their knowledge and experience has helped to argue the case for British interests. In the years that Britain has been a member of the EU there have been only eight UK Permanent Representatives to the EU: Sir Michael Palliser (1973–75), Sir Donald Maitland (1975–79), Sir Michael Butler (1979–85), Sir David Hannay (1985–90), Sir John Kerr (1990–95), Sir Stephen Wall (1995–2000), Sir Nigel Sheinwald (2000–03) and currently Sir John Grant. It is a practice which has meant that British negotiators have regularly been the most experienced among their European counterparts and are therefore often more adept at playing the delicate chess game that is representative of EU negotiations. Reflecting on his period as Permanent Representative, Sir John Kerr was able to comment that 'we are right to send our negotiators for long spells. I had three French and five Greek counterparts. By the time I left, only the Belgian had been there longer. Longevity confers a spurious but useful authority' (cited in Menon 2004: 300).

Exercising influence at the EU level is, however, greatly dependent on the political instructions from government ministers and the wider influence of domestic parliamentarians. For Britain, this has often been the stumbling block that has impacted on its ability to offer proactive leadership. In contrast to the manner by which ministries have adapted their coordinating mechanisms to the impact of European integration, the same cannot be said of Parliament (Bulmer and Burch 1998: 607). This has fed into government decisionmaking, which has suffered from an inability to establish medium-term policy objectives. This was most notable during John Major's premiership and is a state of affairs that has led one official to comment that that 'there's no point in having a Rolls Royce machinery if the driver's a lunatic' (cited in Bulmer and Burch 1998: 607).

Yet, while the negotiating preferences of government have been regularly hampered by domestic political circumstances, British ministers – in particular the Prime Minister – have been able to overcome many of these hurdles in crucial IGC meetings. This is because IGC negotiations attach considerable importance to the need for heads of state and government to 'perform' in key meetings, of which the concluding European Council negotiation is the most important. By all accounts, British Prime Ministers have been among the most impressive performers at the EU level, both in terms of setting out their positions and bargaining over specific issues (Forster and Blair 2002: 98; Young 1998: 322). This is a reflection of their debating skills that have been honed in the combative atmosphere of the House of Commons where they have had to respond to questions without official support. Other heads of government have, by contrast, rarely experienced the same degree of domestic confrontation. Thus, while Britain's ability to play a leading role in Europe has at times been hampered by the domestic political system, it is nevertheless the case that British negotiators benefit from significant informational and organizational resources. Indeed, although the first-past-the-post system of British politics can be viewed as an influential factor behind the awkwardness debate that has dominated British European policy, it is not automatically the case that coalition governments in other member states result in a more effective method of coordinating European affairs. If anything, the opposite is the case. This is because coalition governments tend to result in ministers from different political parties having quite distinct views on policy matters and thereby makes the task of co-ordinating policy more difficult. It is a feature that has been particularly noticeable in Germany, where the co-ordination of policy has often lacked the more neutral mechanisms that have been apparent in member states such as Britain and France. To explore these issues further we will now move on to consider the strategies that British governments have used in IGC negotiations and to reflect on the manner by which these negotiating strategies have evolved over the years.

10.4   Negotiating strategies

In common with other member states, the negotiating strategies advanced by successive British governments have had as their primary aim the maximization of Britain's influence and the minimization of its marginalization within the EU. In achieving these aims, governments have been conscious of the constraints imposed by the domestic political environment – in particular, public opinion, the media and the views of parliamentarians. This has influenced the manner by which governments have managed the domestic level and the way in which they have engaged in debates at the European level.

At the domestic level, as a result of the complexity of the parliamentary dimension and the lack of support for EU membership among the electorate, successive governments have sought to try and distance themselves from the cut and thrust of parliamentary debate in Westminster where IGC negotiations have invariably created the opportunity for awkward questions. A need to square the Parliamentary angle of the Treaty negotiation and respond to the sensitivities of a Euroskeptic electorate is accentuated by the fact that IGC negotiations bring to the fore discussions about the future of European integration. Governments consequently not only have to establish a clear set of priorities, but also have to consider the extent of the concessions that they are willing to make. This has, however, at times led to negotiators having little room for flexibility. This was most apparent towards the end of John Major's period as Prime Minister when the constraints of a Euroskeptic Conservative parliamentary party hindered the ability of British negotiators to effectively engage in the Amsterdam Treaty discussions. It was a situation that changed with the election in 1997 of the Labour government and as the then Permanent Representative, Sir Stephen Wall, recalled, 'my instructions changed from "Just say no" to "Start saying yes" between 30 April and a week later' (cited in Menon 2004: 303).

What can be seen from these points is that as a general rule British governments have adopted a cautious approach to EU negotiations, whereby there has been a tendency to advocate a limitation in the transfer of sovereignty away from nation-states. But while there has been a preference for intergovernmental rather than supranational solutions, it is nevertheless the case that successive governments have been willing to accept the need for deeper European integration when this has been in accordance with British interests. Margaret Thatcher acknowledged the necessity of extending the practice of qualified majority voting (QMV) in the SEA as she understood that it was essential to the success of the single market program. Her 1988 Bruges speech was just as much concerned with arguing the case for an enlarged Community as it was with criticizing the influence of the supranational institutions. In the Maastricht Treaty John Major was willing to accept an extension in the use of QMV and an increase in the European Parliament's powers through the co-decision procedure (which meant that the European Parliament had the ability to veto legislation that was subject to this method of decisionmaking) because he recognized that they were part of an overall agreement that satisfied British interests. Tony Blair too has similarly accepted the further development of QMV and the widening in the use of the co-decision procedure, while a deepening of cooperation on judicial and foreign policy matters has also occurred. At the very least, a willingness to compromise and accept developments such as a widening in the use of QMV and a strengthening in the European Parliament's powers via the co-decision procedure have helped to provide the UK with more goodwill on the part of other member states so as to secure more important negotiating priorities.

Concessions such as these have been made by British governments because of the very nature of IGC negotiations where agreement on the final Treaty is taken on the basis of 'common accord' among all governments. Thus, given that each government can potentially veto the final Treaty, every government is compelled to compromise to achieve an agreement that satisfies all interests. In practice, governments therefore establish a set of priorities on which they are unwilling to compromise as well as to outline those where they are prepared to be flexible. It is, however, rare for the lists to remain fixed and as a result negotiating preferences – and in particular the ranking of priorities – can evolve in the course of a negotiation. Large member states, such as the UK, are naturally able to exercise influence across a broader range of policies than smaller member states. In other words, smaller member states can usually only have one policy on which they can threaten to disrupt the treaty negotiation through an unwillingness to compromise. Given that such compromises are highly politically sensitive, they are often undertaken by heads of state and government at key European Council meetings, of which the greatest prominence is usually attached to the final European Council meeting of the IGC negotiation.

The limiting of concessions to the endgame of the negotiations has been a tactic employed by British governments that has been based in a preference to tackle IGC negotiations on a case-by-case basis, with there being an aversion to accept linkages between different issues. It is a feature that stems from the fact that successive governments have considered that the qualities of each policy should be able to be defended at the domestic level. Policy issues have therefore been addressed on their own merits rather than as part of a broader view of European integration (Wallace 1997: 686). It is a strategy that has also been based in a tendency to be reactive rather than proactive in IGC negotiations. As a result, British governments have often been more willing to react to the proposals of other member states rather than to offer their own policy proposals.

This has in turn influenced British negotiating tactics which have attached emphasis to diluting the significance of proposals from integrationist member states so that they reflect a more modest set of proposals: 'That is to say British negotiators continually ask what proposals really mean, how they fit into existing policies and how much they cost' (Forster and Blair 2002: 106). In contrast, other member states generally do not enter into the same degree of discussion over the minutiae of each individual policy and this in part stems from the fact that they are often in favor of treaty reform and consequently attach a strong commitment to the overall objective. Therefore, they are more able to stress the advantages of an overall agreement (even if it is an imperfect one). In this sense, Britain's 'awkwardness' has been grounded in an unwillingness to concede ground in response to concessions from other member states.

The combination of these factors has meant that Britain has not always been best placed to construct strategic alliances with other countries. Britain has therefore not been able to replicate the special nature of the Benelux or French–German relationships. Being aware of this situation, British governments have at times attempted to culture individual alliances on specific topics as a means of either undermining or offering an opposing force to the French–German axis. Yet such a strategy has never been successful in the long term because of the recognition among other governments that British governments have been unable to offer the same level of commitment to the European cause. In this context, the history of Britain's relationship with European integration has severely hindered the extent to which any government can be seen to be an 'honest broker.'

At the heart of this situation has been the difficulty that British governments have had in establishing medium-term policy objectives in the EU (Bulmer and Burch 1998: 608). This has in turn led to some criticism that British governments have often adopted a blinkered approach to EU negotiations and have failed to recognize the evolving nature of the EU. Put another way, IGCs are regularly viewed in the specific context of the negotiation and 'red lines' are therefore drawn which the government is unwilling to move beyond. And when longer-term priorities have been apparent, such as British support for enlargement and economic competitiveness, the media has regularly overlooked them and has instead tended to concentrate on the extent to which Britain has been isolated on specific policies.

10.5   The nature of British engagement

Having discussed the manner in which leadership resources and the domestic political environment have impacted on British negotiating strategies within the EU, the task of examining the influence that Britain has had in IGC negotiations can be taken up in a more direct mode. In examining the history of British engagement in IGC negotiations, three broad points stand out. First, it is evident that the deepening in European integration that has taken place with successive Treaty reforms has challenged the ability of successive British governments to portray the outcome of the negotiations as having met its negotiating objectives. In other words, as IGCs have been part of an ongoing process of European integration, it is difficult to portray them as some form of 'zero-sum' game. Second, the evolving nature of the EU policy process has meant British governments have gone through a learning process where they have had to reassess their traditional unwillingness to allow the transfer of sovereignty to the EU level. Third, British influence – and leadership – within the EU has been most strongly felt on those policies that have chimed with its own domestic political preferences.

Taking these points as our guide, it is evident that in examining the history of IGCs from the SEA to the Constitutional Treaty, the SEA is the one nego-tiation which stands out as an example of British leadership. It is a situation that was greatly assisted by the SEA's objective of creating a single market (with its aim of promoting free trade) reflecting the free market ideology that dominated Conservative government thinking. This achievement did, nevertheless, result in the government having to acquiesce to the extension of QMV because it was viewed as essential for the objective of creating a single market, as certain measures could have otherwise been blocked by other member states. The UK's success in offering leadership in the SEA negotiations was soon lost as the desire of other member states to seek integ-ration in other policy areas gathered speed. This particularly applied to the progress towards political union and economic and monetary union (EMU) that provided the basis for the 1990–91 IGC negotiations that resulted in the Maastricht Treaty on European Union. These objectives did not sit well with Prime Minister Thatcher who, through an increasingly abrasive dialogue with the EU institutions and other member states, considered it imperative to water down the integrative policies. It was a situation which contributed to her own downfall and John Major, her successor as Prime Minister, was able to comment that 'I had been shocked at my early European Councils to discover that Margaret's strength of will, so admired at home, was used against us abroad. It was the butt of sly little jokes. Most of the other leaders utterly disagreed with her' (Major 1999: 265).

As Prime Minister, John Major's negotiating strategy toward the Maastricht Treaty negotiations were shaped by three key factors. First, a desire to offer a more constructive European policy that was reflective of his own position of being 'a pragmatist about the European Community' (Major 1999: 265). His Chancellor, Norman Lamont, thought he 'was inclined to sympathise with those who felt a more emollient, constructive negotiating style would be more productive' (Lamont 1999: 111). As a result, Major developed a closer friendship with the German Chancellor, Helmut Kohl, and he stressed in March 1991 that Britain should be at the 'heart of Europe.' It was, however, a position that was shaped by the reality of the negotiating process: the breadth of the policies being discussed meant that the government would have to compromise on its traditional unwillingness to permit integration to proceed in certain policy areas over which it had no influence. Second, Major acknowledged that he was unable to dominate the Conservative Party – and in particular the Cabinet – in the manner that Thatcher had. Since Major considered himself to be *primes inter pares* with his Cabinet colleagues, rather than someone who towered over the rest, the government's negotiating position on certain policies was shaped by the view of key Cabinet colleagues. This particularly applied to the case of Michael Howard who, from his position as Secretary of State for Employment, argued that Britain should not accept the introduction of the Social Chapter (Blair, A. 1999: 93–120; Forster 1998). It was also easier for Conservative MPs to unite behind an argument that the introduction of the Social Chapter threatened the labor market reforms that were central to Conservative policies in the 1980s rather than more complex IGC topics, such as foreign policy, interior affairs and institutional reform. Third, Major was aware that the parliamentary party had become ever more fractious and he wanted to maintain unity in the face of an impending general election campaign (Blair, A. 1998a: 178). Domestic political priorities were therefore paramount in the Prime Minister's mind (Major 1999: 275–6). As he would later comment: 'In a foretaste of what I was to encounter in 1997, I also wanted to prevent my backbenchers from binding themselves to an anti-European posture that could either blow our election chances apart or, if we won, undermine my future negotiating strategy' (Major 1999: 293).

A consequence of this was that on certain policies, such as the Social Chapter and EMU, the government was relatively clear of its objectives whereby it did not want to be committed to these policies. The government was aware that the desire of the majority of the other member states to proceed with these policies meant that it was powerless to stop them. This was particularly evident on the EMU discussions where Britain had been unsuccessful in its efforts to convince other member states of the viability of the 'hard ECU' proposal that it had launched in June 1990 (Blair, A. 2002: 124–42). This was principally because Britain had viewed the hard ECU as an alternative towards monetary union rather than forming part of the three-stage prescription towards monetary union that had been set out in the Delors Report of May 1989. As a result, the proposal, which sought to transform the existing ECU into a parallel currency and which had been influenced by concerns in government and the City of London that Britain should engage in the debate on monetary union, had very few supporters among the other member states from whom the central rationale of monetary union was the very creation of a single currency. Thus, since the hard ECU did not resolve the problem of there being other currencies in circulation, very few member states were supportive of it. It can therefore be seen that while the hard ECU plan represented an attempt by Britain to offer leadership within the EU, it reflected a propensity by British governments to direct the behavior of other member states after the very die had been cast in the debate that it sought to shape. In other words, the lateness of the plan in entering the debate combined with its inability to offer a viable alternative to monetary union meant that its chance of success was minimal from the outset.

The implication of this was that barely one month into the Maastricht Treaty negotiations, the British government's priorities changed from trying to sell the hard ECU to ensuring that a single currency would not be imposed upon Britain. In essence, Britain was faced with having to accept a form of flexibility so as to ensure that its influence over the final Treaty was maximized, while at the same time the impact of its non-commitment was minimized. On the question of EMU, the then UK Permanent Representative, Sir John Kerr, reflected that 'our Maastricht aim was to ensure that we did have a say, could ensure that monetary union took a UK-friendly form, and would have a ticket of entry should we ever decide' (cited in Menon 2004: 302).

On other topics the government's position was less clear. This was evidenced by its decision not to produce a White Paper that set out its objectives prior to the commencement of the negotiations through fear of causing division within the government. Prime Minister Major was aware that from the moment he entered Downing Street that 'there was a split in the ground, and that the Conservative Party had a foot on either side of that split and it was growing wider on European policy' (cited in Blair 1999: 210).

As a result, the government's response to the IGC negotiations was very much taken on a case-by-case basis rather than as part of an overall strategy. Alliances were sought with member states on individual topics. The Netherlands supported Britain's preference for the development of a European foreign policy that reflected the central role to be played by NATO, yet at the same time did not share Britain's view that certain elements of the Treaty should be subject to an intergovernmental structure. British influence was most keenly felt in the area of European foreign policy, where any attempt to develop a defense dimension hung on the participation of London and Paris as they were the only member states with both the necessary quantity and quality of military resources. This accordingly gave them greater negotiating leverage. Britain was also able to ensure that its vision of a Treaty design that had less of a federal design was secured, although as Colette Mazzucelli indicates in her case study of the Dutch Presidency, it was a position that was also shared by a majority of other member states. As a result Britain's vision of an intergovernmental pillar structure for cooperation on justice and home affairs (JHA) and common foreign and security policy (CFSP) was secured.

In its achievement of the key negotiating objectives, the opt-out from the Social Chapter and EMU, the government acknowledged that it would have to acquiesce on other aspects of the Treaty. This included an acceptance of an extension in the number of policies covered by QMV and an enhancement of the European Parliament's influence via the co-decision procedure.

While both of these issues posed more significant developments for British sovereignty, it was a view that was not shared by Cabinet Ministers who were more concerned with securing agreements on those issues which had a higher media profile, and which by their very nature would have subjected the government to the greatest criticism. The end result was that although Major regarded the Maastricht agreement to be 'Game, Set and Match' for Britain, the expansion in the supranational design of the EU created a backlash among Euroskeptic Conservative MPs who considered that they had been duped into an understanding that Britain had obtained all of its objectives. John Major would later reflect that 'in the Commons, a legacy of resentment lingered that flared up often enough to overshadow nearly everything the government tried to do' (Major 1999: 584).

As a result, the government's strategy toward the Amsterdam IGC negotiations of 1996–97 was even more constrained and limited than had been the case during the Maastricht negotiations. Matters were not helped by the government having announced in May 1996 that it would adopt a policy of non-cooperation with the EU until a ban on the export of British beef was lifted. It was, however, a short-lived policy of non-cooperation, with the government having reversed its position only a few weeks later in June. This change of tactic was influenced by the fact that the policy of non-cooperation provided Britain with no leverage over other member states, while there were at the same time a perverse effect of the policy included policy proposals that had been advanced by Britain failing because of the non-cooperation policy. Such developments had a considerable impact in limiting the room for maneuver that British negotiators had and also further diluted the government's negotiating capital.

The net effect of this was that from the commencement of the Amsterdam IGC negotiation in March 1996 until the election of a new Labour government in May 1997, Britain essentially just said 'no' to proposals for further European integration. Constrained by the lack of a parliamentary majority and a Euroskeptic Conservative Party, John Major's government was unable and unwilling to play any constructive part in the negotiations and had essentially expended all of its negotiating capital. Sir Stephen Wall, the UK Permanent Representative at the time, was able to reflect that 'we had reached a point where our partners had begun to ask themselves whether it was possible for the British government to sustain its commitment to the basic precepts of membership' (cited in Menon 2004: 304).

Within a matter of days this state of affairs changed with the election of a Labour government in May 1997. This immediately brought benefits at the EU level, and with only a matter of seven weeks until the June Amsterdam European Council the new Labour government was not shackled by the parliamentary divisions that had beset the previous Conservative administration. Strengthened by a parliamentary majority of 178 – the largest since 1945 – Tony Blair's government was able to set out a more positive

European policy. In June 1997 Prime Minister Blair announced that Britain 'shares the goal of a constructive partnership of nations in Europe' (Blair, T. 1997). This vision was reflected in the outcome of the Treaty of Amsterdam, whereby the government overturned Britain's exclusion from the Social Chapter and agreed to a strengthening of foreign policy cooperation. At the same time, the government also accepted a widening in the scope of the co-decision procedure and an extension in the scope of QMV to 16 additional policy areas.

The Labour government's ability to play an influential role at the EU level was noticeable in the 2000 IGC negotiations that resulted in the Treaty of Nice: it was able to secure agreement on a Common European Security and Defense Policy (CESDP) that emerged out of the Franco-British meeting at St Malo on December 4 1998. That meeting had produced a Letter of Intent on defense cooperation and a joint declaration on European defense, which Tony Blair regarded as 'historic' (House of Commons, December 7 1998, col. 8). But while British influence was reflective of its importance to the success of an EU foreign policy, the deepening of cooperation also demonstrated the extent to which Britain has also been drawn further into European integration as a result of a 'ratchet effect' (Forster and Blair 2002: 114).

Outside the area of foreign policy, the Treaty of Nice made changes (albeit of a limited nature) to the institutional design of the EU so as to prepare the Union for future enlargement. This included a redistribution of votes within the Council and a readjustment of the number of seats within the European Parliament. The Treaty also made changes to the structure of the European Commission and extended the process of QMV to an additional 31 policy areas. This extension of QMV was viewed to be necessary to ensure that in an enlarged EU of 25 (or more) states decisions could not be held up by an individual state.

In the wake of the Treaty of Nice the British government showed no appetite for further institutional reform and was initially opposed to the idea of a constitutional Convention that would set out recommendations for the basis of Treaty reform. This was not least because the government was anxious that the idea of an open Convention would mean that the outcome would be out of national governments control. Such a view was influenced by the government having been taken aback by the way in which the Convention that drafted the Charter of Fundamental Rights produced a text that was adopted by member states at the Nice European Council of December 2000 (Menon 2000: 964). However, by the time that agreement had been reached at the December 2001 Laeken European Council that a Convention would be established, the British government had come to accept its necessity and took the decision to make a full contribution to its discussions. As has been pointed out elsewhere (Menon 2003; Kassim 2004), the government's change of tact arose out of a reassurance that the Convention's agenda reflected its priorities (such as the role of national parliaments and simplification of the treaties) and that its concerns would be defended by British citizens having a key role within the Convention. For instance, Sir John Kerr, a former Permanent Secretary of the FCO, was appointed secretary general of the Convention.

In an effort to shape the nature of the debate, the government offered its vision as to what the mission of the Convention should be. Central to this was a view that member states should remain the cornerstone of the European integration process. In a speech to the European Policy Centre in Brussels in January 2002, the Minister for Europe, Peter Hain, stressed 'the EU is primarily a union of member states' and that EU reform needs to have 'its feet on the ground of the nation state, not its head in the sky of a super-state' (Hain 2002). As part of an effort to advance its views, the government sought to cultivate alliances with other member states prior to the commencement of the Convention. This included developing links with the accession countries. Yet while the government was proactive in attempting to influence the debate, the nature of the message was of course reflective of Britain's preference for national rather than supranational solutions.

During the Convention discussions from March 2002 to June 2003, the British representative, Peter Hain, and his alternate, Baroness Scotland, stressed that Britain was a full and active member and played an important role in building up good relations with other member states. As a mark of British engagement in the process, the government sought to advance positive proposals. For example, Britain argued that the continuity of EU policies was hindered by the six-monthly rotating Presidency and there was therefore a need for greater continuity in the handling of policy. As a result, the government initially advocated for the creation of 'team presidencies' and subsequently pressed for a permanent presidency (Menon 2003: 969). Yet while such proactive engagement mirrored Tony Blair's view that 'we must be whole-hearted, not half-hearted, partners in Europe' (Blair, T. 2001), this did not stop the government from setting out 'red-lines' that were key negotiating objectives (Kassim 2004: 273). This included an insistence that the government would block proposals relating to QMV on tax fraud and social security, while it also expressed concerns over the powers (and the very name) of an EU Foreign Minister.

A hardening of the British position became apparent after the publication of the draft treaty articles in February 2003, to which the government either offered an objection or proposed an amendment to 15 of the 16 articles (Menon 2003: 974). This included a concern about the extent of the EU's role in matters of foreign and economic policy, as well as the fact that the Charter of Fundamental Rights was identified as integral to the Constitutional Treaty. The projection of these concerns through amendments to the treaty had been influenced by the publication of the first draft treaty 'awakening' Whitehall lawyers to the Convention as they were able to work on the 'meat' of the text rather than the ideas that had dominated the discussions. As a result, Britain's objections to the draft treaty represented a return to the 'old way' of approaching EU negotiations whereby texts are subjected to the 'proof-reading' treatment. Matters were compounded by a backlash against the proposed Constitutional Treaty by much of the popular press in Britain, which only further assisted in a hardening of the government's negotiating tactics. While this opposition resulted in the government securing a number of its objections by the time the draft Constitutional Treaty was presented in June 2003, there were nevertheless certain provisions of the Treaty to which the British continued to be opposed. These would be the subject of discussion in the IGC negotiations that commenced in October 2003 and concluded at the Brussels European Council of June 2004. This included opposition to the introduction of QMV on tax.

Tony Blair's comment in the government's White Paper on the IGC nego-tiations that 'the Convention's end product – a draft constitutional treaty for the European Union – is good news for Britain' (United Kingdom 2003), consequently did not reflect the complete picture. Nevertheless, in a depar-ture from the approach that had been employed by Britain in previous IGC negotiations, the government set out in one paragraph of its White Paper (Paragraph 66) the so-called 'red lines' that it was unwilling to accept as well as indicating those policies that it was willing to accept. The government emphasized that it was insistent on the maintenance of unanimity on issues relating to tax, social security, defense, criminal procedural law, the system of own resources, and that unanimity should remain the general method of decisionmaking for CFSP. At the same time the government was prepared to accept the use of QMV as a general rule for legislative proposals and agreed to an extension in the use of the co-decision procedure (Paragraphs 65 and 67). Such a strategy reflected the fact that policymakers in London recognized the political pressure that had built up and that the government could therefore not re-open every aspect of the points that had come out of the Convention, as this would inevitably result in a backlash from other member states.

In the course of the IGC negotiations the government proved remarkably successful in defending many of these objectives, which in many senses contrasted with its experience in the Convention. The outcome of the IGC negotiations was agreement on a Constitutional Treaty at the Brussels European Council of June 2004. This included key initiatives such as the new post of EU President that would be elected by heads of government for a term of two- and-a-half years, and the creation of a new EU Foreign Minister that would combine the existing positions of the Council's High Representative for CFSP and the European Commissioner for external rela-tions. Britain's acceptance to the use of the term 'Foreign Minister' had, in fact, contradicted the position that it had advanced in the Convention when the government had argued for 'European foreign affairs representative.' Although such a term reflected London's preference for a term that would limit the potential for domestic criticism, there was little support for this cause among other member states. Thus, as IGC negotiations force member states to concentrate in defending those issues that are of greatest concern, the British government was therefore faced with having to acquiesce to a number of the policies that it had opposed in the Convention, such as the incorporation of the Charter of Fundamental Rights. A consequence of this was that whereas the government was prepared to be flexible on some issues, it was successful in securing its key goals through maintaining the national veto on matters relating to social security, tax, defense and foreign policy, criminal procedural law, and the system of own resources. The very achievement of these objectives owed a great deal to the Labour government's constructive engagement as well as to the fact that many of the issues that were debated were reflective of British preferences.

10.6   Conclusion

In assessing the evidence of Britain's engagement in IGC negotiations, it is hard to disagree with Anand Menon's conclusion that it 'has never felt particularly comfortable with EU treaty negotiations' (Menon 2003: 964). In terms of the specific nature of IGC negotiations, three key points can be concluded. First, IGC negotiations bring to the fore discussions about the future direction of European integration which have created specific problems for Britain because of the tendency for governments to view integration through the lens of the impact on national sovereignty. A second and linked factor is that the trend of British governments to stress the 'win–win' nature of IGC negotiations adds further fuel to problems over European integration because it ensures that that there is an absence of informed discussion on the true implication of integration. Finally, since IGC negotiations have specific timetables and clear deadlines for completion, as well as being under intense media coverage, they accentuate those policies which member states find particularly troublesome.

Britain has, nevertheless, been able to win a number of important battles. This has included the Maastricht Treaty's pillarization of CFSP and JHA, and opt-outs on joining the single currency and the Social Chapter. And although the Labour government subsequently accepted the Social Chapter in the Amsterdam Treaty, the very process of achieving an opt-out has led to a more flexible approach to European integration. Such an approach is a reversal of traditional British hostility toward a two-speed Europe, whereby the likes of Margaret Thatcher argued that member states *should not* be permitted to make advances in certain areas of integration that Britain would have no influence over because in the end Britain would be forced to join.

Set against this viewpoint, John Major concluded that flexibility was a necessity of securing British objectives. This position was taken forward into the Amsterdam negotiations whereby flexibility in the form of enhanced cooperation would permit some member states to move forward with closer cooperation. And in a reversal of Britain's negative viewpoint, by which flexibility would protect British interests through a process of non-commitment, Britain along with France prepared to use flexibility in the Nice Treaty as a means of securing the development of the Anglo-French initiative on foreign and security policy so as to overcome opposition from neutral member states such as Austria, Finland and Sweden.

The attainment of these outcomes has in part been a product of the nature of the negotiations: because all member states have to agree to the outcome by a process of 'common accord' there is a general consensus that 'an imperfect agreement is better than no agreement.' Thus, the key interests of member states tend to be reflected in the eventual Treaty text. Yet, it is also the case that the extent to which the outcome reflects the interests of individual member states is dependent upon the degree of preparedness of each member state and the negotiating skills of key officials and heads of government. In all categories, Britain is generally regarded as being particularly impressive.

Although achievements, such as the intergovernmental pillar structure, have helped to secure British negotiating objectives, the dramatic changes in the nature of European integration over the last two decades have meant that governments have had to reassess the broader nature of decisionmaking within the EU. Thus, whereas British governments had traditionally viewed the maintenance of the national veto over the majority of policy objectives to be a primary objective of securing national sovereignty, the expansion in member states and the broadening (and deepening) of the EU's policy remit has resulted in a reassessment of this point of view.

This was first evident in the SEA negotiations whereby the Thatcher government agreed to an extension of majority voting so as to achieve its single market goal because of the acceptance that the maintenance of the veto would provide an opportunity for other member states to undermine this objective. Tony Blair agreed to the extension of majority voting to 37 new policy areas in the Nice Treaty, and today in excess of 80 per cent of all decisions taken in the Council of Ministers are decided on the basis of QMV. A direct implication of these developments has been that there has been a move away from British governments defending the veto in all policy areas to instead arguing for its maintenance in what it considers to be crucial policy areas, such as tax, and at the same time favoring an adjustment of voting weights in the Council of Ministers in order to ensure that the larger member states are given greater influence, thereby making sure that Britain is able to oppose potential future alliances. Such a strategy was once again evident in the IGC negotiations on the Constitutional Treaty, whereby the British government argued that decisions in the fields of tax, social security policy, judicial cooperation and EU financing should be taken by unanimity. At the same time, the government was more relaxed on questions relating to the composition of the Commission and the allocation of seats in the European Parliament.

Based on the preceding analysis it is apparent that while British governments have been largely successful in ensuring that the outcome of IGC negotiations take into consideration key national priorities, the overall process has tended to be a reactive rather than a proactive one. The exceptions to the rule are policy initiatives on the single market and foreign policy, both of which have reflected national priorities. Yet, outside of set-piece IGC negotiations, it is evident that British influence has been considerable. The EU increasingly reflects key British preferences of economic liberalism rather than *dirigisme* as the way forward. In this sense, those member states which had previously advocated the European social market model, such as France, are, in the face of swollen budget deficits and rising unemployment, having to retreat to a set of policies that are reflective of British preferences. It is in these and other areas of the EU that British leadership is most widely felt.

11
The Constitutional Treaty and Poland – A New Laggard in the EU?

Krzysztof Bobiński

11.1 Introduction

Rarely does a new member of any organization challenge the existing members with the threat of a veto right from the moment it joins, or even before it has taken its place at the decisionmaking table. Yet this is the course Poland chose in the intergovernmental conference negotiations to draft the European Union's draft Constitutional Treaty, which were finally concluded at the Brussels European Council in June 2004 and signed in Rome on October 29 by leaders of the Union's 25 member states. Why was Poland's entry to the European Union accompanied by such a high-profile controversy over the Constitutional Treaty, and, more specifically, the provisions in the draft document on the decisionmaking procedures in the European Council and Council of Ministers? Was this attempt by Poland to exercise leadership counter to the wishes of those member states that held infinitely greater resources, like Germany or France, doomed to failure? And, if so, were the Poles right to undertake this course of action, convinced that they were defending their interests within the Union, notwithstanding their lack of experience in treaty negotiations? Furthermore, what are the consequences of a policy choice by Warsaw that raised hackles in many European capitals and demonstrated that the present enlargement from 15 member states to 25, bringing in eight former Soviet satellite states, was not merely a quantitative leap, but a qualitative one, for the EU?

What follows in this chapter is a narrative that seeks to explain the internal and external factors that shaped Polish policy towards the IGC on the Constitutional Treaty. The narrative aims to contribute to an understanding of a policy choice taken by a new, albeit large, member state which was faced at the beginning of its membership in the European Union with a challenge to what it perceived as its basic interests and a fundamental change in the rules of membership of the club it had agreed to join.

As will be explained, Poland set out like the Pied Piper of Hamelin on its attempt to lead member states away from the Council voting formulas proposed by Valéry Giscard d'Estaing's Convention with the support of France and Germany. Poland could count on two important advantages. One was its government's own strongly held conviction that its case was just and that European law gave a member state the right to veto treaty agreements without prejudicing that country's position in the Union. The second was the support that Poland saw coming from Spain, which adopted an identical position on the issue of retaining the voting system agreed at Nice. This was boosted by the conviction held in Warsaw and based on a straw poll conducted by the Poles at the Convention that as many as 17 member states were unhappy with the proposed change in the Nice formula.

Initially, Poland had several other proposals for changing the Convention draft treaty. These included the retention of one Commissioner per member state and the introduction of the notion of group Presidencies. Secondly, Poland wanted to make sure that the draft treaty in no way undermined NATO's collective security role in Europe. One high-profile demand was that the role of Christianity in building Europe's traditions should be reflected in the Preamble. In the end, what Poland really wanted to achieve at the IGC was the retention of the Nice voting system.

As this chapter explains, Poland could not rely on issue linkages to strengthen its case for retaining the Nice formula. Indeed, the country's position was made vulnerable by the fact that starting in 2004 it faced negotiations on the 2007–13 financial perspective, which was crucial to its chances of boosting growth and modernizing the country's infrastructure. Poland also had no direct experience in previous treaty negotiations. Its highly qualified government team would only win the respect of its negotiating partners once the talks had started and they were able to show their mettle. Until then they had been treated with scarcely disguised irritation by their colleagues, especially once it became apparent that Poland was determined to stick to its position in the face of well-resourced member states such as Germany and France.

Initially there was no hint of flexibility in the Polish position – a fact which Włodzimierz Cimoszewicz, then foreign minister, made a point of underlining both in public and in private. The political opposition was rock solid behind the government, and the hyperbolic statement about 'dying for Nice' came to symbolize the Polish position. This statement was attributed to Jan Rokita, the head of the Civic Platform (PO), an opposition party. However, the tough stance which Poland adopted was decided by Leszek Miller, the then Prime Minister, who had learned, during Poland's accession negotiations at the summit in Copenhagen, that being tough brought results. He was also well aware that Poland was not alone. On this question, Poland worked in parallel with Spain, which had almost twenty years of largely successful negotiation experience to its credit. In the background was Jacek Saryusz-Wolski, a former European affairs minister, whose stubborn approach to any negotiation has become legendary in Brussels. Saryusz-Wolski was influential with the opposition. He credibly explained that Poland should not worry about its image in the eyes of EU decision-makers 'who always wring their hands when faced with a tough stance but who in the end accept the result of a given negotiation and soon forget the ill feelings previously generated'.

Poland's negotiating strategy came down to explaining in bilateral talks that the country's position was aimed at defending the ability of the new member states to defend the EU's redistributive functions by retaining the ability to block collective decisions. This was accompanied by assertions that Poland's case was just. These were arguments, as will be seen, which failed to win support among the other member states; even the newest and poorest ones. However, even though Poland did have the right of veto, this was seen as a weapon that was only effective if never used. Yet the thought that it might be used irritated decisionmakers in both France and Germany to no end, and probably has resulted in a negative influence on the thinking in these countries about further enlargements.

11.2 Prologue

When the Convention on the Future of Europe, which authored the Constitutional Treaty, was originally conceived, there was little to suggest that Poland would engender so much controversy at the beginning of its sojourn in the Union. At the time, Poland was busy completing its membership negotiations and keeping its head firmly below the parapet on issues other than those directly relevant to the talks. The assumption was that a successful candidacy needed the approval of all 15 member states. It was thus better not to reveal policy preferences on issues such as further integration, the future of common policies, or liberalizing the European economy in order not to make enemies before the accession process was completed.

Nor did Poland set out any firm policy options during the Intergovernmental Conference, which ended with the Nice European Council in December 2000. At Nice, Poland was the happy beneficiary of a scrimmage between France and Germany on vote weighting in the Council which saw four countries – France, Germany, Italy and the United Kingdom – emerge with 29 votes each. Close behind came Spain and Poland with 27 votes; putting the Poles, to their delight, in the European big league. In the run-up to Nice, enhanced cooperation and not the weighting of votes had been the issue which had particularly concerned Poland; yet even here the country had eschewed a confrontational stance. Indeed, in a speech to the Centre for European Policy Studies in Brussels on July 25 2000, Foreign Minister Wladyslaw Bartoszewski said that Poland was ready to see vanguard groups formed within the European Union, but that 'the group of countries wanting to create the vanguard of integration must always be ready to accept new members' (Bartoszewski 2000: 60).

Bartoszewski also implied that 'fundamental changes in the institutional order' should be left to the next IGC, by which time the candidates would have become full members and would be fully empowered to participate in decisionmaking. He failed to mention the issue of weighted voting. However, earlier that year his predecessor, Bronislaw Geremek, had replied to a request for views on the subject matter of the IGC from the Portuguese Presidency. There the Polish Foreign Minister did mention weighting. Indeed in the official letter to Jaime Gama, his Portuguese counterpart, Geremek admitted the coming enlargement would see the 'influence of states with large populations systematically decrease' (ibid.: 17). The letter also noted that EU enlargement 'will lower the blocking minority threshold expressed in percentage terms in relation to the size of the population and to the number of votes in the Council.' Geremek suggested that 'the demographic criterion should remain the principle governing the distribution of votes in the Council of the European Union' while adding that 'correcting disproportions' of the member states' representation on the Council is also 'essential'. Finally, he said that changes in weighting could be either 'effected independently' or combined with the establishment of a double majority system. It was a stance that implied changes were necessary. Yet this answer did not make it clear exactly what Poland wanted. Not that Poland's position mattered all that much. Claus Giering, a German political scientist from the Centre of Applied Policy (CAP) in Munich, later reassured the Poles that they should not worry too much about the outcome of the IGC. Spain, he told them, would be pushing to improve its weighting in the Council and that 'all provisions for Spain are likely to apply also to Poland as both states are of a similar size' (ibid.: 36).

This is what happened at the European Council in Nice. The outcome can be interpreted as being in line with Polish thinking as presented in the letter to Jaime Gama. Nevertheless, attempts by France at the seaside resort to lower Poland's weighting in relation to Spain were scuppered. This was accomplished not only by other member states, but also by an energetic diplomatic campaign led by Prime Minister Jerzy Buzek, by using the argument that Spain and Poland, as Mr Giering remarked, 'are of a similar size.' It was this campaign, led by the center right officials of the Polish government, which was one of the factors that explains later Polish intransigence when it came to 'defending Nice.' There were urgent phone calls to EU leaders by Jerzy Buzek who was competently backed by Jan Kułakowski, the chief negotiator. Kułakowski brought into play his extensive network of contacts. In Warsaw Jacek Saryusz-Wolski, then head of the European Integration Ministry (UKIE), set up a crisis center.

This allowed the Poles to claim that they had won the 27 votes for Poland regardless of the moves by the member states' leaders actually present at the

Nice Council. Jerzy Buzek's administration was replaced in 2001 by a center left government led by Leszek Miller. Like the budget rebate won for the United Kingdom by Margaret Thatcher, which successive administrations could not give up, Jerzy Buzek's successor could not have easily 'given up on Nice' – even if he had wanted to do so.

The Polish authorities gave a guarded welcome to the results of the IGC. In a speech at Warsaw University on February 22 2001, Foreign Minister Władysław Bartoszewski said that the European Council voting formula in the Nice Treaty provided a 'stronger linkage between vote weightings and the member states' demographic potential' while it continued to 'over represent' the smaller states in the EU (Bartoszewski 2001: 154). Bartoszewski noted an increase in the qualified majority threshold and 'a strengthening of the democratic legitimacy of qualified majority voting (QMV)' by 'introducing a minimum population threshold of two thirds of the number of countries'. Bartoszewski concluded that 'the Treaty provisions are favorable to Poland. 'Being assigned the same number of votes as Spain, Poland will be able to play an important role in the Council of the EU. To large states we will come as a natural ally in their exercise of the leading role in shaping the EU; to smaller states, we will remain a welcome partner, both in building majority coalitions and in forming blocking minorities,' he said.

The authorities accepted that Nice had given Poland a comfortable pivotal role in future EU relations. Moreover, the argument that 'we have nearly as many votes as Germany or France' was a powerful one in the coming accession referendum campaign in which the opponents of EU entry were arguing that Poland would enjoy second-class status in the EU. Above all, the Treaty of Nice was seen as a necessary prerequisite for enlargement and thus for Polish membership. This impression was reinforced when the Irish said 'No' to Nice in their first referendum. NGOs like the Polish Schuman Foundation then put all their energy into appealing to the Irish to vote 'Yes' the second time around – for the sake of enlargement. In addition, the great and the good, including Lech Wałsa, the former Solidarity leader and former President of the Republic, signed impassioned open letters with the same message. In the second referendum the Irish voted yes. Nice, the Polish public had been led to assume, had been good for Poland.

11.3   The Convention and the IGC

There the issue lay for the following few months. The Convention opened at the beginning of March 2002 and went through its 'listening stage' with scarcely a hint that anyone was intending to open up the decisionmaking procedures for the European Council enshrined in the Nice Treaty. The main issue, once the institutional debate was under way, seemed to be whether or not the Council would have a President, to match the Commission Chairman. The Polish government was represented by the consensual Danuta Hübner, the head of the European Integration Office (UKIE), while the wily Jozef Oleksy, a senior figure in the post-Communist Left Democratic Alliance (SLD), represented the Sejm, the Lower Chamber and Edmund Wittbrodt, a well-meaning right-of-center university professor from Gdansk, represented the Senate, the Upper House. The Polish delegates and their substitutes diligently attended the Convention. The process was rarely covered in the media, however, and the reports written by the Foreign Ministry team of officials working for Danuta Hübner did not attract much attention within the government.[1] The Convention failed to interest Parliament. After all, Poland was still negotiating its accession agreement. The talks ended at the cliff-hanging Copenhagen European Council in December 2002. At this meeting the Polish Prime Minister, Leszek Miller, negotiated hard and obtained sufficient concessions from the European Council which allowed him to present the result as a success on his return to Warsaw. The following spring was dominated by the run-up to the accession referendum held on 8–9 June 2003. Here obtaining a majority for EU entry was at least as important as persuading over half of the adult population to vote since this was the condition for the result to be binding. Otherwise the Parliament would have had to ratify Polish entry with a consequent loss of popular legitimacy for the membership process. In the end, 77.45 per cent of the population voted for entry based on a 58.85 per cent turnout – a satisfactory result.

Meanwhile few in Poland noticed that the Convention was beginning to gather speed. In November 2002, the French and German Foreign Ministers became delegates, showing that these two countries were taking the Convention more seriously. Poland failed to follow suit and kept Danuta Hübner in place although Wlodzimierz Cimoszewicz, the foreign minister, could have been brought into play. Nor did any alarm bells ring when the European Commission proposed to the Convention in December 2002 that it review 'the complex decisionmaking system stemming from the Treaty of Nice and replace it by the simple dual majority scheme. The Council's decisions would be deemed to have been adopted if they had the support of a simple majority of the Member States representing a majority of the total Union population' (Commission 2002c: 16). A few weeks later the Praesidium of the Convention put out a reflection paper on the Functioning of the Institutions. This implied that something ought to be done about the decisionmaking procedures, but went no further than to remind Convention delegates that the Commission had recently 'proposed introducing a double majority system' (CONV 477/03). The Praesidium's note explained that 'the Nice Treaty adopted a new triple system requiring a majority of weighted votes, a majority of the members of the Council, and a majority representing at least 62 per cent of the Union's population. The system has been criticized as excessively complex and making it slightly more difficult to achieve a qualified majority. It has also been pointed out that, since the allocation of votes, like the system for seats in the European Parliament, remains degressive, the views of the less populated Member States carry greater weight relative to population than do those of more populated Member States.'

These hints failed to be noted by Poland's delegates from the Senate, Edmund Wittbrodt and his deputy, Genofewa Grabowska, an academic who specialized in constitutional law. Neither Wittbrodt nor Grabowska mentioned them in a report on the Convention that was debated by the Senate on 16 January 2003. However, in her speech to the Convention dated 20 January 2003, Danuta Hübner, the government's representative, intriguingly suggested that Poland might be open to a revision of the decisionmaking procedures. She said of the Union's institutions, 'it is also worth reconsidering the triple system of voting introduced in the Nice Treaty. A double majority – of votes and citizens – would be a much more transparent way to make decisions,' she said. The statement may have suggested to observers that Poland was ready to accept a change in the formulas agreed at Nice. However the speech was titled 'personal remarks' and later developments showed that this was an accurate description.

At this point, the Convention was still a low priority in the eyes of the Polish authorities. Reports from the Convention, distributed by the Foreign Ministry down to the level of relevant departmental directors in Polish ministries, tended to languish in 'less important' trays. That only changed when, at the end of April, the Praesidium of the Convention discreetly proposed that the Nice voting formula be dropped and replaced by a 'double majority' process. By May 2003, Foreign Minister Wlodzimierz Cimoszewicz was reading his Convention dossiers.

The Convention endgame

Nevertheless, it seems clear that the proposal to scrap the Nice voting formula caught the Poles by surprise. The fact that one of their compatriots, Agnieszka Bartol, was a member of the Praesidium's secretariat did not mean that information about the inner workings of the Convention's steering body was readily available.[2] But even when the Poles[3] realized that a change of the formula had been put on the agenda, publicizing the fact became extremely inconvenient in the light of the two-day accession referendum scheduled to begin on June 8. This was because the 27 votes allocated to Poland in the Nice Treaty had become one of the more important arguments against the Euroskeptics who were telling their supporters that Poland would enjoy 'second-class status' in the EU. A public campaign, which showed that a change in the terms of membership had even been suggested, would have undermined the 'yes' camp's efforts.[4] It was left to the Spanish member of the Praesidium, Alfonso Dastis, repeatedly to express opposition to the change while the Poles kept a low profile, especially at home. Indeed it was only in the final days of the Convention that Danuta Hübner took polls to ascertain that among the national delegations as many as 17 were unhappy with the proposed changes in the decisionmaking formula for the

European Council. This straw vote was important because it was one of the key elements in the Polish decision to adopt a hard line against the change in the coming months. Even if it engendered optimism as to the prospects of success in defending the Polish position, it was also highly unreliable. When push came to shove, among the 17, only Spain came out against the changes. The other countries changed their stance once the IGC began.

The government takes a stand

The Polish position on the draft constitutional treaty became clear in June. On 3 June 2003 the Council of Ministers[5] debated a 'preliminary report on the Convention' and a week later accepted an official 'position for the European Council in Thessaloniki.' On June 20 Leszek Miller told the European Council in the Greek city that the Nice decisionmaking formula for the Council should be kept in place.[6] 'The Convention has proposed a change which will disturb the balance between small, large and medium sized member states', he said. At the subsequent press conference, the Polish prime minister backed by W³odzimierz Cimoszewicz added that 'there had been no change in circumstances between Nice and the Convention which meant that a change in the formula was required.' It was the opening shot in what was to prove a long and punishing campaign.[7]

Leszek Miller recalls that his speech in Thessaloniki, which signaled that Poland would be questioning the draft Constitutional Treaty's conclusions on Council voting procedures, had raised eyebrows amongst his colleagues.[8] He also remembers waiting tensely for José Maria Aznar, the Spanish Prime Minister's speech, to see if Spain was still opposing the change in the Nice formulas. 'I was relieved when I heard Aznar raising questions on this issue. Then I was certain that we would not be alone'. This should come as no surprise because the fact that Spain was ready to work alongside Poland to 'defend Nice' was one of the crucial factors shaping the Polish position.[9]

Leszek Miller identifies three reasons why Poland decided to go out on a limb despite the fact that the country was a new member state in the Union. (In fact, for most of the debate over the Constitutional Treaty Poland had not even been a member of the club.) The first was that the government had cited the 27 Council votes allocated to the country as a major argument in the referendum in favor of membership. 'We would have been very dishonest to say before the referendum that this was important and then after the referendum said that the voting procedure did not matter', he says. Secondly, Miller cites the fact that Poland had identified Spain as an ally. 'We had an alliance with Spain on defending Nice and I saw no reason to worsen Poland's position by accepting the double majority proposed by the Convention.' Third, there was the prior experience of the accession negotiations where Miller held out for a better deal for Poland and believed he had obtained that result. 'In Copenhagen we won out by adopting a tough stance. I have seen member states demanding things and getting them. Why should Poland have behaved any differently? Why should we say Yes when we could get more by refusing to say Yes'? The other lesson of Copenhagen was in Miller's view that 'Poland is a large country with major political potential' – and that this potential allowed Poland to resist pressure from the other big countries – 'and win'.

It is in the context of Poland's political potential that Miller mentions the USA and the divisions in Europe over the Iraq war, which overshadowed so much of the negotiations over the draft Constitutional Treaty. The former Polish Prime Minister denies that Polish intransigence was influenced in any way by its close support for the US administration's policy in Iraq. 'The US did not have a position on the European Constitution,' he says. However, the fact that Poland had backed the war in Iraq and sent troops there was a source of pride for the government. This also gave Miller the extra self-confidence necessary to challenge the French and the Germans over the Constitutional Treaty.

Of course, by the start of the IGC in October 2003 Poland was already in the bad books of major member states like France and Germany. The previous December the Poles had opted to purchase the F-16 fighter from Lockheed Martin, a US firm, and angered the Europeans by shunning their offers of military aircraft. Iraq and the 'Letter of the Eight' supporting the US made Berlin and Paris angrier still. Meanwhile President Jacques Chirac's ill-advised public remarks aimed primarily at the Poles that the interests of future member states would be better served by their 'choosing to remain silent' strengthened Warsaw's recalcitrant mood. The feeling that Poland was being bullied merely fuelled their determination to resist the proposed changes in the decisionmaking formulas agreed at Nice.

Leszek Miller was crucial in taking the decision to defend Nice. Yet he had strong backing from Włodzimierz Cimoszewicz who, as a lawyer, was outraged that Poland had agreed to accede on the basis of the Nice formulas only to see these formulas changed without any good explanation as soon as the country joined. 'We were genuinely shocked and felt cheated. We also authentically believed that right was on our side', an official at the Foreign Ministry recalls.[10] The Foreign Ministry had noted the position of 17 countries against the change in the Nice formula.[11] Its personnel thought it possible to build on this to mount effective resistance in the IGC to the shift to a double majority. Thus it would appear that decisions such as that to purchase the F-16 and the debate over Iraq deepened the divisions over the draft constitutional treaty. If it had not been for Iraq, the crisis would not have gone as deep. Yet, it still would have been evident.

In the summer the Polish Government took the initiative in shaping a response to the draft Constitutional Treaty. By the beginning of September, the Opposition came into play as a factor hardening the Government's already tough stance. The issue also came to be hotly debated in respected newspapers. A number of open letters for and against the official position showed that pro-European elites, which only a few months earlier had worked together in the accession referendum, stood divided over the draft Constitutional Treaty.

The Opposition comes into play

The draft Constitutional Treaty became a subject of debate in the plenary sessions of the Sejm. Whereas the Convention was debated in plenum by the Sejm only once in 2002, the subject came up six times in the 12 months between June 2003 and the summer of 2004. In September of 2004 that Jan Rokita, a leader of the free market Platforma Obywatelska (Civic Platform – PO), outlined the reasons why his party was ready to support the government in its efforts to defend Nice. Rokita charged that double majority had been brought into the negotiations in an underhanded way by the Praesidium of the Convention, and summed up his position as '*Nicea o muerte*' ('Nice or death'). Rokita argued that Nice had given Poland a place in the EU's 'big six' while the double majority broke that group down into 'one enormous state, three large ones and at best two medium-sized, including Poland.' 'We have been reduced from a country which had an influence over decisions to a country which will be influenced by the decisions of others', he continued (Sejm Stenograms 18 September 2004: www.sejm.gov.pl).

Rokita added that the introduction of the double majority marked a major shift in power in the EU away from the small and medium-sized member states toward the biggest and richest countries. The principle of solidarity had always been the foundation of the Union and this principle is now being undermined, he said. The shift also meant member states would no longer be equal in the Council. Finally he argued that Poland had accepted poor financial conditions of entry on the understanding that a strong political position would allow the country to improve its economic position. Therefore, keeping Nice in place was vital for a successful Polish membership in the European Union. This debate and subsequent meetings of the Sejm devoted to the draft Constitutional Treaty showed that the whole political spectrum represented in Parliament was united in its support of the government from the center right PO to the nationalist right-wingers in the anti-European Liga Polskich Rodzin (League of Polish Families – LPR). The degree of accord was unprecedented for Polish politics and contrasted sharply with the weakness of the efforts made during accession talks to unite the political spectrum behind the Polish negotiators. Some observers even argued that the Opposition was determined to trap Leszek Miller in his tough stance and see him fail to achieve results, and thus see his position weakened. Miller denies that he faced pressure from the Opposition.[12] Instead he claims that his position on Nice was his own, and the stance of the Opposition merely served to help him in his talks with other member state leaders. It has to be said that he was diligent in keeping Opposition leaders informed of what was going on during the negotiations. In turn they came to the hospital to congratulate him when he returned from the December 2003 Brussels European Council, which had failed to reach a compromise. Miller was suffering severe back pains after being injured in an earlier helicopter accident.

Critical voices of the official Polish position amidst the parties represented in Parliament were rare. One was that of Andrzej Olechowski, another PO leader and a former Foreign Minister. He argued that the Nice formula was based on false premises and that even if it was retained, it would not stand the test of time. He also warned that if Poland was only backed by Spain, the country risked being isolated in the European Union if Poles continued to defend the Nice formula. His, however, was a comparatively isolated voice. Politicians such as Jaroslaw Kaczyński from the Prawo i Sprawiedliwość (Law and Justice – PiS) right-of-center party were more typical. It was he who popularized the 'party of the white flag' slogan to describe all those who were willing to accept the draft Treaty. He said in a newspaper interview in September 2003 that 'the draft Treaty proposals are unacceptable. The European Constitution in its present shape means that we as a nation will no longer be able to decide about the most important issues facing us. . . . The new Europe appears to be one in which the large and strong countries take all the decisions. Zero solidarity, 100 per cent hegemony.' Jacek Saryusz-Wolski a former European affairs minister who, following his election to the European Parliament in June 2004 on the PO list has become a deputy chairman of that institution, was influential behind the scenes. Saryusz-Wolski's support for Nice was total. He was proud of his role in acquiring 27 votes for Poland at the December 2000 European Council. As the top EU affairs person in the PO, he set the uncompromising tone for party leaders such as Rokita and Donald Tusk. Saryusz-Wolski argued that the shift to a double majority meant the end of the traditional EU, which placed a premium on the redistribution of funds and in which there existed a benign balance between small, medium-sized and large members. Most persuasively, he explained that Nice gave Poland a good chance of building a blocking minority based on new members, especially once Bulgaria and Romania joined in 2007, plus one or two allies from the 'old' member states. Under the double majority provision the views of the new member states could be ignored because they would be unable to achieve a blocking minority.[13]

The stance of the Opposition politicians was based partly on conviction and partly on calculation. None of the Opposition parties wanted to appear too enthusiastic about the EU, as there were national elections due in 2005 and expectations that the aftermath of the accession on 1 May 2004 would bring some negative repercussions, such as price increases. Instead they preferred to play the patriotic card, positioning themselves as defenders of the national interest against a European Union dominated by Germany and France.

However, the issue also produced a major cleavage among intellectual elites, which up until the referendum had been united in support for Polish membership. This surfaced in the form of two open letters. The letter which first appeared was titled an 'Open Letter to European Public Opinion' that basically criticized the approach of the government and the Opposition parties to the draft Constitutional Treaty. It expressed the view that the Treaty presented an opportunity for Poland to develop and modernize within the Union. Slawomir Sierakowski, the youthful editor in chief of *Krytyka Polityczna*, a quarterly magazine and one of the organizers of the letter, warned that government policy could lead to 'the western Europeans abandoning Poland on the margins of a united Europe' (*Krytyka Polityczna* 5 2004: 13). Sierakowski went on to say that Poland was dividing into two speeds. 'One speed, that of Rokita and Miller, and the other, of all those who want a modern and open Poland, free of complexes and megalomania.' The letter provoked a response from supporters of the official Polish position on Nice. One of the signatories who had also helped organize the reply was Marek A Cichocki, a political scientist who was also from the younger generation. He argued that at issue is a redefinition undertaken by Germany since 1998 of its role in the EU (Cichocki 2004: 92). Germany is now aiming to increase its measure of influence over the EU and the fight for a double majority is an expression of this, Cichocki notes. Meanwhile Poland, Cichocki says, wants to be 'treated as one of the more important political players in the shaping of the integration process. From this point of view the draft Constitutional Treaty is not acceptable' (ibid.: 124).

The debate on the Polish stance in Parliament, in the quality newspapers, and in the think tanks was widespread. It spilled over into the electronic media with items on the wireless and the television news signaling to the population at large that the nation's future was at stake. In the late autumn of 2003, opposition to EU membership mounted to 30 per cent as many of the 'undecided' came down on the side of Euroskepticism. Yet support for membership, which had reached 67 per cent in the month of the accession referendum, dipped only slightly towards the end of the year as the debate reached fever pitch. By the May 2004 accession date, the level of support had fully recovered, as the opponents also began to lose ground.[14]

The Brussels European Council and its aftermath

The image of Poland's dogged determination was strengthened after Leszek Miller's helicopter crash in November 2003, which put the Polish Prime Minister into hospital in the weeks preceding the December European Council in Brussels and saw him arrive there, in considerable pain, in a wheelchair. Copenhagen had taught Miller that playing tough brought results, but he also knew full well that keeping Spain as an ally was crucial if the Polish position was to stand any hope of success. 'At Brussels the other leaders would come to our room because of my problems with my back' Miller remembers.[15] And as he listened to Jacques Chirac reminiscing about the Algerian war and talked to Gerhard Schroeder about bilateral relations, Miller was in touch with José Maria Aznar, checking if the accord with Spain was still in place.[16] As things developed, both Spain and Poland did have compromise proposals. However, these did not go further than variations on the Nice formula. It seemed, however, that other member state leaders were in no mood for a long negotiation and decided to call it a day. The European Council meeting broke up with everyone asking everyone else not to blame anyone for the fiasco and assuring themselves that IGCs usually take longer than just under three months.[17]

New thinking needed

Leszek Miller returned to Warsaw determined to hold out. However, officials in the Foreign Ministry realized that the Brussels European Council had been a turning point. Indeed some maintain that, during or just after that meeting, they learned that the Spanish had been ready to make a deal either with or without the Poles. 'The Spaniards went to Brussels ready to do a deal on the basis of the double majority,' a junior Polish Foreign Ministry official involved in the process claims.[18] In contrast to the autumn, when Włodzimierz Cimoszewicz had been adamant that Poland would not compromise on the Nice voting formula, Foreign Ministry statements turned to the search for a compromise solution. 'We understood we had to start thinking in different ways' another Foreign Ministry official says. Indeed as early as January 16 2004, Włodzimierz Cimoszewicz published a simultaneous article in *Le Monde*, the *Financial Times*, *Expansion*, the *Frankfurter Allgemeine Zeitung* and the *Gazeta Wyborcza* in which he said that Poland's position was unchanged but that 'we will not be blind to the interests, arguments and expectations of our partners. In view of the substantial differences, reaching agreement will still be a formidable task – but not an impossible one' (*Financial Times*, London 16 January 2004: 15).

Polish compromise proposals won little favor with the defenders of the double majority formula enshrined in the draft Constitutional Treaty. Berlin and Paris showed little interest in the idea of seeing how the Nice voting formula would work and then deciding in 2009 whether to stick to it or change it; known as the 'rendezvous proposal.' On 3 February 2004, Jan Truszczyński, the deputy Foreign Minister, told a meeting in Warsaw 'we are ready to be flexible but the fundamental principles of the Polish position remain the same. As there is no proof that a system based on the double majority is more effective, more democratic and gives added value to the member states, Poland sticks by its position that the Nice formula, however much it is criticized, should be given a try.'[19] Another Polish idea, which was scarcely considered in other EU capitals, was a proposal by two mathematicians from the Jagiellonian University in Krakow, Wojciech Słomczyński and Karol Życzkowski. They proposed a more equitable and scientifically designed weighting formula (*Rzeczpospolita* 30 January 2004 Warsaw: A4).

The climate changed in March when the Council Secretariat came up with a proposal for a blocking minority made up of four countries containing between 12 and 15 per cent of the enlarged Union's population (see also chapter 5). The mechanism would accompany the double majority that would come into play in special circumstances when national interests were deemed to be under threat. Leszek Miller liked the idea and recalls that he had to explain it to Gerhard Schroeder, who had not been informed of the proposal.[20] On March 4, while on a visit to Brussels, Longin Pastusiak, the president of the Senate, said that Poland was ready to discuss possible compromises on the basis of a double majority. He withdrew the statement amidst media uproar at home, and within hours claimed he had been misunderstood. The trial balloon had however gone up.

The breakthrough

However, it was the bomb attack in Madrid on March 11 by Islamic extremists which provided the breakthrough. An ill-starred attempt by Aznar's Popular Party to capitalize on the atrocity by blaming it on Basque separatists swung popular opinion around to the opposition socialists, who won the election on March 14. Secondly, the blast underscored the need for greater unity in the EU and made the Constitution seem more urgent. While the Poles knew that Aznar had been ready for compromise they realized that they faced the danger of complete isolation once his socialist rival Jose Louis Rodriguez Zapatero took office. A meeting at the funeral of the bomb victims with Zapatero convinced Leszek Miller that this was a real possibility.[21] Also there was a palpable change of mood at the European Council meeting that month. Leszek Miller has no doubt that the events in Spain changed everything. 'The departure of the Popular Party was caused by the tragic attack and the tragic attack made everyone see things differently. People understood better that Europe must integrate more quickly and deeply than before. There must be more cooperation. There was a feeling of determination at the European Council in Brussels in March 2004 that the draft Treaty was needed quickly.'[22]

Meanwhile, Leszek Miller was losing political support at home and was soon forced to declare that he would be resigning on May 2. The events in March saw him decide that acceptance of a double majority with higher thresholds and a blocking minority as proposed by the Council Secretariat was a formula Poland could accept. Poland's position was weakened by the fact that the Spaniards were not interested in the blocking minority formula, but wanted to hold out for higher thresholds. After accession Miller handed power to Marek Belka, who had been to that point his finance minister. Belka agreed to head an interim government until national elections in 2005. It was Belka who traveled to Brussels in June 2004 to agree to a draft constitutional treaty, which raised thresholds, but watered down the blocking minority concept to become a mere cooling-off mechanism. Leszek Miller later wondered, if he had still been prime minister, would he have accepted the deal? Belka had not been to Copenhagen nor did he have the Spaniards backing him. These were the two main factors, which had shaped the Polish position in the last twelve months.

11.4 Epilogue

The decision to accept the compromise was greeted with anger by the right-wing Opposition. Jacek Saryusz-Wolski was quick to criticize the deal and argue that Poland had lost out. Behind the scenes he had been arguing that Poland should have held out and waited for elections in coming years – certainly in Germany and maybe in France, where leadership changes would have brought in politicians who were more amenable to the Polish position. Later in Parliament, Jan Rokita declared that if he became prime minister his government would do everything to ensure that the draft treaty would not come into force in 2009. It was a foregone conclusion that Poland would hold a referendum on the issue. There was a fair chance that the right-wing parties would have asked their supporters to reject the Constitutional Treaty. An opinion poll taken after the conclusion of the Treaty, however, is revealing in its outcome. While just over half of Poles thought that the government had achieved little in its fight for the treaty, and the same number thought that the weaker member states would have little say in the enlarged EU, as many as 43 per cent thought that the EU would function more efficiently as a result. Also 64 per cent said they would vote in a referendum while over half of those said they would support the Constitutional Treaty.[23]

In hindsight, officials at the Foreign Ministry conclude that Poland should never again risk being isolated, as was potentially the case in the dispute over the Constitutional Treaty. The process had also hardened skeptical feelings toward the EU among elites and risked eroding support for the Union among the general public. 'If we had known that the effect would be to create a group of Euro-skeptics, then we would not have chosen this path' stated one middle-ranking ministry official. Also while the experience has shown Polish officials that the power game inside the European Union can be brutal, they have also learned that the most painful of all are head-on clashes. In the future, Polish officials will play a more subtle game, trying not to leave traces when they hit out and, most of all, trying not to leave psychological scars on their partners. It is a lesson though that the politicians have yet to learn.[24]

Notes

1. Prime Minister Leszek Miller admitted as much in an interview with the author in July 2004. 'We all understood that the Convention was important but the negotiations stood higher in the order of priorities at least until Copenhagen.' (Interview with Leszek Miller, July 2004). Alfonso Dastis, the Spanish government delegate to the Convention who was also a member of the Praesidium had a

similar problem. The Spanish diplomat told the author that he felt as early as the beginning of 2003 that a change in weighting would be proposed. 'I reported this to Madrid but the government was too busy with issues like Iraq to take much notice.' (Conversation with AD, April 2005).

2. 'Agnieszka Bartol behaved most of the time as if she was a member of a more privileged 'inner circle' so she wasn't of much use to us' a Foreign Ministry official told the author.

3. This should not suggest that the Polish delegates to the Convention were unaware of what was happening. One of the officials working with them told the author that the Polish group had a 'growing feeling of frustration and of being manipulated by the Praesidium.'

4. Foreign Ministry officials confirm that with the Euro-skeptic League of Polish Families calling for the referendum to be postponed until after the new constitutional treaty had been finally agreed, it was inopportune to raise the issue of the change in the decisionmaking formula.

5. Leszek Miller (LM interview) states that the Council of Ministers was the main decisionmaking body in the entire process. According to him, discussions on the Polish position took place at this level and that this was not a mere rubber-stamping body. It seems safe to assume that until his resignation on May 2 2004 Leszek Miller was the key player in the decisionmaking process. Other opinion-forming centers were involved. These include President Aleksander Kwasniewski and his office, which initially assumed a tough stance, but during the course of 2004 began to push both in private (at meetings of a group of experts called the 'Reflection Group') and in public at a series of conferences titled 'For a Strong Poland in a Strong Europe' for a compromise. Miller remembers the President 'acting more elastically.' Next there was the Foreign Ministry led by Włodzimierz Cimoszewicz, a lawyer who specialized in international law and who early on, and with full conviction, nailed his colors to the 'defense of Nice.' He was backed by a highly expert and experienced team, including Jan Truszczynski, a deputy minister and former chief negotiator as well as ambassador to the Commission and Pawel Swieboda, the able head of the ministry's European Department. Adam Rotfeld, another deputy minister and the former head of SIPRI, the arms control institute in Stockholm, took part in policy meetings at the ministry. Before and during the IGC, the ministry loyally defended their minister's and the government position despite misgivings as to the wisdom of adopting a confrontational stance toward almost all the member states and the Commission. Indeed it was Cimoszewicz who, on the government side, embodied the Polish position, explaining both in public and in private that it was non-negotiable. The remaining opinion-forming institution was the Parliament where the opposition gave its full support to the government position. It was in the Sejm, the Lower Chamber, in September 2004 that Jan Rokita, a leader of the pro-market Platforma Obywatelska, formulated the 'Nice or Death' slogan, which came to symbolize the Polish position in the IGC. Also it was in Parliament that Leszek Miller met regularly with Opposition leaders to keep them up to date on the negotiations.

6. The preliminary Polish government position also mentioned that the Preamble to the draft Constitutional Treaty should mention 'Christian traditions.' Later the government added other demands, including one that defense policy provisions in the draft should not affect the position of NATO. This chapter concentrates deliberately on the voting procedure issue because this was the main as well as the most difficult of the questions raised by the Poles.

7. Speaking after a compromise had been reached at the Brussels European Council in June 2004, Leszek Miller noted that the Constitutional Treaty would not in all probability go into force since it would not be ratified in 'one or several countries.' He named Poland and the United Kingdom as possible casualties. 'That will mean a lot of effort will have been wasted' he suggested adding on reflection 'maybe not, we all went through an important learning process' (LM interview).

8. LM interview.

9. 'Aznar was very sure of himself and that was infectious' a Foreign Ministry official told the author.

10. This feeling of being in the right strongly informed the Polish position. Leszek Miller (LM interview) also reiterates that the strength of the Polish position was that Poland had 'good arguments.'

11. In taking its decision to defend Nice the Foreign Ministry ignored reports from key Polish embassies abroad, which warned of the negative consequences of such a move and the slim chances of success. One of these was the Polish delegation do the Commission headed by Marek Grela, an experienced diplomat. Another theme which ran through the whole conflict was that Poland would suffer in other fields namely the forthcoming negotiations over the 2007 to 2013 financial perspective where Germany, as a major net contributor, could be expected to have its say on EU spending. Jan Truszczynski, a deputy foreign minister, told the author in an interview for this chapter that he simply ignored the issue because 'there had never been any discrimination of such kind before.' 'There were veiled threats from the Germans but I didn't take these seriously as I could not see how these threats could be carried out in practice. How could the Council accept discrimination against one member state?' However the minister does admit that were Poland to remain recalcitrant after the June 2004 Brussels European Council, then it might have suffered in the next budgetary redistribution.

12. LM interview.

13. Leszek Miller, when asked why Poland failed to get the backing of other candidate states for her position on Nice, said, 'their stance amazed us. Cimoszewicz and I talked to them even drawing diagrams to show them that they would not gain from the new system. Yet they appeared to think that the choice of voting system made no difference to them. They didn't appear to care. And they didn't want to get on the wrong side of the Germans, This was particularly evident among the Czechs while the Hungarians were counting on the French. Indeed they viewed us with admiration, but disbelief that we would get anywhere' (LM interview).

14. Centrum Badania Opinii Publicznej (CBOS) Warsaw. Communique BS/115/2004: 2. The same survey conducted in June 2004 asked Poles which factors determined a member state's position in the EU. Just over half noted a country's economic development while the second factor pointed to by 33 per cent was 'the efficacy of a country's politicians.' A mere 16 per cent suggested that population, the criterion around which the weighting debate revolved, was an important factor. However, in the same survey 82 per cent of Poles pointed to Germany as the country that had the greatest influence over the functioning of the Union. France, Great Britain, Italy followed by Spain came next as Poles de facto recognised the demographic factor as the most important. The survey saw Poland come first among the new member states and before Portugal, Finland and Greece.

15. LM interview.

16. Accord is perhaps too strong a word, but the Spanish government led by Jose Maria Aznar's right wing Popular Party had long before the Convention decided that Poland was to be a strategic partner for Spain in the Union. Spanish diplomats in

Warsaw had instructions to build strong bilateral relations and Spanish advisers were brought to Poland as regions in both countries established links with each other. Spain also encouraged Polish seasonal workers to come to the Iberian Peninsula. In another sign that the relationship had not been just limited to Treaty related issues, Spain agreed to send a contingent to Iraq to serve under Polish command. At the same time Miller says he was constantly being warned by fellow prime ministers that Poland would be left in the lurch by the Spaniards. Spain was happy to go it alone and paid little attention to what the Poles were doing. An article written by four authors at the Spnish institute, Real Institute Elcana, failed to mention Poland's stance as a factor in Spanish thinking. ('Spain and European Constitution Building', Raj S Charii, Alfonso Egea de Haro, Kenneth Benoit and Michael Laver www.realinstitutoelcano.org/documentos/imprimir/133imp.asp) An analysis of the Spanish press at this time done by the Warsaw Institute of Public Affairs showed very few references to Poland in this period (Mateusz Fałkowski (ed.), *Pierwsze kroki w Unii. Polityka polska w praise europejskiej* (Warsaw: ISP, 2004)).

17. A few weeks before the December European Council a senior French diplomat mused aloud in the presence of the author 'maybe we should let the Poles bounce off the wall' in Brussels. Indeed the abrupt way in which the French and the Germans with the support of the UK's Tony Blair told Silvio Berlusconi, the Italian Prime Minister holding the Presidency, to wrap up the proceedings would suggest that this was the case. A few weeks later when the French, German and Polish Foreign Ministers met in Berlin on January 16, Polish foreign ministry officials recall Dominique de Villepin dazzling the assembly with loquacious and eloquent interventions, which were nevertheless short on substance. 'They had wanted to teach us a lesson and in January that was still true' he recalls.

18. In the interview the unnamed Foreign Ministry official the source stated 'We knew the Spaniards had been ready to do a deal in Brussels because they told us so.'

19. *Relacja z Wydarzen. Nicea albo i nie.* 6 February 2004. www.ngo.pl. In a concession to the Spanish and the new member states, Giscard d'Estaing and the authors of the draft Constitutional Treaty kept the Nice voting formula in place until 2009. This gave Poland the argument, enshrined in the proposed rendezvous clause, that if it was to be used for five years anyway, then why not see how it worked and then consider its revision.

20. LM interview.

21. LM interview.

22. LM interview.

23. CBOS Warsaw July 2004. BS/123/2004: 1. The same poll showed that as many as 65 per cent of supporters of Jan Rokita's PO would vote for the Constitutional Treaty in a referendum and 40 per cent of the even more radical anti constitution PiS would vote for the Treaty. Only the LPR could count on a majority of its supporters to vote against the Treaty.

24. The Foreign Ministry team handling the negotiations was well prepared. Though they often had the feeling that they were patronized as newcomers by their old member state partners, who sometimes even failed to listen to Polish arguments, they were of first class caliber. Unfortunately, politicians who were heavily involved in the process lacked that level of sophistication. 'We found that they became fascinated by the possibilities of blocking Council decisions thanks to the 27 votes Poland was allocated at Nice. They failed to notice that the EU and that includes Poland, needs decisionmaking majorities if it is to work at all,' says one official.

12
Is There Anyone in Charge? Leadership in EU Constitutional Negotiations

Renaud Dehousse and Florence Deloche-Gaudez

In the 1970s, Andrew Shonfield described European integration as a 'Journey to an Unknown Destination' (Shonfield 1973), to highlight the uncertainties surrounding what Joschka Fischer was later to call the *finalités politiques* of the process. If anything, the description is more accurate today than it was at that time. The resounding 'No' votes of the French and Dutch people signal that a very deep *malaise* is developing in the population of EU member states. The derailing of the Constitutional Treaty and the European Council's difficulty in deciding on a common response to this unexpected development have left the Union without a clear road map for the first time since the launching of the single market program by the Delors Commission. This is not the place to discuss the factors that have brought about this scenario. The contributions to this volume shed light on one possible cause of the current situation: the weakness of leadership in the EU, not least on the occasion of the 'grand bargains' that are supposed to set the course to be followed by the Union.

In these concluding remarks, our ambition is not to summarize in a systematic fashion the findings of the project; it is rather to provide a more impressionistic reading of what appears to be one of the key variables of the past 15 years, namely the dispersion of leadership in Europe, and its implications for the future.

12.1 The fragmentation of leadership

In reviewing the history of EU institutional development, it is difficult to avoid the impression that leadership is a most contingent commodity. The main resources actors can use to provide leadership are identified in chapter 1: material resources; informational resources, including content and process expertise; internal and organizational capacity; and reputation.

The evidence presented in this volume demonstrates that these assets are rarely to be found in the hands of any one single actor.

Large countries may have significant material resources, notably at the political and administrative level. Contrary to liberal intergovernmentalist assumptions, they may even be relatively unconstrained by demands from domestic actors when it comes to constitutional negotiations, as the French case demonstrates (Jabko 2005). Even then, their influence may be limited; precisely because they have consistently relied on material resources, French negotiators often lack negotiation skills and attempt to impose their views rather than to persuade. True, they may occasionally add institutional powers to their weaponry. Thus, during the Nice Treaty negotiations in 2000, the French government took advantage of the chair to pursue its own interests (see chapter 2). Yet France's impact on the eventual outcome appears to have been limited. Its neglect for the norm according to which presidencies are supposed to stick to a neutral position raised severe criticism. Moreover, its biased attitude damaged its reputation, a key asset for would-be leaders. This criticism could explain the relatively low profile shown by France during the first months of the European Convention. Then, to avoid the Nice scenario, the French gave priority to the partnership with Germany – ultimately accepting the double majority system which broke with the formal parity between the two countries for which they had bitterly contended in Nice. This tends to confirm the existence of a 'feedback loop', introduced in chapter 1, between the perception of leadership strategies by the parties and their ability to provide future leadership.

In a situation where even large countries enjoy at best limited leadership power, independent institutional actors might be expected to enjoy more leeway, at least in areas where their own institutional interests are not directly at stake. While there is evidence to suggest this may be the case for the Council secretariat (see chapter 5), the position of the Commission, analyzed by Kassim and Dimitrakopoulos, appears significantly weaker (chapter 6). Similarly, even though Valéry Giscard d'Estaing has widely been described as one of the most influential figures in the Convention (Magnette 2005) as he concentrated in his hands a variety of powers (information, control over the agenda of the Convention and the drafting process, ability to shape the decisionmaking rules), his eventual weight was less decisive than some had feared. He was able to influence considerably the proceedings, putting off till the end of the Convention the drafting of concrete articles and reducing the time devoted to the discussion of salient articles, notably the institutional provisions and the revision clause (Dehousse and Deloche-Gaudez 2005). However, the president of the Convention did not possess the whole range of leadership resources. His controversial nomination and his 'aristocratic' image, fueled by press reports on his financial requests, tarnished his reputation. His neutrality was regularly questioned, as he displayed on several occasions a strong bias in favor of large member states. Thus, for all the organizational power at his disposal, he was not the only one at the helm. He had to deal with powerful actors, such as the Convention Secretariat, the two other vice-presidents and the dozen of *Conventionnels* forming the Praesidium of the Convention (Deloche-Gaudez 2004). At the end of the day, if one makes an exception for the change in the rules governing majority voting, he was forced to renounce most of his pet reforms or to water them down significantly (Dehousse and Deloche-Gaudez 2005). In other words, his influence was stronger over processes than over the eventual outcome.

All these elements suggest that the deconstruction of the notion of leadership into distinct analytical sub-categories advocated in this volume is indispensable to make sense of the influence of all actors taking part in the institutional reform process. Additional categories might be considered. Thus, the ability to put forward ideas that appeal to a large audience can be a key leadership resource. All ideas are not equal: some are more likely to fit in with common assumptions and to gain support. For instance, the idea that the democratization of the Union goes hand in hand with the increase in the EP powers is widespread, even though the originality of the European polity could lead one to question it. So is the view according to which national parliaments should be given a greater voice in EU decisions. The latter view explains why the proposal to involve them in assessing subsidiarity, through the so-called 'early warning system', received near-unanimous support in the Convention. In contrast, Giscard d'Estaing's proposal to establish a 'Congress' composed of MEPs and national parliaments was widely criticized because it was perceived by many to be a potential competitor to the European Parliament.

12.2 Institutional reform as a polycentric process

What clearly emerges from this analysis is a contrasted picture, suggesting a relative dispersion of leadership resources. No participant in the constitutional reform exercise is able to exert a decisive influence over the whole process. Most contributions to the volume insist on the contingency of leadership. For Derek Beach, the Council Secretariat influence 'is always contingent upon the role that a given Presidency allows it to play.' Likewise, one of the arguments put forward by Hussein Kassim and Dionyssis G. Dimitrakopoulos is that the ability of the Commission to exercise leadership is 'highly dependent on external factors' and that the extent to which it can exercise it 'is still more contingent and depends to a large degree on the personal qualities, style and standing within the organization of the Commission President.'

As a result, grand decisions can only be explained by the combination of different kinds of leadership (mostly structural and instrumental) exerted by different kinds of actors, or indeed by the absence of any durable leadership.

During the Maastricht Treaty negotiations, the institutional contours for economic and monetary union have, of course, been strongly shaped by Germany's hegemonic role in monetary policy, which has enabled it to dictate its own conditions. Yet without the instrumental leadership displayed by Jacques Delors and the Commission in the run-up to the IGC, it is far from clear that monetary union would have seen the light of day.

The fragmentation of leadership also explains some of the most remarkable features of recent attempts at treaty reform. First, there is the piecemeal character of the exercise. IGCs unavoidably end up as a big marketplace where concessions are traded in large package deals. As a result, the final compromise generally looks like a long list of discrete decisions reflecting the preferences of a large number of participants instead of a coherent blueprint for the future development of the EU. This horse-trading character was so pronounced in the Amsterdam Treaty that the European Council attempted to limit the subsequent Nice IGC negotiations to the so-called 'Amsterdam leftovers.' Yet centrifugal forces prevailed, and the Nice Treaty ended up with the usual exchange of favors.

Secondly, the polycentric nature of the reform process creates opportunities for unintended developments. Thus, one of the most striking trends of two decades of institutional reforms is the emergence of the European Parliament, which has gradually acquired a status of co-legislator as well as strong oversight powers *vis-à-vis* the Commission. During each IGC, the Parliament harvested a series of changes that consolidated its influence. Remarkable as this evolution may be, it cannot be traced back to any kind of leadership exerted by one of the negotiating partners. The Parliament itself was not a party to the negotiations, and though it could count on the support of an influential actor like Germany, there is no evidence that the German government had to cast its political weight in the balance to impose an increase in the Parliament's powers. What appears to have been decisive instead was a loose convergence in ideational schemes, with national governments being inclined to accept that parliamentary oversight is a key aspect of democratic legitimacy in Western European political culture (Rittberger 2003). In other words, active leadership does not appear to have played a decisive role in one of the most striking institutional developments of the last twenty years.

Similarly, one could argue that the last three rounds of IGCs were characterized by an inherent weakness of leadership. True, as exemplified in several contributions to this volume, some of the participants could exert leadership of a certain kind in relation to some of the issues that were debated. However, none of them enjoyed decisive influence over a significant range of issues. The French-German tandem, though being the most likely candidate to exert structural leadership, did not really succeed in imposing its own 'model' on other EU member states, in spite of sporadic successes (see chapter 9). Occasionally, governments could exploit the position of the Presidency to score a few points, and in areas where its own interest were not directly at stake, the Council Secretariat could exert strong influence thanks to its expertise; recognized by all participants (see chapter 5). However, this falls far short of the grand convergence between structural and instrumental leadership that characterized the Single Act and the Maastricht Treaty negotiations. Indeed, in the period under review, France and Germany were at pains to identify areas of convergence, while the Commission's policy line fluctuated between the fear of exposing itself (during the Santer Presidency) and a complete inability to create stable alliances with national governments under Prodi (see chapter 6). In such a context, it is hardly surprising that the grand debate on the institutional adjustments made necessary by enlargement was so chaotic, with a failure to agree in Amsterdam, then an agreement perceived by all participants as suboptimal in Nice, immediately followed by the new round of negotiation that gave birth to the Constitutional Treaty.

Finally, in such a context, what often appears to be decisive is the ability of actors holding key leadership resources to unite their forces. Here again, episodes from the last round of negotiations provide good examples. Large states were often not trusted by most other EU members; this is especially true when they attempted to strike a deal among themselves. And the Commission's instrumental leadership was of little avail as it failed to enlist the support of a sufficient number of governments. Conversely, when there is a convergence of views between holders of structural leadership and those of instrumental leadership, it will prove harder to resist as exemplified by the EMU negotiation.

12.3   Is leadership on the wane?

Several chapters in this volume fuel the idea that leadership is in short supply these days. The inability of large countries to rally broad support around their plans, the systematic weakness of the Commission and the perceived 'failure' of key Presidencies (France in 2000, Italy in 2003) all combine to suggest the absence of any lasting leadership. It is therefore tempting to argue that the phase of uncertainty the EU is currently enduring is a byproduct of a 'crisis of leadership.' However, this judgment needs to be qualified in several respects.

First, we have to distinguish structural factors from contingent ones. There may be a crisis of leadership in the sense that current national leaders do not seem to attach the same importance to Europe than their predecessors. Yet this phenomenon could change in the future.

Secondly, it could be argued that the outcomes of the intergovernmental conferences analysed in this volume were influenced by agenda considerations. Contrary to earlier steps in the integration process, which essentially took the form of discrete political projects – achieving the single market, paving the way towards the single currency – these IGCs had as their main object institutional reform in its own right. This clearly made it more difficult for an agreement to emerge. Addressing institutions in the absence of more concrete stakes, the former tend to become an end in and of themselves, national suspicions awaken, and the negotiation ends up in a zero-sum game, making agreement uncertain. Such was the case in Nice as well as in the 2003–04 IGC (Dehousse 2001). The artificial divide between 'large' and 'small' states, which had been largely absent in past decades, as noted by the convention's trio presidency, became a central problem. This dilemma assumed center stage, and was aggravated by the growing number of small countries among the new member states (Amato *et al.* 2003). National representatives' positions in the negotiations were strongly influenced by their political culture or their institutional interests. The French were sensitive to the need for a strong President, whereas the Germans insisted on the idea of a catalogue of respective EU and member state powers. Compromises between these various models were made all the more difficult as the institutions themselves bear political symbolism; although it has had, so far, less real importance than is usually believed, the distribution of Council votes is perceived as an indicator of each nation's importance. Which government could give up its rank without consequences at the national level?

All this arguably had implications for the kind of leadership that could be provided. Structural leadership could not emerge easily as it was difficult to conceive of side payments that could be used in relation to the kind of issues that were addressed. Thus, although Spain and Poland as 'cohesion countries' were potentially exposed to financial pressures, they did not hesitate to block a compromise on the Constitutional Treaty in December 2003.

Other elements have altered the negotiating context of EU constitutional politics even more radically. The European Union of the early twenty-first century is radically different from the European Community at the time of the Single European Act. It has grown in number and in diversity. The Union now unites countries that have followed a radically different course in the post-1945 period. This heterogeneity makes negotiations much more complex than in the past.

The changes introduced in view of the last round of institutional reform have further complicated the provision of leadership in the negotiations. As is known, the 2003–04 IGC was preceded by a Convention, which significantly widened the number and variety of participants in the process. Whereas IGCs only comprise national governments' representatives, the Convention included of representatives of three other types of institutions: national Parliaments, the European Parliament and the European Commission. Representatives from candidate countries were also present, which brought the number of delegates to 207, if alternate members are included. This mere fact made it difficult to know the preferences of all the parties and to keep track of the successive proposals they contributed. Second, as the Convention quickly decided to draw up a text that would replace the current treaties, the number of issues dealt with increased accordingly. Lastly, as the rules of the game were new, and the actors were expected to 'deliberate,' it was difficult to resort to any process expertise.

National government representatives were the only actors to take part both in the Convention and the subsequent IGC, which had to 'take the ultimate decisions.' This is the reason why, towards the final stage of the Convention, their views sometimes appeared to be more acknowledged. However, this does not necessarily amount to supplying leadership. Although the joint French-German proposal regarding institutions attracted much attention, it did not really lead the other parties to agree to its terms.

Finally, as the Union has developed, so have points of resistance. The 'benign neglect' which surrounded European integration up until the mid-1980s has given way to forms of deep sensitivity to what 'Brussels' may be doing – or, indeed, may be supposed to be doing, since the information available to the public is often distorted. As a result, the number of veto points has grown. Not only institutions, such as the German *Länder*, but also social actors, be they trade unions, business interests, or even artists (for instance in the case of the French debate over the so-called *exception culturelle*) may try to influence their government's position in EU constitutional negotiations. All this makes it more likely that whichever form of leadership is exerted, the countervailing forces will, as a rule, be stronger than in the past.

The defeat of the Constitutional Treaty, by providing evidence that a varied coalition of specific interests can block a fundamental reform, will probably unleash centrifugal forces. Paradoxically, at the very moment that the difficulty of the endeavor makes leadership more necessary, its emergence is also made more problematic.

12.4 Conclusion

In closing, we argue that constitutional politics are becoming more and more polycentric, as was illustrated by the Convention process. Despite the obvious difficulties entailed, one should not necessarily deplore this evolution. Polycentrism is in part the result of a process that has become more open and transparent than in the past, not least with the establishment of the Convention. Moreover, European integration has deliberately been conceived as an anti-hegemonic process, in which no country should be able to exert decisive influence on its own.

In 'ordinary' EU decisionmaking, this polycentric character is compensated by devices aimed at ensuring a form of 'neutral' leadership, thanks to the Commission's monopoly of legislative initiative, or at avoiding excessive bargaining costs through the possibility of majority voting. Such devices are conspicuous by their absence at the level of IGCs; no stable instrumental leadership is explicitly foreseen and unanimity remains the rule. The case studies in this volume make one wonder if such a system can lead to satisfactory results in the context of an enlarged Union.

Admittedly, leadership cannot be created by a political decree. Although the powers of Commission Presidents have been considerably reinforced after the Delors era, few would argue that this has sufficed to make the Commission stronger. The context is so radically different that the changes in question have not prevented a gradual decline of the institution's influence relative to ordinary issues and in constitutional politics. Yet, as has been argued in various contributions to this volume, the conditions in which a negotiation takes place clearly impinges upon the leadership resources of the various participants.

While bearing this in mind, one possible path could be to rethink the institutional constraints in which IGCs take place, notably by drawing on the lessons of the Convention experience. This could take two forms. First, instrumental leadership might be provided for systematically, for instance with the creation of a full-time IGC Presidency, possibly strengthened by some kind of secretariat. However, the suspicion that surrounded the Presidency of Valéry Giscard d'Estaing during the European Convention suggests that governments will not tread lightly on this path. At the very least, they can be expected to demand guarantees in order to preserve the 'neutrality' of that body against the risk of capture by strong national interests. Another possible remedy would be to relax the twofold unanimity constraint that bears upon institutional reforms: unanimity on the proposed changes as well as at the ratification stage. In all likelihood, this would make it easier for an agreement to emerge without necessarily threatening the consensual character of decisionmaking, as suggested by the practice of majority voting in the Council of Ministers. Will the wreck of the draft European Constitutional Treaty be sufficient to convince national governments to do away with their veto power? At the time of writing, the question is still open.

13
Conclusions

Derek Beach and Colette Mazzucelli

13.1 Introduction

European Union constitutional negotiations are complex and often quite messy and chaotic affairs.[1] The final deal is by no means a given when governments sit down at the negotiating table to discuss sensitive constitutional reforms on an often large range of complex topics. A mutually acceptable compromise does not materialize by itself; it is the result of a long and often complicated negotiating process. This volume asserts that leadership is a crucial factor in overcoming the strong collective action problems and high bargaining costs that exist within these history-making constitutional negotiations. Leadership is defined relatively broadly as any action undertaken by an actor in order to attempt to solve *collective* action problems through the use of leadership resources. The provision of leadership is often motivated by an interest in *collective* gains. Often it is also directed at influencing outcomes for *private* gain.

The chapters in this book argue that leadership is necessary in these negotiating processes to help governments find and agree upon a mutually acceptable final treaty. Leadership often improves the *efficiency* of final agreements (see Figure 1.1). This means that leadership usually results in deals being reached that are closer to the Pareto frontier than would otherwise have been the case, or, in other words, no potential gains were left on the negotiating table. Yet leadership can come from many different actors, and who provides leadership matters. Successfully providing leadership grants the leader opportunities to skew the final outcome closer to his/her preferred outcome, affecting the *distribution* of gains from the final deal. Therefore, final outcomes tend to look different depending upon whether it was the French–German axis, the European Commission, or a small member state Presidency that supplied successful leadership.

The research design of this book was to create a structured series of case studies analysing the role and impact of potential leaders in a variety of different negotiating contexts. The volume aimed to create a focused inquiry by addressing the same questions in all of the chapters. The questions were answered by a team of distinguished scholars in European integration who were asked to focus on explaining both when and why potential leaders were successful in providing leadership, and, equally importantly, when potential leaders failed in their leadership attempts.

How, then, did we know successful leadership when we saw it, and how did we determine the effects of leadership upon agreements? Chapters in this volume tackled these problems in two ways. First, counterfactual argumentation was used extensively to make plausible claims that the leadership provided by an actor was significant/insignificant, and to determine the effects of that leadership. For example, chapter 2 directly addressed the question of whether the pro-French institutional provisions in the Treaty of Nice would have looked the same with another government at the helm. Tallberg answered negatively, providing strong counterfactual arguments for why French leadership affected the distribution of gains in the final outcome. Second, comparative analysis was used in order to determine the effects of the provision of different types of leadership in similar circumstances. For instance, in chapter 4 Crum compared the provision of leadership by the Italian and Irish Presidencies, which dealt with the same issues, although there arguably is some endogeneity between the cases. That is, the two cases are not necessarily independent of each other, as the results of the Italian Presidency, or perhaps lack thereof, impacted upon the ability of the Irish to provide effective leadership during their Presidency.

The leadership theory developed and tested in this volume was an attempt to go beyond the supranational–intergovernmental dichotomy that is still plaguing studies on European integration. The introductory chapter first answered the basic question of why leadership is necessary in EU constitutional negotiations by demonstrating why governments cannot sit down and easily find and agree upon a mutually acceptable outcome. While the bounds of agreement are determined by the preferences and relative power of governments, these bounds are often very broad due to the fact that governments often have vaguely defined preferences and due to high bargaining costs. Leadership therefore can be necessary to help governments find a mutually acceptable deal within this fog of uncertainty. Furthermore, it was also argued that who provides leadership matters. Outcomes do not merely reflect patterns of governmental preferences. By successfully providing leadership, a leader also gains opportunities to skew outcomes closer to his/her own preferences.

The chapter then developed a set of strong behavioral microfoundations for the leadership theory. It was argued that the assumptions of high bargaining costs, bounded rationality and collective action problems are empirically realistic; making leadership a necessary factor for constitutional negotiations to reach a conclusion.

The first stage of the leadership theory hypothesized that four types of leadership resources were relevant for treaty reform negotiations: material, informational, reputational, and internal capacity resources. The theory posited that a potential leader must possess strong leadership resources. Material resources, such as Germany's economic weight, allowed that country until recently to offer larger contributions to the EU budget in order to bankroll side payments given to recalcitrant parties. Informational resources are often crucial in constitutional negotiations, with expertise and bargaining skills the most relevant. Furthermore, a reputation for providing 'acceptable' leadership is often a resource. However, as explained in the French case analyzed in chapter 2, it is not always necessary to be seen to be 'neutral' to be a successful leader. Finally, the potential leader must have the internal capacity to mobilize all of his/her relevant resources behind any leadership attempt.

Second, whether a specific actor is able to translate resources into leadership depends upon the negotiating context. Here four factors were seen as critical. First, does the potential leader possess a *privileged institutional position* that can grant him/her advantages in supplying leadership? Second, are the *issues* under negotiation technically or legally *complex*? Third, is the *negotiating situation complex* with many issues and many parties? Given an increase in the complexity of the issues and the complexity of the negotiating situation, we expected the demand for instrumental leadership to forge agreement out of chaos to increase.

Finally, in terms of an actor's ability to provide leadership, *distribution and intensity of governmental preferences* matter in a given constitutional negotiation. When no area of possible agreements exists, only strong structural leadership provided by materially powerful actors can potentially shift governmental preferences in order to create a zone. In very sensitive issues, informational resources become less relevant because governments have incentives to mobilize the necessary resources to fully understand the issue. Finally, when governments are strongly interested in reaching a deal, they may have difficulties in agreeing upon a specific solution. This often creates a strong demand for instrumental leadership to help governments reach a deal.

In the following pages, the findings of the volume are discussed in more detail and related to the existing findings and theorizing in the literature. The chapter concludes with a discussion of the future of leadership in the European Union. As the EU-25 expands, and the policy scope of the union extends to new areas, such as the fight against terrorism, the provision of leadership is likely to be an increasingly important function in negotiations, be they constitutional or other history-making EU decisions.

13.2 The findings

The overall conclusions of the chapters in this book were that who provides leadership in EU constitutional negotiations mattered for both the efficiency and the distribution of gains in constitutional agreements. Structural leadership by leaders with 'muscles' was often found to be necessary to provide the EU with overall direction (Figure 1.3). This type of leadership was often supplied in the past by the French–German tandem, with the best example being the French–German compromise that led to the Treaty of Maastricht (chapter 9 and Mazzucelli 1999). Furthermore, when governments are faced with politically sensitive issues, structural leadership can be necessary in order to push governments towards viable compromises.

Instrumental leadership was defined as setting and shaping the agenda and then engineering consensus. This type of leadership was also often necessary to find and agree upon mutually acceptable outcomes in complex EU treaty negotiations. The importance of instrumental leadership is perhaps most evident in situations where the demand for it was strong and yet this type of leadership was not supplied effectively. One example was arguably during the Italian Presidency in the fall of 2003, when the Italians did little to engineer consensus on the key issues under negotiation (Chapters 4 and 5).

What factors determined which actors were successfully able to provide these two types of leadership? The following pages initially discuss the findings regarding the impact of leadership resources upon the ability of actors to provide leadership, and next turn to discuss how the negotiating context mattered.

Leadership resources

Material resources were necessary for actors that attempted to provide structural leadership; they were almost never sufficient given the consensual nature of EU constitutional politics and the sensitivity of many of the issues under discussion (see Table 13.1). Material resources were found to be especially useful as a means of offering side payments to isolated holdouts in specific issue areas. For example, Spain was given a side-payment in the form of cohesion funds to 'buy' its acceptance of EMU in the 1990–91 IGC.

Yet, except in isolated circumstances, no potential leader can, for example, merely muscle other governments to accept the transferal of sovereignty to the EU in those areas to which they are strongly opposed. Clearly there is a limit to the success side payments and hard bargaining can bring in EU constitutional negotiations. This was seen in chapter 9, in the instances where France and Germany were unable to muscle other governments to compromise their positions due to the sensitive nature of many of the issues on the table.

At the other end of the spectrum, due to the need for unanimity in intergovernmental conferences, the United Kingdom was effectively able to act as a 'laggard leader' in several rounds of treaty reform. However, strong material resources were a key factor in the success of the British 'laggard leader' strategy. If a smaller country such as Denmark attempted the same

Table 13.1 The impact of material leadership resources

Leadership resource	Impact of the variable in the empirical cases
Material resources	• French Presidency (ch. 2) – possession of strong material resources was a very significant factor for the success of the French Presidency in the 2000 IGC; • Italian/Irish Presidencies (ch. 4) – possession of strong material resources was not a significant factor in explaining the relative failure/success of the two Presidencies; • European Parliament (ch. 7) – ability of the EP to link its powers in daily EU policymaking with outcomes was unsuccessful in the 1996–97 IGC; • Big vs Small (ch. 8) – crucial resource that was vital for the success of the 'bigs' leadership on the institutional balance of power in the Constitutional Treaty negotiations; • French–German tandem (ch. 9) – was a necessary, but not sufficient factor for successful French–German leadership; • UK and Poland (chs 10 and 11) – strong material resources were important for the ability of both the UK and Poland to act as 'laggard leaders'.

strategy as the British, we would expect that the weak laggard would be unsuccessful in its leadership attempt as they have no credible unilateral alternative to agreement (Schneider and Cederman 1994).

One possible exception to the lesson that material leadership only goes so far was seen, however, in the negotiation of the Constitutional Treaty. As chapter 8 explains, the bigger member states had such a preponderance of material resources that their aggregate strength enabled them to 'bully' the smaller member states into accepting a fundamental shift in the institutional balance of power in the Council. The result was the shift to a system in the Constitutional Treaty where the overrepresentation of the smalls in the Council was reduced in favor of the larger member states through the double majority procedure (Article I-25). In this case, however, specific concessions were given to the smalls in order to sweeten the pill, further demonstrating the limits of 'great power' leadership in EU constitutional negotiations.

Informational resources are often crucial to the ability of potential leaders to provide leadership. EU constitutional negotiations are often complicated affairs. It can take substantial expertise in the issues and bargaining skill in order first to find and then to craft consensus around a mutually acceptable final deal. Given this complexity, there is often a high demand for instrumental leadership to help the parties find and agree upon a mutually acceptable outcome.

Table 13.2 The impact of informational leadership resources

Leadership resource	Impact of the variable in the empirical cases
Informational resources	• Dutch Presidency (ch. 3) – learning curve evident from experiences in fall of 1991 to their next Presidency in spring 1997; • Council Secretariat (ch. 5) – possession of unrivaled bargaining skills and experience with EU treaty negotiations made the Secretariat an indispensable assistant to the Presidency; • Commission (ch. 6) – possessed technocratic expertise, yet these skills were less relevant in the context of the negotiation of the Constitutional Treaty in 2002–04; • European Parliament (ch. 7) – experience with negotiating in 'parliamentary-like' EU-level setting was a key factor in explaining the relative success of the EP in the European Convention; • UK (ch. 10) – relatively successful despite outlier position due to preparedness and the bargaining skills and experience of key officials;

The importance of informational resources was illustrated in the chapters on the Council Secretariat, the UK, and the EP. Table 13.2 summarizes the conclusions. Chapter 5 described the role and impact of the Council Secretariat in intergovernmental conferences. The Council Secretariat has unrivaled bargaining skills, which have enabled it first to identify and then to craft acceptable compromises that elude other actors. The Secretariat sits at the center of a web of communication and has a vast institutional memory. As an institution, the Secretariat has a vision of the state of play in the negotiations that is often beyond that possessed by any other actor, even the government holding the Presidency. These skills and knowledge can be successfully translated into leadership when: (1) there is a demand for instrumental leadership; and (2) the Presidency decides to delegate functions to the Secretariat.

The United Kingdom, despite having outlier preferences, has been relatively successful in several rounds of treaty negotiations due to the preparedness as well as the bargaining skills and experience of key officials, including Prime Ministers. For instance, British Permanent Representatives are often posted for longer stays in Brussels than their counterparts in other member states. This means they possess greater experience of how EU compromises are made, and, in particular, how EU treaty negotiations are conducted.

The European Parliament has traditionally played an outsider role in constitutional negotiations (chapter 7). However, when the Parliament was brought into the fold in the European Convention on the Future of Europe in 2002–03, key MEPs were able to exploit their familiarity with operating in a 'parliament-like' setting at the EU level to craft compromises and build coalitions that eluded other actors.

However, informational advantages have to be relevant to the specific negotiation in order for them to be a leadership resource. As explained in chapter 6, in the European Convention the Commission found that despite possessing unrivaled technical expertise, this expertise was not what was 'in demand' in the debates on institutional reforms. Therefore, Commission representatives could not translate their technical expertise into leadership on most issues.

The *reputation* of a potential leader was found to have an impact upon the ability of a potential leader to provide leadership successfully (Table 13.3). As we argued in chapter 1, a reputation for providing 'acceptable' leadership is based upon either the recognition of the utility of the potential leader's contributions or the legitimacy possessed by the potential leader.

Table 13.3 The impact of reputational leadership resources

Leadership resource	Impact of the variable in the empirical cases
Reputation for 'acceptable' leadership	• French Presidency (ch. 2) – The French ignored norms of neutrality and impartiality throughout their Presidency, yet were still able to act as a successful leader; • Dutch Presidency (ch. 3) – Dutch excessive partiality in 1991 did not adversely affect the prospects for effective Dutch leadership in the chair during the 1996–97 IGC endgame; • Council Secretariat (ch. 5) – a vital resource for the Council Secretariat. In issue areas where the Secretariat was viewed by the Presidency to be acting partially (for instance, the Dutch view of the Secretariat in spring 1997), the Secretariat was not allowed to play its role acting as a key instrumental leader; • Commission (ch. 6) – the Commission's reputation as a technocratic actor was a key factor in securing acceptance of a strong European Commission role in the 1985 IGC, whereas it significantly weakened the Commission in the European Convention; • European Parliament (ch. 7) – also vital for the EP's ability to provide leadership. In the 1996–97 IGC, a stronger EP role in the IGC was unacceptable for several governments; • French–German tandem (ch. 9) – during periods where French–German leadership effectively bridged major cleavages, their leadership was perceived as 'acceptable;' yet their reputation has been tarnished in recent years as Germany, in particular, has increasingly ignored the interests of smaller member states;

There are rarely, if ever, 'neutral' leaders in the Union, as all of the potential leaders have stakes in the outcomes of EU treaty negotiations. It must, therefore, be stressed that 'acceptable' is *not* always synonymous with neutrality, and that a partial leader can sometimes provide 'acceptable' leadership. This was arguably the case with the French Presidency in 2000. Chapter 2 argued that the French were partial to their own national position on the key institutional issues, and exploited their Presidency to protect French interests. In this case, the French never crossed the invisible line of 'excessive partiality,' although they were arguably very close at several instances during the final Nice European Council (Beach 2005: 149–51). If the French had crossed this line, negotiations would have broken down. In the 2000 IGC, other governments did not openly reject French leadership by packing their bags and leaving Nice. The end result was a final deal that protected the key French priority – parity in Council voting weights with Germany.

In contrast, the Dutch Presidency overstepped this line of 'excessive partiality' in September 1991. The Presidency chose to discard the Luxembourg draft treaty, which had been approved by all governments as the basis for negotiations, replacing that text with a more federal single-pillar Dutch draft. This open breach of protocol to further national aims led to an open rebellion by the other governments, forcing an embarrassing retreat by the Dutch back to the Luxembourg draft (chapter 3).

A reputation for providing 'acceptable' leadership was found to be especially crucial for EU institutions since they are not officially parties to EU treaty negotiations. The Commission enjoyed this acceptability in the 1985 IGC, and governments saw it as natural that the Commission would play a key agenda-setting role since the issues under negotiation were core areas of Community cooperation. This acceptance led the Luxembourg Presidency to delegate the agenda-setting role to the Commission, thereby also granting Delors many opportunities to translate the Commission's considerable expertise into leadership (chapter 6).

The case of the EP further illustrates the key importance of 'acceptability' (chapter 7). Despite being the only directly elected EU institution, both France and the UK resisted giving the EP more than an observer role in the 1996–97 IGC. Both countries feared the EP would push pro-federal solutions in the negotiations. After the failures at Nice and the way in which EP representatives played a useful contributing role in the Convention that drafted the EU Charter in 2000, the question of granting the EP a role in the next round of constitutional reform was more digestible. In other words, the 'acceptability' of the EP had substantially increased, which allowed key MEPs to play influential leadership roles during the Convention.

The *internal capacity* of a given actor to mobilize relevant resources behind his/her leadership attempts was found to be an important factor in the cases under investigation. The findings are summarized in Table 13.4.

Table 13.4 The impact of internal capacity as a leadership resource

Leadership resource	Impact of the variable in the empirical cases
Internal capacity	• Dutch Presidency (ch. 3) – divisions during the initial months of the Presidency in the fall of 1991 affected the ability of the Dutch to provide effective leadership; • Commission (ch. 6) – internal divisions prevented the Commission from providing leadership in the European Convention; • French–German tandem (ch. 9) – internal divisions in both France (*cohabitation*) and Germany (pressure from the *Länder*) significantly impacted upon their ability to act as the motor of integration; • UK (ch. 10) – strong internal preparation and coordination of British positions has been a key resource;

The ability to mobilize resources – in other words, whether the actor has the actual *capacity* to provide leadership – is dependent upon the actor's internal organization. The impact of this leadership resource was best illustrated in the two cases where there is the most variance. Regarding the case of the Commission in the European Convention, the internal splits and lack of internal leadership effectively led the Commission to go 'missing in action' (chapter 6). In contrast, the UK was often successful in its 'laggard-leader' strategy due to the strong internal coherence and 'will' demonstrated in building coalitions supporting British outlier positions.

The impact of the negotiating context

The literature analysing leadership in EU constitutional negotiations has been split into an either-or dichotomy regarding whether or not leadership is necessary in this context, and which actors are able to provide leadership. These two schools are the intergovernmentalist, state-centric view and the supranational agency approach. As chapter 1 explains, the intergovernmentalist position articulates that governments are relatively easily able to sit down and find a Pareto-efficient outcome. Given the sensitive nature of many of the topics in EU constitutional negotiations, governments will have incentives to mobilize all of the necessary resources in order to understand the issues and the state of play. Bargaining costs are seen as low relative to the potential gains of agreement (Moravcsik 1999a). Those governments with the strongest interests in specific issues act as leaders. Yet they argue that, given the ease with which leadership can be supplied, the supply of leadership by any one actor is redundant, and will not impact upon outcomes. Intergovernmentalists conclude that EU treaty negotiations are 'naturally efficient' (ibid.: 273). The distribution of gains in EU treaty negotiations is determined solely by the distribution of relative power, resulting in agreements skewed toward French–German interests, with the UK acting as a brake.

On the other side of this dichotomy is the supranational agency approach, which argues that the provision of leadership by the Commission is often significant, and sometimes necessary, for the achievement of efficient EU constitutional agreements (chapter 6; Beach 2005 provides further descriptions and discussions of the different theories within this overall approach). Here constitutional negotiations are understood as more complex affairs. The Commission is viewed as possessing significant informational resources, which allow the institution successfully to provide leadership by creating and exploiting demands for further integration. Most prominent is neofunctionalist theory, which sees the European Commission as playing a key leadership role by cultivating demands for more integration (Haas 1958, 1961; Lindberg 1963; Tranholm-Mikkelsen 1991; Stone Sweet and Sandholtz 1998). Further, it is argued that the Commission can help governments go beyond a Pareto-inefficient lowest common denominator and, by acting as a mediator, is able to help governments 'upgrade their common interests' (Haas 1961).

The leadership theory developed in this volume attempts to go beyond this dichotomy that still plagues integration theory by specifying under which specific circumstances we expect different types of leaders to play important roles. The introductory chapter detailed four different contextual variables that can affect the demand for leadership and the ability of potential leaders to provide leadership (see Table 13.5).

First, it was theorized that the institutional role an actor plays in a given negotiation is significant; different institutional positions grant actors a range of powers that can be exploited to better offer opportunities to supply leadership that matches the demand. We expect the provision of successful leadership varies depending upon the strength of the institutional position enjoyed by the potential leader. Chapters 2 to 4 discussed the advantages accrued by governments possessing the Presidency during EU treaty negotiations. Jonas Tallberg's chapter analysed what he describes as the 'power of the Chair.' These are the potential channels for leadership enjoyed by the Presidency, including procedural powers, such as control of the agenda, along with access to privileged information (chapter 2; Tallberg 2003, 2004a).

The empirical analysis in chapters 2 to 4 clearly illustrated the impact of possessing a privileged institutional position such as the Presidency. In the 2000 IGC, France exploited its procedural control over the negotiations to ensure that the final deal reached in Nice protected key national interests. In particular, the French Presidency took advantage of its control over the negotiating process to assure that the French position on parity with Germany

Table 13.5 The impact of the negotiating context

Contextual variable	Impact of the variable in the empirical cases
Institutional position	• The Presidency was a key institutional position that gave the holder significant procedural powers that could be used as a channel for the provision of successful leadership. In particular, the ability of Presidencies to structure the agenda and conduct of the negotiations proved to be an essential factor for all of the Presidencies investigated; • Delegation of functions by the Presidency to the Council Secretariat was crucial to the ability of the Secretariat to act as an instrumental leader, helping improve the efficiency of agreements by drafting texts, and helping to find and broker compromises;

Demand for leadership created by the negotiating context (technicality of issues, complexity of negotiating situation, distribution and intensity of governmental preferences)	• 1996–97 IGC – there was a demand for instrumental and structural leadership;
	
	  – instrumental leadership was necessary due to the many technically complex issues under discussion, and the large number of issues on the agenda;
	  – regarding the sensitive institutional issues, there was also a need for structural leadership to pressure reluctant governments to compromise, although arguably these issues were not 'ripe' for settlement because enlargement was still years in the future;
	
	• 2000 IGC – strong demand for structural leadership;
	
	  – there was a lower demand for instrumental leadership since there were only relatively few simple issues on the agenda;
	  – in contrast, there was a need for 'great power' (structural) leadership in order to pressure reluctant governments to compromise on institutional issues;
	
	• European Convention – strong demand for leadership;
	
	  – instrumental leadership was necessary in order to forge order out of the chaos of over 200 delegates debating thousands of different amendments and proposals on hundreds of often very technical institutional and policy-related issues;
	  – there was also a demand for structural leadership when dealing with the key institutional 'balance of power' questions;
	
	• 2003–04 IGC – there was a demand for instrumental and structural leadership;
	
	  – despite the fact that the IGC only dealt with a handful of salient issues, these were of a sensitive nature, which demanded pressure on governments to concede;

emerged victorious in the negotiations. Here the combination of strong material resources and holding the Presidency allowed the French to skew outcomes towards their own preferences, which affected the distribution of gains in the final agreement.

The case of the Dutch Presidency in the 1990–91 IGC showed, however, that there are limits to what can be achieved with a privileged institutional position. In September 1991, the Dutch Presidency unilaterally decided to move away from the Luxembourg draft. The Presidency exploited its control of the agenda by tabling a new single-pillar draft treaty, which was shot down by other governments in what has come to be termed 'Black Monday.' The Dutch learned lessons from this debacle. Although they also promoted Dutch national interests during their Presidency in the endgame of the 1996–97 IGC, the Dutch used their position in the Chair that spring mostly to engineer consensus. This led to the successful negotiation of a mutually acceptable Treaty of Amsterdam, in which Dutch leadership primarily impacted upon the efficiency of agreements.

The contrasting cases of the Italian and Irish Presidencies in the 2003–04 IGC provided evidence that who holds the Presidency matters, and that the procedural powers of the Presidency can be used for very different purposes. The Italian government was interested in maintaining the Convention's text 'as is,' and therefore exploited its procedural control to prevent the reopening of the package. This had the adverse effect of not preparing the way for agreement, leaving the Irish Presidency to pick up the pieces after the inevitable breakdown in Brussels in December 2003.

Institutional position was also found to be central to the ability of EU institutions to provide leadership. Since the Commission, Council Secretariat and European Parliament have no *formal* roles in intergovernmental conferences, all three were dependent upon the delegation of functions. In chapter 5, we saw that the Council Secretariat was able successfully to provide leadership when it was delegated functions by successive Presidencies. This was seen during the 1996–97 IGC, where both the Irish and Dutch used the Secretariat to provide draft texts, and to help broker behind-the-scenes compromises. This gave the Secretariat a privileged institutional position from which to attempt to provide instrumental leadership.

Furthermore, during the European Convention the chair of the Convention was a key function that allowed the holder, Valéry Giscard d'Estaing, firmly to control the debates and the drafting of texts. Giscard was an advocate of the large member states on key institutional issues. This fact created an indirect privileged position for the large member states in the Convention, and helped those actors put their stamp on the final draft Constitutional Treaty provisions, especially those concerning the re-weighting of Council votes and the European Council Presidency (chapter 8).

The chapters also discussed the impact of the negotiating context regarding the demand for leadership. The impact of this factor can best be illustrated by contrasting the two extremes. The 2000 IGC was a relatively simple negotiation, with only a few non-technical issues under discussion among 15 governments. There was a relatively low demand for instrumental leadership. In contrast, the European Convention was an immensely complex affair. There were hundreds of salient issues on the agenda. Thousands of amendments and proposals were on the floor. The Convention was comprised of 207 delegates and chairmen, creating a situation in which no one actor had a fully synoptic overview of the situation. Here there was a strong demand for instrumental leadership to guide the proceedings, which was supplied by the chairmen, and more secondarily by key governments and MEPs.

The demand for structural leadership varied depending upon the political salience of the issues. There was little demand for structural leadership in low salience issues, such as the majority of issues in the 1996–97 IGC. In the 2000 IGC, however, the deal-breaking issues were very sensitive questions of institutional power. These issues were only resolved when the French Presidency, backed by the other big member states, leaned on the smalls to make them accept the Nice compromise (chapters 2 and 8).

In conclusion, for leadership to be successful the potential actor had both to possess strong relevant leadership resources, and to provide the type of leadership that matched the specific demand created by the negotiating context. A privileged institutional position was also often a key factor that allowed a potential leader to provide leadership. The successful provision of instrumental leadership, where the leader shaped the agenda and helped engineer consensus, usually only affected the efficiency of agreements. In the cases investigated in this volume, this type of leadership was usually provided by the Presidency, assisted by the Council Secretariat. Structural leadership, in comparison, was often aimed at the distribution of gains from an agreement, and was usually provided by 'great power' actors like the French–German tandem. Given the nature of EU cooperation, some form of acceptability or legitimacy was a necessary condition for successful structural leadership. Otherwise, this type of leadership would be perceived as a form of 'hegemonic' leadership, and would result in the weaker powers using their veto powers to block the 'hegemonic' leaders.

13.3 Comparing the leadership model to existing studies of EU constitutional negotiations

How does this leadership theory, and the evidence provided in this volume, relate to existing studies of European integration? The first point that must be made is to discuss what the leadership model does not do. The leadership model is not a general 'theory' of integration; it is a more limited mid-range theory that focuses specifically upon how leadership affects the ways in

Figure 13.1 The analytical stages of EU constitutional negotiations

which governmental preferences are translated into outcomes in EU constitutional negotiations. This is depicted in Figure 13.1 as the middle box between governmental preferences and outcomes. This volume, therefore, does not make propositions about the process of national preference formation. Nor does it discuss the extent to which events in constitutional negotiations feed back into national preferences (the dotted line with the question mark in Figure 13.1). The studies in this volume take national preferences as given and are interested in focusing specifically upon the process of negotiation and the impact of leadership therein.

Liberal intergovernmentalism (LI), in comparison, does develop mid-range theories for both domestic preference formation and what Moravcsik terms the 'inter-state' bargaining phase (Moravcsik 1993, 1998). LI draws upon international political economy theory and liberal interdependence theory to argue that governmental positions reflect patterns of economic policy externalities, and how they impact upon significant domestic actors such as producer groups (Moravcsik 1998: 35–50). An interesting critical attempt to make LI's preference formation theory more realistic has been developed by Dimitrakopoulos and Kassim (2004), where they include factors neglected by LI, such as the impact of domestic political arrangements, domestic opportunity structures, the impact of membership, and national policy style and culture.

Other integration theories are less explicit regarding the preference formation process. It is dealt with in both neo-functionalist and social constructivist work on the EU, but neither develops an explicit theory of preference formation for what interests governments start with in the integration process. Instead, each argues that participation in a strong supranational institution like the EU gradually changes actor preferences in a more cooperative, pro-integrative direction. In neo-functionalism this is termed political spillover (Lindberg 1963); in social constructivism it is termed 'social learning' (Checkel 1999, 2001).

Turning to look specifically at the model of EU constitutional negotiations, the following section compares the leadership model and the results of the case studies to liberal intergovernmentalism's theory of inter-state bargaining, principal–agent theorization, and realist accounts of European integration.

In comparison to LI, the leadership model developed testable hypotheses about how the negotiation context matters. In contrast, LI ends up 'black boxing' the analytical significance of the actual negotiation process. Moravcsik's theory of inter-state bargaining holds that: (1) governments are close to comprehensively rational; (2) bargaining costs are low relative to the gains of agreement; and (3) there are no factors internal to the negotiating process, such as the possession of a strong institutional position, that affect how relative power and preferences are translated into outcomes. Therefore, drawing upon cooperative game theory, Moravcsik argues that it is possible to predict the outcome of a negotiation *solely* based upon the relative dependence of governments upon an agreement (Moravcsik 1998: 61–4, 1999a).

Yet the evidence produced in this book shows that factors such as the institutional position of actors matter. The Presidency is the best example of an institutional position that affects how preferences are translated into outcomes. It gives the holder a range of procedural powers that can be exploited to provide leadership. While a substantial portion of this leadership provided by the Presidency affects the efficiency of agreements, the chapters on the French and Dutch Presidencies clearly showed that the Chair can also be exploited for private gains.

Another area of contention with LI is that the leadership resources, or, in LI terms, power resources, of actors are not solely determined by the relative dependence of actors upon agreement. The French–German chapter clearly showed that when France and Germany are unable to mobilize their significant material resources due to internal disagreements, they are unable to provide direction and leadership despite their preponderance in terms of relative power.

LI also posits that there are no 'bottlenecks' regarding information and ideas in IGCs. In the words of Moravcsik, 'Why should governments, with millions of diverse and highly trained professional employees, massive information-gathering capacity, and long-standing experience with international negotiations at their disposal, *ever* require the services of a handful of supranational entrepreneurs to generate and disseminate useful information and ideas?' (Moravcsik 1999a: 273).

This volume questioned this assumption regarding information, and extended the argument more broadly to encompass governments as well. We found that there are often significant differences in the level of expertise and bargaining skills possessed by actors in EU constitutional negotiations. The possession of informational advantages can in certain contexts be an asset for attempts to provide leadership. For example, the high level of preparedness and the skill of British officials and ministers significantly assisted British 'laggard leadership.' Regarding EU institutions, the Council Secretariat, which on paper has no formal 'power' resources, possessed the bargaining skills and drafting experience that allowed the institution to provide instrumental leadership, which substantially increased the efficiency of the agreements reached.

As the leadership model developed draws upon Principal–Agent reasoning, it is very relevant to compare it with Principal–Agent (PA) theory as it has been applied to the EU (Pollack 1997, 2003; Tallberg 2003). PA's basic argument in comparison to LI is that delegated institutional positions matter. The influence that can be gained from possessing a privileged institutional position that varies according to: (1) the strength of the powers delegated to the agent; (2) whether effective control mechanisms are available to the principals; (3) the distribution of principal preferences; and (4) the extent to which the agent possesses informational advantages *vis-à-vis* the principals. While these factors echo the leadership model developed in this volume, there are three key differences. First, on a theoretical level, the leadership model provides a more general model of negotiations that analyzes a wider range of actors than just agents. P–A's focus is on how agents with delegated institutional positions can provide 'leadership,' but the leadership model goes beyond this to discuss how other types of actors, such as governments, also can exploit informational and material advantages in complex negotiations to provide leadership. Second, the leadership model develops an explicit set of hypotheses based upon the negotiating context for when informational advantages can matter. This is something that P–A theorization unfortunately does not do. Thirdly, when Pollack does look at the role of EU institutions in constitutional bargaining, he focuses solely upon *formal* institutional powers, thereby defining away the types of *informal* delegation of powers that has given the Council Secretariat the ability to provide successful instrumental leadership in IGC negotiations (Pollack 1999 as compared with Chapter 5 and Beach 2004, 2005).

Finally, realism has focused upon 'great power' leadership in the EU. Pedersen's theory on 'cooperative hegemony' is the most complete attempt to explain the history-making decisions of the EU using realism (Pedersen 1998, 2002). Pedersen sees the integration process as driven by the major powers, where there is an inter-state bargain regarding European cooperation. The theory is based upon the 'cooperative hegemony' thesis. A potential hegemon that does not have sufficient material resources to dominate other states will choose a more cooperative strategy to prevent lesser powers from balancing against the hegemon. The 'weak' hegemon, in this case, Germany, will therefore choose cooperative hegemony, creating a legitimate power-sharing institution such as the EU. In this institution, smaller states bandwagon *with* the hegemon in order to gain 'voice,' whereas the hegemon, Germany, uses the institution as both an instrument to achieve goals by institutional means and to prevent balancing against it by France and other EU countries.

Pedersen's theory provides an interesting and important contribution that can help us understand the long-term evolution of the Union. Yet the conclusions of this volume differ from his thesis in three important ways. First, while 'great power' leadership was shown to be influential,

French–German leadership was found to be most effective when: (1) French–German compromises neatly bridged the main cleavages in the given negotiations; and (2) the 'great powers' had the internal capacity to mobilize their resources behind their leadership attempts. Second, the two chapters in this volume that explicitly tackled the question of 'great power' leadership in the EU both found that, given the consensual nature of EU constitutional politics, the ability of the 'bigs' to push the smaller states around was limited. Finally, Pedersen's theory can be subjected to the same critique as Moravcsik's LI theory, namely that it makes no provision for the importance of institutional positions, such as the importance of holding the Presidency, or being delegated certain functions by governments.

13.4   The implications – leadership in EU constitutional negotiations

This volume explained under which circumstances we should expect certain types of actors to be able to exercise leadership in EU constitutional negotiations. What are the implications of these findings? What do they tell us about the nature of the Union? Do they shed light on possible future developments?

First, given the increasing complexity of EU politics, we expect a greater demand for leadership as time passes. In terms of instrumental leadership, or the management of complexity to help governments find mutually acceptable outcomes, it has become increasingly apparent that the Presidency is a vital institution. However, greater dependence upon instrumental leadership provided by the Presidency has 'costs' for governments, as the Presidency also gains the opportunity to exploit the chair to promote its own national priorities that do not necessarily reflect majority views. Equally important, it also shows that when a Presidency does not effectively supply leadership, it is often difficult, if not impossible for, the EU to reach crucial compromise deals.

Secondly, structural leadership can be vital to give the EU direction. There are two different types of situations where structural leadership is necessary. First, structural leadership is often necessary in intractable negotiating situations, and a certain amount of 'pushing' by powerful governments can be necessary to force other governments to accept compromises. Yet the use of this resource by the 'bigs' since the late 1990s to pressure the smaller states to compromise on institutional questions has also led to forms of 'balancing' on the part of the 'smalls,' as seen in the European Convention. If this tendency continues, this would upset the fundamental 'cooperative' compromise between the 'bigs' and 'smalls' in the Union. Furthermore, given the consensual nature of EU politics, it is usually not very effective. This was evidenced in most instances during the Constitutional Treaty negotiations.

Further, structural leadership can be necessary to give the integration process an overall sense of direction. Whether the EU has reached an institutional plateau where further integration is no longer necessary, or whether the EU is similar to a bicycle that needs to keep moving in order not to fall down, is a debate that is outside of the scope of this chapter (See e.g. Moravcsik 2005a, 2005b). What may be concluded, based upon the volume's findings, is that we should not expect direction from the French–German tandem, as the duo has increasingly moved away from the original 'motor' role, to act of late much more like an 'improbable core' (chapter 9).

One could argue, however, that strong structural leadership to provide the EU with a sense of overall direction has not been, and will not be, necessary. The constitutional process in the past two decades has only been a minor 'tinkering' with the fundamental compromise made in Rome almost 50 years ago. There have been no major constitutional changes to alter fundamentally the Union's institutional balance-of-power similar to, for example, the transition from the Fourth to the Fifth Republics in France. This may well be a blessing for which to be thankful. The lesson from domestic constitutional reform processes is that *major changes* are usually not the product of 'leadership;' they are primarily the result of *major crises*, such as the one France faced in the late 1950s (Hine 2001).

Another take on this situation is that the EU is presently leaderless, and that there is an unmatched demand for structural leadership. Therefore, one could interpret the recent history of the Union as a listless drift from one suboptimal outcome to another, illustrated by Euro-fudges like the 'reform' of the Growth and Stability Pact, the French and Dutch rejections and 'reflection period' of the Constitutional Treaty, and the disputes over the financial perspective for 2007–13.

In our view, we can conclude this discussion on a pragmatic positive note by stating that although the Constitutional Treaty failed in the Dutch and French referendums, it cannot be denied that the Union still works. Effective leadership is still possible that can help governments 'solve' important problems. For instance, the Danish Presidency, assisted extensively by the Commission and the German government, ensured that the complicated enlargement negotiations were concluded in December 2002 with the ten accession states (Beach 2005). Moreover, 'great power' structural leadership is still possible when governments choose to adopt a 'cooperative' strategy that attempts to bridge key cleavages, leading to a compromise that all member states can accept. A good example of this was the British–French initiative in St Malo in 1998, which neatly bridged the cleavages separating the Europeanists from Atlanticists on EU defense policy. France accepted that European defense integration would complement NATO, whereas the British accepted that the cooperation would take place *within* the Union.

On the other hand, we must recognize that there are challenges that confront the Union. Many of the member states that represent the traditional 'core' of the Union have internal problems that raise questions about their capacity to supply leadership. In Germany, political stalemate is likely to linger as long as the needed economic reforms have not been implemented. Disorder in France is symptomatic of a much deeper *malaise* for a country struggling with the integration of immigrants, structural reforms in its economy to address high unemployment, and a clear reluctance to embrace the services economy in a global environment. In the Netherlands, a country that remains firmly committed to integration, dissatisfaction with the governmental leadership and a clear gap between parliamentary elites and the population is coupled with an unwillingness to remain a net contributor to the Union's budget. Political instability is likely to mark Italian politics for some time to come, hampering its ability to play a pro-European card and even calling into question the country's commitment to the single currency. In Britain, the ability to supply leadership is also in question as a weakened prime minister faces lingering doubts about the country's involvement in the Iraq war. Even though leadership in a larger Union is clearly about more than the contributions of these member states, the challenge is that their difficulties may be symptomatic of a broader generational dilemma *vis-à-vis* integration throughout the Continent.

Equally importantly, as long as domestic leaderships are unable to inspire member state populations, the 'democratic deficit' is likely to pose genuine obstacles to further constitutional reform. After the rejection of the Constitutional Treaty in two referenda, the basic question is whether there is a mismatch between the demands for and supply of leadership at the elite level, and what actually can be ratified by voters. The million-dollar question here is how we can bring voter demands for integration and the elite supply of leadership into balance. Should voters be 'educated' in order for them to be more supportive of further integration? There is, however, no clear correlation between levels of 'knowledge' among voters and preferences toward Europe: both Denmark, with one of the highest levels of voter knowledge, and Ireland, with one of the lowest, have rejected EU treaties.

Should constitutional processes be changed in order better to match elite and voter demands? The Convention method was an attempt to do so, where it was hoped that the more transparent and democratic setting would result in a more democratic and deliberative process that would result in popular constitutional reforms. Yet what we saw was that, in the words of Moravcsik: 'Few citizens were aware of the 200 conventionnels' deliberations. When testimony from civil society was requested, professors turned up. When a youth conference was called, would-be Eurocrats attended' (Moravcsik 2005b). There is little to indicate that a future Convention would be any different. After only several months of the so-called 'reflection period' after the French and Dutch no's, the question of the future of Europe has all but disappeared from public discourse.

All this requires member states and European institutions to rethink fundamentally their strategy of constitutional reform and to match their rhetoric with the reality of domestic expectations. The so-called Convention process is in fact no substitute for what are essentially still treaty reform negotiations. Moreover, a constitutional process that moves too far and too fast in the eyes of general publics cannot be accepted via direct democracy in spite of the ready supply of elite leadership illustrated in the chapters of this volume.

There is no doubt that leadership is necessary in an increasingly complex Union. This volume demonstrated that there are many potential leaders, and that the Union possesses the required institutions that can assist them in supplying leadership to match most demands. Regarding future constitutional reforms, the problem is not primarily the supply of leadership, but should be seen at the level of preference formation, where there is a notable lack of demand for further constitutional reform.

Note

1. The terms constitutional and treaty are used synonymously in this chapter.

References

Albert, M. (1993) *Capitalism against Capitalism.* London: Whurr.

Allen, D. (2004) 'The Convention and the Draft Constitutional Treaty', in F. Cameron (ed.) *The Future of Europe.* London: Routledge, pp. 18–34.

Allison, G.T. (1969) 'Conceptual Models and the Cuban Missile Crisis', *American Political Science Review*, 6(3): 689–718.

Allison, G.T. (1971) *Essence of Decision: Explaining the Cuban Missile Crisis.* Boston: Little, Brown.

Allison, G.T., and M. Halperin (1972) 'Bureaucratic Politics: a Paradigm and Some Policy Implications', *World Politics*, 24: 40–79.

Amato, Giuliano, Jean-Luc Dehaene and Valéry Giscard d'Estaing (2003) 'L'Europe de demain. La fausse querelle entre "grands" et "petits" ', *Le Monde*, November 14.

Arnauld, A. (2003) 'Normenhierarchien innerhalb des primären Gemeinschaftsrechts', *Europarecht*, 2: 191–216.

Aspinwall, M. (2000) 'Structuring Europe: Powersharing Institutions and British Preferences on European Integration', *Political Studies*, 48: 415–42.

Aspinwall, M. (2004) *Rethinking Britain and Europe. Plurality Elections, Party Management and British Policy on European Integration.* Manchester: Manchester University Press.

Baldwin, R. and M. Widgrén (2003) *The Draft Constitutional Treaty's Voting Reform Dilemma*, CEPS Policy Brief Number 44. Brussels: Centre for European Policy Studies.

Barrett, Michael and Raymond Duvall (2005) 'Power in International Politics', *International Organization*, 59: 39–75.

Bartoszewski, W. (2000) *Poland's Position on the 2000 Intergovernmental Conference: A Critical Evaluation.* Warsaw: Konrad Adenauer Foundation in Poland.

Bartoszewski, W. (2001) The Future of the European Union, The Polish Point of View. Warsaw.

Bassompierre, G. de (1988) *Changing the Guard in Brussels: An Insider's View of the Presidency.* New York: Praeger.

Beach, Derek (2001) *Between Law and Politics: The Relationship Between the European Court of Justice and EU Member States.* Copehhagen: DJØF Publishing.

Beach, Derek (2002) 'The Negotiation of the Amsterdam Treaty – When Theory Meets Reality', in Finn Laursen (ed.), *The Amsterdam Treaty: National Preference Formation, Interstate Bargaining, Outcome and Ratification.* Odense: Odense University Press, pp. 593–637.

Beach, Derek (2003) 'Towards a New Method of Constitutional Bargaining? The Role and Impact of EU Institutions in the IGC and Convention Method of Treaty Reform', Constitutional Online Papers Number 13, 2003. The Federal Trust.

Beach, Derek (2005) *The Dynamics of European Integration: Why and When EU Institutions Matter.* Houndmills: Palgrave Macmillan.

Beach, Derek (2006) 'The Commission and the Council Secretariat in the negotiation of the 2000 IGC', in Finn Laursen (ed.) *The Treaty of Nice: Actor Preferences, Bargaining and Institutional Choice.* Leiden: Brill.

Bender, B. (1991) 'Whitehall, Central Government and 1992', *Public Policy and Administration*, 6(1): 13–20.

Bengtsson, R., O. Elgström and J. Tallberg (2004) 'Silencer or Amplifier? The European Union Presidency and the Nordic Countries'. *Scandinavian Political Studies*, 27(3): 311–34.

Bercovitch, Jacob (1996a) 'The Structure and Diversity of Mediation in International Relations', in Jacob Bercovitch and Jeffrey Z. Rubin (eds), *Mediation in International Relations*. New York: St Martin's Press, pp. 1–29.

Bercovitch, Jacob (1996b) 'Introduction: Thinking About Mediation', in Jacob Bercovitch (ed.), *Resolving International Conflict: The Theory and Practice of Mediation*. London: Lynne Rienner Publishers, pp. 1–9.

Bercovitch, Jacob and Allison Houston (1996) 'The Study of International Mediation: Theoretical Issues and Empirical Evidence', in Jacob Bercovitch (ed.), *Resolving International Conflict: The Theory and Practice of Mediation*. London: Lynne Rienner Publishers, pp. 11–35.

Beuter, Rita (2001) 'Germany: Safeguarding the EMU and the Interests of the *Länder*', in Finn Laursen (ed.), *The Amsterdam Treaty: National Preference Formation, Interstate Bargaining, Outcome and Ratification*. Odense: Odense University Press, pp. 93–120.

Bjurulf, B. and O. Elgström (2004) 'Negotiating Transparency: The Role of Institutions', *Journal of Common Market Studies*, 42(2): 249–69.

Blair, Alasdair (1998a) 'UK Policy Co-ordination During the 1990–91 Intergovernmental Conference', *Diplomacy and Statecraft*, 9(2): 159–82.

Blair, Alasdair (1998b) 'Swimming with the Tide? Britain and the Maastricht Treaty Negotiations on Common Foreign and Security Policy', *Journal of Contemporary British History*, 12(3): 87–102.

Blair, Alasdair (1999) *Dealing with Europe: Britain and the Negotiation of the Maastricht Treaty*. Aldershot: Ashgate.

Blair, Alasdair (2001) 'Permanent Representations to the European Union', *Diplomacy and Statecraft*, 12(3): 173–93.

Blair, Alasdair (2002) *Saving the Pound? Britain's Road to Monetary Union*. London: Prentice Hall.

Blair, T. (1997) 'Speech to the Party of European Socialists Congress', Malmö, June 6.

Blair, T. (2000) 'Prime Minister's speech to the Polish Stock Exchange', 6 October. http://www.number-10.gov.uk/output/Page3384.asp.

Blair, T. (2001) 'Britain's role in Europe', speech to the European Research Institute, University of Birmingham, 23 November. http://www.number-10.gov.uk/output/Page1673.asp.

Bourgignon-Wittke, R. *et al.* (1985) 'Five Years of the Directly Elected European Parliament, Performance and Prospects', *Journal of Common Market Studies*, 24(1): pp. 39–59.

Budden, P. (2002) 'Observations on the Single European Act and the "Relaunch of Europe": a Less "Intergovernmental" reading of the 1985 Intergovernmental Conference', *Journal of European Public Policy* 9(1): 76–97.

Bulmer, S and M. Burch (1998) 'Organizing for Europe: Whitehall, the British State and European Union', *Public Administration*, 76: 601–28.

Cameron, F. (2004) *The Future of Europe: Integration and Enlargement*. London: Routledge.

Carnevale, Peter J. and Sharon Arad (1996) 'Bias and Impartiality in International Mediation', in Jacob Bercovitch (ed.), *Resolving International Conflicts: The Theory and Practice of Mediation*. London: Lynne Rienner Publishers, pp. 39–53.

Charlemagne (1994) 'L'equilibre entre les etats membres', in *L'équilibre européen. Etudes rassemblées et publiées en hommage B. Niels Ersbøll*. Brussels. Edition provisoire, pp. 69–78.

Checkel, Jeffrey T. (1999) 'Social Construction and Integration', *Journal of European Public Policy*, 6(4) Special Issue: 545–60.

Checkel, Jeffrey T. (2001) 'Why Comply? Social Learning and European Identity Change', *International Organization*, 55(3): 553–88.

Christiansen, Thomas (2002) 'The Role of Supranational Actors in EU Treaty Reform', *Journal of European Public Policy*, 9(1): 33–53.

Christiansen, T., G. Falkner and K. Jørgensen (2002) 'Theorizing EU Treaty Reform: Beyond Diplomacy and Bargaining', *Journal of European Public Policy*, 9(1): 33–53.

Christiansen, T. and M. Gray (2003) 'The European Commission and Treaty Reform', *Eipascope*, 3: 10–18.

Christiansen, Thomas and Knud Erik Jørgensen (1998) 'Negotiating Treaty Reform in the European Union: The Role of the European Commission', *International Negotiation*, 3(3): 435–52.

Church, Clive H. and David Phinnemore (2002) *The Penguin Guide to European Treaties*. London: Penguin Books.

Cichocki, Marek A (2004) *Porwanie Europy*. Kraków – Warszawa: CSM.

Clarke, M. (1992) *British External Policy-making in the 1990s*. Basingstoke: Macmillan/Royal Institute of International Affairs.

Closa, C. (2002) 'An Institutionalist Interpretation of the Formation of Preferences in the EU: The Debate on the Future of the EU in Spain', Minda de Gunzburg Center for European Studies, Harvard University Scholars Seminar, unpublished paper.

Closa, Carlos (2004) 'The Convention Method and the Transformation of EU Constitutional Politics', in Erik Oddvar Eriksen, John Erik Fossum and Agustín Menédez (eds), *Developing a Constitution for Europe*. London: Routledge, pp. 183–206.

Commission of the European Communities (2002a) *Communication from the Commission: a Project for the European Union*, COM (2002) 247 final, 22 May. Brussels: European Commission.

Commission of the European Communities (2002b) *Feasibility Study*: Contribution to a Preliminary Draft Constitution of the European Union, Working Document http://www.europa.eu.int/futurum/documents/offtext/const051202_en.pdf (accessed on 7 November 2003)

Commission of the European Communities (2002c) *Peace, Freedom, Solidarity: Communication of the Commission on the Institutional Architecture*, COM (2002) 728 final, 4 December. Brussels: European Commission.

Coombes, D. (1998) 'The Commission's Relationship with the Presidency'. Paper presented at the conference The Presidency of the European Union, Belfast, October 15–16.

Corbett, Richard (1998a) *The European Parliament's Role in Closer EU Integration*. Houndmills: Macmillan Press Ltd.

Corbett, Richard (1998b) 'The Council Presidency as seen from the European Parliament'. Paper presented at the conference The Presidency of the European Union, Belfast, October 15–16 1998.

Costa, O., Couvidat, A. and Daloz, J.-P. (2003) 'The French Presidency of 2000: An Arrogant Leader?'. In O. Elgström (ed.), *European Union Council Presidencies: A Comparative Perspective*. London: Routledge.

Council Secretariat (1997) *Council Guide. 1. Presidency Handbook*. Luxembourg: Office for Official Publications of the European Communities.

Cox, Robert W. and Harold K. Jacobsen (1973) 'The Framework for Inquiry', in Robert W. Cox, Harold K. Jacobsen *et al.*, *The Anatomy of Influence: Decision Making in International Organizations*. London: Yale University Press, pp. 1–36.

Craig, P. (1997) 'Democracy and Rulemaking within the EC: An Empirical and Normative Assessment', *European Law Journal*, 3(2): 105–30.

Crum, Ben (2004) 'Politics and Power in the European Convention', *Politics*, 24(1): pp. 1–11.

Crump, Larry and A. Ian Glendon (2003) 'Towards a Paradigm of Multiparty Negotiation', *International Negotiation*, 8(2): 197–234.

Dehousse, Renaud (2001) 'Rediscovering Functionalism', in Christian Joerges, Yves Mény and Joseph Weiler (eds), *Which Constitution for Which Kind of Polity?* Florence: European University Institute.

Dehousse, Renaud and Florence Deloche-Gaudez (2005) 'The Making of a Transnational Constitution: An Institutionalist Perspective on the European Convention', *Cahiers européens de Sciences Po*, no. 2/2005. http://www.portedeurope.org/rubrique.php3?id_rubrique=52&lang=fr.

Dehousse, R., A. Maurer, J. Nestro, J.-L. Quermonne and J. Schild (2003) 'The Institutional Architecture of the EU: A Third Franco-German Way?', *Research and European Issues*, 23.

Deloche-Gaudez, Florence (2003) 'La présidence de la Convention européenne', *Annuaire Français des Relations Internationales*, Bruylant, 2003. http://www.france.diplomatie.fr/cap/1388.html.

Deloche-Gaudez, Florence (2004) 'Le Secrétariat de la Convention européenne: un acteur influent', *Cahiers européens de Sciences Po*, no. 3/2004. http://www.portedeurope.org/rubrique.php3?id_rubrique=52&lang=fr.

Dempsey, J. (2005) 'In a New Turn for Kohl, He's Favored Once More,' *International Herald Tribune*, April 5, p. 2.

de Schoutheete, P. (1990) 'The European Community and its Sub-Systems,' in William Wallace (ed.) *The Dynamics of European Integration*. London: Royal Institute of International Affairs, pp. 106–24.

Dewost, J.-L. (1984) 'La Présidence dans le Cadre Institutionnel des Communautés Européennes', *Revue du Marché Commun*, 273: 31–4.

Dimitrakopoulos, Dionyssis G. and Hussein Kassim (2004) 'Deciding the Future of the European Union: Preference Formation and Treaty Reform', *Comparative European Politics*, 2(3): 241–60.

Dimitrakopoulos, D.G. and H. Kassim (2005) 'Inside the European Commission: Preference Formation and the Convention on the Future of Europe', *Comparative European Politics*, 3(2): 180–203.

Dinan, Desmond (1999) *Ever Closer Union: An Introduction to European Integration*. Houndmills: Macmillan Press.

Dinan, Desmond (2000) 'The Commission and the Intergovernmental Conferences', in Neill Nugent (ed.), *At the Heart of the Union: Studies of the European Commission*, 2nd edition. London, Macmillan Press Ltd., pp. 250–69.

Dinan, Desmond and Sophie Vanhoonacker (2000–01) 'IGC 2000 Watch.' Parts 1–4, in *ECSA Review*, 13(2–4) and 14(1).

Dinan, Desmond (2004) 'Governance and Institutions', *Journal of Common Market Studies*, 42 Annual Review: 27–42.

Dinan, D. (2005) 'Governance and Institutions: A New Constitution and a New Treaty', *Journal of Common Market Studies*, 43 (annual review): 37–54.

Drake, Helen (2000) *Jacques Delors: Perspectives on a European Leader*. London: Routledge.

Duff, Andrew (1995) 'Building a Parliamentary Europe', in M. Télo (ed.), *Démocratie et Construction Européenne*. Bruxelles: Edition de l'Université de Bruxelles, pp. 253–4.

Duff, Andrew (2003) 'Der Beitrag des Europäischen Parlaments zum Konvent: Treubende Kraft für einen Konsens', *Integration*, 26(1): 3–9.

Dupont, Christophe and Guy-Olivier Faure (2002) 'The Negotiation Process', in Victor A. Kremenyuk (ed.), *International Negotiation: Analysis, Approaches, Issues*, 2nd edn. San Francisco: Jossey-Bass Publishers, pp. 39–63.

Eckstein, Harry (1975) 'Case Study and Theory in Political Science', in Fred I. Greenstein and Nelson W. Polsby (eds), *Handbook of Political Science: Scope and Theory*. Reading, MA: Addison-Wesley.

Elgström, Ole (2001) ' "The Honest Broker"? – The EU Council Presidency as a Mediator', Paper presented at the 4th Pan-European International Relations Conference, Canterbury, September 8–10.

Elgström, Ole (ed.) (2003a) *European Union Council Presidencies: A Comparative Perspective*. London: Routledge.

Elgström, Ole (2003b) 'The Honest Broker? The Council Presidency as a Mediator', in O. Elgström, (ed.), *European Union Council Presidencies: A Comparative Perspective*. London: Routledge.

Elgström, Ole and Christer Jönsson (2000) 'Negotiation in the European Union: Bargaining or Problem-Solving?', *Journal of European Public Policy*, 7(5): 684–704.

Endo, Ken (1999) *The Presidency of the European Commission under Jacques Delors: The Politics of Shared Leadership*, Basingstoke: Macmillan.

Epstein, Lee and Jeffrey A. Segal (2000) 'Measuring Issue Salience', *American Journal of Political Science*, 44(1): 66–83.

Ersbøll, Niels (1994) 'The European Union: The Immediate Priorities...' *International Affairs*, 70(3): 413–19.

Ersbøll, Niels (1997) 'The Amsterdam Treaty – II', *CEPS Review*, 4 (Autumn): 12.

Europaudvalget (2000) 'Europa-Kommissionen præsenterer ekspertrapport om todeling af EU-traktaterne', Info-note, bilag 152, 1999–00.

European Council (2001) *The Future of the EU: Declaration of Laeken*. SN 273/01, December 15.

European Council (2003) *Presidency Conclusions – Thessaloniki European Council – 19 and 20 June 2003*. 11638/03, Brussels, 1 October.

European Council (2004) *Brussels European Council – 12 and 13 December 2003 – Presidency Conclusions*. 5381/04, Brussels, 5 February.

European Parliament (1988) Rapport fait au nom de la Commission institutionnelle sur le déficit démocratique des Communautés européennes, par Michel Toussaint, PE DOC A 2276/87 of 1 February.

European Parliament (1995) Opinion of the Committee on Foreign Affairs, Security and Defence Policy for the Committee on Institutional Affairs on the operation of the Treaty on European Union with a view to the Intergovernmental Conference in 1996, Rapporteur: Enrique Barón Crespo, PE 211.022/fin., 21 February.

European Parliament (1996a) *Summary of the Positions of the Member States and the European Parliament on the 1996 Intergovernmental Conference*. Luxembourg, 30 September.

European Parliament (1996b) *Summary of the Positions of the Member States and the European Parliament on the 1996 Intergovernmental Conference*. Luxembourg, 4 December.

European Parliament (1999) Report on the Decision-making Process in the Council in an Enlarged Europe, Rapporteur: Jean-Louis Bourlanges, Doc. No. A4-0049/99.

European Parliament (2001a) Report on Reform of the Council, Rapporteur: Jacques F. Poos, Doc. No. A5-0308/2001.

European Parliament (2001b) Resolution on the Treaty of Nice and the Future of the European Union, Doc. No. A5-0168/2001.

European Parliament (2002a) Report on the legal Personality of the European Union, Rapporteur: Carlos Carnero Gonzalez, A5-0409/2001, 21 November.

European Parliament (2002b) Report on Relations between the European Parliament and the National Parliaments in European Integration, A5-0023/2002 Rapporteur: Giorgio Napolitano, 23 January.

European Parliament (2002c) Report on the Division of Competences Between the European Union and the Member States, A5-0133/2002, Rapporteur: Alain Lamassoure, 24 April.

European Parliament (2002d) Report on the Typology of Acts and the Hierarchy of Legislation in the European Union, Rapporteur: Louis Bourlanges A5-0425/2002, 3 December.

European Parliament IGC Monitoring Group (2003) 'Comparative Tables Concerning the Positions of the Member States in the IGC, IGC Monitoring Group, The Secretariat, PE 337.089, November 6.

Falkner, Gerda (2002a) 'Introduction: EU Treaty Reform as a Three-Level Process', *Journal of European Public Policy*, 9(1): 1–11.

Falkner, Gerda (2002b) 'How Intergovernmental are Intergovernmental Conferences? An Example from the Maastricht Treaty Reform', *Journal of European Public Policy*, 9(1): 98–119.

Fearon, J. (1991) 'Counterfactuals and Hypothesis Testing in Political Science', *World Politics*, 43(3): 169–95.

Felsenthal, D. and M. Machover (2004) *Population and Votes in the Council of Ministers: Squaring the Circle*. EPC Issue Paper Number 10, Brussels: European Policy Centre.

Finnemore, Martha and Kathryn Sikkink (1998) 'International Norm Dynamics and Political Change', *International Organization*, 52(4): 887–917.

Fischer, J. (2000) *Vom Staatenverbund zur Föderation – Gedanken über die Finalität der europäischen Integration*. Speech delivered at Humboldt University, Berlin, 12 May, http://www.auswaertiges-amt.de/www/de/infoservice/presse/presse_archiv?archiv_id=713 (accessed on November 2 2003).

Forster, A. (1998) 'Britain and the Negotiation of the Maastricht Treaty: a Critique of Liberal Intergovernmentalism', *Journal of Common Market Studies*, 36(3): 347–68.

Forster, A. and A. Blair (2002) *The Making of Britain's European Foreign Policy*. London: Longman.

Forster A. and W. Wallace (2001) 'The British Response: Denial and Confusion?', in Robin Niblett and William Wallace (eds), *Rethinking European Order: West European Responses, 1989–1997*. Basingstoke: Macmillan, pp. 124–51.

French Government (2000) *Priorities of the French Presidency of the European Union, 1 July–31 December 2000*.

Friend, J.W. (1991) *The Linchpin: French–German Relations, 1950–1990*. New York: Praeger with CSIS.

Friis, L. (2003) 'An "Emperor Without Clothes"?', *Cooperation and Conflict*, 38(3): 283–290.

Galloway, David (2001) *The Treaty of Nice and Beyond: Realities and Illusions of Power in the EU*. Sheffield: Sheffield University Press.

Garrett, Geoffrey and Barry Weingast (1993) 'Ideas, Interests, and Institutions: Constructing the European Community's Internal Market', in Judith Goldstein and Robert O. Keohane (eds), *Ideas and Foreign Policy: Beliefs, Institutions, and Political Change*. London: Cornell University Press, pp. 173–206.

Garrett, Geoffrey and George Tsebelis (1996) 'An Institutional Critique of Intergovernmentalism', *International Organization*, 50(2): 269–99.

Geddes, A. (2004) *The European Union and British Politics*. Basingstoke: Palgrave.

George, S. (1998) *An Awkward Partner*, 3rd edn. Oxford: Oxford University Press.

Giering, C. (2000) 'Der Europäische Rat,' in Werner Weidenfeld and Wolfgang Wessels (eds), *Jahrbuch der Europäischen Integration 1998/1999*. Bonn: Europa Union Verlag, pp. 51–60.

Goetz, K.H. (1996) 'Integration Policy in a Europeanized State: Germany and the Intergovernmental Conference', *Journal of European Public Policy*, 3: 23–44.

Goulard, S. (2005) 'France Allemagne: pour une initiative qui aille au-delà des apparences.' *Visions franco-allemandes* no. 5, juin.

Gowland, D. and Turner, A. (2000) *Reluctant Europeans: Britain and European Integration 1945–1998*. London: Longman.

Grabitz, E. et.al. (1988) *Direktwahl und Demokratisierung. Eine Funktionsbilanz des Europäischen Parlaments nach der ersten Wahlperiode*. Bonn: Europa Union Verlag.

Granger, Marie-Pierre (2005) 'The Future of Europe: Judicial Interference and Preferences', *Comparative European Politics*, 3(2): 155–79.

Grant, Charles (1994) *Delors: Inside the House that Jacques Built*. London: Brealey.

Gray, Mark (2001) 'The European Commission and Treaty Reform', Speech given to Nuffield College, University of Oxford, May.

Gray, Mark (2002) 'Negotiating the Treaty of Amsterdam: The Role and Influence of the European Commission', in Finn Laursen (ed.), *The Amsterdam Treaty: National Preference Formation, Interstate Bargaining, Outcome and Ratification*. Odense: Odense University Press, pp. 381–404.

Gray, Mark (2004) 'The Convention's Internal Dynamic', in Anna Michalski (ed.), *The Political Dynamics of Constitutional Reform*. The Hague: Clingendael, pp. 39–60.

Gray, Mark and Alexander Stubb (2001) 'The Treaty of Nice: Negotiating a Poisoned Chalice?', *Journal of Common Market Studies*, 39 Annual Review EU 2001: 5–23.

Grevi, G. (2003) *Gloves off: the Going gets Tough in the Convention*. Brussels: European Policy Centre.

Grieco, J. (1995) 'The Maastricht Treaty, Economic and Monetary Union and the Neo-Realist Research programme', *Review of International Studies*, 21: 21–40.

Guérot, U. (2004) 'Frankreich und Deutschland – Lokomotive ohne Anhänger?', in Johannes Varwick and Wilhelm Knelangen (eds), *Neues Europa – alte EU*. Opladen: Leske + Budrich, pp. 285–98.

Haas, Ernst B. (1958) *The Uniting of Europe*. Stanford: Stanford University Press.

Haas, Ernst B. (1961) 'International Integration: The European and the Universal Process', *International Organization*, 15(3): 366–92.

Haas, Ernst B. (1990) *When Knowledge is Power: Three Models of Change in International Organizations*. Berkeley: University of California Press.

Häberle, Peter (2003) 'Die Herausforderungen des europäischen Juristen vor den Aufgaben unserer Verfassungs-Zukunft: 16 Entwürfe auf dem Prüfstand', *Die öffentliche Verwaltung*, 11: 429–43.

Hain, P. (2002) 'The Future of Europe: Time for a New Vision', Speech to the European Policy Centre, January 29.

Hall, Peter and Rosemary C.R. Taylor (1996) 'Political Science and the Three New Institutionalisms', *Political Studies*, 44(4): 936–57.

Hampson, Fen Osler (1995) *Multilateral Negotiations: Lessons from Arms Control, Trade, and the Environment*. Baltimore: The Johns Hopkins University Press.

Hartley, Trevor (2003) *The Foundations of European Community Law*, 5th edn. Oxford: Oxford University Press.

Hayes-Renshaw, F. and Wallace, H. (1997) *The Council of Ministers*. London: Macmillan.

Hine, David (2001) 'Constitutional Reform and Treaty Reform in Europe', in Anand Menon and Vincent Wright (eds), *From the Nation State to Europe? Essays in Honour of Jack Hayward*. Oxford: Oxford University Press, pp. 118–38.

Hix, Simon (1995) 'Parties at the European Level as an Alternative Source of Legitimacy', *Journal of Common Market Studies*, 33(4): 527–54.

Hopmann, P. Terrence (1995) 'Two Paradigms of Negotiation: Bargaining and Problem-solving.', *Annals of the American Academy of Political and Social Science*, 542: 24–47.

Hopmann, P. Terrence (1996) *The Negotiation Process and the Resolution of International Conflicts*. Columbia: University of South Carolina Press.

Hurrell, A. and A. Menon (1996) 'Politics Like Any Other? Comparative Politics, International Relations and the Study of the EU', *West European Politics*, 19(2).

Jabko, N. (2004) 'The Importance of Being Nice: An Institutionalist Analysis of French Preferences on the Future of Europe', *Comparative European Politics*, 2(3): 282–301.

Jabko, Nicolas (2005) 'Comment la France définit ses intérêts en Europe', *Revue Française de Science Politique*, 55(2).

Janning, J. (2001) 'Bundesrepublik Deutschland', in Werner Weidenfeld and Wolfgang Wessels (eds), *Jahrbuch der Europäischen Integration 2002/2003*. Bonn: Europa Union Verlag. pp. 317–24.

Janning, J. (2003) 'Bundesrepublik Deutschland', in Werner Weidenfeld and Wolfgang Wessels (eds), *Jahrbuch der Europäischen Integration 2002/2003*. Bonn: Europa Union Verlag. pp. 327–34.

Jensen, M. (1985) 'The Presidency of the Council of Ministers of the European Communities: The Dutch and the Presidency', in Colm O Nuallain (ed.), *The Presidency of the European Council of Ministers*. London: Croom Helm. pp. 209–36.

Jones, Bryan D. (2001) *Politics and the Architecture of Choice: Bounded Rationality and Governance*. London: The University of Chicago Press.

Kapteyn, P.J.G. and P. VerLoren van Themaat (1998) *Introduction to the Law of the European Communities*, 3rd and rev. ed. by L.W. Gormley. London: Kluwer.

Kassim, H. (2000) 'The United Kingdom', in H. Kassim, B.G. Peters and V. Wright (eds), *The National Co-ordination of EU Policy Making: The Domestic Level*. Oxford: Oxford University Press, pp. 22–53.

Kassim, H. (2004) 'The United Kingdom and the Future of Europe: Winning the Battle, Losing the War', *Comparative European Politics*, 2(3): 261–81.

Kassim, Hussein (2006) 'The Secretariat General', in David Spence (ed.), *The European Commission*. London: John Harper Publishing.

Kassim, Hussein, G. Peters and V. Wright (eds) (2000) *The National Co-ordination of EU Policy: The Domestic Level*. Oxford: Oxford University Press.

Kassim, Hussein, A. Menon, G. Peters and V. Wright (eds) (2001) *The National Co-ordination of EU Policy: the European Level*. Oxford: Oxford University Press.

Kassim, Hussein and Anand Menon (2003) 'The Principal–Agent Approach and the Study of the European Union: Promise Unfulfilled?', *Journal of European Public Policy*, 10(1): 121–39.

Kassim, Hussein and A. Menon (2004) 'EU Member States and the Prodi Commission', in D.G. Dimitrakopoulos (ed.), *The Changing European Commission*. Manchester: Manchester University Press, pp. 89–104.

Kerremans, Bart and E. Drieskens (2003) 'The Belgian Presidency of 2001: Cautious Leadership as Trademark', in O. Elgström (ed.), *European Union Council Presidencies: A Comparative Perspective*. London: Routledge, pp. 155–72.

Kirchner, E. (1992) *Decision-Making in the European Community: The Council Presidency and European Integration*. Manchester: Manchester University Press.

Kohler-Koch, B. (1997) 'Die Europäisierung nationaler Demokratien: Verschleiß eines europäischen Kulturerbes?', in M. Greven (ed.), *Demokratie – eine Kultur des Westens?*

20. *Wissenschaftlicher Kongreß der Deutschen Vereinigung für Politische Wissenschaft.* Leske & Budrich: Opladen.

Kressel, K. and Dean G. Pruitt (1989) *Mediation Research: Process and Effectiveness of Third-Party Intervention.* San Francisco: Jossey-Bass.

Krotz, U. (2002) 'Structure as Process: The Regularized Intergovernmentalism of Franco-German Bilateralism', Program for the Study of Germany and Europe, Working Paper 02.3. Cambridge, MA: Harvard University Center for European Studies.

Laffan, B. (2003) *Ireland and Europe: Continuity and Change. The 2004 Presidency.* Notre Europe Studies and Research Notes, Number 30, Paris: Notre Europe.

Lamont, N. (1999) *In Office.* London: Little, Brown and Company.

Lax, David A. and James K. Sebenius (1986) *The Manager as Negotiator.* London: The Free Press.

Lequesne, Christian (2001) 'The French Presidency: The Half Success of Nice', *Journal of Common Market Studies*, 39, Annual Review: 47–50.

Lindberg, Leon N. (1963) *The Political Dynamics of European Economic Integration.* Stanford: Stanford University Press.

Lindberg, Leon N. and Stuart A. Scheingold (1970) *Europe's Would-Be Polity: Patterns of Change in the European Community.* Englewood Cliffs: Prentice-Hall, Inc.

Lipsius, Justus (1995) 'The 1996 Intergovernmental Conference', *European Law Review*, 20(3): 235–67.

Lodge, Juliet (1998) 'Negotiations in the European Union: The 1996 Intergovernmental Conference', *International Negotiation*, 3: 481–505.

Lübbe, H. (1994) *Abschied vom Superstaat. Die Vereinigten Staaten von Europa wird es nicht geben.* Berlin: Siedler.

Luce, R.D. and Raiffa, H. (1957) *Games and Decisions.* New York: Wiley.

Ludlow, Peter (2001a) 'The European Council at Nice: Neither Triumph nor Disaster', *Background Paper*, CEPS International Advisory Council, February 1–2.

Ludlow, P. (2001b) *A View from Brussels: A Commentary on the EU. 2004 and Beyond.* Brussels: CEPS.

Ludlow, P. (2002) *The Laeken Council.* Brussels: Eurocomment.

Ludlow, P. (2004) *The European Council and IGC of December 2003.* EuroComment Briefing Note, Volume 2, Number 8, Brussels: EuroComment.

Magnette, P. (2005) 'Leadership in European Constitutional Politics'. Paper presented at the 2005 ECPR Joint Sessions, Granada, April 14–18.

Magnette, Paul and Kalypso Nicolaïdis (2004a) 'Coping with the Lilliput Syndrom: Large vs Small Member States in the European Convention', *Politique Européenne*, 14.

Magnette, Paul and Kalypso Nicolaïdis (2004b) 'The European Convention: Bargaining in the Shadow of Rhetoric', *West European Politics*, 27(3): 381–404.

Major, J. (1999) *The Autobiography.* London: HarperCollins.

Maurer, A. (2001) 'Democratic Governance in the European Union: The Institutional Terrain after Amsterdam', in J. Monar and W. Wessels (eds), *The European Union after the Treaty of Amsterdam.* London/New York, Continuum Publishers, pp. 96–124.

Maurer, Andreas (2002a) 'The European Parliament', in Finn Laursen (ed.), *The Amsterdam Treaty: National Preference Formation, Interstate Bargaining, Outcome and Ratification.* Odense: Odense University Press, pp. 405–50.

Maurer, A. (2002b) *Parlamentarische Demokratie in der Europäischen Union. Der Beitrag des Europäischen Parlaments und der Parlamente der Mitgliedstaaten.* Baden-Baden: Nomos.

Maurer, A. (2003) 'Orientierungen im Verfahrensdickicht? Die neue Normenhierarchie der Europäischen Union', *Integration*, 4: 440–53.

Maurer, A. (2004) 'The Convention Method for Enhancing EU Democracy', in C. Closa and J.E. Fossum (eds), *Deliberative Constitutional Politics in the EU*, Arena Report, No. 5. Oslo.

Maurer, A. and D. Nickel (eds) (2005) *Das Europäische Parlament. Supranationalität, Repräsentation und Legitimation*. Baden-Baden: Nomos.

Maurer, A., D. Kietz and C. Völkel (2005) 'Interinstitutional Agreements in the CFSP: Parliamentarization through the Backdoor?', *European Foreign Affairs Review*, 2: 175–95.

Mazzucelli, Colette (1999) *France and Germany at Maastricht: Politics and Negotiations to Create the European Union*. New York: Garland Publishing, Inc.

Mazzucelli, Colette (2001) 'Much Ado about Amsterdam: CDU–CSU Politics, Länder Influence and EU Treaty Reform', *German Law Journal*, 2(15).

McDonagh, Bobby (1998) *Original Sin in a Brave New World: An Account of the Negotiation of the Treaty of Amsterdam*. Dublin: Institute of European Affairs.

Meier, Kenneth J. (1989) 'Bureaucratic Leadership in Public Organizations', in Bryan D. Jones (ed.), *Leadership and Politics: New Perspectives in Political Science*. Lawrence: University Press of Kansas, pp. 267–88.

Menon, Anand (2003) 'Britain and the Convention on the Future of Europe', *International Affairs*, 79(5): 963–78.

Menon, A. (2004) 'Britain and European Integration: the View from Within', *Political Quarterly*, 75(3): 285–317.

Metcalfe, David (1998) 'Leadership in European Union Negotiations: The Presidency of the Council', *International Negotiation*, 3: 413–34.

Metz, W. and A. Möller (2001) 'Kommentierte Chronologie von Amsterdam bis Nizza', in Werner Weidenfeld (ed.), *Nizza in der Analyse*. Gütersloh: Verlag Bertelsmann Stiftung, pp. 305–50.

Meunier, S. and K. Nicolaïdis (2001) 'Trade Competence in the Nice Treaty', *ECSA Review*, 14(2): 7–8.

Midgaard, Knut and Arild Underdal (1977) 'Multiparty Conferences', in Daniel Druckman (ed.), *Negotiations: Social-Psychological Perspectives*. London: Sage Publications, pp. 329–46.

Moravcsik, A. (1991) 'Negotiating the Single European Act: National Interests and Conventional Statecraft in the European Community', *International Organization*, 45(1): 19–56.

Moravcsik, A. (1993) 'Preferences and Power in the European Community: A Liberal Intergovernmentalist Approach', *Journal of Common Market Studies*, 31(4): 473–524.

Moravcsik, Andrew (1998) *The Choice for Europe: Social Purpose and State Power from Messina to Maastricht*. Ithaca: Cornell University Press.

Moravcsik, Andrew (1999a) 'A New Statecraft? Supranational Entrepreneurs and International Cooperation', *International Organization*, 53(2): 267–306.

Moravcsik, Andrew (1999b) 'Theory and Method in the Study of International Negotiation: A Rejoinder to Oran Young', *International Organization*, 53(4): 811–14.

Moravcsik, Andrew (2005a) 'The European Constitutional Compromise and the Neofunctionalist Legacy', *Journal of European Public Policy*, 12(2): 349–86.

Moravcsik, Andrew (2005b) 'Europe Without Illusions', *Prospect*, 112.

Moravcsik, Andrew and Kalypso Nicolaïdis (1999) 'Explaining the Treaty of Amsterdam: Interests, Influences, Institutions', *Journal of Common Market Studies*, 37(1): 59–85.

Nickel, D. (1993) 'Le Traité de Maastricht et le Parlement européen: Le nouveau paysage politique et la procédure de l'article 189b', in J. Monar, W. Ungerer, and W. Wessels (eds), *The Maastricht Treaty on European Union*. Brussels: EIP.

Nickel, D. (1997) 'The Amsterdam Treaty – A Shift in the Balance between the Institutions!?' Paper submitted for a lecture at the Harvard Law School.

Nickel, D. (1999) 'Beyond Treaty Revision: Shifts in the Institutional Balance?' Unpublished paper presented at the ECSA Sixth Biennial Conference, Pittsburgh, June 2–6.

Nicolaïdis, K. (2004) 'We, the Peoples of Europe', *Foreign Affairs*, November/December: 97–110.

Noël, E. (1985) 'Reflections on the Community in the Aftermath of the Meeting of the European Council in Milan', *Government and Opposition*, 20(4): 444–52.

Norman, Peter (2003) *The Accidental Constitution: The Story of the European Convention*. Brussels: Eurocomment.

Norman, P. (2005) *The Accidental Constitution: The Making of Europe's Constitutional Treaty*, 2nd edn. Brussels: EuroComment.

Notre Europe – European Steering Committee and A. Padoa-Schioppa (1998) 'From the Single Currency to the Single Ballot-Box,' *Agence Europe*, 2089, May 27.

Notre Europe – European Steering Committee (1998). 'Politicising the European Debate,' *Agence Europe*, 2089, May 27.

Nugent, Neill (1999) *The Government and Politics of the European Union*. London: Macmillan Press.

O Nuallain, C. (ed.) (1985) *The Presidency of the European Council of Ministers*. London: Croom Helm.

Padoa-Schioppa, A. (1998) 'The Institutional Reforms of the Amsterdam Treaty'. *The Federalist* No. 1.

Palacio, A. and P. Hain (2003) 'Les institutions de l'Union', Brussels, February 28, CONV S91/03, CONTRB 264.

Pedersen, Thomas (1998) *Germany, France and the Integration of Europe: A Realist Interpretation*. London and New York: Pinter.

Pedersen, Thomas (2002) 'Cooperative Hegemony: Power, Ideas and Institutions in Regional Integration', *Review of International Studies*, 28: 677–96.

Peterson, J. (1995) 'Decision-making in the European Union,' *Journal of European Public Policy*, 1: 69–93.

Peterson, J. (2004) 'The Prodi Commission: Fresh Start or Free Fall?', in D. Dimitrakopoulos (ed.), *The Changing European Commission*. Manchester: Manchester University Press, pp. 15–32.

Peterson, J. and Bomberg, E. (1999) *Decision-Making in the European Union*. Houndmills: Palgrave Macmillian.

Petite, Michel (1998) 'The Treaty of Amsterdam' NYU School of Law, Jean Monnet Working Papers, no. 2. Available at http://www.jeanmonnetprogram.org/papers/98/98-2-html.

Petite, Michel (2000) 'The IGC and the European Commission', in Edward Best, Mark Gray and Alexander Stubb (eds), *Rethinking the European Union: IGC 2000 and Beyond*. Maastricht: European Institute of Public Administration, pp. 61–6.

Pierson, Paul (1998) 'The Path to European Integration: A Historical Institutionalist Analysis', in Wayne Sandholtz and Alec Stone Sweet (eds), *European Integration and Supranational Governance*. Oxford: Oxford University Press, pp. 27–58.

Pijpers, Alfred (1983) 'The Netherlands: How to Keep the Spirit of Fouchet in the Bottle', in Christopher Hill (ed.), *National Foreign Policies and European Political Cooperation*. London: Allen & Unwin, pp. 166–81.

Piris, Jean-Claude (1999) 'Does the European Union have a Constitution? Does it Need One?', *European Law Review*, 24: 557–85.

Pliakos, A. (1995) 'L'Union européenne et le Parlement européen – y a-t-il vraiment un déficit démocratique?', *Révue du droit public et de la science politique et France et à l'Étranger*, no. 3.

Pollack, Mark A. (1997) 'Delegation, Agency, and Agenda Setting in the European Community', *International Organization*, 51(1): 99–134.

Pollack, Mark A. (1999) 'Delegation, Agency and Agenda Setting in the Treaty of Amsterdam', *European Integration online Papers (EIoP)*, Volume 3 (1999), Number 6, published at Internet site: http://eiop.or.at/eiop/texte/1999-006a.htm.

Pollack, Mark A. (2003) *The Engines of European Integration: Delegation, Agency and Agenda Setting in the EU*. Oxford: Oxford University Press.

Powell, G. Bingham (2000) *Elections as Instruments of Democracy*. New Haven: Yale University Press.

Presidency of the European Union (2003) *Intergovernmental Conference. Note for the attention of Foreign Ministers*, s.l., September 1.

Raiffa, Howard (1982) *The Art and Science of Negotiation*. Cambridge, MA: Harvard University Press.

Raunio, T. and M. Wiberg (1998) 'Winners and Losers in the Council: Voting Power Consequences of EU Enlargements', *Journal of Common Market Studies*, 36(4): 549–62.

Reich, C. (1992) 'Le Traité sur l'Union européenne et le Parlement européen', *Révue du Marché Commun*, No. 357.

Riker, William (1980) 'Implications from the Disequilibrium of Majority Rule for the Study of Institutions', *American Political Science Review*, 74(2): 432–46.

Risse-Kappen, T. (1996) 'Exploring the Nature of the Beast: International Relations Theory and Comparitive Policy Analysis Meet the European Union', *Journal of Common Market Studies*, 34(1): 53–80.

Ritberger, Berthold (2003) 'The Creation and Empowerment of the European Parliament', *Journal of Common Market Studies*, 41(2): 203–25.

Rosamond, Ben (2000) *Theories of European Integration*. London: Macmillan.

Rosati, Jerel A. (2001) 'The Power of Human Cognition in the Study of World Politics', *International Studies Review*, 2(3): 45–75.

Ross, George (1995) *Jacques Delors and European Integration*. Cambridge: Polity.

Sandholtz, Wayne (1992) *High-Tech Europe: The Politics of International Cooperation*. Berkeley: University of California Press.

Sandholtz, Wayne and John Zysman (1989) '1992: Recasting the European Bargain', *World Politics*, 41(1): 95–128.

Scelo, M. (2002) 'Le Parlement européen face à l'avenir de l'Europe. De la Convention européenne à l'adoption d'une Constitution pour l'Europe', *Révue du marché commun et de l'Union européenne*, 462: 578–82.

Scharpf, Fritz (1997) *Games Real Actors Play: Actor-Centered Institutionalism in Policy Research*. Oxford: Westview Press.

Schepsle, Kenneth (1979) 'Institutional Arrangements and Equilibrium in Multi-dimensional Voting Models', *American Journal of Political Science*, 23(1): 27–60.

Schild, J. (2001) 'Den Rhein vertiefen und erweitern? – Deutsch-französische Beziehungen nach dem Nizza-Gipfel', *Aktuelle Frankreich-Analysen*, no. 17 – February. Ludwigsburg: DFI.

Schild, J. (2004) 'La France, l'Allemagne et la Constitution Européenne: Un bilan mitige, un leadership contesté', *Note du Cerfa* no. 10, Mars. Paris: IFRI.

Schoo, J. (1997) 'Kommentar zu Art. 189b–189c', in Groeben, Thiesing and Ehlermann (eds), *Kommentar zum EU/EG-Vertrag*, Band 4 (Art. 137–209a EGV). Baden-Baden: Nomos.

Schout, Adriaan and Sophie Vanhoonacker (2001) 'The Presidency as Broker? Lessons from Nice'. Paper presented at the 4th Pan-European International Relations Conference, Canterbury, September 8–10.

Schout, Adriaan and Sophie Vanhoonacker (2006) 'Nice and the French Presidency', in Finn Laursen (ed.), *The Treaty of Nice: Actor Preferences, Bargaining and Institutional Choice*. Leiden: Brill.

Schröder, M. (1994) 'Das Bundesverfassungsgericht als Hüter des Staates im Prozeß der europäischen Integration', *Deutsches Verwaltungsblatt*, no. 6.

Schröder, G. and J. Chirac (2003) 'Deutsch-Französischer Beitrag zur institutionellen Architektur der EU', January 15 2003, Pressemitteilung Nr 21.

Schunz, Simon (2005) 'Das Europräische Partiament in Konvert zur Zukunft Europas', in Andreas Maurer and Dietmar Nickel (eds), *Das Europäische Parlament*. Baden-Baden: Nomos, pp. 47–64.

Sebenius, James K. (1984) *Negotiating the Law of the Sea*. Cambridge, MA: Harvard University Press.

Sebenius, James K. (1991) 'Negotiation Analysis', in Victor A. Kremenyuk (ed.), *International Negotiation: Analysis, Approaches, Issues*. Oxford: Jossey-Bass Publishers, pp. 203–15.

Sebenius, James K. (1992) 'Challenging Conventional Explanations of International Cooperation: Negotiation Analysis and the Case of Epistemic Communities', *International Organization*, 46(1): 323–65.

Sebenius, James K. (2001) 'Negotiation Analysis', in Victor A. Kremenyuk (ed.), *International Negotiation: Analysis, Approaches, Issues*, 2nd edn. Oxford: Jossey-Bass Publishers, pp. 229–55.

Sherrington, P. (2000) *The Council of Ministers: Political Authority in the European Union*. London: Pinter.

Shonfield, A. (1973) *Europe: Journey to an Unknown Destination*. London: Allen Lane.

Simon, Herbert A. (1997) *Administrative Behavior: A Study of Decision-Making Processes in Administrative Organizations*, 4th edn. New York: The Free Press.

Simonian, H. (1985) *The Privileged Partnership*. Oxford: Clarendon Press.

Sjöstedt, Gunnar (1999) 'Leadership in Multilateral Negotiations: Crisis or Transition?', in Peter Berton, Hiroshi Kimura and William I. Zartmann (eds), *International Negotiation: Actors, Structure/Process, Values*. New York: St Martin's Press, pp. 223–53.

Smith, Mitchell P. (1996) 'Democratic Legitimacy in the European Union: Fulfilling the Institutional Logic', *Journal of Legislative Studies*, 2(4): 283–301.

Smyser, W.R. (2003) *How Germans Negotiate*. Washington, DC: USIP Press.

Soetendorp, Ben and Rudy B. Andweg (2001) 'Dual Loyalties: The Boundary Role of the Dutch Permanent Representation to the EU', in Hussein Kassim, Anand Menon, B. Guy Peters and Vincent Wrights (eds), *The National Coordination of EU Policy*. Oxford: Oxford University Press, pp. 211–27.

Stenelo, L.-G. (1972) *Mediation in International Negotiations*. Lund: Studentlitteratur.

Steppat, S. (1988) 'Execution of Functions by the European Parliament in its First Electoral Period', *Révue d'integration européenne*, No. 1.

Stone Sweet, Alec and Wayne Sandholtz (1998) 'Integration, Supranational Governance, and the Institutionalization of the European Polity', in Wayne Sandholtz and Alec Stone Sweet (eds), *European Integration and Supranational Governance*. Oxford: Oxford University Press, pp. 1–26.

Stubb, Alexander (1998) *Flexible Integration and the Amsterdam Treaty: Negotiating Differentiation in the 1996–97 IGC*. Dissertation submitted for the degree of Doctor of Philosophy at the London School of Economics and Political Science, December.

Stubb, A. (2000) 'Negotiating Flexible Integration', in K. Neunreither and A. Wiener (eds), *European Integration after Amsterdam*. Oxford: Oxford University Press, pp. 153–74.

Stubb, Alexander (2002) *Negotiating Flexibility in the European Union*. Houndmills: Palgrave.

Svensson, A.C. (1998) 'Negotiating IGCs: The Role of the Presidency.' Paper presented at the 3rd Pan-European International Relations Conference and Joint Meeting with the International Studies Association, Vienna, September 16–19.

Svensson, A.C. (2000) *In the Service of the European Union*. Uppsala: Acta Universitatis Upsaliensis.

Sverdrup, U. (2000) 'Precedents and Present Events in the European Union: An Institutional Perspective on Treaty Reform', in K.-H. Neunreither and A. Wiener (eds), *European Integration after Amsterdam*. London: Routledge, pp. 241–65.

Sverdrup, U. (2002) 'An Institutional Perspective on Treaty Reform: Contextualising the Amsterdam and Nice Treaties', *Journal of European Public Policy*, 9(1): 120–40

Tallberg, Jonas (2001) 'Responsabilité sans Pouvoir? The Agenda-Shaping Powers of the EU Council Presidency'. Paper presented at the 4th Pan-European International Relations Conference, Canterbury, September 8–10.

Tallberg, Jonas (2002) 'The Power of the Chair in International Bargaining.' Paper presented at the 2002 ISA Annual Convention, New Orleans, March 24–7.

Tallberg, Jonas (2003) 'The Agenda-Shaping Powers of the EU Council Presidency', *Journal of European Public Policy*, 10(1): 1–19.

Tallberg, Jonas (2004a) 'The Power of the Presidency: Brokerage, Efficiency and Distribution in EU Negotiations', *Journal of Common Market Studies*, 42(5): 999–1022.

Tallberg, Jonas (2004b) 'The Power of the Chair: Formal Leadership in International Cooperation'. Paper presented at the Annual ISA Convention, Montreal, March 17–20.

Tallberg, Jonas (2005) *The Power of the Chair: Leadership and Negotiation in the European Union*. Unpublished book manuscript.

Thatcher, M. (1993) *The Downing Street Years*. London: HarperCollins.

Thielemann, Eiko R. (2004) 'Dividing Competences: Germany's Vision(s) for Europe's Federal Future', *Comparative European Politics*, 2.

Three Wise Men (1979) Report on European Institutions. Report presented by the Committee of the Three to the European Council, Brussels, October 1979.

Tiilikainen, T. (2003) 'The Finnish Presidency of 1999: Pragmatism and the Promotion of Finland's Position in Europe', in O. Elgström (ed.), *European Union Council Presidencies: A Comparative Analysis*. London: Routledge.

Troy Johnston, M. (1994) *The European Council: Gatekeeper of the European Community*. Boulder, CO: Westview Press.

Tsebelis, G. (1994) 'The Power of the European Parliament as a Conditional Agenda Setter', *American Political Science Review*, 88(1): 128–42.

Underdal, Arild (1983) 'Causes of Negotiation "Failure" ', *European Journal of Political Research*, 11: 183–95.

Underdal, Arild (1994) 'Leadership Theory: Rediscovering the Arts of Management'. In I. W. Zartman (ed.), *International Multilateral Negotiations: Approaches to the Management of Complexity*. San Francisco: Jossey-Bass.

United Kingdom (2003) *A Constitutional Treaty for the EU: The British Approach to the European Union Intergovernmental Conference 2003*, Cm 5934.

Vogel, W. (2004) 'Neue Dynamik im alten Europa. Deutsch-Französische Beziehungen zwischen Jubiläum und Osterweiterung der EU', *Aktuelle Frankreich-Analysen*, February.

von Gossler, S. Zervakis, P. (2003) '40 Jahre Elysée-Vertrag: Hat das deutsch-französische Tandem noch eine Zukunft?', *Aus Politik und Zeitgeschichte*, B 3–4: 6–13.

Wall, James A. and Ann Lynn (1993) 'Mediation: A Current Review', *Journal of Conflict Resolution*, 37(1): 160–94.

Wall, James A., John B. Stark and Rhetta L. Standifer (2001) 'Mediation: A Current Review and Theory Development', *Journal of Conflict Resolution*, 45(3): 370–91.

Wallace, H. (1997) 'At Odds with Europe', *Political Studies*, 45(4): 677–88.

Wallace H. (1993) 'A Critical Assessment of the Styles, Strategies and Achievements of the Two Presidencies', in Emil J. Kirchner and Anastassia Tsagkari (eds), *The EC Council Presidency: The Dutch and Luxembourg Presidencies*. London: UACES Secretariat in conjunction with the Centre for European Studies.

Walton, R.E. and R.B. McKersie (1965) *A Behavioral Theory of Labor Negotiations*. New York: McGraw-Hill.

Watkins, Michael (1999) 'Negotiating in a Complex World', *Negotiation Journal*, 15(3): 245–70.

Wehr, Paul and John Paul Lederach (1996) 'Mediating Conflict in Central America', in Jacob Bercovitch (ed.), *Resolving International Conflicts – The Theory and Practice of Mediation*. London: Lynne Rienner Publishers, pp. 55–74.

Weidenfeld, Wolfgang (2002) 'Europäische Einigung im historischen Überblick,' in Werner Weidenfeld and Wolfgang Wessels (eds), *Europa von A bis Z*. Bonn: Bundeszentrale für politische Bildung.

Weidenfeld, Wolfgang (ed.) (2001) *Nizza in der Analyse*. Gütersloh: Verlag Bertelsmann Stiftung.

Weidenfeld, Wolfgang (ed.) (2005) *Die Europäische Verfassung in der Analyse*. Gütersloh: Verlag Bertelsmann Stiftung.

Weiler, Joseph (1997) 'Legitimacy and Democracy of Union Governance', in A. Pijpers and G. Edwards (eds), *The Politics of European Treaty Reform: The 1996 Intergovernmental Conference and Beyond*. London: Pinter, pp. 249–87.

Weiler, Joseph H.H. (1995) 'The State "über alles" – Demos, Telos and the German Maastricht Decision', in Ole Due, Marcus Lutter and Jürgen Schwarze (eds), *Festschrift für Ulrich Everling*, Vol. II, Baden-Baden: Nomos, pp. 1651–88.

Wessels, W. (1996) 'The Modern West European State and the European Union: Democratic Erosion or a New Kind of Polity?', in S.S. Andersen and K.A. Eliassen (eds), *The European Union: How Democratic is It?* London: Sage.

Westlake, Martin (1999) *The Council of the European Union. Revised Edition*. London: John Harper Publishing.

Williamson, David (1997) 'The European Union in Transition', European Union Studies Center, The Graduate Center of the City University of New York, December 12.

Willis, F.R. (1968) *France, Germany and the New Europe*. London: Stanford University Press.

Wright, V. (1989) *The Government and Politics of France*. London: Routledge.

Wurzel, R.K.W. (1996) 'The Role of the Presidency in the Environmental Field: Does It Make a Difference which Member State Runs the Presidency?', *Journal of European Public Policy*, 3(2): 272–91.

Young, H. (1998) *This Blessed Plot: Britain and Europe from Churchill to Major*. Basingstoke: Macmillan.

Young, Oran R. (1967) *The Intermediaries: Third Parties in International Crises*. Princeton: Princeton University Press.

Young, Oran R. (1991) 'Political Leadership and Regime Formation: On the Development of Institutions in International Society', *International Organization*, 45(3): 281–308.

Young, Oran R. (1999) 'Comment on Andrew Moravcsik, "A New Statecraft? Supranational Entrepreneurs and International Cooperation"', *International Organization*, 53(4): 805–9.

Zartmann, I. William (1991) 'The Structure of Negotiation', in Victor A. Kremenyuk (ed.), *International Negotiation: Analysis, Approaches, Issues*. San Francisco: Jossey-Bass Publishers, pp. 65–77.

Zartman, I. William (2000) 'Regional Conflict Resolution', in Victor A. Kremenyuk (ed.), *International Negotiation: Analysis, Approaches, Issues*, 2nd edn. San Francisco: Jossey-Bass Publishers, pp. 348–61.

Zartman, I. William (2002) 'The Structure of Negotiation', in Victor A. Kremenyuk (ed.), *International Negotiation: Analysis, Approaches, Issues*, 2nd edn. San Francisco: Jossey-Bass Publishers, pp. 71–84.

Zartman, I. William (2003) 'Conclusion: Managing Complexity', *International Negotiation*, 8(1): 179–86.

Zartman, I. William and Maureen R. Berman (1982) *The Practical Negotiator*. New Haven: Yale University Press.

Zimbardo, P. and M. Leippe (1991) *The Psychology of Attitude Change and Social Influence*. New York: McGraw-Hill.

Index